THE BORZOI
HISTORY OF ENGLAND
VOLUME THREE
1450–1640

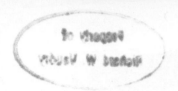

The Borzoi
History of England

General Editor
ARTHUR JOSEPH SLAVIN
University of California at Los Angeles

ANGLES, ANGELS,
AND CONQUERORS
Volume I: 400–1154
Joel T. Rosenthal
State University of New York at Stony Brook

THE COMMUNITY
OF THE REALM
Volume II: 1154–1485
Michael R. Powicke
University of Toronto

THE PRECARIOUS BALANCE:
English Government and Society
Volume III: 1450–1640
Arthur Joseph Slavin
University of California at Los Angeles

A CERTAINTY IN THE SUCCESSION
Volume IV: 1640–1815
Gerald M. and Lois O. Straka
University of Delaware

Volume V: 1815–the Present
J. B. Conacher
University of Toronto

THE BORZOI
HISTORY OF ENGLAND
VOLUME THREE
1450-1640

THE PRECARIOUS BALANCE

ENGLISH GOVERNMENT AND SOCIETY

ALFRED A. KNOPF   NEW YORK

ARTHUR JOSEPH SLAVIN

University of California
at Los Angeles

THIS IS A BORZOI BOOK
PUBLISHED BY ALFRED A. KNOPF, INC.

First Edition
987654321

Copyright © 1973 by Alfred A. Knopf, Inc.

All rights reserved under International and Pan-American Copyright Conventions. No part of this book may be reproduced in any form or by any means, electronic or mechanical, including photocopying, without permission in writing from the publisher. All inquiries should be addressed to Alfred A. Knopf, Inc., 201 East 50th Street, New York, N.Y. 10022.
Published in the United States by Alfred A. Knopf, Inc., New York, and simultaneously in Canada by Random House of Canada Limited, Toronto.
Distributed by Random House, Inc., New York.

Library of Congress Cataloging in Publication Data

Slavin, Arthur Joseph.
  The precarious balance.
  (The Borzoi history of England, v. 3)
  Bibliography: p.
  1. Great Britain—Politics and government—1485–1603. 2. Great Britain—Politics and government—1603–1649. 3. Great Britain—Economic conditions. 4. Great Britain—Social conditions. I. Title.
  II. Series.
  DA26.B65 vol. 3   [DA315]   942 [942]   72-11840
  ISBN 0–394–47951–3
  ISBN 0–394–31119–1 (text ed.)

Typography by Jack Ribik

Manufactured in the United States of America

To Walter Richardson, who first opened Tudor history to me

Foreword

The volumes making up the Borzoi History of England spring from the desire the authors share to preserve for the present the excitement of the English past. To a somewhat smaller degree we also share a prejudice against the writing of a history unified artificially by an allotment of "factors" and "forces." We do not think a good consecutive history of England between the coming of the Anglo-Saxons to Britain and the British entry into the Common Market can be made by such stinting of work.

This is not to say that we dismiss the need for a concern over how five volumes by as many historians go to make one history. It is to say that we began by admitting the diverse character of our assignments. We recognized at the outset that what might be central to the history of Anglo-Saxon England might be eccentric, if given the same weight by another author, to a history of industrial England. Moreover, we began in agreement that our own gifts and interests, if followed in a disciplined way, could bring out of many volumes one book.

Professor Rosenthal's history of early English society employs a narrative technique around a political center. Yet his most basic concern is to give the reader a sense of the rudeness of life in Anglo-Saxon England.

Because Professor Rosenthal had so firm a base on which to work in Volume I, Professor Powicke agreed to concentrate his work in another direction. He set out to tell how the medieval realm was ordered. While not altogether abandoning traditional narrative, he thought it profitable to set out in detail the shape and character of the various communities that constituted the medieval realm—royal, ecclesiastical, urban, and manorial.

The aim of the medievalists was thus to establish and explain the institutions and culture in a broad way, while telling how they worked. Their working order was profoundly challenged over a period of time stretching from

Chaucer's age to that of Milton, or, reckoning politically, from Edward III's time to that of Charles I. It was my concern to describe and explain how a series of shifts in the social basis of politics led the English to reorder a turbulent commonwealth.

The efforts at establishing political, religious, and social stability undertaken by the Tudors proved more daring than durable. Professor Straka and his wife wished to deal with the undisputed establishment of political stability between the Puritan Revolution and England's wars to contain the expansion of revolutionary France in Napoleon's time. Where Volume III sought to base an analysis of government and society in the economic and religious life of the era, the Strakas thought it essential to tell how stability was achieved in terms narrative and political at heart. They felt they could build confidently on the descriptions already achieved in Volume III, just as Professor Powicke thought to thicken the texture of the society whose shape was defined by Professor Rosenthal.

This alternation was acceptable to all because we accepted in principle the existence of three great revolutionary situations in English history—that surrounding the Norman Conquest, another focused on the Reformation, and a third based on the transformation of a mixed commercial-agrarian society into an industrial one. It fell to Professor Conacher to take forward into our time the account of the revolution that made aristocratic England into the liberal, industrial democracy of the empire and the welfare state.

Hence this History has taken shape around two concerns: giving scope to narrative, where the story of change was itself dramatic in social terms rather than in dynastic ones; and allowing room for more analytical work, where this seemed to point to an understanding of why changes took place rather than merely what changed and how.

Our historical assumptions reveal a pluralism rather than the ideas of a "school." Our concerns and styles differ, and we hope this difference is appropriate to our problems. We felt we would work best if we marched to the drum each heard best, whether it was the steady one of ordinary people working the land and the common rhythm of factory pistons or the subtler one beating to political tunes in high places. It has been our hope thus to avoid the mere repetitious noise of texts cut to cover uniformly every aspect of society. Philosophers say nature does nothing by leaps. History, however, is constantly surprising; it is alive precisely because of its variety, its stubborn refusal of any lockstep.

Between the extremes of Alfred's tight little island and the august empire ruled by Queen Elizabeth I's heirs and successors, English history lies, a polyglot thing, nurturing our own civilization and its discontents. Since the time when Ranke spoke of national histories as a perfect guide to a people's consciousness, the sense of history has profoundly altered. Yet narrative—description and analysis centered in political life as widely defined to make room for religion, economics, and popular culture—has not yielded its central place. We therefore offer this History: of a country bound in by her triumphant sea; a sepulchre for famous men; an often bleak workshop; a place that sent blacks into slavery in 1562 in a ship named *Jesus*; frankly political.

Contents

LIST OF MAPS AND ILLUSTRATIONS

Introduction

In his *Utopia* Thomas More gives a detailed account of a society markedly English in its setting and in certain details but markedly un-English in its perfections. After setting the island geographically and topographically, his narrator, Hythlodaeus, elaborates. He gives a picture of the society's agricultural basis; passing from the farm to the city, he describes its commerce and industry. Only then does he give details of Utopian government, on the national and local levels, before relating anything of religion and recreation. The frame of work and family contains and defines society and government.

I mention this because my own progress through England in this book takes roughly the same turns, and also because I want to dispel the notion that my method imposes a modern prejudice on the reality of an old society. Thomas More took it as axiomatic that to understand Utopian government in relation to Utopian society you had to know first the way of getting and spending. This old-fashioned analysis has recently come under some heavy fire from powerful guns, chiefly because such elaborate scene-setting is supposed to detract from the main purpose of political history.[1] I do not agree with Professor Elton on this matter, but in most things I have to admit that my idea of narrative thickened by description and analysis owes much to his inspiration.

Any historian concerned with things Tudor has dipped into other men's harvest. I am especially conscious of having taken corn from many barns in putting on paper my account of England in the stretch of time running from the great dislocations of the fourteenth century to the circumstances of Caroline society. I have borrowed in the hope of generating new capital, mortgaging myself to generous friends and distant colleagues in the desire to give students a share in their stock.

The debt I have incurred will be obvious from the extensive bibliographic notes. Because the debt is so vast, errors of payment are inescapable. I must

[1] See especially G. R. Elton, *Political History* (New York: Basic Books, 1970), pp. 165–70.

therefore thank those who go unrecognized but who have allowed their goods to be common in the Utopian way. I want also to thank Bill Frohlich for suggesting this book and the editorial staff at Knopf for seeing it into press.

Lastly, I want to explain the dedication. Professor Richardson first opened to me books of history, especially Tudor history. Nearly twenty years ago he was my teacher. He has remained an unstinting friend. Now, having tickled students' tender wits as well as the tougher ones of the readers of his many books, he verges on academic retirement. This book is my thank offering to Walter Richardson, written for my students in the spirit of Francis Lenton, once a member of an Inn of Court, and dedicated to Professor Richardson as from "an infant newly crept from the cradle of learning to the Court . . . from his tutor to the touchstone of his wits . . . ."

Chapter One
THE PRECARIOUS BALANCE

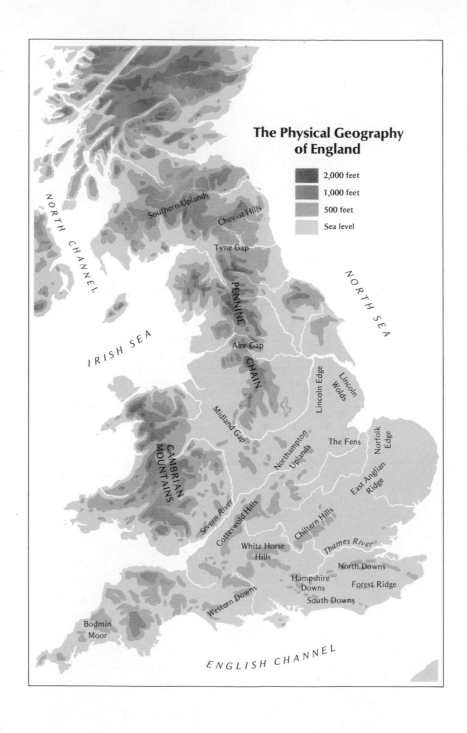

The Physical Geography of England

2,000 feet
1,000 feet
500 feet
Sea level

NORTH CHANNEL

NORTH SEA

IRISH SEA

Southern Uplands
Cheviot Hills
Tyne Gap

PENNINE

Aire Gap

CHAIN

Lincoln Edge
Lincoln Wolds

Midland Gap

CAMBRIAN MOUNTAINS

Northampton Uplands

The Fens

Norfolk Edge

East Anglian Ridge

Severn River

Cottswold Hills

Chiltern Hills

Thames River

White Horse Hills

North Downs

Hampshire Downs

Forest Ridge

Western Downs

South Downs

Bodmin Moor

ENGLISH CHANNEL

Villeinage Ceases but the Poor Law begins.

R. H. TAWNEY
The Agrarian Problem in the Sixteenth Century, p. 46

Englishmen in 1450 were uncommonly nervous. Their political, economic, intellectual, and social systems were delicately balanced between two worlds. One was feudal and aristocratic in its culture, dying but not yet dead. Its inhabitants viewed decadence and ambition rather differently than did rising wool merchants, lawyers, and peasants. They feared the world that was then coming to birth, and even more the upstarts who were its heralds. Fear deepened their social conservatism. They preferred present dangers to future ones, the traditional agrarian society to one braced by the expanding commercial capitalism that was to characterize England by 1640.

In large measure the revolutionary social tension in 1450 stemmed from the consequences of two basic shocks to late medieval economic life. These were the collapse of seigneurial exploitation of demesnes (estates) before the pressures that favored a *rentier* economy of rural capitalism, and the consequent shift in relations binding the classes associated with the land. By the late fifteenth century the demesnes had been leased, serfdom had declined markedly, and peasant living standards had climbed steadily, not to fall until after 1510.

The relationships of land and agriculture to technique, population, and capital modeled English society, as it responded to brute material force, human decisions, and inventiveness. Occupations and wealth varied from region to region, partly because of the details of a relief map, which starkly contrasts lowland and upland regions, areas that are crop oriented and those that are stock oriented, the dry eastern areas and the plentifully watered West and North. The land thus lent itself differently to human use in Yorkshire and Kent. But its precise employment depended on the adaptability, the efficiency, and the changing numbers of the men using it.

Fifteenth-century agrarian life turned chiefly on the shifting population patterns that occurred after 1348. Consider only for a moment the movement of the center of textile production from the southeast to the west and north, between about 1275 and 1520. Wool raising, gathering, and processing dominated English trade. Any shift in its locale or purposes must necessarily have affected the order of society, as did the consequent abandonment of cropland for pasture or the destruction of peasant villages to accommodate sheep. This complaint was heard in Hertfordshire in 1506:

About eighty years before, Pendley was a great town. . . . There was in the town above 13 ploughs besides diverse handi craftesmen, as tailors, shoemakers and card-makers. . . . The town was afterwards cast down and laid to pasture by Sir Robert Whittingham who built . . . Pendley Manor at its west end.[1]

Hence to study the physique of England in relation to her population in the fifteenth century, her soil, and her profile is central rather than eccentric. The land was the frame of society. For us it is also an open-air museum. There Englishmen once saw heaven mirrored, and there we may see the history of a changing social order.

By 1450, England had witnessed a century of rapid changes in the value of land and money, movements of population, and swift shifts in social obligations rooted in the soil. She was recovering from a century of decline and stagnation in the agrarian economy. A slowing of prosperity early in the 1300s had given way to a downward plunge after the onset of plague in 1348–9. The demand for food contracted. Death waxed fat. Shortages of labor were alarming. Apocalyptic speculations flourished.

There is now general agreement on what happened in English society because of these grave dislocations. As population decline set in, the economy shifted against demesne agriculture. A reduced demand for food, and wage inflation caused by labor shortages, raised the hazards of large-scale seigneurial agriculture. Estates were broken up. Some lords abandoned labor-intensive crop farming for pastoral farming and mixed-stock raising.

An Expanding Agrarian Economy

On most estates there was a pronounced shift from dependent peasant labor services toward tenants farming leaseholds with wage labor. Lords compromised their power and direct control over the peasant population in return for money rents. Fixed obligations grounded in servile tenures yielded to contractual bonds connecting lords, farmers, and the labor force. Stagnation, depression, and retrenchment ruled.

These are the bare bones of an agreed-upon skeleton. How these transforma-

[1] Quoted in Maurice Beresford, *The Lost Villages of England* (London: Lutterworth Press, 1954), pp. 147–8. On the contribution made to understanding the countryside by local historians, see W. G. Hoskins, *The Making of the English Landscape* (London: Hodder and Stoughton, 1955).

tions took place, what their background was, and why they should occupy our attention require more detailed examination. To understand how the agrarian balance shifted between 1350 and 1450 and what consequences this shift had between 1450 and the 1540s, we must briefly examine the relationships between land and labor in two distinct periods of agrarian history: the period of bust and stagnation (1350–1450) and that of consequent recovery and reflation (1450–1540).[2]

Villages and agrarian hamlets in medieval England were neither self-sufficient nor self-contained. Even in the Anglo-Saxon age external factors—nonlocal elements—frequently transformed the countryside. Population changes profoundly affected farming; so did disturbances in trade, the failure of government to preserve the peace, and the prices brought by corn and wool. Neither lords nor peasants had much control over such things. But lords had the freedom to react denied to peasants. They kept records of their estate policies, through which we may often reconstruct broad economic movements. From accounts and surveys of estates and royal court records, it is clear there was an enormous transformation in agriculture after the Black Death. Evidence suggests that before 1300 there had been a tremendous extension of seigneurial exploitation; the area of demesnes increased substantially. Administrative technique improved, helping to maximize profits. Baronial incomes rose more than 60 percent between 1150 and 1220. The buoyancy of agriculture continued; and between 1220 and 1260 baronial incomes increased by amounts between 51 and 64 percent.[3]

Other data tell similar stories. In the thirteenth century, more than 3,000 grants of markets were made to manorial lords. Between 1154 and 1250, some eighty-eight new towns grew up on baronial and ecclesiastical estates, six of them within lands controlled by the rich bishop of Winchester. A campaign was waged to attract settlers to previously uncultivated lands, and the internal

[2] The best general introduction to the economic history of England in the later Middle Ages may be found in the following books: Sidney Pollard and David Crossley, *The Wealth of Britain* (London: Batsford, 1968), pp. 1–82; J. R. Lander, *Conflict and Stability in Fifteenth Century England* (London: Hutchison University Library, 1969), esp. Chap. I; E. F. Jacob, *England in the Fifteenth Century* (Oxford: Clarendon Press, 1961); Joan Thirsk, ed., *The Agrarian History of England and Wales, IV: 1500–1640* (Cambridge: Cambridge University Press, 1967); and the brilliant early chapters of F. R. H. DuBoulay, *The Age of Ambition* (New York: Viking, 1970). On the expansion before 1300, see especially R. Lennard, *Rural England 1086–1135* (Oxford: Clarendon Press, 1959); H. E. Hallam, *Settlement and Society* (Cambridge: Cambridge University Press, 1965); H. C. Darby, *The Medieval Fenland* (Cambridge: Cambridge University Press, 1940); W. G. Hoskins, *The Midland Peasant* (London: Macmillan, 1957); and B. H. Schlicher von Bath, *The Agrarian History of Western Europe, 500–1850* (London: Arnold, 1963).

[3] The figures relate to two different periods: the 1150–1220 increases averaged 60 percent, and the 1220–60 increases from the new base went as high as 64 percent, and as low as 51 percent.

colonization of England went forward rapidly. Estate documents show this assarting—bringing woodland, marsh, or waste under the plow—occurring at a fever clip in the 1200s. The king's forest records reveal a steady encroachment by peasants on royal parks, forests, and villages. There were no signs of a slowing of expansion until nearly 1300.

Now this fantastic increase in land clearance, baronial and ecclesiastical income from agriculture, and what we may call the "national output," implies a need for vast increases in food supplies to feed a rapidly growing population. Whether the evidence is economic or bears directly on population data, it agrees with the hypothesis of a violent upward demographic surge between about 1100 and 1300, with perhaps a slowdown and a new balance in the period 1280–1340.[4] Since there was no revolution in agrarian technique in England, the new demand for food was met extensively rather than through more intensive cultivation, breed improvement, or increases in yield per acre of grown crops. Fertilizer supplies were slender. This meant that soil exhaustion, which kept yields low, was always a problem. It is likely that the forced use of marginal lands from the 1290s through the 1340s decreased average yields slightly. This of course had an effect on stock raising, by limiting feed. There was thus a natural limit on fertilizer supplies. Livestock and food production were locked into the extension of cultivation in a negatively reciprocal way.

The view that the condition of the English peasantry had declined markedly by 1300, that perhaps the vast majority of Englishmen lived at or near the subsistence level, was formulated by M. M. Postan many years ago.[5] His belief was that the expansion of population after 1100 was not accompanied by an equal expansion of production. Despite an extensive reclamation of land with the primitive techniques available, by 1300 the limit of expansion had been set by the marginal caliber of the latest assarts. Since population was still expanding, if perhaps at a slower rate than in previous centuries, the early fourteenth century witnessed a condition of relative overpopulation—in proportion, that is, to available food resources. The subthesis, which holds that especially after 1270 marginal land was cultivated under extreme pressure, led to a second major hypothesis. Long before the Black Death struck, Englishmen had been

[4] For the so-called demographic hypothesis and the analysis that is based on it, see especially J. C. Russell, *British Medieval Population* (Albuquerque: University of New Mexico Press, 1940); H. E. Hallam, "Some 13th Century Censuses," *EcHR* (1958), X, pp. 340–61; J. Z. Titow, "Some Evidence of the 13th Century Population Increase," *ibid.* (1961–2), XIV, pp. 219–23; and M. M. Postan and J. Z. Titow, "Heriots and Prices on Winchester Manors," *ibid.* (1958–9), XI, pp. 392–417.

[5] Some illustrative data may be studied in the index of prices given in the Appendix, Figure 1, where the rise in prices is shown against the curve of population.

prepared for it. Even had there been no plague, the lowering of their living standard forced them to a largely carbohydrate diet, made them more susceptible to disease, and ensured higher mortality rates. A lower work efficiency and poor land reduced harvests somewhat. When the terrible cold and rains of 1315–17 produced widespread crop failure, famine ensued. This was enough to alter further the movement of population. In the 1320s, stock epidemics added to the woes of an already narrow margin of existence. The paradox of the pre-plague epoch ran deep: there coexisted a striking increase in wealth and a tragic fall in the well-being of most Englishmen. Higher profits for some meant higher prices, while wages, though on the rise, lagged behind. There was progressive land shortage and a labor supply that favored the lord against the peasant.[6]

The crucial element in these conclusions is the alleged rise of population. Recent research on tax records and other documents that list heads of households in 1086, 1279, 1337, and 1377 has provided figures for aggregate populations. These vary widely because the multipliers employed represent different estimates of family size and also different views on rates of mortality between 1348 and 1377, as we can see from two sets of figures:[7]

	Russell (mult. = 3.5)	Postan–Hallam (mult. = 4.5)
1086	1.1 million	1.6
1279–1337	3.7 million	6.25
1377	2.25 million	3.75

Studies of other data from numerous manorial communities also show wide variations without being inconsistent with a large overall growth. It is especially significant that replacement rates—the likelihood of a son surviving his father into adulthood—were often as high as 1.6–2.34 before the 1340s.[8] In the early 1400s such rates fell as low as .29 in some communities; they were not to reach unity (1.0) until the 1480s. That is consistent with a very large rate of change in the total population.

[6] This and what follows are based on M. M. Postan, "Some Economic Evidence of Declining Population in the Later Middle Ages," *EcHR* (1950), II, pp. 221–46; J. C. Russell, "The Pre-Plague Population of England," *Journal of British Studies* (1966), V, pp. 1–21; S. L. Thrupp, "The Problem of Replacement Rates in Late Medieval English Population," *EcHR* (1965), XVIII, pp. 101–19; B. F. Harvey, "The Population Trend in England, 1300–1348," *TRHS* (1966), XVI, pp. 23–42; and H. S. Lucas, "The Great Famine of 1315–1317," *Speculum* (1930), V, pp. 343–77.

[7] See the Appendix, Figure 2, for further population data.

[8] The decimal expresses the likelihood of any father being replaced in the population by an adult son. See Sylvia Thrupp's studies for this and other measures.

Whichever estimates we accept—and I think some figures are better than none—*there is no disagreement about the grand proportions of the increase before 1348–9.* What population expansion meant to the living standard can be grasped easily from other social facts. In 1086 there were 71,785 "plow teams," of 120 acres each, cataloged in the *Domesday Book,* or roughly 8.6 million acres under cultivation in England. If we adjust the plow team to 100 acres, as some insist we must, we have the smaller total plowed acreage of 7.2 million. Official English agricultural statistics for 1914 showed 7.7 million arable acres in cultivation. Each acre in 1914 probably yielded four bushels of grain for every one yielded around 1300. Furthermore, during the expansion nearly 50 percent of the land was under seigneurial exploitation, which meant it yielded nothing to the well-being of 90 percent of the people, the peasant masses, whether free or not. It is hard to escape the obvious conclusion. Unless an unchronicled revolution increased yields fourfold or brought 30 million acres under cultivation, by the 1340s the area of arable land per capita had progressively declined along with the standard of living. There was a swamping of resources, land, and foodstuffs.

As we have seen, economic evidence supports this view. So does the bulk of the manorial records. These show a fall in the average size of peasant holdings and the concomitant growth of a large landless, or semilandless, peasantry. The fragmentation of holdings, slender yields, and stock constituted a cycle of poverty. Since wage supplementation through day labor was not a good source of alternate income in a market already labor-redundant and characterized by tenures with servile labor, the peasant's lot was hard indeed. While by 1300 the *range* of peasant wealth had doubtless widened—there had emerged already a peasant aristocracy of perhaps 1 percent of the peasant population—free, wealthy peasants living in five-bay houses were not typical. Far more common were one-bay or two-bay houses, with rooms 12 feet by 10 feet, where large families resided and deep poverty prevailed. On the other side of the coin was landed baronial and church prosperity. The demesnes of the bishop of Winchester's lands marketed 82 percent of their grain for profit in the 1280s. Baronial incomes that averaged £202 (fifty-four) in 1180 had reached £668 (twenty-seven) in 1300. Luxurious buildings, almsgiving, noble living, and armed and liveried retainers marked the aristocratic existence. But the peasants knew best Death, Judgment, Heaven, and Hell. Most were living on pieces of land of smaller size than the quarter-virgate ($7\frac{1}{2}$ to 10 acres) thought to mark the line of mere subsistence.[9] Evidence from widely different sources with great geographical spread shows that around 1300 about 45 to 50 percent of all peasants worked less than a quarter-virgate of land. In some

[9] R. H. Hilton, in *The Economic Development of Some Leicestershire Estates* (Oxford: Oxford University Press, 1947), would set the line at half a virgate!

Winchester manors, 85.9 percent fell below the subsistence level, the lowest common denominator of an agrarian society.

The Black Death and Earlier Checks to Growth

The grim effects of rising population and falling real wages were reversed by human tragedy on a grotesque scale. Between 1348 and 1377, England lost population because of plague and related causes at the rate of four lives in ten. Between 1348 and 1485, there were thirty "plague-years," highlighted by countrywide epidemics in 1348–9, 1361–2, 1369, 1375, 1390, 1407, 1413, 1434, 1464, 1471, and 1479. Those of the fifteenth century were primarily urban phenomena. The severest sieges were the first two. The people infected usually suffered severe pneumonic complications, which varied with age, sex, density of population, and previous exposure. After 1348–9, the young, lacking the immunity of parents who had survived the same siege, were more severely affected. This sharply reduced the replacement potential of the whole population. The shrinkage of population had important social effects; it encouraged early marriages and enhanced the personal freedom of many. It severely strained the human resources of the church, causing severe shortages of clergy. But its economic impact was even more profound and had wide-ranging social consequences for rural England.

Direct evidence of the slaughter is not wanting. On some Crowland Abbey estates in Essex adult tenants died in these proportions in 1348–9: Oakington, 35 out of 50; Dry Drayton, 20 out of 42; Cottenham, 33 out of 58. At Blackmore in Sussex, the rate was 50 percent. At Petworth, Sussex, the number of heriot payments—tributes due to a lord upon the death of a tenant—rose from 4 in 1347–8 to 58 in 1348–9. Vocations leading to the vows for priesthood in the Cistercian Abbey of Quarr on the Isle of Wight, Hampshire, stood at an average of 3.7 per year in 1347–9. Between 1367 and 1403 the annual average of males professing vows fell as low as .58.

W. G. Hoskins has shown, in his study of Wigston Magna, that the pre-plague (1348) population of about 500 tenants fell to 110 by 1377 and did not recover until about 1600. Leicester City, which had 4,800 inhabitants in 1327, had only 3,152 survivors in 1377. Similar suggestions of decline emerge from studies of the turnover in names of families occupying tenements in certain villages between the 1340s and the 1390s. Hertfordshire evidence culled from widely scattered towns and villages shows replacement rates as low as .29 and .42 early in the fifteenth century. One historian showed that on a Hampshire manor, Bishop's Waltham cum Burseldon, 13 of every 20 tenants had died between 1348 and 1362! The average mortality on 22 manors of Glastonbury Abbey, Somerset, was 54.6 percent, with a range of 33.3 to 69.4 percent.

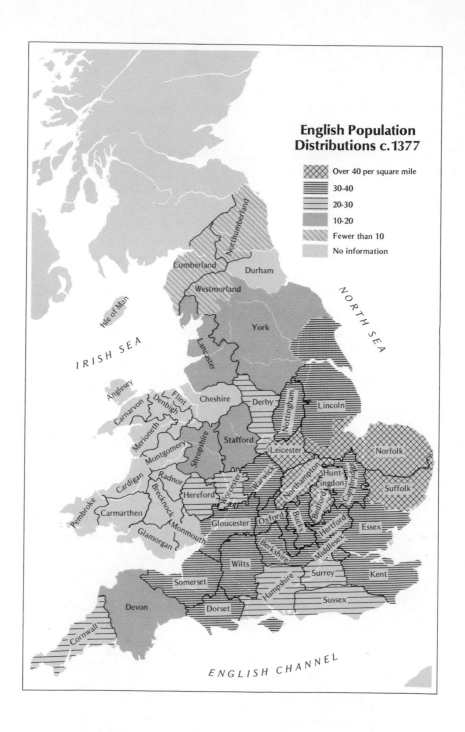

**English Population
Distributions c.1377**

Over 40 per square mile

30-40

20-30

10-20

Fewer than 10

No information

NORTH SEA

Northumberland

Cumberland

Durham

Westmorland

Isle of Man

York

IRISH SEA

Lancaster

Anglesey

Flint

Carnarvon

Denbigh

Cheshire

Derby

Nottingham

Lincoln

Merioneth

Montgomery

Shropshire

Stafford

Leicester

Norfolk

Cardigan

Radnor

Worcester

Warwick

Northampton

Hunt-
ingdon

Cambridge

Suffolk

Pembroke

Brecknock

Hereford

Bedford

Carmarthen

Monmouth

Gloucester

Oxford

Bucks

Hertford

Essex

Glamorgan

Berkshire

Middlesex

Wilts

Somerset

Hampshire

Surrey

Kent

Devon

Dorset

Sussex

Cornwall

ENGLISH CHANNEL

These figures are compatible with our claim that overall mortality *c.* 1348–62 was about 40 percent. England and Europe as a whole had experienced a catastrophic change in population and in the relationship between land and labor. It was without precedent in historical times. The decline continued well into the fifteenth century. Available data suggest that strong growth began only in the later fifteenth century—slowly at first, and then rapidly. Yet most scholars believe the pre-plague level was not regained until 1600.

The Black Death brought into bold relief some grotesque correlations—often noted in modern agrarian societies—between land-hunger, famine, and disease. Food supplies and death rates run together. Estates had been pushed to the limit before 1348. Competition among laborers had been intense. But disaster drove seigneurial profits down and *improved* the lot of peasant survivors. Entry fines began to fall; the size of peasant holdings showed an increase; wages rose, especially agrarian wages and those paid to unskilled workers. These rises were the more marked because they were larger than increases in the prices for consumables. This of course meant a reversal of the downward trend in real wages. Real wages increased and remained stable from about 1348 until 1510, when the precarious balance that was struck about 1450 turned once more against workers, and population and prices began to increase faster than production.

There is some dispute among historians as to whether these trends, which dominated the period 1350–1450, did not in fact begin earlier in the fourteenth century. We have already called attention to the famines of 1315–17, livestock epidemics, the end of assarting, and some evidence of population stagnation before 1348. In some shires—Cambridge and Huntingdon, for example—perhaps 25 percent of all land was already out of cultivation by 1341–2. Rents there and in Yorkshire, Bedfordshire, Buckinghamshire, and the southeast Midlands as a whole were falling. Some landlords were already reexamining the assumptions of the age of expansion. Here and there demesnes were leased out, labor was scarcer, food prices were down. These things are arguable before 1348, but they are certain after the Black Death struck, whether "trends" were magnified or not. At first the backlog of land-hungry men among the tenantry was sufficient to ensure the taking up of a plow as soon as a dying man relinquished it. This meant that in the 1350s and 1360s—perhaps even in the 1370s or 1380s in some places—the reversal in relationships between lords and peasants came more slowly. By the 1390s, pace was irrelevant, and all England had been engulfed in a decline and depression in agriculture that was to last into the 1440s.[1]

---

[1] The literature on the changes in agrarian society in England *c.* 1350–1540 is vast, ranging from general studies of social groups to particular accounts of manors, counties, regions, social classes. I have drawn data from dozens of monographs and journal articles and cannot cite them all here.

Landed income for lay lords, ecclesiastical corporations, and the crown fell. Between 1350 and the 1380s seigneurial incomes were off by as much as 10 percent. They were somewhat artificially maintained by the pent-up demand for land; as the progressive deterioration of population and demand set in, sharper falls were common. The Percy estates in Cumberland, Northumberland, and Yorkshire showed losses of 25–33 percent, 55 percent, and 25 percent, respectively, between 1375 and 1460. As great a magnate as Richard, duke of York, lost 15 to 30 percent of his landed revenue by the 1440s. The Mowbray dukes of Norfolk experienced similar losses on their Forncett lands in their titular county. When assessing wealth in hard-hit counties and villages, the king's tax collectors took the general depression in agriculture into account. Leicestershire, for example, a center of prosperous free-peasant farming, paid £757 in subsidy in 1334. In 1433, a rebate of £79, or just over 10 percent, was given, followed by another of over £50 in 1446. Rebates for the county ran from lows of 2½ percent to highs of over 40 percent. The grounds were stated to be the impoverishment of agriculture. The national figures for taxes actually collected declined from £37,000 to £33,000 between 1334 and 1433, and sank to £29,000 in 1446. The real revenue from crown land fell by 36 percent between 1422 and 1432, in the nadir of the depression. Loughborough Manor rent totals fell from £5 in 1348 to £2 in 1413. At Markfield, rents declined by over 50 percent, and 289 good arable acres, because they had no tenants, returned nothing. Grave declines in land revenue have been traced on ecclesiastical estates: Durham Cathedral Priory, Ramsey Abbey, Glastonbury Abbey, Quarr Abbey, and some Canterbury episcopal and priory lands.

While it is true that the Gray family of Ruthin, the inhabitants of Tavistock Abbey, and other individuals kept landed incomes up, the general trend was downward at a time of rising costs for labor, industrial goods, and estate management. The data vividly show the lords caught in the scissors of declining rents and rising prices. Accounts show also that meanwhile, among some

---

Instead, I will mention some of the most illuminating contributions of book length: R. H. Hilton, *op. cit.*; H. P. R. Finsberg, *Tavistock Abbey* (Cambridge: Cambridge University Press, 1951); P. D. A. Harvey, *A Medieval Oxfordshire Village* (Oxford: Oxford University Press, 1965); E. Miller, *The Abbey and Bishopric of Ely* (Cambridge: Cambridge University Press, 1951); J. A. Raftis, *The Estates of Ramsey Abbey* (Toronto: Pontifical Institute, 1957); R. H. Tawney, *The Agrarian Problem in the Sixteenth Century* (London: Longmans, 1912); J. Thirsk, *English Peasant Farming* (London: Routledge and Kegan Paul, 1957); L. Hockey, *Quarr Abbey* (London: Leicester University Press, 1969); J. M. W. Bean, *The Estates of the Percy Family* (Oxford: Oxford University Press, 1958); F. R. DuBoulay, *The Lordship of Canterbury* (London: Nelson, 1966); E. A. Kosminsky, *Studies in the Agrarian History of England* (Oxford: Blackwell's, 1956); F. M. Page, *The Estates of Crowland Abbey* (Cambridge: Cambridge University Press, 1934); J. A. Raftis, *Tenure and Mobility* (Toronto: Pontifical Institute, 1964); G. A. Holmes, *The Estates of the Higher Nobility in 14th Century England* (Cambridge: Cambridge University Press, 1957).

great lords, *expenditures* did not fall. Indeed, for the duke of York and the earl of Northumberland they rose steeply against the curve of income. Prices tended to stabilize around levels lower than the increase in wages. If the land-owners were suffering, artisans, laborers, and small farmers were not. Food prices ran ahead of rents, while wages tended to advance even after prices became stable in the mid-1400s.[2] The pattern set was thus one of increased real wages, or of some rise in the living standards of the lower social orders.

Depopulation Alters the Use of Land and Labor

(These developments, taken together, helped change English society in the period stretching from 1350 through the rebellion of Jack Cade (1450) and the onset of the Reformation in England. They included a general abandonment of demesne farming for leasing; a shift in the balance of agriculture from corn to grass, from arable to pastureland; destruction and desertion of hundreds of peasant communities under the pressures of pastoral farming; a general enfranchisement of the peasantry; upward pressure from yeomen and lower gentry elements, socially and politically; a general increase in social mobility; and marked changes in the geographical distribution of both wealth and population.)

The evidence seems beyond dispute. The Abingdon Abbey Manor of Lewknor, Oxfordshire, had in 1536 no demesne or home farming. All had been leased in the fifteenth century for money rents. Labor services had been commuted. While deeds do not show when the earliest leases were drafted, it is certain that 50 percent of the village tenants were lessees in the early fifteenth century. In 1279 these lands were worked by many villeins and a few free-holders. On Ramsey Abbey estates, between 1350 and 1450, every possible encouragement was given to artisans and wage laborers in an effort to get them to take up tenements once occupied by villeins. The *arrentata*—a money rent that commuted all customary work dues and services—was devised. Under this system, 50 percent of the manorial village of Houghton came under leases in a few years. Until well into the 1380s, Christ Church, Canterbury, made a determined attempt to hold onto direct exploitation through peasant labor. On some estates of Christ Church, the "seigneurial reaction" actually increased *praedial* duties. Yet by the 1440s all the best lands were in leasehold. Tavistock Abbey, with its exceptional balance of grain, wool, dairying, and industry (tin), successfully resisted the trend toward leasehold, as did some lay estates in the East Midlands and East Anglia. The Ruthin *Valor* shows the Grays increasing their profits on manors in eight counties by 34 percent be-

[2] See the Appendix, Figure 3.

tween 1420 and 1440, the most intense period of depression. But too much should not be made of the exceptions to the rule. Leicester Abbey surrendered to leasehold. On the Norfolk manor of Forncett, demesne agriculture collapsed by the 1420s. The situation on Ramsey estates was so serious that by the 1470s the abbatial treasury took the unusual step of acknowledging as hopeless all arrears in rents from rebellious, striking peasants.

The movement to lease the demesnes had three general phases: (1) resistance and partial surrender, the 1350s to the 1390s; (2) wholesale leasing, the 1390s to the 1440s; and (3) stagnation and inability to pursue leasing in the poorest lands, the 1440s to the 1480s. All these phases were evident on the Quarr Abbey estates. As early as 1208 the Cistercian General Chapter forbade leasing, and the prohibition was renewed in 1220. Alienation was again prohibited in a decree of 1293, although leasing that did not prejudice the rights of possession was tolerated. In 1315, under the pressure of change, the General Chapter gave new latitude, doubtless because the absence of *conversi*—lay brethren who did farm work—was pronounced. With the late fourteenth century came the beginning of the breakup of the demesnes, which Quarr's historian, Father Hockey, has glossed: "We shall [now] find the abbey having all along the years to acquiesce in an attitude of retreat." He also commented on the new equilibrium of the later fifteenth century:

With the last years of the fifteenth century, before we enter the wider stage of the sixteenth, there is a certain stability. . . . A system of rent economy had been developed . . . just sufficient to maintain the establishment. [Hockey, *op. cit.*, p. 199.]

Leasing the demesne was not, however, the only way to cope with economic adversity and inflated costs. The conversion from arable land to pasture, from labor-intensive grain production to sheep running, would also trim expenses. In addition, wool prices were buoyant because of a great expansion in the English wool trade and a rise in the manufacture of woolen textiles in England. This entailed a marked shift in the balance of grain and grassland in the agrarian economy, as entrepreneurs took advantage of the fact that wool prices ran well ahead of grain prices throughout the fifteenth century.[3]

Sheep farming had always been vital in the English economy. English place names reflect this. It is memorialized in the fact that the chancellor sits on a woolsack in Parliament. The High Streets of what are today historic villages of perhaps a thousand people are still wider than Fifth Avenue, Park Lane, or the Kürfürstendam; wide thoroughfares accommodated the sheep brought to market in the 1400s. And England's customs system still reflects its early basis in taxes on wool and hides. In the countryside one still sees the "wool churches"

[3] See the comparison of animal and grain prices in Figure 4 of the Appendix.

of Lavenham, Chipping Camden, and Ashwell. Since Roman and Saxon times, lords and peasants had kept sheep. The *Domesday Book* reveals a sheep population of perhaps 7.5 million, with peasant flocks in aggregate comprising 80 percent of the total. Yet, in the thirteenth century, arable land ran ahead of pasture by factors varying between ten-to-one and two-to-one, depending on region. Thus, although stock raising had always contributed heavily to wealth, during the age of expansion the premium was on cropland. The balance of price and profit favored grain over wool, even between 1280 and 1310, when exports of raw wool increased from 25,600 sacks to 35,000 under the pressure of Flemish and Italian industrial demand. Yet even before the Black Death, some landlords ran great flocks: the bishop of Winchester, the duke of Lancaster, Pershore Abbey, the Clares, Berkeleys, and certain Cistercian houses ran flocks of between 13,000 and 29,000 heads. Small and large flocks proliferated in the upland areas and in the sandy soils that were inhospitable to grain but that yielded fine wools—a quirk of nature by which poor sheep nutrition produces the best staple!

As the economy shifted against large-scale arable production, especially after the 1380s, landlords who saw the opportunities of grazing began wholesale conversion. The shepherd and his dog made for low wages and high prices. Sheep running could thus compensate for declines in arable yields and facilitate a policy of holding demesnes and resisting peasant demands for higher wages, commutation, and freedom.

How this could happen is illustrated by the way in which the duke of Norfolk and the abbot of Crowland met labor shortages on their estates. Flights of peasants were recorded as follows on the abbatial estates: 1380–1400—16; 1400–15—38; 1425—22; 1425–96—25. These flights, which peaked in the 1420s, coincided with the appearance of sheep on the demesnes. The flights of peasants became a problem for the duke at Forncett in 1375. Soon audacious tenants were enclosing abandoned strips to keep sheep; in 1404, they were fined by the estate bailiffs. A few years later it was the lord who enclosed vacancies for pasture, evicting some usurping peasants in the process. Throughout the rich Midland farming areas, the fall in assized rents and the rise in unfilled tenancies and decaying farmhouses encouraged entrepreneurial shifts to sheep. Although this shift was in some ways objectionable even when it was taking place, its greatest danger, as we shall soon see, was hidden in the future. What would happen if the population were to grow again, sharply and steadily, as it began to do by 1480, while much good arable land went back to waste or was converted to sheepfolds? How would an enlarged population then feed itself?

By the 1440s the transition to demesne leasing and pasture was complete. The land most easily leased in 1450 was that suitable for sheep. The economies of the duke of Norfolk, Sir John Fastolfe, Osney Abbey, Winchcombe Abbey, Gloucester and Dorchester Abbeys, Tavistock Abbey, Canterbury Priory lands in Kent and Sussex, the bishopric of Winchester, the Stonors, Celys, Pastons, Berkeleys, Howards, Hungerfords, and countless lesser names that do not survive, piled profit on profit from sheep, their wool, hides, and meat.

But the land was sadder than such men and their corporation stewards. Not only did the shrinkage of the land under cultivation heap up a crisis for the Commonwealth men of the Reformation era, it also disturbed fifteenth-century observers, because it led to dispossession, the desertion of villages, changes in settlement patterns, and ruthless competition within the peasantry itself.[4]

Fifteenth-century people noticed the strains that were causing villages to decline and die. In 1414, an anonymous writer recalled the process: "There was made great waste in the manor . . . of housing . . . with none left standing there but it were a shepecote. . . ." In 1459, John Rous, the Warwickshire antiquarian, had petitioned Parliament to pass laws against depopulating enclosers. In his *Destructores Villarum*, Rous pointed out the extensiveness of the problem in the Midlands:

If such destructions as that in Warwickshire took place in other parts of the country, it would be a national danger. Yet not all my list is of Warwickshire villages; some, although a few, are in Gloucester and Worcester, but none of them more than a dozen miles from Warwick.

By 1488 there was a statute, limited only to the Isle of Wight, so vital to England's southern defenses, which spoke openly of the dangers of conversion to pasture:

It is to the surety of the realm . . . that the Isle . . . be well inhabited with English people. . . . The whole Isle is late decayed of people by reason that many towns and villages be let down and made pastures. . . .

[4] For what follows, touching on enclosures and reactions to them, see Beresford, *The Lost Villages, op. cit.*, from which come the quotations. See also: R. H. Hilton, "A Study in the Prehistory of English Enclosure," *Studi in Onore di Sapore*, I (Milan: 1957), pp. 673–85; Joan Thirsk, *Tudor Enclosures* (London: The Historical Association, 1959); F. G. Davenport, *The Economic Development of a Norfolk Manor* (Cambridge: Cambridge University Press, 1906); A. H. Johnson, *The Disappearance of the Small Landowner* (Oxford: Clarendon Press, 1909); E. F. Gay, "The Inquisitions of Depopulation in 1517," *TRHS* (1900), XIV, pp. 231–67, pp. 286–303 (a critique of J. S. Leadham, "The Inquisition of 1517," *TRHS* [1892], VI, pp. 167–314). Beresford's explanation of village attrition is criticized in J. D. Gould, "Mr. Beresford and the Lost Villages," *AgHR* (1955), III, pp. 107–13.

A year later a general statute was enacted, but its utility was limited, perhaps intentionally, as we shall see. By 1514, repeated proclamations to bolster the statute had failed. The king's Council examined the problem, and within a year a supplementary statute was passed. Cardinal Wolsey took a keen interest in it, as did reformers in his circle, especially Thomas More, who in *Utopia* (1516) wrote at length against those who multiplied sheep and "ate up men." In 1517, Wolsey launched the great inquiry one modern scholar called "the Domesday of Enclosure." Using his command of Chancery and its court, the cardinal amassed evidence that still survives and helps us to fix with certainty the answers to our questions.

The records of the 1517–18 legal proceedings against malefactors, in Chancery and Exchequer, make it abundantly clear that Rous was no alarmist. They show that the majority of hurtful enclosures took place before 1489, the year in which Parliament made September 1488 the limit of legal memory for actions against offenders. They also show how often enclosures defeated the interests of peasants and husbandmen, inducing conflict and often violence, because Parliament had in fact set the limit in time in a way unhelpful to most victims of enclosure. When John Hales' 1548 commission report on enclosures asserted that the chief destruction had taken place before 1489, Hales must have suspected that the legislators intended to give the appearance of justice while yielding to legal scrutiny nothing that they had done between 1450 and 1489. The chief consequences of their 1489 act had been to limit future competition to the grazing interests that had consolidated their power in the wake of the agricultural depression's depth, especially the 1430s and 1440s.

In the Midlands, where the damage had been greatest, the destruction of villages was all but over by 1520, although legislation enacted between 1535 and 1553 and the polemics of those decades serve to remind us how alive fear was.[5] The years 1485–1517 had witnessed only the tail end of the process. Only 16 percent of Northamptonshire's deserted villages fell before 1450. This was a proportion slightly lower than for Oxfordshire and slightly higher than for Leicestershire at the same date. With regard to the counties hardest hit before the Act of 1489—Bedfordshire, Berkshire, Buckinghamshire, Gloucester, Leicester, Middlesex, Northampton, Oxford, and Warwick—only the smallest communities went under before 1377. The great poll tax of that year shows most places that were alive in 1334 remained vital. Studies of county tax assessments by hundreds[6] and villages show also that most villages lost by September 1488 were not yet defeated in 1428, 1433, or even 1446. Hence the conclusion: it was not the Black Death or its immediate aftermath, but the

---

[5] See Chapter Five.

[6] An administrative and judicial subdivision of a county or shire in England (a unit that exists in some states here, Delaware, for example) that had its own court.

deep depression in agriculture and its consequences *after 1450*, that convinced lords and farmers to convert so swiftly from corn to wool.

We can in fact use the early Tudor evidence and the fifteenth-century tax materials, which remitted sums to villages of fewer than ten households, to trace the process step by step. Concessions to shrinking villages multiply: 1442, 1445, 1449, 1453, 1456, 1463, 1487, 1489, 1491, 1492, and 1497. These assessments were the fever chart that ended in death for whole communities. The darkest days spanned the period 1449–87, a striking vindication of Rous. Half of all Warwickshire casualties occurred between 1460 and 1500. The same was true of Nottingham between 1490 and 1500. In the East Midlands, defeat generally came earlier, while in the southwest the peak occurred in the 1450s and 1460s. Only in the north was the crisis a sixteenth-century phenomenon. Even in Lincolnshire, where, as in East Anglia, a large number of losses came in the 1300s, the whole picture emphasizes the crisis of the 1400s.

Lost before 1348	12
Lost soon after 1348	15
Lost before 1450	18
Lost 1450–1520	27

Evidence confirming the pattern is often found in church records. We can correlate the names of villages having fewer than ten householders and those declining in subsequent assessment with lists of parish churches abandoned because there were no souls to tend!

The Balance Upset

This adds up to a retreat of settlement, spread over more than a century, but most intense between 1450 and 1520. The impact of demographic change was not immediately felt. But over a long period of time the buoyancy of the wool economy defeated the interests of grain production, even after population growth began again about 1480. This exacerbated rural conflict. It upset the always precarious balance between wool and corn in early Tudor society. Cornland tumbled to grass, following the higher price of wool relative to grain. When grain prices did rise—slowly at first and then quickly and steadily from 1510 to 1550—there was no rapid reversal of the balance of production. The mushroom growth of England's textile industries and the boom in exports throughout the 1540s provided a hungry maw that took in wool and put out cloth, thus encouraging new conversions. All this in the face of increased population pressure on the food supply.

Nothing can provide a more striking contrast to the prosperity under York and the early years of the Tudors than the growth of poverty after 1510 and the swelling of the ranks of a new, landless proletariat suffering dispossession and a decline in real wages. The tide that for 150 years had created the "golden age of labor" and thrust forward a sturdy yeoman class drowned others. The balance that had prevailed briefly was insecure by the 1490s and only a memory between c. 1500 and 1550. Only the collapse of the cloth trade in the 1550s shifted the price balance toward wheat, a trend that lasted well into the seventeenth century. As Clement Armstrong commented, after exploring the roots of the shift, husbandmen plow when it is advantageous to do so and run sheep in a wool time.[7]

It comes as no surprise, therefore, to see eagerness among enclosers. In Buckinghamshire, the East Riding, Warwick, East Anglia, and Northamptonshire, local men knew what was true in Leicestershire:

The county gentlemen [of Leicestershire] . . . were not slow to learn from each other the new way of doubling their incomes by turning their estates into sheep and cattle pastures, and driving away their tenants from the one-time arable fields.[8]

The time, late 1400s; the motive, profits; the locale, as we have surveyed it, varied! The internal political disorders of England gave strong men the chance to do what they wished—within the law sometimes, on its fringes at others, or entirely outside it when necessary. Thus the fall in population itself helped create the condition in politics and society that disfigured the countryside and changed the balance of corn and grass. By a reciprocal motion, it provided ever-new causes of local conflicts that, in turn, could escalate into something else. The dominance of wool over wheat and barley was well suited to a period of reduced consumption of foodstuffs and declining population. It was a markedly different balance than that of the thirteenth century, when labor was redundant, food scarce, and the peasantry depressed in spirit and possessions. It was a balance that could not survive a new cycle of population growth and its economic consequences.

It was a balance made precarious not only in the long run. In the short run, land use was unsettled and tenurial relationships were shifting. As the peasants moved restlessly upward socially and outward geographically, capitalist landlords looked for new ways to exploit directly the men with whom they could not as yet live in harmony. Sermons and Star Chamber stories of riots and local rebellions between 1450 and the 1540s tell how delicate was the social order and how threatened society's traditional leaders felt. They feared most the

---

[7] Armstrong was a writer on economic and social questions and one of Cromwell's clients in the 1530s. See the discussion on economic and social questions in Chapter Five.

[8] W. G. Hoskins, *Essays in Leicestershire History* (Liverpool: Liverpool University Press, 1950), p. 129.

Biblical teaching that the last would indeed be first—and not without reason.

Lord and Peasant: Social Relationships Change

The post-plague crisis produced other pressures among lords who had lived off the direct exploitation of their demesnes. The maximum benefits of the agrarian boom had come to those who got the cheapest labor. Peasant redundancy had fostered competition among peasants before 1300, often for small holdings burdened by limitations on social, legal, and economic freedoms. Villein status had become common; indeed, customary peasant tenure became synonymous with the condition of serfs (neifs). Serfs were men without standing in the common law in manorial conflicts over rents and services.[9] Owing labor services became the test of servile status, and the continental customs of paying merchet (a fine paid by a tenant to his lord for liberty to give his daughter in marriage) and heriot were also included in the determination of servitude. A man who had to yield labor and money rents, beg permission for his daughter to marry outside the manor, and pay a fine before he could succeed his father in the family holding, was a villein. Between him and men born villeins (neifs, *nativus de sanguine*), distinctions vanished.

Thus customary tenure of peasant lands had developed *away* from freedom, despite assarts on land never before so burdened. In some areas of the Midlands, in East Anglia, Lincolnshire, and Kent, a free peasantry thrived; in Cambridgeshire perhaps 50 to 70 percent of all peasants were free. But in Oxfordshire fewer than 20 percent enjoyed free-peasant status. The pattern in the southeast and southwest was mainly toward servile status. Even in areas of great peasant freedom the presence of a powerful manorial lord might bring servitude: in fen-edge villages of Spalding Priory, Lincolnshire, and on lands of Bury St. Edmunds in Suffolk, for example. In Hampshire 30 percent of the peasants were free by 1300, yet only 5 percent of Winchester episcopal peasants were. The same pattern of exception existed on some Durham ecclesiastical lands and on the De Lacy estates in Lancashire. By the 1320s most customary tenants owed boon work, labor dues, merchet, and heriot. Although commutation for money dues was common, economic hardship persisted. Lords exacted a variety of payments beyond rents and entry fines; especially common were court fines, poll taxes, fees for mill use, and mortuary dues.

The Black Death accelerated changes in peasant status. Merchets and entry fines fell off; money rents almost universally replaced labor dues. Peasant tenures began to approximate the conditions of free tenure, whether freehold or leasehold. These changes followed closely the chronology of demesne leas-

[9] On the complicated question of the security of unfree tenures and the growth of the doctrine of estates, see the extended discussion in Chapter Seven.

ing and were essentially completed during the depression in agriculture that marked the early 1400s. They brought with them great mobility among the rural population, as tenants and laborers sought the best leases and highest wages. The demand for labor was uniformly strong in nearly all arable farming areas where the slaughter was greatest and demographic recovery slowest. Men of every rank with wits and a little capital increased the size of their holdings. A peasant aristocracy, which had emerged earlier, was now broadened and strengthened. Some peasants living on marginal holdings and some landless peasants moved to towns and took up urban crafts. Rich peasants sometimes invested their rural capital in town enterprises of a wholly bourgeois character, a movement we shall return to in another context.

Examples of this mobility are plentiful in every region of England: East Anglia, the Midlands, the North, the South. The evidence of vacated tenancies, peasant flights, and the enormous turnover in family names in village society thus helps to explain the manifest and growing tensions that produced sharp conflicts between lords and peasants and between the claims of custom and those of freedom.

The most important form of this tension and conflict is what Professor Hilton once called "the seigneurial reaction."[1] Not every lord "rationalized" his economy by freeing peasants, leasing demesnes, and running sheep. Some practiced a self-assertive repression of peasants instead of accommodation. The peasants who rebelled in 1381 complained especially of upward revisions of labor services, one alternate method of making demesne agriculture solvent under the new conditions. That seigneurial incomes fell only 10 percent before 1380 may itself point to intensified exploitation of peasant labor and the coercion of villeins. The evidence of statutes that kept wages down and restricted the mobility of labor gives substance to Chaucer, Gower, and Langland, each of whom complained about peasant threats to the traditional social order. The Commons was an assembly of landlords and guild industrialists in whose hands resided the power of enforcing the laws in the communities that composed the realm. Hence the seigneurial ranks in society were well placed to use political power in a futile effort to perpetuate artificially the cheapness of the labor on which they prospered.

Social change and fierce struggles therefore went hand in hand. Conflict existed among all the groups associated with the land: peasants against peas-

---

[1] For the development of peasant tenures, the seigneurial reaction, and the decline of villeinage in general, see Hoskins, *The Midland Peasant, op. cit.*; R. Hilton, *A Medieval Society* (London: Weidenfeld and Nicolson, 1967); Hilton's "Peasant Movements before 1381," *EcHR* (1949), II, pp. 117–36; and his "Freedom and Villeinage in England," *Past and Present* (1965), no. 31, pp. 3–19. Also see: H. J. Habakkuk, "La disparition du paysan anglais," *Annales: Économies Sociétés Civilisations* (1965), XX, pp. 649–63; and A. Savine, "Bondsmen under the Tudors," *TRHS* (1903), XVII, pp. 235–89.

ants, lords against lords, *rentiers* against their farmers, tenants against wage laborers. This makes the evidence of the seigneurial reaction worth stressing.

Given different mixtures of peasant restiveness, lords' margins of solvency, and real economic factors, bondage showed a striking longevity. In 1492 a woman on a crown manor paid *leyrwite*, the fine levied on an unchaste bondswoman (usually a pregnant but unmarried girl) for derogation from *le droit du seigneur*. On Canterbury estates in Sussex, bailiffs confiscated the savings of bondsmen because a serf's goods were his master's. At Methley, Yorkshire, a manorial jury was fined for not reporting as delinquent a man whose son was sent to school without the lord's permission. In 1458, on the same manor, a man's holding was seized in payment for his rape of a bondswoman (*nativa de sanguine*). On the earl of Warwick's Worcestershire estate, Elmley Castle, *chévage* (a capitation or poll tax) was taken from men absenting themselves from the estate in 1444. In 1495, 1498, and 1509, Elmley stewards collected merchet. On the bishop of Worcester's estates, boon work is recorded as late as 1503. There was also an echo of the labor surplus of 1300 in a Spalding Priory tenant's oath, exacted from bond tenants, "to be the Abbot's man." The court rolls of the liberty (a privilege, immunity, or right enjoyed by grant or prescription) of Tardebigge, in Fechenham forest, Worcestershire, have entries of boon work throughout the fifteenth century.

These estates also provide evidence of primarily fiscal motivations: forced manumissions for a price, as well as leyrwite, merchet, and heriot. Sometimes the case reveals how mobility itself created opportunities for the lords' financial exploitation of peasant tenures. The evidence of the lucrativeness of manumission is strong on some church estates. Heriot could also be especially attractive. William Heynes, a prosperous clothier, died in 1436 at Nethercombe, Worcester. He was by birth a neif. Having escaped villeinage, he prospered and at his death left chattels valued at over 3,000 marks sterling. Sir John Fastolfe, lord of the manor of Castlecombe, cast an eye on that fortune worth £2,000, and finally gained £140 in lieu of other claims that Heynes was *nativus de sanguine*! The pursuit of the fortunes of wealthy villeins into the towns where they prospered was not rare. Celebrated cases scattered about England—London, Norwich, Lincoln, Southampton, and Leicester—occurred in 1308, 1347, 1400, 1413, 1450, 1500, and 1536. Even in Elizabeth's time the courtier Sir Henry Lee played the game. In 1575 he got a grant of 200 bondsmen to be "found" in Duchy of Lancaster lands. This means he assumed the burden of *discovering* them, proving the discovery in law, and making suit in the Duchy Chancery for the instruments of manumission. These men had to accept compulsory manumission, at the cost of one-third of their lands and goods, when Lee sued for charters in the Duchy Chancery. As late as 1601 he was doing just that, having obtained rights to another hundred discoveries. The game must have been worth the candle.

Yet the reaction was doomed to fail. Economic and political conditions ensured that in the long run major changes in villeinage would come and that freer peasant life rooted in new manorial customs would dominate. A very large quantity of land had been removed from demesne cultivation and converted to leasehold, and much of it was taken by peasants. This meant that peasants enjoying customary tenements had not been legally enfranchised. But their holdings lost the taint of servility. It became copyhold, that is, tenure by copy of the custom of the manor, recently changed in order to reduce marks of serfdom. During the fifteenth century, freemen, even gentry, took up this refurbished copyhold, customary land. Much of it was held under fixed, terminable leases. The relationships of copyholders to lords or farmers were contractual and implied freedom. The courts gave protection to such "estates." On some manors—Ramsey Abbey's are good examples—the distinction between serf and nonserf disappeared between 1440 and 1500. After 1450 both common law and equity increasingly protected copyhold estates. Peasants were en masse increasingly law-worthy in a litigious society. They could sublet or alienate land and make their heirs secure in their inheritances.[2]

Despite the development of capitalist farming and the decline of serfdom, farming society retained its hierarchical and patriarchal character. There were strict conceptions of lordship and subordination, a ladder of owner-farmer-laborer. The social and political life of rural England, despite so much movement, was still tipped in favor of property and status, still bound in a framework in which deference determined more than "who–was–who." Land was power.

Yet it did matter then and for the future that legal freedom was increasing. Hereditary and juridical segregation of free and unfree was giving way to a stratified society in which a man's economic condition counted most. To appreciate the significance of this, it is enough to recall that in Catalonia, Prussia, Poland, Russia, and wherever the Teutonic Knights ruled, the seigneurial reaction was a *permanent* success. While peasant freedom waxed in England and France, it waned east of the Elbe River. It was not inevitable, then, that the same economic and demographic changes would produce the same social changes. Peasant freedom in England came at least in part because peasants were conscious of it. This consciousness they showed in 1381; and they were to demonstrate it again in 1450 and in 1549. They refused to accept the implications of serfdom. And the lords were finally unable to coerce them to do so. The reasons for this were partly political, partly psychological, and partly ecological.

There were in the great, dense areas of peasant settlements many communities of free peasants. Wigston Magna, the Leicestershire village studied by

---

[2] See the full discussion of these questions in Chapter Seven.

Professor Hoskins, was one of these. There was no resident lord. A rough village democracy prevailed until the late eighteenth century, when Parliament destroyed it by Enclosure Acts. Only one ninety-sixth of its land was in monastic hands. A numerous free peasantry maintained its open-field economy. Its inhabitants frequently granted and exchanged lands among themselves. Transactions ordinarily involved the larger peasant—the village aristocracy—trading with lesser men. Small parcels came and went. The peasants continually used money, which presupposes successful production of cash crops rather than mere subsistence. The energetic, lucky, or acquisitive few widened the gap between themselves and peasant laborers and small-holders in the fifteenth century. Yet even among such men as these, mobility was marked. Between 1377 and 1510, 90 percent of all family names changed. The outward mobility from Wigston was often that of prosperous free peasants, of men whose capital resources pointed them toward the urban opportunities of Leicester. The life of these people was free, willful, often violent; there were at least six murders in this village of 110 families between the 1340s and 1399. When the economic consequences of a grain depression hit such men, they were as likely to fight for their freedom as were absentee lords. Their struggles and their very presence in every great farming area provided the psychological, legal, and status impetuses needed by men who desired freedom. Consciousness played a role in the transformation of rural society, and this was not only seigneurial consciousness.

In the end, however, we must not celebrate too much either the free peasantry or the upward mobility of serfs. No modern village society came into being after 1400. The total security of copyholders was as precarious as the economic balance of English society. They were strong as long as real economic changes favored labor against lord, kept rent and entry fines down, and encouraged long leases and the free choice of heirs. By 1500 the tide was turning against the mass of poor men in rural society. By 1540 the impact of inflation had eaten up the economic advantages of the peasants and undermined their economic security, no matter what the courts did to protect the tenure of copyholders. In the areas where free peasants were most numerous, a new wave of conversion to pasture began. This helped some peasants and yeomen into the gentry. For most, however, it was a reversal of fortune, although it never meant a return to legal servitude; there was no need of that. In English rural society, capitalist farming using wage labor had become the rule. As prices rose again, real wages were depressed.[3] The landowners and large-scale farmers were entrenched in government, local and central. They controlled the public and private means for coercing tenants at will where necessary and for

[3] See the Appendix, Figure 3.

picking up the small properties of poor men driven to the wall by inflation. The first statute warning the good and the prosperous about "sturdy beggars" —those who had no land but shrugged off work—dates from 1473. When next we look at the countryside, it will be as Tawney said: villeinage will have ceased, and the Poor Law would soon begin.

The Middling Ranks of Rural Society

Upward mobility in rural society affected every rank between serf and aristocrat. One group to whom not enough attention has been paid is the tenant farmers. Throughout the kingdom they leased manorial demesnes; these men were the "thrifty husbandmen," "substantial yeomen," and "gentlemen franklins" we meet in the letters left by the Pastons, Plumptons, and Stonors. Accounts from diverse estates show us these *firmarii* (farmers or lessees of demesnes no longer directly controlled by the lord) over the years of the agricultural depression and the pre-Reformation recovery, c. 1420–1520. Many of their wills have survived and these, along with inquisitions held after their deaths, enable us to know how such men increased their wealth and enhanced their status in rural society.[4]

For the most part these men were resident farmers. The estate councils of great landlords knew that leasing the demesne was sound policy only if those who entered into the agreements were personal occupiers who would exercise care in the upkeep of what was still the lord's property. This applied to mills and buildings as well as to the land itself. The farmers who had the money to take up large leases were sometimes virgaters and rich peasants. But they were most frequently yeomen who had added acre to acre or merchants and gentry who had made money in trade, estate management, or the law. Around 1500 one-third of Canterbury Cathedral lessees were drawn from the local "gentry," while half were prosperous yeomen and husbandmen and the rest either rich peasants or London merchants. The best leases were in yeoman hands. However, the gentry were not slow to rent demesne farms or enter former peasant or yeoman holdings. And they practically monopolized leases in parks or sporting grounds good for hunting.

[4] On the development of the nobility, prosperous gentry, and yeomanry c. 1350–1520, see F. R. H. DuBoulay, "A Rentier Economy in the Later Middle Ages," *EcHR* (1964), pp. 427–38; H. L. Gray, "Incomes from Land in England in 1436," *EHR* (1934), XLIX, pp. 607–39; T. B. Pugh, "Materials for the Study of Baronial Incomes in 15th Century England," *EcHR* (1953), VI, pp. 185–94; A. Simpson, *The Wealth of the Gentry* (Chicago: University of Chicago Press, 1963); Julian Cornwall, "The Early Tudor Gentry," *EcHR* (1965), XVII, pp. 456–75; J. H. Hexter, "Storm over the Gentry," in *Reappraisals in History*, pp. 117–62; L. Stone, *The Crisis of the Aristocracy* (Oxford: Clarendon Press, 1965).

This underlines another facet of rural social change. Men with court connections were prominent among lessees, as were those already entrenched in the management of ecclesiastical estates. Leases were a form of patronage extended to kinsmen, lawyers, stewards, bailiffs, and politicians. Land was used to fashion new ties to hold together rural society in the face of the collapse of seigneurial power and feudal bonds between masters and men.

Social change blurred the lines of authority and obligation. There were peasants indistinguishable from yeomen, like Bishop Latimer's father, who leased a farm worth three or four pounds a year. On it he employed six peasant day-laborers, kept 100 sheep, and had a wife who milked thirty cows daily. Wigston Magna had a number of peasant tenants farming bigger estates. But the greatest confusion of rank and degree comes when we focus on the gentry whose rise in rural society before the Reformation is central to the understanding of society and politics.

The gentry who crystallized from the upper strata of tenant farmers, tradesmen, merchants, and lawyers were a heterogeneous lot. Yet it is possible to distinguish them from other groups in the countryside, partly because of their wealth and partly because of their success in securing tangible signs of their status. Such signs were sometimes political in character and sometimes social in the broadest sense, as if to satisfy this monastic complaint:

So that one person cannot be discerned from another in splendor or dress or belongings, neither poor nor rich, nor servant nor master, nor priest nor layman; but everybody tried to imitate the other, till the magnates had to decide on a remedy.

We can, of course, deal with the gentry from the point of view of economic standing. How many men were involved? How much property did they own? What part of the wealth of England did they enjoy? This approach may enable us to show one basis of differentiation within the gentry. Here the work of Dr. Julian Cornwall is salient. He studied five counties' tax lists and military muster documents dating from the 1520s. The counties include 10 percent of the whole English population of the period, and they represent the gentry *before* the vast flood of monastic lands came into lay hands. Hence the data from his inquiries show us the gentry as they had risen to dominate county wealth and politics in the 150 years *before* their alleged "rise" in the period 1540–1640. Failure to perceive the extent of their domination prior to the Reformation distorts the social and political realities of the Tudor Age and inhibits understanding of its most interesting aspects.

The numbers of gentry are shown in the table on the opposite page.[5]

[5] For the counties with large populations a sampling technique based on select hundreds was employed.

	Gentry	Adult Males	Percentage of Gentry/Adult Males
Rutland	2,000	35	$1\frac{3}{4}$
Suffolk	1,843	17	.9
Bucks.	12,000	72	.6
Sussex	16,000	140–80	.9–1.1
Cornwall	—	76	—

There is some distortion in these figures produced by the fact that some wealthy men in Suffolk satisfied their ambitions without abandoning bourgeois status, whereas in all counties some knights and gentlemen either had more than one principal residence or were taxed in special assessments of either the royal or ministerial households of Henry VIII and Wolsey.[6] What does appear clear, however, is that in the 1520s the gentry population varied above and below the 1 percent mark. Returns from later in the century show a figure of 2 percent as more typical. Thus, while the distribution of church lands did swell gentry ranks after 1536, the change was basically quantitative rather than qualitative. It did not mark a shift in gentry dominance of rural society. The tendency toward the concentration of wealth and power in gentry hands had reached maturity long before any date thought to mark their rise as a result of the Reformation.

In Dr. Cornwall's five counties the gentry possessed, before 1540, the greatest share of all land. They far outstripped the nobility. In Rutland they owned 37.7 percent of all land (by value) and 55.6 percent of land in lay hands. The peers had only 1.3 percent of all land. In Buckinghamshire the figures were 35.7 percent, 57.6 percent, and 4 percent. The margin between resident and nonresident ran in favor of the resident gentry in both counties, but not overwhelmingly so: in Rutland, 30.9 percent–23.7 percent and in Buckinghamshire, 30 percent–27.5 percent. If we differentiate the gentry socially by the ranks that appear in the documents, the real disparities in wealth within the gentry become evident. The data suggest some squeezing out of the weakest members, the "mere" gentlemen, a development that accelerated in the sixteenth century as the consolidation of the new rural aristocracy matured. There is a further correlation between the fortunes of the wealthiest gentry and their connections with the government and the court.[7]

---

[6] Government servants could obtain certificates of nonresidence and thus distort their representation in county lists.

[7] This development in the counties studied by Dr. Cornwall finds support in detailed analyses of the Tudor gentry. See especially the recent books on Lancashire and Yorkshire by Haigh, Smith, and Cliffe, listed in the Bibliography.

Gentry Status in the Feodary Surveys, Reign of Henry VIII

	Number	Minimum	Maximum	Medium
Knights	18	£53–16–8	£1,655	£204
Esquires	124	10–00–0	618– 6–3	80
Gentlemen	42	4–12–8	28–13–4	16–11–4

This tabulation as broken down by ranks within counties is particularly interesting if the results are compared with the assessments of knights and esquires in the households of King Henry VIII, Princess Mary, and Cardinal Wolsey. The court element clearly was richer than the provincial gentry as a whole.

Land Assessments in Subsidy, 1524–5

Ranks	County	Number	Minimum	Maximum	Medium
Knights	Suffolk	12	£20	£400	£130
	Sussex	8	50	460	120
	Bucks.	3	48	200	160
Esquires	Suffolk	27	20	200	50
	Sussex	17	5	180	50
	Bucks.	13	9	120	67
	Rutland	6	31	120	63
	Cornwall	13	20	133	60
Gentlemen	Suffolk	41	2	80	13
	Sussex	39	2	67	15
	Bucks.	28	2	160	17
	Rutland	8	5	42	12
	Cornwall	13	6	30	11
Knights	Court	26	50	1,150	225
Esquires	Court	8	—	—	116

Beyond the disparity between court-connected gentry and provincial gentry there is the obvious wide range of wealth between the knights and the poorest esquires and gentlemen. The knights as a group had few men whose chattels surpassed their land in value. This fact is significant because taxes were not levied on land and goods but on whichever category of wealth was the larger of the two. Not only were the estates of esquires generally only half as great as those of knights, but in a number of cases the goods of both esquires and gentlemen were of greater value than their lands. Yet these distinctions within the gentry were not as important as the fact that practically all gentry were *landowners*. Fewer than 50 percent of yeomen owned land, and estates among those who were freeholders rarely cleared more than five to six pounds a year. This "permanent interest" meant a great deal.

The development of the power of the gentry depended on their owning land. In social and political terms a relatively small fortune in freehold land meant more than an equal fortune in leasehold or a much larger one in chattels. The gentry owned a far smaller share of the entire wealth of their communities than they did of its land. Hence, within the gentry and in their relations with other groups in rural society, marked disparities in the kinds and amounts of wealth could provoke conflict. The lesser gentry were pressed hard from below and tried desperately to avoid slipping out of their position of privilege. The greater knights of the shires worked relentlessly to provide objective measures by which they could be known as the natural rulers of the countryside. They were aristocrats as truly as were the peers of Parliament.

Economic and social change had interjected between peasant and noble a range of men anxious to distinguish their present condition from their origin. Even before the Black Death, war had faded as the mark of honor and personal virtue. Tenurial distinctions had become so blurred as to be without value as the basis of social distinction. Legal and hereditary bases for caste had never existed in England. To avoid wealth's becoming the only measure of merit among men, alternative marks of status had to be elaborated. In the fifteenth century, for example, dress, marriage, education, and political privilege increasingly allowed easy identification of social groups.

Of these, nothing mattered more to the gentry than political privilege. While this often rested on an education in the common law or the universities —an aspect of society we will explore at length later—the rise of the gentry in the sociopolitical sense must be treated here. Their weight in national politics had increased radically from the mid-fourteenth century. By 1429 the county franchise had been redefined to allow only forty-shilling freeholders the vote. Only £100-freeholders were eligible to represent their shires at Westminster. By the force of statute *les gentils* and *les gentilhommes* were achieving a practical monopoly of county politics. Nowhere was this more vital to them than in Parliament; nowhere were its implications more obvious than at home.[8]

Ever since the 1360s the statute book had laid on the backs of the gentry an increasing burden in local government. Their powers as conservators and justices of the peace enhanced the status of a relatively small number of knights

---

[8] See Chapter Two, *passim*, for the significance of the gentry in politics, *c.* 1400–1540.

and gentlemen. County commissions of the peace fell under the headship of ministers and courtiers, but that lead was nominal. Entry into the sphere of authority for the greater gentry was not automatic. But, as we shall see, the crown needed their good will to ensure the peace, make jail deliveries, get loans, collect subsidies, levy soldiers, and control the sewers. The top third or quarter of the country gentry emerged with these honors firmly in their grasp before the Reformation. Of the 120 resident Sussex gentry in 1524–5, 23 were justices of the peace (J.P.s), 36 were subsidy commissioners, and 28 were on the commissions for sewers. The J.P.s almost always served on the subsidy and sewer commissions. The magistrates averaged £100 annually in either land or goods; the subsidy commissioners only about £80, which was chiefly in goods; those nonmagistrates on the commissions for sewers were rated at sums ranging from 100 marks in goods to 40 marks in lands. For those who had the king's confidence or a powerful patron, the access to office satisfied ambition while promoting the image of status justified by function. It also helped to create and sustain the mystique of the gentleman in Tudor society. The proportion of activists among the gentry in Suffolk, Rutland, Buckinghamshire, and Cornwall was similar to that in Sussex. The data indicate that economically, socially, and politically the gentry formed an upper crust in rural society and that among them a *corps d'élite* formed in the years between 1340 and 1540. Throughout the 1400s this elite group insisted on the recognition of their "degree" in every sort of document, especially in litigation. By 1510 the College of Heralds existed under royal patent to cater to the vanity and ambition of the group.

Some of their number achieved fame by reason of their knightly virtue. Others, like Sir John Fastolfe, by their cunning combination of war profiteering, exploitation of peasants, industrial enterprise, and good estate management. Many came to the land from the law. Names of great families spring to mind: Gages, Brudenells, Dudleys. The Pastons recapitulated the cycle by sending their sons to study in the London Inns of Court. Others prospered on speculation: Richard Beauchamp, earl of Warwick, hired an auditor of the royal Exchequer to prove his steward had bilked him of at least £1,860. We know from the letters of the Stonors, Pastons, and Plumptons that all of them had introspective yearnings about their gentility, and that all of them sought objective bases, beyond mere wealth, on which to erect their power and maintain it.

The changing distribution of wealth had not made men gentle. It had created intense pressure. Naturally the redistribution was viewed with varying degrees of favor. Those who fancied themselves the "old aristocracy" positively execrated the showy ways of the gentry, as Chaucer tells us in his " Wife of Bath's Tale":

But for ye speken of swich gentilesse
As is descended out of old richesse
That there fore sholden ye be gentil men,
Swich arrogance is not worth an hen.

Earlier, in 1385, a Benedictine chronicler, Thomas of Walsingham, had
pointed the finger at Michael de la Pole, then earl of Suffolk: "[He] is a man
more suitable for trade than for knighthood." The de la Poles of Hull were
merchants, financiers, and crown moneylenders. Walsingham's disdain, however, did not keep the earl's heirs from receiving a dukedom in the fifteenth
century. They were believable enough as great nobles in Henry VII's reign:
Henry executed John de la Pole as a threat to his Tudor dynasty. Nor were the
1385 complaint and the Tudor murder unique. In 1460 three earls of the
"king's own blood" castigated Lord Rivers: "You were made by marriage!"
 The so-called old nobility protested too much, however. The English
nobility was itself contributing to upward mobility and to the erosion of what
"aristocracy" signified. To get around the law of primogeniture, which restricted the descent of land in the interest of the king's feudal dues and services,
peers practiced "enfeoffment to use." This meant that during their lifetime
they alienated land to a certain man or group of men. These "feoffees" held
the land in trust for the grantor. On his death, therefore, the crown could not
claim what might be termed death duties, since the dead man had had only the
use of the land, and the holders of it were still alive. The holders could then
restrict the land to the use of several heirs, male or female, rather than to the
legally favored elder son. Familial conceptions of posterity made more flexible
the distribution of property and the social power that was its concomitant.
And in this way connections between the nobility, their cadet lines, gentry,
and professionals expanded. A side effect was that the nobility itself was under-
mining the meaning of feudal tenure.
 What was not weakened by social process and family-consciousness might
fall to nature. The idea of the old nobility is biologically suspect, for just as
bourgeois families and peasant families tended toward extinction in the male
line within three generations, so it was among the nobles. Families died out in
the male line almost every third generation; there was no difference among
social groupings or countries. Sylvia Thrupp showed that this fact applied to
London merchants, and Edouard Perroy found it to be true for the nobility in
France in the fifteenth century. Lawrence Stone found a similar span among
the English aristocracy between 1560 and 1640. Of the noble families represented in 1485, half had died out in the male line by 1547. There is no reason
to believe that the figures from about 1350 to 1450 were *more* favorable to
survival. Quite the contrary! The nobility of the fifteenth century was not very

"ancient." Between 1439 and 1504, sixty-eight new peerages were created. Only twenty-one represented honors based on a husband or son who survived an old peer's heiress, that is, re-creation through female descent. Forty-seven were wholly new creations. The early Tudor aristocracy was a thoroughly reconstituted elite.

Thus, like every other social group affected by the upheavals of the century and a half following the Black Death, recruitment from below was the rule of life. The basis of English society had become plutocratic rather than aristocratic. Wealth ruled at every level, and its varying fortunes and migrations linked urban and commercial England to rural England. Rank was no longer power, though it was still validating claims to power. Finally, the political involvement of the nobility in the civil wars of the century had an unwanted result. It ensured that the aristocracy, which was independent of the crown before Edward IV's reign, would be a dependent, courtier-service aristocracy reconstructed by the crown in its image before Edward VI's accession.

The Other England: Trade and Industry

This discussion of upward social mobility calls to mind that fortunes were made in London and the provincial towns from commerce, manufacturing, and the law. What the urban centers of England were like and how commerce and industry developed in this period are matters we must discuss before ending our analysis of economy and society between the Black Death and the Reformation.

There was in England in the fifteenth century some expansion of industry and trade. This buoyancy of the economy in the industrial sector has led some historians, notably A. R. Bridbury, to state that there was something like "economic growth" instead of decline and recovery in that century. This view seems unconvincing, if taken to mean that the growth of industry and commerce alone offset the well-established depression of the agrarian economy. What does seem to be true is this: there was a marked development in certain extractive industries and in the manufacture and export of cloth. These developments were momentous for the future. There was also a shift in the rank (in terms of population and taxable wealth) of English towns and a considerable enrichment of some urban communities, often by the migration of men with rural capital. These developments, and the recovery in agriculture after 1480, did in fact make the economy of 1540 more productive of wealth than it had been in 1450 or 1340.[9]

[9] For the general overview of the early development of industry and commerce in medieval England, see: L. F. Salzman, *English Industries in the Middle Ages* (Oxford: Clarendon Press, 1923); E. Miller, "The English Economy in the 13th Century," *Past and Present* (1964), No. 28, pp. 28–40;

Roughly between 1100 and 1300, English trade and industry were not yet strong enough to relieve the economy by providing jobs for the peasants who were so thickly crowded on the land. Mining clearly expanded, especially that of tin. But wool in its raw form was the chief export. On the Cornish peninsula there was a considerable expansion of towns around the stannaries. It seems that the lead-mining areas of the west and southwest fed an increasing military demand as well as a rising demand for church roofing. In Durham some silver was extracted from lead deposits. Both coal and iron, however, were still small-scale enterprises in the southwest, Wales, Yorkshire, the North Midlands, and the Weald of Sussex. While the output of iron quintupled by 1300, it scarcely exceeded 1,000 tons countrywide. England was in fact dependent on imports from Spain and Sweden for her iron supply. Salt, on the other hand, was a major English extractive export to Scandinavia and the Low Countries, and it was widely used at home as a preservative. On the whole it is possible that the manufacturing sector *declined* during the period of agrarian expansion, perhaps because the fall in real wages and the meagerness of peasant and artisan incomes lessened domestic demand.

The one industry with the potential to right the balance between resources and population was textile manufacture. English cloth was widely esteemed in the twelfth century. Prosperous weavers in the areas of York, Lincoln, Oxford, and Winchester formed strong guilds. But European competition from Flemish towns forced a decline after about 1200. The best English cloth could not compete in price with cloth on the Continent. Lower-quality cloth, worked in rural areas to take advantage of labor redundancy and freedom from guild restrictions, as well as water-powered fulling mills, had little export potential. Hence the textile industry contracted, unable to compete against the Flemish cost advantage and unable to overcome the decline of domestic purchasing power through conversion to low-quality products. Only the upper reaches of the peasantry could have maintained or expanded their consumption before the reversal in real economic factors in the mid-fourteenth century.

Yet the wealth of the church and lay landlords did create a demand for fine craftsmanship on a relatively big scale. Hence in some towns—London, York, Bristol—we see a characteristic urban growth throughout the period before 1348–9. Wool, metal, furs, leather: these were materials finely worked for home consumption. Several towns had specialist reputations—for example,

E. Power, *The Wool Trade in English Medieval History* (Oxford: Oxford University Press, 1942); G. R. Lewis, *The Stannaries* (Boston: Houghton Mifflin, 1908); E. M. Carus-Wilson, "The English Cloth Industry in the Late 12th and Early 13th Centuries," *EcHR* (1944), XIV, pp. 32–50; and Carus-Wilson and O. Coleman, *England's Export Trade, 1275–1547* (Oxford: Clarendon Press, 1963); M. Beresford, *New Towns of the Middle Ages* (London: Lutterworth Press, 1967); E. Carus-Wilson, *Medieval Merchant Venturers* (London: Methuen, 1954).

Coventry for metal goods and Northampton for leather. But in most towns the artisan groups were all well represented.

A few places became hubs of distribution networks. Some were internal, as was the case with York; others were external. Bristol, Boston, and London emerged as centers of international trade. Cloth, wool, and some metals went out to most of Europe. Imports, however, outweighed these, especially wine, dyes for cloth, and luxury goods of every description. The significance of this balance of imports and exports was central to the economy. Primary products were sent abroad. The surge in wool exports of course helped demesne agriculture and conferred a marginal benefit on peasants rich enough to have good flocks. On balance, however, England's imports included the augmentation in price that derives from the cost of labor needed to work a product, while its exports did not.

Thus the period is one of some urban growth, the development of a fairly sophisticated craft-guild system, and the establishment of a commercial network of credit and banking, a stable currency, and facilities for trade. Yet fewer than one Englishman in ten lived in towns in 1381. There had doubtless been a decline, after 1348, from a level inflated by the development of new towns and the growth of established centers. We have already called attention to the new towns of the period and the rise in the number and significance of markets. Many were local development schemes run by land proprietors anxious to build markets for demesne products. This illustrates well the general subservience of the nascent urban economy to rural interests. Towns were not yet industrial centers; they were, with few exceptions, distribution points for agricultural produce, and thus were inhibited by weak demand. Their failure to build craft capital and help an unbalanced economy to rectify itself was therefore not accidental.

Such was the situation of the urban economy, of trade and industry when the age of underpopulation came to England. What changes took place and what new arrays of forces shaped—or rather, reshaped—English trade and industry in the century and a half that preceded the Reformation? How did labor scarcity, coupled with rising real wages, affect an economy that had gone so awry before 1350? What did trade and manufacturing contribute to restoring the precarious balance of the economy between the Black Death and the Reformation?

We may take our cue from two great authorities:

It was obviously in the course of the later Middle Ages, and more particularly in the fifteenth century, that there took place the great transformation from medieval England, isolated and intensely local, to the England of the Tudor and Stuart Age, with its worldwide connections and imperial designs. It was during the same period that [there developed] . . . new methods of commercial organization and regulation, national in scope and at times definitely nationalist in object, and that a marked movement towards capitalist methods and principles took place in the sphere of domestic trade.[1]

The sweep of that judgment made by pioneers in the study of the urban economy in the fifteenth century suggests some subjects best reserved for another place—for example, the diplomatic aspects of commerce and the internal diplomacy by which the Merchants of the Staple helped restore the solvency of the crown through the profits of wool. Here we will sketch the changing nature of trade and industry, with a sharp focus on wool and textiles, the growth of towns, and the changing distribution of wealth before 1540. In this way we can prepare the way for a later examination of the relations between prosperity and politics.

There is a temptation to make a priori statements on industrial development in the fifteenth century. The population did shift downward markedly. This shrinkage of the home market (and markets abroad) and rising labor costs are said to have brought on a drastic slump in production. Some maintain that certain external factors had a compensating effect on extractive industries, especially on the cloth trade. As a result of changing techniques and forms of organization both manufacture and export trade in iron and woolen cloth expanded dramatically. The story is not one of linear progress but rather of two great upward surges separated by trade depressions. There is much physical evidence of local expansion: the resurgence of church building in the 1400s; the multiplication of new coastal villages involved in overseas fisheries; the number of new, enlarged bridges on major inland roads; and important developments in the domestic buildings of provincial towns. Finally, taxable wealth seems to have risen.[2]

[1] See the Introduction in E. Power and M. M. Postan, *Studies in English Trade in the Fifteenth Century* (London: G. Routledge and Sons, 1933).

[2] What follows is based primarily on: A. Bridbury, *England and the Salt Trade in the Later Middle Ages* (Oxford: Clarendon Press, 1965); G. A. Williams, *Medieval London, from Commune to Capital* (London: Athlone Press, 1963); E. M. Veale, *The English Fur Trade in the Later Middle Ages* (Oxford: Clarendon Press, 1966); A. A. Ruddock, *Italian Merchants and Shipping in Southampton, 1270–1600* (London: Southampton University, 1951); E. M. Carus-Wilson, "Evidence of Industrial Growth in Some 15th Century Manors," *EcHR* (1959), XII, pp. 190–205; G. Unwin, *Studies in Economic History* (London: Unwin and Co., 1923); J. B. Black, "The Medieval Coal Trades of North-East England," *Northern History* (1967), II, pp. 1–26; G. D. Ramsey, *English Overseas Trade During the Centuries of Emergence* (London: Longmans, 1957); S. L. Thrupp, *The Merchant Class of Medieval London* (Chicago: University of Chicago, 1940); J. W. F. Hill, *Medieval Growth, England in the Later Middle Ages* (Oxford: Clarendon Press, 1962); and H. Heaton, *The Yorkshire Woolen and Worsted Industries*, 2nd ed. (London: Clarendon Press, 1965). On the distribution of wealth, see the brilliant article of R. S. Schofield, "The Geographical Distribution of Wealth in England, 1334–1649," *EcHR* (1965), XVIII, pp. 483–510; and the paper by E. J. Buckatzsch, "The Geographical Distribution of Wealth in England, 1086–1843," *EcHR* (1950), III, pp. 180–202; as well as the study of early Tudor towns in J. Cornwall, "English County Towns in the 1520's," *EcHR* (1962), XV, pp. 54–69.

The overall statistical base on which statements about the extractive mining industries rest is shaky. It does seem, however, that the production per capita of tin, coal, and iron rose sufficiently to offset declines elsewhere. Tin production is best documented, because of the royal Court of the Stannaries, which represented the crown's vested interest. In 1400, production of tin reached a level whose only precedent was in the 1330s. There was an increasing domestic demand for coal as a fuel, no doubt a reminder that living standards among survivors of population disasters rose sharply. The coastal traffic in coal in the East assumed important proportions in the 1400s—"sea-coal" for London, as contemporaries said. This was complemented by a lively trade to the Low Countries' coastal regions, where timber and other domestic fuels were entirely lacking. The greatest advance was in the iron industry. There higher labor costs spurred invention. Bloomery records after 1350 show the inflation of wages that temporarily crippled English production. The bloomery forge most commonly used at that time was a prehistoric relic that worked by foot and hand power. But by 1400 there was an increasing application of water power, the earliest industrial applications of this sort having been made about 1200, on monastic estates, for grain milling. Bloomeries using water mills for forge and hammer operation cut labor costs to one-sixth of similar costs in hand mills. Production in some ironmonger accounts can be shown to have increased tenfold as a consequence. Iron for domestic use, for agricultural tools, and for export was an important element in the economy after 1400, proof that both external factors of invention and physical geography could offset real economic changes of an adverse character.[3]

The enormous transformation of the textile industry shows those things even more clearly. When we speak of English industry in the period after 1350, we speak primarily of textiles. Cloth manufacture employed more people than any other craft or series of related crafts. We have seen that before 1350 there had been a contraction of the industry under the pressure of shrinking real wages and foreign competition. The result was that the export of raw wool was far more vital to the economy than that of finished cloth. This situation, of course, robbed England of both employment and profit. However, there is some evidence of growth before 1349, as tariffs and the great rebellions in the Flemish cloth towns weakened foreign access to English markets. In the years after 1349, for which the export figures for cloth are available, the long-range upward trend is well documented.[4] In the period 1350–1400 the average annual export of broadcloths was 19,249. In the 1350s the highest total for any year was 10,324. After 1382 there are no figures below 20,000 per year. The

[3] See Chapter Eight for a more complete discussion of the dramatic developments in the extractive industries c. 1570–1640.

[4] See the Appendix, Figure 5.

average over the 1400s was up to 42,000, with no single year after 1410 below 20,000. Thus, although we are ignorant about *total production* and domestic consumption as opposed to exports, the figures and customs data showing declining imports of fine Flemish cloth support the view of a leap forward in the cloth manufacturing industry in England. By the 1520s, over 80 percent of all English exports (by value) was in cloth, and the proportion of sacks of wool to broadcloths, which in the early 1300s had been radically unbalanced in favor of raw wool, was three-to-one, broadcloth over sacks. This was a gain for English labor. As we shall see in the following table, it increased industrial employment until the 1550s. There was, in fact, a prolonged boom between 1500 and 1550.

The booming cloth exports of the early sixteenth century were concentrated in the hands of the Merchant Adventurers, a regulated company that had in effect a monopoly on export to Antwerp and the German and northern European markets. Cloth constituted 92 percent of the total export trade in 1550, with relatively small numbers of lighter cloths—worsteds—going to the Levant and southern Europe. London and the Antwerp-Germany axis thus dominated England's commercial life by 1485, when 70 percent of all cloth exports passed through the capital, a figure that rose to 88 percent in 1541. How complete this dominance was can be seen in the following table showing London's trade between 1503 and 1509:[5]

% of total cloth exports	60
% of total wool exports	69
% of total wine imports	36
% of goods paying petty customs	73
% of goods paying poundage	51

The year 1500 was of vital importance in England's mercantile economy. Thereafter, Southampton's trade with the Mediterranean declined steadily, as London's with the Germans expanded. London's proximity to the Atlantic and the Baltic, as well as to Antwerp, the early sixteenth-century trade center of Europe, added to its advantages as a political capital. The great port was also the legal and administrative center of England, the focal point of its land and marriage markets, and the hub of its banking facilities.

There were disadvantages inherent in London's metropolitan status and the slow development of the outports. The threat of war in areas under the Empire produced depressions in trade in 1504, 1511–12, 1521–3, 1530–1, and 1542–4. Londoners themselves resented the concentrations of privileged foreigners who lived in the city, as we learn from the apprentices who rioted against them on "Evil May Day" in 1517. And provincial commercial men

[5] T. S. Willan, *Studies in Elizabethan Foreign Trade* (Clifton, N.J.: Kelley, 1959), p. 66.

constantly pushed against the Merchant Adventurers' privileges and those of London in general. English trade was unbalanced both geographically and with regard to its internal structure. The outports watched profits accrue to the capital city while their varied, smaller trades received no comparable favor. There was nothing wrong with slate from North Wales, pilchards from Plymouth, herrings from Great Yarmouth, wooden billets from Rye, beer from Ipswich, grindstones from Newcastle, grain from King's Lynn, saffron from Dover, coal from Milford, or gold and silver lace from Chester. But when efforts were made to diversify markets in the 1520s, Henry VIII asked the Londoners to finance new companies to trade overseas. When trade boomed, grievances were stilled; but any setback, especially the collapse of 1551–2, woke again the cries against restrictions.[6] And men everywhere were sharply aware that prosperity rode on the backs of sheep and in the pockets of clothiers, staplers, and Merchant Adventurers.

A number of factors must have influenced this radical shift in the economy. Crown policy provided for duties that gave English cloth a heavy advantage over Flemish cloth in Europe. The wholesale application of water power in the crucial operation of fulling the cloth, which increased its body and tensile strength, created huge cost savings. English woolen cloth went out fulled but usually undyed, to take full advantage of cheap processes while avoiding as much as possible the great costs inherent in a dyeing operation dependent on imported dyestuffs. This use of water power brought about a great shift in the locale of cloth production, from the southern and eastern towns to hilly rural areas in the West Country, the Marches, and the northern uplands, so plentifully supplied with rapid streams and sheep. Textiles are thus a perfect example of the mobility of industry, as it seeks the right blend of materials, labor, power, technique, markets, and transport. Labor was especially anxious for employment in upland regions before 1350 and again after 1480, when population growth in areas of marginal arable prosperity caused hardship. The government had played a role also, especially with its essentially tolerant attitude toward the mobility of industrial labor, at least until the mid-Tudor crises forced a rise of anti-industrial policies among councillors acutely aware of the danger of industrial unemployment. Throughout the boom years, moreover, capital had flowed into the clothing industry. There was also a vast multiplication of the money going into commerce and the "broker" or middleman skills vital to the expanding export markets.

The movement of the industry to rural sites brought activity and prosperity to the countryside and also helped the growth of provincial towns. The wool trade reflected this. Two fifteenth-century price lists, the best one dated 1454,

[6] These problems are dealt with in different chapters at some length: the commercial polemics of the mid-century in Chapter Five, and the emerging solutions in Chapter Eight.

record fifty-one different grades of wool, exclusive of the staples of the North and Southwest! The finest wool came from the Welsh Marches and brought 14 shillings a sack, or 6 pence a pound. Cotswold wool ran close to March wool, which William Camden, in his *Britannia*, called "Lemster gold." The wool of most Midland districts was of middle grade, fetching 3½ pence per pound, while the cheapest wool for coarse cloth, that from Sussex Downs, ran at 1¾ pence per pound. Market towns in such areas grew quickly, as the combination of water, wool, and workmen brought thriving industry to Wiltshire, Gloucestershire, York's West Riding, Worcester, and Warwick, while traditional centers declined, especially at Oxford, Lincoln, and York City. In East Anglia the old industry maintained itself through specialization and vertical integration between growers, yarners, worsted-makers, and shippers. Wool knitted together town and country. We have evidence of huge transactions among graziers, local "woolmen," and the provincial buyers of the Merchants of the Staple. In one late fifteenth-century account book, that of Richard Cely, there are recorded purchases, in single deals, of £753. Transactions in Oxford of £840 and in Lechdale-on-Thames of £1,078 appear in other sources. When William Wyggeston the Younger died in Leicester in 1536, he was owed £3,500 by merchants of Antwerp, Malines, Delft, and Bruges. His fortune reminds us not only of upward mobility among peasants but also of their movement to the towns.

William was the lineal descendant of Simon de Wikston, from the "Viking town" of Wigston Magna, Leicestershire. Several successive generations of Simons and Williams lived in the open-field village south of Leicester. In 1334 the current William had over ten virgates of land. Then the family name vanishes from the village records. But it reappears in Leicester, where a franchise roll of 1344–5 notes that William Wyggeston, Ironmonger, was admitted to the freedom of the city. This peasant-aristocrat's tribe increased and prospered; in the 1400s the Wyggestons went into the wool business, became Merchants of the Staple, and supplied mayors of Leicester as well as burgesses at Westminster. After the 1440s they were joined in Leicester by the Randulls, prosperous wholesale grocers, and by the Henrichs, who in the 1470s made the familiar migration into trade and industry and emerged as prominent goldsmiths. This interdependence of rural and urban wealth was part of a cycle that took rural capitalists to town and great prominence, often with the result that "bourgeois" great-grandsons took this "urban" capital back into the land market after the dissolution of the monasteries.

A survey of overseas trade yields impressive evidence of its variety and growth. Throughout the 1400s, England traded with the whole of northwestern and western Europe. There was the short sea route to the Low Countries, the commercial center of Europe and England's nearest neighbors. Apart from this, most prominent trade ventures to Normandy and Brittany were regular, despite breaks due to war and piracy. Merchants from the southern and southwestern parts of the country traded with the north of France even during the Hundred Years' War. And the great wine regions south and east of Brittany—Poitou, Aquitaine, Gascony, and the Bordeaux center—made Bristol shipping synonymous with the import of good wines. This "Gascon" trade was in fact second only to the Flemish commerce in wool and cloth. The Mediterranean south supplied sweet wines, fruits, and the transit points for Oriental luxuries, although English ships, restrained by Italian pressure, did not penetrate beyond the Straits of Morocco. Thus the Italian "factors" of Southampton, the entry port for southern commerce, loomed as large in the 1400s as had Italian bankers a century earlier. To the west, a good trade with Ireland existed. East and north of Flanders, merchants from Yorkshire and the ports of East Anglia and Lincolnshire pursued a diminishing Scandinavian trade, compensated for in part by the expansion of commerce with Ireland. Expansion into the Baltic took place, only to bring about a confrontation with the superior economic and political power of the Hanseatic League, zealous in its protection of the great northern trading littoral.

Surveyed chronologically, rather than from the point of view of either a product or the map, English commerce in the 1400s underwent two cyclical movements. Early in the century there was a depression, lasting until about 1425. This was followed by a marked recovery, which ran parallel to the worst part of the agrarian depression, stretching from about 1425 to 1450. But this time of prosperity gave way to a second severe depression, which spread over the decades that were most convulsed at home by civil war. Then, about 1475, concomitant with the solid retrenchment in government achieved by Edward IV, and spreading over the first Tudor reigns, a renewal of prosperity in commerce came and lasted for more than three decades. After a brief reversal, the great boom set in and stayed for fifty years.

Overall, England's wealth from foreign trade rose during the 1400s. Perhaps the most notable transformation came in the shift in the balance of this trade from deficit to surplus. Before the second depression, which set in after 1448, the surplus ran as high as £37,700 between 1446 and 1448. On the leading edge of the second restoration, c. 1478–82, the annual surplus on visible trade (that is, excluding piracy, war booty, ransoms, and profits or losses on transport and investment) ran about £15,300. The prime reason for this shift was the changeover from the export of raw wool to the overseas sale of cloth. By 1450, half of the English wool went out as cloth; by 1540, the figure had risen to 86 percent. This meant more jobs at home and the addition of labor costs to the sale price abroad.

The missed opportunities that were complained of in *The Libelle of Englyshe*

Policye in 1436 had been largely grasped by the early 1500s. New markets had been opened. More carriage was undertaken in English bottoms. The Merchant Adventurers had become firmly established at Antwerp in the 1490s. Institutional facilities had improved. The return of political stability and the "merchants'" policy of the Yorkists and Henry VII helped. Foreign bankers retreated, giving London goldsmiths the chance to develop the banking functions stipulated in the 1327 charter. The establishment of the Wool Staple at Calais had brought the dominant trade into English hands, although Italians were excepted and continued to handle the trade to Italy's northern textile cities. And the merchant marine developed accordingly. All of this prepared the way for the fantastic Tudor expansion of commerce and the experience and daring that mastered the Spanish Armada in 1588.[7]

The Urban Society: The Social and Geographical Distribution of Wealth

These developments had important consequences for the growth of urban wealth and the general distribution of wealth in England, the character of English towns, and the establishment of a more diversified economy between 1350 and 1540. The greatest developments were crowded into the unsettled decades after 1480, when yet another change of dynasty and a wave of criticism of the church underscored the delicacy of the social order.

The face of provincial England changed, while the metropolis, London, attained the status of a great city. In 1335, London had measurable wealth three times that of the richest provincial town, Bristol; in 1520, the proportion had grown to fifteen-to-one. When the Scottish poet William Dunbar came to London, he gawked at her size—she had a population of about 70,000—and dubbed her "the flower of cities." By comparison, Norwich, which had become by 1540 the second city in the kingdom in wealth and population, had perhaps 12,000 people. London was at once a legal and political capital, a marriage market, a center of services and commercial distribution, and a teeming warren of traders, gentlemen, pimps, and prostitutes, already fully possessed of the elegance and underworld that have made her a marvel since early Tudor times.

Nothing in the provinces could compare with London. But all over the country during the 1400s and early 1500s provincial towns had risen and their wealth had expanded in proportion to commerce and industry. In the *Italian Relation of England* (*c.* 1500), it was observed that "there are scarcely any towns

---

[7] Yet there was still in commerce an exceedingly dangerous dependence on foreign shipping and a vast concentration of trade on the London–Antwerp–Germany axis—a bottleneck that repeatedly proved disastrous after 1550.

of importance in the kingdom" apart from London, Bristol, and York, but this was simply an error. True, England's towns might have failed to impress an Italian who knew the rich profusion of city-states, each with its hinterland and walled fortress, that distinguished his own countryside. But Englishmen of Norwich, Coventry, Exeter, Salisbury, Boston, Ipswich, Lynn, and Canterbury were already wealthier than their fellows at York. And Englishmen considered their town their "country," looking askance at "foreigners," by which they meant men from beyond their gates. Whether their town "standeth all by clothing" or by a "good quick market" varied from place to place. Some thrived because of a specialized industry: Birmingham was known for its smiths and Fowey for its cockleshells, fish, and great oysters. Patriotism and pride were local in character, although perhaps not reaching to the sublimity of Pia dei Tolomei, who cried aloud "*Siena mi fe*" ("Siena made me"— *Purgatoria*, v. 134). But they were solid nonetheless. Men showed their affection tangibly, and it is hard to move about in any considerable country town today without bumping into a fifteenth-century grammar school, hospital, almshouse, or the remnant of a refurbished church or market hall.

Most of this growth came between 1450 and 1540, after the population decline of the late fourteenth century. Early Tudor tax records and related documents tell a striking tale when compared with similar sources in the fourteenth century. Apart from the greatly enhanced economic strength of London, there is evidence of a shift to the West in the distribution of important towns. However, eastern England's share of wealthy towns among the country's top twenty-five did not shift much—there were sixteen in 1334 and fifteen in 1523. Exeter, Totnes, and Worcester reflected the westward migration of the clothing industry. Exeter and Coventry had also emerged from relative obscurity, so that the order of importance ran: London, Norwich, Bristol, Coventry, Exeter, where once it had been London, Bristol, York, Newcastle, and Boston. Only Bristol had ranked among the greatest provincial towns in 1334; in 1523, seven of the top fifteen (by wealth and population) lay west of London. And among the next rank—those with populations of perhaps 3,000–4,000—West Country regions like Plymouth and Taunton were newly prominent.

The sociopolitical structure of these towns generally reflected the distribution of wealth. Several rich men in Coventry elevated the whole town to prominence in England's commercial life. William Wyggeston dominated Leicester, as did the Spring family Lavenham, where Thomas Spring III was assessed for £1,333 in the 1524 subsidy—a figure larger than that for any person outside London and the peerage. The Norwich grocer Robert Jannys paid more taxes than the whole city of Rochester, but in a large city of great wealth he was part of a merchant oligarchy that was widely based. Like Exeter,

Ipswich, and London itself, some towns realized an oligarchic dispersion of power within guilds of wholesale merchants, whether staplers, tailors, vintners, coopers, grocers, butchers, ironmongers, or chandlers. Recruited from the upper peasantry and the lesser gentry of the hinterland, merchants who succeeded returned to the land within a century. Often the male line failed within three generations. Hence, whether the return was to dust and ashes or crops and stock, the pattern was constant. While town society was hierarchic and oligarchic, it was not patrician: no long-lasting patrician class formed in English towns. This was as true of London, whose leaders came from the younger sons of small landed families in the provinces, as it was of York or Leicester. It was an exceptional business that endured for as long as a century between 1350 and the 1520s, and the exceptions are few enough to underscore the continuing mobility of rural and urban populations in this period—mobility that brought together town and country and promoted the sense of community.

Unlike continental towns, whose oligarchies often rose on the base of early possession of town lands and rent speculation, urban England was not primarily a landscape of great *rentiers*. It was commercial in character, studded with merchant and artisan populations, with little control exercised by the men who grew rich in real-estate speculation. There was instead a merchant oligarchy, an industrial craftsman population, and a wage-labor proletariat drawn from the mobile elements of peasantry, husbandmen, and gentry.

Business growth and the fluidity of the land market in the fifteenth century promoted litigation and, with it, the need for lawyers. The legal profession expanded rapidly. Training was concentrated in four great London Inns of Court: Lincoln's, Gray's, Middle Temple, and Inner Temple. There, clustered around the Chancery offices and only a mile from Parliament and the courts of common law, the sons of gentlemen and merchants learned their craft. In 1500, there were not more than forty admitted to each of the Inns. By 1600, this number had risen to an average of one hundred. The law was not only lucrative in itself; it was the gateway to court and official careers. Thomas More, Thomas Audley, and Thomas Cromwell went that way to high office. So did countless others. Twenty-one speakers of the Commons prior to 1555 were common lawyers. Although some barristers and attorneys went back to the provinces and lived on fees and provincial administrative jobs, others made fortunes. Cromwell's income from all sources ran close to £8,000 in 1535–6. (This compared favorably with the average income of any peer—£600–1,500 a year around 1540.) And his father was a blacksmith and small landholder in Putney!

Only the destitute escaped the subsidy, since about half of all urban residents were wage earners. The wage earners and the hopelessly poor who paid no tax constituted nearly seven of ten urban Englishmen and lived at or near the line of subsistence. A tax certificate or a dole was their only passport to immortality. The members of this broad base of the towns owned no property but the clothes they stood in, and their hunger was a danger to the community. Above them the pyramid of town society rose to a point, through layer upon layer of artisans, merchants, and professional men, up to the few great families. In Leicester, for example, six of the families in a city of perhaps 5,000 owned 33 percent of the taxable wealth, and twenty-five people, or 6 percent of the taxable population, disposed of 60 percent of Leicester's riches. Figures for Coventry and Exeter are similar. In the Warwick town 2 percent of the ratable adults had 45 percent of the assessed wealth; 7 percent had 66 percent. At Exeter 7 percent of the taxed had 67 percent of the rated wealth.

England in 1540 was thus a very different country than that greeted by the dogs of war in 1450. As John Leland (1506–52)[8] wandered over England in the years 1538–43, compiling his *Itinerary*, he must have observed how the towns were spreading into the countryside. The population had swelled to perhaps 3.2 million, well below the level of 1340 but half again as high as 1377. England's face was different too. Parks were everywhere. The changes in agriculture had altered the relationship between arable and pasture land. Enclosure had reduced the size of the champion country in fielden England. Regional isolation because of poor roads and inland river traffic promoted provincialism, but to a lesser extent than in Chaucer's time. Jealousy of the capital among provincial men was acute. So was the inequality in the distribution of wealth, as deeply rooted in the city as in the country. Shifts in the social pyramid had changed social relations. Yet the pyramid remained broad at the base, despite some blunting of the apex. Mobility was sometimes decried. But men also cursed the darkness, which was everywhere. So was social tension. Agrarian and urban poverty had become the chief problem by the 1540s. The onset of the Reformation exacerbated change, and the politics of the mid-Tudor Age were made critical by the clash of opinion over these two kinds of poverty.

Yet it would be wrong to say that movement in economy and society justified the attitude that *plus ça change, plus c'est la même chose!* In agriculture the shrinkage of arable acres emphasized the reflation of population. And the "Commonwealth men" of the Reformation decades would roundly debate the unsettling influence of the cloth trade and the necessity of a policy favorable to grain and inimical to wool. Competition for land was certainly keen, and it provoked much suffering. The recovery of population in England and in Europe had spurred manufacture and trade, however. On balance it would be wrong to paint too dark a picture of the whole era between 1350 and 1540. For whatever the past crises in agriculture, or those to come with the collapse

[8] Celebrated antiquary, historian, and librarian to Henry VIII.

of the export boom in 1551, taxable wealth in England had been increased in the aggregate and had been somewhat redistributed socially and regionally. Runaway inflation threatened the fruits of that increase everywhere, as the age of price stability in the 1400s gave way to one of rapid augmentation after 1510. This doubtless sharpened social struggles and perhaps accelerated social change. But it did not ruin the community of the realm. Nor did it undo the constructive work of Yorkists and the Tudor Henrys in reknitting the raveled sleeve of England as she emerged from the troubled decades of the Wars of the Roses.

Chapter Two
THE LOSS OF ORDER

We believe that the king our sovereign lord is betrayed by . . .
certain false and unsuitable persons who . . . duly inform him that
good is evil and evil is good. . . . Also, the law serves no other
purpose in these days except to do wrong. . . . His false council has
lost his law; his merchandise is lost; his common people are
destroyed; the sea is lost; France is lost; the king himself is so
placed . . . that he owes more than ever any king of England ought.

JACK CADE
Proclamation, June 4, 1450

The issues raised by Cade's *Proclamation* indict the monarchy of Henry VI for failing to govern. Cade and his fellow rebels charged the king and his court with not giving direction to political life and stability to social ambition, with not distributing justice and not keeping the peace. These grievances reflected the traditional view of the king: that he was the lens that gave focus to government and society. When his powers were clouded or cracked, the kingdom was a kaleidoscope of broken images. Personal failure for him was in fact a catastrophe for his people.

To talk of failure in 1450 implies past success in governing. Hence our immediate concern is twofold: to sketch the later medieval system of government in the community of the shire and that of the realm, and to see how and for what causes that order grew corrupt. These tasks will take us into the world of sheriffs and justices of the peace (J.P.s), knights and burgesses, great lords and Everyman, in order to see what the men of Kent who followed Cade thought was amiss. But disorder and its roots are no more our ultimate objects than is a static picture of good government. What we want to stress most is that men became aware of the value of order in society because of the disorder in which they lived. That awareness itself helped Edward IV, Henry VII, and Henry VIII. For the revival of the medieval monarchy under them was more a resurrection than a new birth. What they achieved restored the historical role of the monarchy and made it again the focal point of political life and the guarantor of peace and justice. This they did by putting government finance right, by nurturing the law and its administration, by ending the dream of empire in France, by invading franchises, and by making an official and courtier class out of an aristocracy of blood and iron. During his reign, Henry VIII completed these achievements and also carried the kingdom into the uncharted waters of the Reformation, where once more the order of society was threatened with dissolution.

The achievements of these rulers satisfied the burgesses of Bristol, who in 1486 prayed for pardon, peace, and prosperity. And these rulers were lauded by the philosopher and statesman Lord Bacon. He called them the *Magi*. Their accomplishments were credited to Henry VII only by the Tudor chronicler Edward Hall, who wrote:

The old divided controversy . . . was suspended and . . . made perpetually extinct. So that all men may perceive, that as by discord great things decay and fall to ruin, so the same by concord be revived and erected. In likewise also all reigns . . . be by union and agreement . . . pacified and enriched. . . .[1]

Hall was a spokesman for the "Tudor idea"—that only the accession of Henry Tudor had ended the decline of governance—and preferred to ignore York's foundation for most of what the Tudors built. We shall see that the restoration of order and its reconciliation with what men then called their "liberties" began on March 4, 1461, when Edward of March took from an abbot's hands St. Edward's scepter, after promising all Englishmen to keep the realm and maintain its peace.[2]

Central Government: King, Court, Council

Men understood Edward's promise in diverse ways. Few doubted that a strong kingship was necessary for security and prosperity, or that the essence of political unity lay in justice. Good kings struck this balance between royal power and the rights of subjects. In practice this meant the limitation of royal power along with the acceptance of the fact of that power in the shire communities. Coronation oaths recorded the theme of a king obedient to God and the law—*sub Deo et sub lege*. The usurper Henry IV used the form of oath taken by Edward I, "the English Justinian," and Edward IV emulated him. But he also added to his obedience to God and the law a promise to sustain the "commonweal." This last he said was the burden of all men, while he and his father had taken it as their special concern in the political manifesto of 1460. In it York pledged especially to put an end to officials who

[1] Quoted in Sydney Anglo, *Spectacle, Pageantry and Early Tudor Policy* (Oxford: Clarendon Press, 1969), p. 2.

[2] The discussion of Edward IV's accession and the character of his politics relies chiefly on E. F. Jacob, *England in the Fifteenth Century* (New York: Oxford University Press, 1961); J. R. Lander, *The Wars of the Roses* (New York: Putnam, 1965); C. J. Kingsford, *English Historical Literature in the Fifteenth Century* (Oxford: Clarendon Press, 1913); Cora L. Scofield, *The Life and Reign of Edward IV*, 2 vols. (London: Frank Cass, pub. 1923; reprinted 1967); and Bertie Wilkinson, *The Constitutional History of England in the Fifteenth Century* (London: Longmans, 1964).

practiced extortion and to men of any sort who robbed and murdered or did violence to the least member of church and commonweal.[3]

What the new king said found theoretical expression in the writings of Sir John Fortescue. This celebrated judge and theorist thought the English kings ruled in a way that was *political* as well as regal.

A King of England can not, at his pleasure, make any alterations in the laws of the land, for the nature of his government is not only regal, but political. Had it been merely regal, he would have a power to make what innovations . . . which sort of government the Civil Laws points out, when they declare *Quod principi placuit legis habet vigorem*:[4] but it is much otherwise with a king, whose government is political, because he can neither make any alteration, or change in the laws of the realm without the consent of the subject . . . that is, when the sovereign power is restrained by political laws.

Here Fortescue referred to Parliament. Not all the people found their voice there, but the lords spiritual and temporal did, as did the knights of the shire and the burgesses. Behind them stood the masses of inarticulate men who had no active citizenship but for whom the law secured life and property. Lord and peasant alike were under the king's law, even in the great franchises where the bailiff who enforced the law was not the king's immediate agent but acted for a privileged magnate or corporation. Ultimately every writ ran in the king's name and was subject to political limits. Men who failed to exercise proper care in their liberties or franchises could be deprived of their jurisdictions to nourish peace and strengthen justice. The king, under the law, was the fountain of justice.

The wisdom he generated was in fact channeled through his Council and Court into the law courts and every other institution of government.[5] The close connection between the Council and the court was subject to abuse. The court was an entourage of politicians, officeholders, and decorative courtiers gathered about the king. Men there traded friendship and skill for power, patronage, and the profits of office. Their gaze centered on the king. It was his prerogative to do acts of grace: to reward and ennoble or cast down and disgrace. Wise kings dispensed this grace sparingly and guarded against the

---

[3] Wilkinson, *op. cit.*, pp. 134–6.

[4] The frequently quoted "absolutist" maxim means "what pleases the prince has the force of law." It is found in Fortescue, *De Laudibus Legum Angliae* (Cincinnati: Robert Clark & Co., 1874), Chap. 9, pp. 26–7, tr. Francis Gregor.

[5] On the Court and Council see R. L. Storey, *The End of the House of Lancaster* (London: Barrie, Rockliff, 1966), esp. Chaps. 1 and 2. Also: J. F. Baldwin, *The King's Council in England during the Middle Ages* (Oxford: Clarendon Press, 1913); A. R. Myers, *The Household of Edward IV* (Manchester: Manchester University Press, 1959); and Wilkinson, *op. cit.*, pp. 214–54.

THE COURT OF KING'S BENCH.
DuBoulay, op. cit., *p. 113.*

advance of private aspirations inimical to the common good. If the king were weak, incompetent, or unwise, the potential for harm in the court was magnified. The routine of government separated the king from the actual work of the great partially bureaucratized offices of state—secretariats, courts of law, the Exchequer, and the Chancery. Hence later medieval kings sought advice within their entourages. This sometimes gave a decisive weight to the collective will of the magnates who made up the king's Council. But it also gave scope to courtier-politicians and even to mere favorites, a circumstance that proved especially dangerous when a senseless ruler like Henry VI conferred power on bad men who misused first his trust and then both him and his kingdom. Sometimes a faction of courtiers was able to dominate the Council itself. In theory, court and Council were complementary, and personnel overlapped between them. Events could undermine the balance, however.

The Council was the executive board of the monarchy, led directly by the king or by those to whom he gave confidence. This body was indispensable in government. It gave advice on policy and coordinated the center of government and the counties. Its business was multifold. Throughout the 1400s and the 1500s its judicial work steadily expanded under strong kings. Lawbreakers might be called to answer before the magnates. No malefactor was too great to feel the Council's power, since the king protected it from factionalism and used its strength to arbitrate disputes. The councillors also spearheaded royal initiative in Parliament at a time when the Lords still dominated that assembly and managed its legislative functions. War and peace were also the Council's business. This potential omnicompetence was itself not an element of distortion in politics and society. But its abuse *was*, especially after 1437, when Henry VI showed his weakness the moment he attained his majority. One of his first acts was to give the Council the power to determine every important piece of business, subject to his advice and their coherent agreement.

The king quickly undermined the collective nature of the delegated authority he had given the Council. Since the central question of conciliar power was always its relationship to government's purposes, it was essential that the Council maintain the *sub Deo et sub lege* tradition. In fact the king gave his confidence to a mere faction of the magnates who in the 1440s were bent on self-interested misrule. Perhaps it is true that events conspired in that direction, that magnates would in any case have misused government to recoup fortunes lost in economic upheavals, and that the endless wars in France and the king's minority gave scope to perverse men. But the evidence is conclusive on a different point: government under Henry VI's majority was marred by the serious flaws in his judgment of men, by his lack of interest in government, and most of all by his mental instability. It was his failure as a king that helped turn economic dislocation, aristocratic feuds, and military defeat into anarchy and civil war. It was his contribution to confide in a band of courtier-politicians who usurped the Council's power, drove the magnates out of government and into opposition, and brought down the House of Lancaster.

The politics of Henry IV's reign had increased the Council's power, since his usurpation of the throne was an aristocratic coup dependent on magnate support. Henry V's absences during the French campaigns stabilized magnate rule without conceding power to unworthy men. Then, during the long minority of Henry VI from 1422 to 1437, a sharp contest developed between the senior uncle of the king, "The Good Duke" Humphrey of Gloucester, and the majority of the magnates grouped around the Beaufort descendants of John of Gaunt. The contest opposed the duke's wish to be regent—thus wielding alone the authority, patronage, and prerogatives of the crown—and Bishop Beaufort's desire for collective rule by the magnates. The duke's ostensible motive was to keep intact royal power and so pass it on undiminished to his nephew. Bishop Beaufort distrusted Gloucester, as did other councillors. Beyond this motive was their desire to consolidate real control over the royal administration and distribute the profits of government among themselves.[6]

This was not abnormal; it was the nature of politics in a personal monarchy under a mature king. However, mature kings did not allow the system to strip authority from the monarch. The Beaufort victory over Gloucester brought about the establishment of a stable core of government that fostered both the disaffection among magnates and the alienation of the integral power of the crown. While it is true that Henry VI's minority was not marked by unusual social disorder, it is equally true that the regime established before he came of age in 1436–7 was not dislodged during his majority. Indeed, the character of the Beaufort faction's leadership degenerated after 1437, when Henry was forced to reappoint the councillors then ruling. During the next decade the true magnate Council of Cardinal Beaufort's hegemony gave way to a narrower ruling group led by William de la Pole, earl and then duke of Suffolk. Suffolk built a faction based on the king's confidence. When it was strong enough, he kept many magnates away from the Council board. And in the end he used the executive authority of the crown to destroy the stable core of government that had justified magnate rule in the first place. By so doing, his regime gave rise to the motifs that dominated government and society for a generation: oligarchic misrule, widespread social disorder, the escalation of feuds into civil war in the absence of royal arbitration, and the adhesion of some

---

[6] See B. Wilkinson, "The Duke of Gloucester and the Council," *BIHR* (1958), XXXI, pp. 19–20; J. S. Roskell, "The Office and Dignity of Protector of England," *EHR* (1953), LXVIII, pp. 193–233; and Storey, *The End of the House of Lancaster, op. cit.*, pp. 29–60.

magnates to Richard of York in their desire to redress the balance of government and society.

The Crown, Commons, and Local Communities

In good times Fortescue's "dominion regal and political" operated especially in matters of finance. The crown and the Council knew the urgency of a "tractable Commons"—that is, of burgesses and knights willing to supply the needs of the government. Henry IV and Henry V took a keen interest in financial matters and in general followed a policy of not making grants that would deplete royal resources and increase the need for taxes without conciliar approval. This practice gave the great officers of state who were always councillors—the chancellor, the lord privy seal, the treasurer, and the barons of the Exchequer—an opportunity to defend the crown's income, side by side with other lords, against those whom Fortescue criticized: "men of his [the King's] chambre, of his household." A Council of public officers and servants of the commonweal was the best check on courtiers and others who were prone to let the "complaints of the kingdom go unheeded."

Clamores regni! This phrase has in it the essence of the relationship between government and society. All grievances could be settled in the Council or in the ordinary courts of law. But those touching finance, public order, and foreign relations were so basic to the king's right to govern and the subjects' rights to be well governed that the Council took a special interest in them. The Council was not a representative assembly, however, despite the summoning of knights and burgesses to its sessions at odd times. Hence, in periods of special stress, the crown buttressed conciliar advice with that of the Commons in Parliament.[7]

If the Commons were men with their hearts in their pockets, Parliament was the high court of the realm, the political forum of the country. There the communities of the shires sent stout men to petition and plead for the satisfaction of their *clamores*. They joined their voices to those of the *comites*—great lords lay and spiritual—and the burgesses from numerous boroughs. In their own house (*domus communis*), they were decidedly inferior in initiative and power, compared with the Lords. When Henry Bolingbroke and his aristo-

---

[7] For Parliament see H. L. Gray, *The Influence of the Commons on Early Legislation* (Cambridge, Mass.: Harvard University Press, 1932); M. McKisack, *Representation of English Boroughs in the Middle Ages* (London: Oxford University Press, 1932); H. G. Richardson and G. O. Sayles, "Parliaments and Great Councils in Medieval England," *Law Quarterly Review* (1961), LXXVIII, pp. 213–36 and pp. 401–26; J. S. Roskell, "The Medieval Speakers for the Commons in Parliament," *BIHR* (1950), XXIII, pp. 31–52; and his "The Social Composition of the Commons in a 15th Century Parliament," *BIHR* (1951), XXIV, pp. 152–72.

cratic partisans revolted against Richard II, the Commons acknowledged a *fait accompli*, as they did on Edward IV's accession. Commons was not yet the place where Queen Elizabeth met assentors to policy and others praised dissent from it, nor yet the house where regicides tried a king and voted the abolition of episcopacy. The fifteenth-century members of Commons were petitioners and complainers.

They were also something more. Intimately familiar with their communities, they knew that the countryside and neighborhoods were the keys to their increasing power. From the time of Edward I's reign, kings found it necessary to be in touch with these men. Their cooperation made government possible, since they were the operative agents of local self-government at the king's command. They were the Council's eyes and ears as well as the mouths of their own diverse communities, by whom they were commissioned to deal with "worldye policye." That they thought of themselves as charged to present grievances is made clear by the unknown member of Parliament (M.P.) who wrote the political poem *Mum and the Soothesegger* (1405–6). The truthteller of the title speaks of the harm done by diplomatic silence in the face of abuses, and he chastises the sort of M.P. who sat in Parliament "like a nought in arithmetic, that marks a place but has no value in itself."

This contempt for silence reflects the change in the role of the Commons early in the 1400s. During the reigns of Henry IV and Henry V most parliamentary petitions originated there. The share of legislative work done by knights and burgesses increased, until by the 1450s the Commons complained that Henry VI did not consult them as he should or heed their advice. Long before that, a speaker of the Commons had told Henry IV that his chief treasure was his subjects' hearts. This claim was perhaps pretentious in an age of aristocratic rule. Yet it reflected the social changes we have already detailed, and Edward IV's 1467 manifesto took pains to court the Commons. For this, the king's critics among the magnates gave him the contemptuous name of "merchants' king." Not that he called many Parliaments or made concessions to the bourgeoisie. But he did understand that for his triumph in 1461 he owed something to them. Yorkist propagandists stressed the integration of the Commons in government. A monastic chronicler reported dryly: "As he had in time of need found great comfort in his commons, he ratified and confirmed all the franchises given to cities and towns." How accurate the monk was we shall soon see. Certainty does adhere to this proposition: Lancastrian legislation had rarely mentioned the Commons in the assent clauses of new acts. Early Tudor statutes often mentioned the Commons' role in the authority of Parliament. Edward IV's laws sometimes did. The qualification shifted and in so doing reflected both the slow integration of Parliament as a political body and the growing political unity. It was this dual achievement under York and the early Tudors that ended the Commons' detachment from politics. And it underlay the Reformation statutes, which proclaimed England a unitary state of diverse ranks of subjects. Edward IV realized all this in 1467, when he remarked that the Commons were in Parliament on behalf of the "commune of the realm."

The men who heard their king praise their patriotic role were transformed from their fourteenth-century character. As early as 1376 petitions took up the question of elections. A 1406 statute required free and impartial elections in the shires. Every freeman attending the county court, whether in the open air or in the shire hall, could cry out for his man. The consolidation of gentry power led in 1429 to an act of disenfranchisement, however. Landless freemen and freeholders with estates that cleared less than forty shillings a year lost their voice. Then, in 1445, the right to represent the shire was confined to knights and squires of "reputation" and "sufficient" estate to support the dignity of knighthood. These facts reflect another: the rise of the Commons and their making common cause with the Lords depended on the power of the landed aristocracy and the gentry elements of that aristocracy to acquire enough seats in the Commons. Throughout the 1400s magnates extended their own influence by securing the election of their gentry dependents. This too Cade complained of, noting how great men prevented "free" elections. Evidence drawn from every section of England supports this contention, without obscuring some genuinely free contests.

In fact, the rise of the Commons lay in the usurpation of borough seats by gentry whose ambitions were not satisfied by the relatively few shire seats. The reasons for this usurpation are clear. In the 1300s the Commons consisted of nearly eighty knights of shires and roughly four times as many burgesses. Tradition gave to the boroughs two representatives, men whose claim derived from the royal prerogative of creating new parliamentary boroughs. Methods of borough election were often left to local decision, with the result that franchises varied from the narrowly oligarchic to the relatively democratic. In every case, a law of 1413 required that burgesses be residents of their boroughs. Yet by 1422 one-fourth of them were not resident townsmen, while another one-fourth were only burgesses in a technical sense. These were not traders, guildsmen, or lawyers, but local landed men, country gentry getting the "freedom" of a borough, often by severe pressure. Returns for the fifty-seven Parliaments held between 1399 and 1509 are incomplete. What does survive, however, clearly shows the steady rise in the number of parliamentary boroughs[8] and the takeover of burgess seats by the aristocracy. Aristocratic

---

[8] The figures for the different reigns ran as follows: Richard II, 83; Henry IV, 75; Henry V, 80; Henry VI, 87; Edward IV, 98; Richard III, 101; Henry VII, 111. Note that Edward IV and Henry VII made the most new boroughs. As we stress, however, this was no favor to the bourgeoisie.

pressures within political factions resulted in demands for the king to make new boroughs and for towns to put in men nominated elsewhere. John Paston recognized this when he urged that many boroughs that were not returning men ought to do so. He implied that "pocket boroughs" were on his mind.

Aristocratic interest in creating M.P.s testifies to the changing role of the Commons. Magnates would not bother about an impotent group. Their determination to undermine borough independence had first taken the form of favor for narrow borough franchises. The slow gathering of power by urban oligarchs made influence from the outside easier in towns than in shires, where the freemen were too numerous and the gentry too powerful to be overawed. The extension of the magnates' tactics to borough manipulation on behalf of client-gentry ensured that English Parliaments for several centuries would speak with the accents of the landed classes. Sitting to make laws and grant taxes, the aristocracy of peers and gentry controlled the political nation. They were powerful enough to control the bourgeoisie and homogeneous enough to ensure that Parliament would serve the interests of the land. Thus, while the Commons became increasingly powerful, this was no victory for urban England and signified no alliance between the crown and the bourgeoisie. This triumph simply completed the integration of power at the center and in the shire.[9]

Rule in the shires depended on the law courts and on finances. Originally the maintenance of order and the collection of the king's shire revenues were combined functions of sheriffs. Shrieval office (the shire reeve) developed out of the old English ealdorman or earls. During the twelfth and thirteenth centuries royal government grew by adding to the sheriff's burdens. Through the chance survival of a Bedford sheriff's working papers we are shown how large a staff was needed to do the business of the crown in about 1340: keepers of writs, receivers of monies, constables and various jailers, and several assorted clerks. From the sheriff's offices in the County Castle, orders went to the hundreds or to other variously named divisions of the shire. In each of those units a bailiff and his staff coped with the work. Sometimes these men worked for a lord with a royal franchise that included fiscal and juridical rights of government. In such cases, the king's writs ran in his name only to the borders of the liberty. But within the liberty the lord had to dispense justice and collect taxes. Government was in the last resort the king's government, even where privileges prevailed. Even the bishop of Durham could lose his franchisal rights for malfeasance.

[9] For the medieval development of royal power expressed in institutions of local government, see especially the works of Helen Cam: *The Hundred and the Hundred Rolls* (London: Methuen, 1930); *Lawfinders and Law-makers in Medieval England* (London: Merlin Press, 1962); *Liberties and Communities in Medieval England* (Cambridge: Cambridge University Press, 1944).

In the 1300s the power of gentry sheriffs was more worrisome to the crown than that of franchised lords. This had been true for Edward I as well. In a vast survey made in 1274–5, Edward sent inquiries to every hundred and comparable unit, asking which sheriffs were corrupt and oppressive. The evidence of the answers on the Hundred Rolls shows that corruption and oppression were general problems. Nor could it be otherwise. Neither treatises nor swelling statute books could transform the crown's inability to control fully the local governors. Men regarded local office and the law as means toward private ends. Impoverished agrarian societies generally exhibit a high degree of fierce litigation and armed conflict over land and its use, and England in the later Middle Ages was no exception. Strife was the stuff of politics and government, a fact clearly shown in Paston, Stonor, and Plumpton letters, as well as in central and county court records. Where the processes of law were slow, technical, and expensive, suits were well ended where men were well friended. Hence the potential for shrieval abuse, since it was to the sheriff that every writ ran from the Chancery and other courts.

Of course the remote root of the difficulty was the poverty of the monarchy. The ability to govern meant the execution of the law to make the propertied classes secure in their property and the poor free from oppression and docile before their social superiors. To stay the fury of the inferior multitude was an impossible task, a conceit rather than an achievement, for governments that were too poor to pay staffs of disinterested crown servants. English government in the shire relied on amateurs drawn from the local aristocracy. And men so burdened were encouraged to take their rewards by making public office the source of private profit. While sheriffs were not thereby thugs, every man sold his wares at the highest price. This was enough to create problems, but matters were made worse by the fact that rich men were governing a poor people. They were conservative in an aggressive way, made bold by the license given them by a crown that lacked adequate coercive force and that was forced into reliance on aristocratic good will. In such circumstances competition was likely to degenerate into violence. This likelihood was increased by the ignorance in which the central government worked. How could there be honesty and efficiency when the king's ministers had to ask a corrupt official whether his port could accommodate large ships, or where, in 1371, the government thought there were 40,000 taxable parishes—there being no more than 8,500 in England at the time. Not even printing changed this lack of information sufficiently to ensure good government. Lacking wealth enough to pay honest and well-informed men, medieval governments stood before a constant indictment, whether that of Fortescue or the humanist Thomas More in *Utopia*:

Therefore when I consider and weigh in my mind all these common wealths, which now a days any where do flourish, so God help me, I can perceive nothing but a certain conspiracy of rich men procuring their own commodities under the name and title of the common wealth. . . . These devices, when the rich men have decreed to be kept and observed under color of the commonalty, that is to say, also of the poor people, then they be made laws.

The response to shrieval abuse was typically medieval: one class of officials was checked by superimposing another class on them. The hope was that the zeal of new men would balance the malice of old ones. As early as 1258, the baronial war against Henry III provoked the appointment of *custodes pacis*, keepers of the peace. These men were asked to exercise police power in the shires most ravaged by local conflicts. Edward III sporadically renewed this office, as his predecessors had done. After 1350, however, he initiated legislation that began the great career of the J.P.s and made their clerks the most frequent visitors to the sheriffs' offices. In that year he named "commissioners" of the peace to enforce the Statute of Laborers.[1] He also gave them authority to hear and determine certain felonies. At a stroke he cut away the sheriffs' vast power at law; he undermined their control of juries and their influence over verdicts. In 1362, these commissioners gained power over all labor laws. By 1414 they replaced the justices of trailbaston[2] and commissioners of oyer and terminer in the shire courts, except in extraordinary emergencies. In such times they were subordinated to the magnates and their dependents, who might be the only check against open warfare. But in ordinary times of disorder the J.P.s ruled in the countryside in the king's name.

We have already shown who the J.P.s were and the fact that they represented the rise of the same landed classes who were gaining power in Parliament. There was thus no separation of law-making from law-enforcing in England in the 1400s or 1500s—or even 200 years later in Fielding's time, as we know from *Tom Jones*. Nor was there a separation of executive power from legislative and judicial power. Just as the curia regis derived every sort of power from the king's presence, his officers in the shire shared in that undifferentiated authority. The J.P.s were the legatees of shrieval power. But unlike sheriffs, who were forbidden to be M.P.s while in office, the J.P.s sat in Commons. In 1461 they confidently established by law that all indictments and presentments of offenses taken on the sheriff's *tourn*, or tour of the countryside, should be theirs. They also ceded to themselves powers of arrest and imprisonment and the making of "process upon indictment."

---

[1] The legislation of 1350, in which wages, hours, and other conditions of labor were fixed at pre-Plague levels.

[2] Trailbastons were a special set of lawless men who carried or trailed *batons*. The articles of trailbaston were special commissions directed against such men (from *trahere*: to carry or drag).

In plain language, they became trial judges. This development perhaps sprang from the distrust of Henry VI's "household" sheriffs. In the 1440s and early 1450s an extraordinary number of sheriffs were named from the royal household. In effect they were promoted by Suffolk and his faction to give the duke control over county administration through the household. Suffolk had abused the king's feeblemindedness and misruled the kingdom through such men as Sir Thomas Tuddenham and Thomas Daniels.[3] The men of the shires gathered in 1461 to make a recurrence impossible. And both Edward IV and Henry VII aided them with a spate of statutes that left to the sheriffs only the terrible burden of answering in the Exchequer for the king's country revenues, while making the J.P.s the bulwarks of local government. Men who in 1300 paid to be sheriffs in the early 1500s paid to be exempt from the office. The competition under the Tudors was to be a member "of the commission of the peace."

Pauper Regimes

The main interests of the county thus found expression in the Commons as well as in the county courts. Often these interests centered on money and taxes, on "the matter of the Exchequer." And in such matters lay the greatest failure of Lancastrian government. The three Henrys of Lancaster ran pauper regimes.[4]

Fortescue considered their poverty the deepest root of the sorrows of their house. He had anticipated Machiavelli's advice to princes: have the appearance of liberality at all times, and in time of need ruin the few and spare the many. Only well-endowed rulers could long withstand "exquisite means" to extort money from men mired in poverty. And only well-endowed men could be mighty in their bouts with rich subjects. The records of income and borrowing

[3] There is a valuable study of this aspect of government in R. M. Jeffs, "The Late Medieval Sheriff and the Royal Household, 1437–1547" (Oxford, D. Phil., 1961, unpublished), where it is made clear that York and Tudor used reliable men of different character in much the same way, especially in areas with reputations for disorder. Sir Thomas Tuddenham was head of Suffolk's ducal council, a royal official, and a sheriff of incredible corruption.

[4] For Lancastrian finance and the evidence of Exchequer partiality, see S. B. Chrimes, *Introduction to the Administrative History of Medieval England* (Oxford: Blackwell's, 1952); J. L. Kirby, "The Issues of the Lancastrian Exchequer and Lord Cromwell's Estimates of 1433," *BIHR* (1951), XXIV, pp. 121–48; G. L. Harriss, "Preference at the Medieval Exchequer," *BIHR* (1957), XXX, pp. 17–40; B. P. Wolfe, "Acts of Resumption in the Lancastrian Parliaments," *EHR* (1958), LXXIII, pp. 603–10; and A. Steele, *The Receipt of the Exchequer, 1377–1485* (Cambridge: Cambridge University Press, 1954).

between 1399 and 1455 show clearly the crown's fiscal failure: both ordinary revenue and credit fell far short of expenditures.

The income of English kings consisted of parliamentary taxes, feudal dues, customs, the profits of justice, regalian rights, the ancient "farm" of towns and shires, and revenue from crown lands. These were never wholly adequate to cover the costs of government, particularly when adventures in France increased these costs. Hence any serious abuse of crown income by courtier-politicians enhanced the imbalance and usually drove the monarchy toward excessive tax demands. Men sensible of good government paid willingly. But when there was little peace and less justice, the Commons reluctantly granted taxes. This forced the king's government into desperate borrowing, anticipating incomes spent before they were collected. The spurious loans obtained were in fact often not repaid. Men who got the king's "tallies" from the Exchequer tried unsuccessfully to redeem them for cash, often getting fresh "tallies" instead. Recent study of crown finances in the 1400s fully justifies the view that Henry VI was progressively less able to collect his nominal income. This shift in the balance of resources made the crown poor in relation to all the greater magnates together.

Richard II's government owed £18,000 in false loans accepted outside his household. Henry IV owed £95,000 to members of his court for false loans and £39,000 to outside lenders. He had come to power on the promise to relieve the crown's fiscal distress, posing as the champion of property and the savior of society. Financially, his revolution was a failure. Henry V fared better. He restored crown income, paid his bills in cash, and enjoyed good credit. Under Henry VI, revenue declined sharply, and the index of fictitious loans rose by 75 percent in 1432. Simultaneously, the king's ability to borrow fell by 17 percent. This meant that after 1422 government increasingly had to rely on the good will of its wealthier subjects for financial aid. The magnates, great clergy, and gentry at first lent readily, along with merchants and urban corporations. But it soon appeared that the more public-spirited a man was, the more he was victimized by bad tallies. The Percies held over £20,000 of them and York nearly twice that total. The first result of this was the retreat of small lenders among the king's subjects. This detachment of the Commons eroded popular support and emphasized how precarious it was to be Lancaster's creditor; it was also a gloss on these telling figures:

Decade	Nominal Revenue	Real Revenue
1422–32	£95,000 p.a.	£75,000 p.a.
1433–42	115,000 p.a.	75,000 p.a.
1443–52	85,000 p.a.	54,000 p.a.

Not all of the drastic decline after 1442 can be laid to Suffolk's machinations. The war in France no longer provided triumphs and booty. The great agrarian depression hurt all landlords. But Suffolk's regime was corrupt, and his influence signaled a catastrophic fall in income that ran parallel to the decline of government. Men said openly that it was harder for the government to get money from its collectors than it was to get taxes. Public confidence in Henry VI's regime was collapsing, and the king was without the attributes of kingship. Peace in France and retrenchment at home were required; but the first was unpopular with the people and the second possible only for rulers who showed some Homeric virtue. Henry VI, however, lacked the valor of an Ajax, the splendor of an Achilles, or the power of an Agamemnon. Nor was he as wise in council as Ulysses or Nestor. And during his tutelage, Suffolk was no Mentor. Events in fact moved away from such solutions. Relations with Scotland soured and produced war. As the domination of Suffolk increased, so did the cost of the royal household and court. The Chancery and Exchequer could not pay the routine costs of government. These things had the sinister effect of alienating from government the official classes who could not detach themselves from it but who could no longer profit from it.

The means that the crown could stretch to cover the crisis were failing. Alienation threatened tax revenue. Customs, generally buoyant as the cloth trade expanded, were endangered by war and by the renewal of taxes on alien merchants. Loans from every source—even from the City of London—declined. Cardinal Beaufort and Bishop Chichele were gone. The staplers and other merchant groups with an interest in order continued to lend money, but their loans were no more an adequate base for government than were loans for the same cause from magnates and churchmen. In fact they were analogous to drugs that check fever and hide the signs of more serious malaise. And the failure to repay loans—or, worse, the discriminatory repayment of tallies—created rivalries within those classes whose unity was vital to government. The danger was great. The house of Lancaster was growing too poor to govern and too unpopular to prevent others from doing so in its name.

This state of affairs excited the Commons. They knew that crown resources were being dissipated, as they had been when, from 1399 to 1406, Parliament forced Henry IV to make a limited resumption of crown lands. The monarchy had once used the royal demesne to finance government. It had "lived of its own." But by 1300 the vast majority of crown manors had been granted away —to the church, officials, magnates, and favorites. After 1290 the crown relied for its solvency on customs and taxation. Henry IV's deep debt prompted the cry for resumption: the crown should take back estates and alienated revenues and should retrench. This cry, of course, was merely a revival of the ancient demand by baronial opposition elements. But in the 1400s knights and burgesses led the way to acts of resumption. Theirs was a conservatism rooted in the hope of averting anarchy by making the crown strong again and thereby protecting their own interests. Magnates who were likely to be victims joined in this intelligent conservatism against Henry IV, and then, between 1449 and 1455, against Henry VI. Opposition came chiefly from the bishops, who throughout the century feared that lay motives might buttress Lollard demands for the disendowment of the Church. Against that fear and the courtiers who carelessly pulled "the pears off the royal tree," Soothesegger had appealed to good men to force the crown toward solvency. York took up the complaint of 1405–6 in the 1450s, as did other magnates opposed to Suffolk. Lands and regalian rights were not to be granted in lieu of wages. These were to be a permanent endowment to enable the Exchequer to pay the costs of government, while letting them at true economic rents.

Henry IV yielded gracelessly. His fear was that a general revocation of all grants made since 1366 would destroy the credibility of his government and the prestige of his dynasty. And he resented the idea of the magnates in Council exercising control of the royal prerogative to reward. But the Commons backed the magnates, and even added a revolutionary demand for sanctions against favorites who diminished the crown's estates for selfish reasons.

Henry VI raised similar objections when his magnates, and later the Commons, pressed for acts of resumption. He was especially rich in lands, thanks to a series of escheats (confiscated lands) and to the accident of his long minority. He had neither wife nor children to support, and not too many kinsmen. Ralph Lord Cromwell, the treasurer, stressed this in 1433 when he departed from past practice and gave a "state of the treasury" report, which he then had put on the Parliament roll. This was a grave step, in effect a veto of Bolingbroke's boast that "kings do not render accounts." The Commons, armed with the "state" of 1433, considered the report a precedent, and in other years secured similar enrollments: 1435, 1447, 1449 (twice!), 1453, and 1455. This tactic reinforced their bargaining power in the campaign to force the crown to a policy of resumptions. It was also a vital weapon in their armory against Suffolk in 1449–50. But before these efforts fully matured, the situation had so far deteriorated as to make men wonder whether reform must not give place to revolution.

Rebellion and Common Complaint

The Parliament that met at Leicester early in 1450 impeached Suffolk. While they sat and ordinary people sang of his fall (to the ballad "Now is the fox driven to hole"), the rebels in Kent rose; despite the duke's fall and subsequent murder, Jack Cade complained about other ministers, who blocked resumptions and bilked the crown. The upshot was the impoverishment of the "poor Commons." Serious dangers though they were, the impeachment and rebellion were but the tip of an iceberg whose mass was the loss of order, confidence, and prosperity. As spring gave way to summer, a new series of popular risings in several counties threatened civil war.[5]

The men who followed Cade in the convulsion in the southeast and forced London's gates in 1450 were neither peasants nor vagabonds. Their leaders came from the classes whose rise we earlier traced among the consequences of the Black Death. Some believed Cade to be a Mortimer cadet sprung from Edward III. They were conservative men, unmoved by ideology and anxious for specific reforms in government. They wanted especially to have law and order, some reduction in taxes, the dismissal of corrupt councillors, and some end to the French wars. Above all else, they stood for the security of property. Even the peasants in the "army" wished for the just enforcement of customary law or the extension of the common law and equity to cover their causes. They were partisans of true monarchy, far from the rogues of Shakespeare's fancy. The poet had transformed Cade into an antinomian router: "Burn all the records of the Realm. My mouth shall be the Parliament of England!" Had he been that it is hard to believe his followers would have included the abbot of Battle, a sprinkling of gentry, some lawyers, many prosperous bourgeoisie, as well as a number of poor people sunk in poverty and despair. Cade's *Proclamation* was no millennial shout. It was merely the voice of men who wanted peace in the microcosm of the manor or town and in the great world of England. They had come to fear and resent a monarchy so debt-ridden as to be unable to reward good men, punish malefactors, arbitrate disputes, or contain the excesses of armed bands.

Serious disorder, together with the novel theory that the king should live on the Commons while courtiers wasted the common wealth, contributed to Cade's rebellion. Conditions in Kent and Sussex were not unique, however. They were indicative of the nature of the degeneration of social order and its relationship to the militancy of armed retainers and their lords. Nothing better reveals the character of a society than its institutions of warfare. In Eng-

---

[5] There is now no good full-length study of Cade's rising and the other rebellions associated with it. The defect will soon be remedied by a book in preparation by Professor Eleanor Searle, a chapter of which she generously showed me. The best available works on the situation in 1450 are: H. M. Lyle, *The Rebellion of Jack Cade* (London: Historical Association, 1950); R. L. Storey, *The End of the House of Lancaster,* Chap. 3; and R. Virgoe, ed., *Documents Illustrative of Medieval Kentish Society* (Maidstone, 1964), "Some Ancient Indictments in King's Bench . . . 1450–1452," Kent Archaeological Society, *Record Publication* XVIII, pp. 215–43. On the general disorder, see the literature cited by Storey, *passim.*

land these constituted an indictment of Henry VI's government. The real danger to government was aristocratic, not popular.

Neither the *Manifesto* of 1460 nor Cade's *Proclamation* in 1450 exaggerated in their claims that robbery, riot, and murder had taken the place of justice under Henry VI. Offenders arose in all ranks of society, but aristocrats charged with upholding the law were most culpable in its destruction. Their feuds grew into private warfare. Liveried retainers practiced mayhem and murder and ruined property in their masters' quarrels. No section was immune to the virus, although the worst epidemics were in the North, the Welsh Marches, and East Anglia. Sir William Talbois terrorized southern Lincolnshire. In Bedfordshire the J.P.s dared not hold quarter-sessions by the shire court, so intimidated were they by Lord Grey and Lord Fanhope. We have the witness of the Pastons for Norfolk and Suffolk. In Oxfordshire warring factions conducted small campaigns. Such towns as Norwich and York were engulfed in feuds and in the riots that grew out of them. And the crown more often than not failed to bring either offenders to sentence or disputes to agreement. Local justice fell before maintenance and embracery, while the records of the king's bench show how little danger there was of a great malefactor being found guilty by juries.

The Commons thought Suffolk particularly to blame for the anarchy in the countryside. Since 1437 his primacy in household and Council had enriched him and his agents while excluding others from power. He ruled by "faction." When the Commons charged Suffolk with such crimes on March 9, 1450, they merely reflected local evidence. The duke's influence maintained a set of "loyal predators" in the counties—to match the party he built at court—composed principally of such churchmen as Moleyn, Ayscough, Stafford, and Lumley. Together with the household sheriffs, these men engrossed wardships, offices, and every fruit of patronage. In practice this meant that the sheriffs and other agents "overset" the duke's affinity in each county, so that every matter he wished sped would be sped and "true persons" would be "set back."[6] Misrule multiplied through the duke's manipulation of the royal pardon at the center and the running or stopping of writs on the periphery.

This was most true in East Anglia, where his estates were concentrated. There his agents used force to extort loans, fraudulently usurped titles to lands, prevented legal redress by frightening juries, and even resorted to murder. Since 1435, the "Tuddenham gang" had conspired to rule East Anglia by monopoly of office, force, and fraud. In the Paston *Letters* a score of men cite oppressive practices of the Tuddenham gang, including murder. After Suffolk's fall, Tuddenham lost his practical immunity from prosecution. The

[6] The Commons charged Suffolk with elevating his henchmen and using them to hold back justice from the subject not of his "affinity."

records of the commission that investigated his activities led to over 300 indictments, among them charges of murder, blackmail, forgery, maintenance, cruelty to children, and fraud. The jury that took part in the inquest uncovered conspiratorial agreements between Suffolk and Tuddenham dating from 1435.

Where Suffolk had less immediate power and land on a large scale he intervened dramatically. In Cheshire and Warwickshire he prevented the law from dealing with his client Sir Robert Harcourt, who (allegedly) had murdered Sir Humphrey Stafford's son Richard. In Norfolk he favored the Wingfields against the Mowbrays—dukes in their titular county! In Devon and Cornwall, which challenged the North and the Welsh Marches as centers of faction and disorder, he built his power on the local feuds between Sir William Bonville and the Courtenay earls of Devon. There, as elsewhere, he favored the upstart against the magnates. In the North he favored the Nevilles, who had gained land and power at the expense of the Percies, earls of Northumberland and "kings of the North." Their feuds in the 1440s involved alignments of forces in Northumberland, Cumberland, Westmorland, and Yorkshire, and opposed the Nevilles to their own cadet lines as well as to the Percy lords, Dacre of Gilsland, Baron Greystoke, Lord Lumley, the Cliffords, and the powerful knight Sir William Parr.

I mention these alignments to emphasize two things: the consistency with which Suffolk's actions and those of his successor—Somerset—alienated magnates and helped form a circle of "ins" and "outs"; and how aristocratic ambitions, which to some extent always divided the countryside, were focused and magnified by those of Suffolk. Moreover, detailed studies have demonstrated that these alignments have no explicable connection to the dynastic claims that allegedly divided York and Lancaster and so produced anarchy and civil war. On the contrary, local struggles seem to have stemmed from local causes. We hear nothing in them of dynasticism, much less of finespun constitutional ideas. What is clear is that already existing feuds were spurred on by Suffolk's purposes and the crown's inability to play its traditional role as arbiter among the aristocrats. In fact, in the 1450s the court's favor shown to a faction fashioned the court's enemies into an opposition. What Suffolk began, Somerset continued. Those who hoped that casting down Suffolk would end England's troubles hoped in vain. The immediate consequence of his death was rebellion and a reign of terror on a small scale. Between May 2, 1450, and May 22, 1455, when the Yorkists and the Lancastrians clashed at St. Albans, disorder grew into anarchy and civil war. These years were the most turbulent of the century. But strife was truly the "father of all things." And from the welter of events Richard, duke of York, emerged, first as the champion of his king, and then as the savior of the kingdom from Henry VI's effete court.

While we cannot narrate in detail the campaigns of the 1450s and the political machinations, some account is essential to our analysis of the restoration of order.[7]

The Magnates' Dilemma: The Rise of York

A reign of terror began even before Suffolk's fall. On January 9, 1450, a crowd fell on his colleague Bishop Moleyn at Portsmouth and murdered him. In February, insurrectionary movements were suppressed and certain leaders executed, among them characters calling themselves "Bluebeard" and "Robin Hood." From May through July, Cade's men ruled the approaches to London. At Edington, in Wiltshire, a mob of 600 dragged Bishop Ayscough from the altar where he had said Mass and beheaded him. From the Salisbury Plain to the Isle of Wight, men were riotous. In Gloucester, clergymen who had supported Suffolk were sacked, and Bishop Booth of Lichfield was threatened by crowds of angry men. Essex rose in strength to join Cade. In August and September there were further uprisings in Sussex, Wiltshire, Essex, and Kent. The situation was finally so severe that fearful magnates of all factions temporarily united to put down the rebellious common people. In this effort the gentry and burgesses supported them.

Stories circulated implicating York in Suffolk's fall. Common sailors slew the duke in Dover Road as he was sailing for Burgundy with a royal safe-conduct. When the crew of the *Nicholas of the Tower* took de la Pole, he showed his safe-conduct, in Henry VI's name, and demanded clear passage. His captors "did not know the said king," but they knew the "crown of England." They further explained that the crown "was the community of the realm and that the community of the realm was the crown of the realm." This extraordinary populist outburst was accompanied by a dark hint from one of the assassins. He said he knew of "another person beyond the sea," a man fit to be made king if all hope of reform perished.

This oblique reference was probably to York. But more important than

---

[7] The account that follows is based principally on: R. Virgoe, "The Death of William de la Pole, Duke of Suffolk," *BJRL* (1965), XLVII, pp. 489–502. See also: C. L. Kingsford, *Prejudice and Promise in Fifteenth Century England* (Kingsford: Clarendon Press, 1925; reprinted 1962, Frank Cass); K. B. McFarlane's important Raleigh lecture, *The Wars of the Roses* (London: British Academy, 1965); G. L. Harris, "The Struggle for Calais," *EHR* (1960), LXXV, pp. 30–53; J. R. Lander, "Henry VI and the Duke of York's Second Protectorate," *BJRL* (1960), XLIII, pp. 46–69; "Marriage and Politics in the Fifteenth Century," *BIHR* (1963), XXXVI, pp. 119–51; C. A. J. Armstrong, "Politics and the Battle of St. Albans, 1455," *BIHR* (1960), XXXIII, pp. 1–63; and R. L. Storey, "The Wardens of the Marches of England towards Scotland, 1377–1489," *EHR* (1957), LXXII, pp. 593–615. By far the best synthetic account of the troubles leading to St. Albans is Storey's, *op. cit.*, Chaps. 4–13.

efforts to construe a conspiracy from it was the open challenge to Henry VI.[8] The records of the king's bench yield numerous similar examples of seditious speech. York's own view—that the king was "an idiot and by God's doom of small intelligence"—was common enough. York was the only son of Richard, the earl of Cambridge, who was executed in 1415 for conspiring against Henry V. York thus sprang on his father's side from the fifth of Edward III's sons, Edmund of Langley, duke of York, and on his mother's side from Lionel of Antwerp, duke of Clarence, whose daughter established the Mortimer line.

His career had been a successful effort to overcome his father's infamy. In the 1430s he had served as Henry VI's lieutenant in France. He was the richest peer in the realm. He had married Cicely Neville, eldest daughter of Ralph, earl of Westmoreland. In 1440 York was for a second time king's lieutenant in France, a command that lasted until 1445, when Suffolk's growing policy of excluding the magnates from the Council affected York. He was denied the resumption of the French command in 1447 and sent to Ireland for ten years as lieutenant. Ireland was the graveyard of military reputations and an exile from politics. There York stayed until the wild summer of 1450, when he left his command without license and forced his way into the king's Council and national politics, claiming the right to be protector of the monarchy. He was the heir presumptive.

York was like nearly every man of property in wanting an end to the regime of upstarts and bastards—the popular label for de la Pole and the Beauforts. In him the grievances of men were epitomized. He had had to mortgage a part of his vast estates, concentrated in Hertford, East Anglia, the East Midlands, South Wales, the Marches, and Yorkshire, in order to pay the wages of his soldiers. He held unredeemed tallies worth £48,666. Contemporaries conceded to him a primacy in keeping intact his patrimony and that of the monarchy. And now Somerset had grasped power, a thing York could not tolerate.

He charged Somerset with the same crimes the Commons alleged against Suffolk: the loss of France, misrule, and the destruction of confidence in the monarchy. Moreover, there were rumors that Suffolk intended to marry Margaret Beaufort, Duke John's daughter, and, if the king died without heirs, make her queen of England and their son king.[9] Yet when York forced himself on Henry VI, *he* made no claim to the throne. He did not quarter the royal arms. He raised no dynastic issue. Instead, he asked four things: that he be held guilty of no treason for his actions, that his tallies be paid, that royal finances be reformed, and that law and order be restored in the countryside. Henry VI

---

[8] The Kent jury that tried the case in 1451 found no evidence of a conspiracy.

[9] Descended illegitimately from John of Gaunt, the Beauforts were barred from the succession in 1407.

promised only to convoke a "sad substantial council" in which York would have a place. He also rebuked York for presuming to advise the king.

York appealed from the king to the Commons and gave his support to the parliamentary campaign for resumptions of crown lands and charges against the Somerset clique. His interests and those of men hungry for good government coincided. The removal of his enemies from power would redistribute offices and influence and give substance to the propaganda in which he espoused the complaints of the "Commons of Kent." Most of the magnates remained aloof, however, more concerned with their own influence and popular risings than anything else. Hence York's "populist" campaign in 1450 was in effect a political blunder. The way to power lay not in the Commons but in the support of the most powerful vested interests of a hierarchical society. Lacking magnate support, York could be turned aside by the court in 1450–1.

Two linked themes thus dominated the 1450s: the government's failure to control local magnate feuds, and the contest at the center—between York and Somerset before 1455, and between York and the queen afterward. The first was nothing new; the second was decisive. This central conflict accounts for the wars in which York came to power. It kept politics at a boil in the 1460s, until the final destruction of the queen's party established the conditions in which Edward IV could begin the thorough reconstruction of the monarchy.

Before the capture of the king by Warwick at St. Albans in 1455, a series of satellite struggles reflected the illuminating contest at the center. In the Southwest the ancient enmity between Courtenay and Bonville grew completely out of control, and until 1456 the countryside was convulsed with their feuds. In East Anglia, Somerset had restored to local influence the leaders of the Tuddenham gang. Tuddenham was arrested while Somerset continued in power, despite guarantees to the contrary. When York attempted a second time to force Somerset from power, he was again decisively rebuffed. The Commons in 1453 correctly construed York's second political failure. They eschewed any show of support for him and treated his resort to force as no harbinger of peace. This attitude made York's isolation total. The king was now promising good government. Most of the magnates sat on the fence, while the Nevilles still associated with Somerset. The Nevilles joined Lord Cromwell and Norfolk in the commissions formed to try York's adherents. The policy of coercing the crown through the power of the common people had failed.

There was thus no effective Yorkist plan or party in 1453. However, two events helped to revive York's aspirations in that year. The quarrels in the North between Percy and Neville broke the peace on a large scale. And the king lost his sanity.

The heads of the two great northern families were kinglets enjoying vast delegated powers in the various border wardenships granted to them. They ruled northern society. Lesser men had little alternative but to choose one affinity or the other. Traditionally, the Percy earls of Northumberland had been "kings of the North." But the revolt of Sir Henry Percy ("Hotspur") against Henry IV weakened their hold on power. They had lost the wardenship of the West March to Ralph Neville, earl of Westmoreland. In the ensuing decades, successive Percy earls tried to recoup their power by spending lavishly on retainers and elaborately patronizing local gentry. These efforts weakened Percy finances decisively, without accomplishing their objective. The Nevilles had impeccable Lancastrian connections, since Earl Ralph's second marriage had been to a Beaufort. His son from the Beaufort alliance, Richard, received offices, lands, and the earldom of Salisbury from Henry VI, and fathered Warwick, "the Yorkist kingmaker."

The career of the Nevilles illustrates perfectly how wrong it is to see the struggles of the 1450s as a dynastic fight for the crown between "parties" loyal to Lancaster and York. The Nevilles rose in the reflected glory of Lancaster. They were advanced to balance the Percies. More eager courtiers there were none. Court was their natural place. Then, in 1453, Somerset fell out with Warwick and drove Salisbury to take his son's side.

The initial impulse was given to this massive centrifugal force by the ambitions of cadets in the older northern dynasty. Thomas Percy, Baron Egremont, was determined to destroy the dominance of the Nevilles. When he surveyed the North he saw a vast network of power in the hands of the hated "Beaufort" upstarts and their Neville clients. This included vast lordships, a near monopoly of local offices, the bishopric of Durham (virtually a Neville fief), and great influence in Yorkshire, a county ruled for decades by Percy and his Clifford clients. In the late 1440s several feuds were unsuccessfully arbitrated, chiefly because the Percies felt the weight of court support for the Nevilles to be fatal to genuine arbitration. And in the early 1450s the struggles between York and Somerset made the crown both more ineffective as arbitrator and more suspect. Henry VI had been reduced to the status of an undermighty ruler surrounded by overmighty subjects. By 1453 Egremont was beyond containing, as became evident in a series of Yorkshire fights and, later, in a more direct challenge to the Nevilles, in which armies of over 10,000 men were involved.

The utter loss of order in the North doomed the peace already weakened by the conflicts in the Southwest, East Anglia, and the Welsh borderlands. At court Somerset feuded with Warwick. Warwick withdrew from the Council and openly indicated his opposition to the Beaufort duke. This forced Salisbury to decide whether the alignment of his family with the court, which had raised his power and exalted that of his house, was viable. The time was inopportune, owing to the depredations of Egremont, far from London, in campaigns that made access to the royal grace the more valuable. He could not lightly go against the court. What Salisbury did was play for time, unable to desert his son and unwilling to surrender his influence at court. He knew the fragility of York's position; and he had no stomach to be another Devon, a victim of court machinations. Then Somerset, by giving signs of a rapprochement with the Percies, tipped the balance.

While these intrigues made Salisbury consider supporting York in his determination to bring down Somerset, the king went mad. Somerset and his friend hid the fact for nearly two months, before admitting the necessity of some regency settlement. The outcome of this settlement he hoped to control through a great council to be held on October 24, 1453, from which he planned to exclude York. Shortly before that date, Queen Margaret gave birth to Henry VI's heir, Prince Edward. York was no longer heir apparent. Somerset saw an altogether new political situation in this fortuitous reduction in York's position. The magnates were aghast at the transparency of Beaufort's design: to ally himself with the queen and reduce magnate influence during the king's madness and his son's minority. Norfolk and Worcester spoke quietly about the danger and went to see York in London. Salisbury and Warwick decided the time was ripe for an understanding with York. Devon and two obscure Welsh earls, Pembroke and Richmond—Jasper and Edmund Tudor, half-brothers of the king—now saw the advantage of siding with Somerset's enemy. Hence there emerged from the welter of events in the most troubled corners of the kingdom and at court the lineup that decided the regency crisis of 1453. The Tudor Beauforts and the Neville Beauforts joined the traditional "outs" —York, Devon, Cobham—against the Beaufort duke and the swelled Lancastrian family. We must surely think this a strange "Yorkist" party. And the Percy rebels and their followers—the Cliffords, Dacres, and Parrs—were indeed stranger Lancastrians!

These alignments represented nothing more than the self-interest of men caught up in a revolution in domestic diplomacy. Some of the "ins" saw opening under their feet the same abyss that had always threatened to swallow the "outs" before 1453. They sided with York only because his elevation with their support seemed the best way to prevent the ruin of the baronial oligarchy. The war in France was over and lost and this fact gave a new primacy to the settlement of domestic power in a way safe to the magnates. Only by weakening Somerset could they avoid open war between York and the court, or truly hope to arbitrate the local feuds and baronial struggles that also threatened civil order.

Their decision found acceptance in the Commons, which ratified and proclaimed York's first Protectorship. This was, after all, a victory for the Commons too. The Commons had triumphed over the profligate court, a foreign queen, and the misrule of Somerset.

Peace glittered on the horizon, a prize that would be, paradoxically, the issue of an unbalanced mind and an unexpected heir. A true magnate Council led by York might banish faction and feuds and restore good government by placing the kingship in commission. But the prospect that cleared the sight of some bleared that of Baron Egremont. He saw the preoccupation with peace as inimical to his coup against the Nevilles in Yorkshire. Rallying to his standard, his brother, the bishop of Carlisle, and York's unhappy son-in-law, the desperate and quixotic Henry Holland, duke of Exeter, Egremont battered the North. York and the Council reacted with a commission to put down the "Exeter Conspiracy," so called because Holland allegedly claimed the crown for himself. York took the duke out of sanctuary and then commissioned Salisbury to capture Egremont and Carlisle. Success came quickly, but at a price. Somerset was in the Tower, Exeter in jail, and York in command. But York's alliance with Neville against the Percies turned the Percies against him and gave them a vested interest in Somerset's restoration. York had fined the Percies £11,000.

The return of the king's sanity early in the winter of 1454–5 tumbled York's power. Pardons went to Egremont, Carlisle, and Exeter. The magnates stood by helplessly, witness to the fragility of *political* efforts to reform Henry VI's regime, and wondering what their fate might be. The troubled regions of the country were soon enmeshed in feuds as unbridled as any before 1453. But now developments at the center had fused two sets of enemies and disputes. York and the Nevilles fled from London, while Somerset laid plans for their ruin in a great council set to meet in Leicester on May 21, 1455. Thus began the Wars of the Roses.

Revolution

Somerset could not trust a Parliament or a genuine magnate gathering because of his weakness in the country and his lack of support among the greater nobles. York and Neville certainly would not trust Beaufort. When they came south in May, it was in arms. They intercepted the king's entourage at St. Albans, Hertfordshire, entered the royal camp, slew Somerset, Clifford, and Northumberland, and took Henry VI prisoner. The slaughter at St. Albans on May 22, 1455, was highly selective, with the grandees named being honored in a list of some sixty victims. This was not so much the beginning of a vast civil war as it was the continuation of politics by other means. These political murders and the capture of the king raised no cry of "York the king." Duke Richard had no intention of claiming the throne; nor would he have had support for such a move. The magnates were no more "Yorkist" than he was. Although they applauded St. Albans, they were alienated by Warwick's violence against the king's standard. This made it necessary for York and the Nevilles to conciliate the nobility by restoring collective magnate power in the Council.

York's second Protectorship was based on the king's alleged mental relapse, for which there is no good evidence. York and his supporters tried to strengthen their rule with an appeal to the country. This they made in a Parliament that met in July 1455. The appeal succeeded; the Commons put the blame for the "sorrows" squarely on Somerset, from whose corpse there was no answer. York and his friends proved moderate in their use of power. While they rewarded their friends, they practiced no monopoly of patronage. And they began to develop a program to pacify the borders, keep the seas, advance trade, pay arrears for crown servants and soldiers, and retrench royal finances through new acts of resumption.

York's second Protectorship was too short-lived, however, for us to evaluate which of his promises he might have achieved. Against the magnates seeking peace, Queen Margaret and the remaining Beauforts, Cliffords, and Percies wanted revenge. Their need was the political legacy of St. Albans. Hence they rallied to make the "Queen's party." Ironically, this move cast them against their king, for Henry VI was willing to continue York's rule in exchange for York's renunciation of the Protectorship. York would simply be styled "chief councillor" and "the king's lieutenant," precisely the role the duke had fought for since 1450. The queen, however, looked upon York as a threat to her power and to the eventual succession of her infant son. York wanted power, but nothing in his actions before 1460 can convict him of usurpation. His plans to assume the dignity of kingship stemmed from Margaret's refusal to accept the result of St. Albans. The struggle had always been for peace, power, prosperity, and profit. And now the queen showed herself to be anxious to reverse their distribution in a new round of hostilities.

She built her hopes on the turbulent southwest and Wales. In 1455 she had made an alliance with the Tudors, using Margaret Beaufort, Duke John's daughter, as the pawn of her internal gambit. The Tudor line derived from the marriage of Queen Catherine, Henry V's widow, to Owen Tudor, an obscure Welsh courtier. The two sons of that union were Edmund and Jasper, the earls of Richmond and Pembroke. It was Edmund who married the Beaufort heiress. This step detached the Tudors from York and made them, along with Henry Stafford (Beaufort's heir), Shrewsbury, and Wiltshire, the nucleus of a powerful court faction. To this center Margaret recruited the Westmorland cadets of Neville's first family—men bitter over the favor shown to the children of Neville's Beaufort marriage—and other men who thought to profit from her cabal. Buckingham (Stafford) alone acted for reasons of loyalty to Henry VI and the integrity of the crown.

Between the summers of 1456 and 1457, the queen had secured York's disgrace and had gained control over government. Her pretense that Henry VI ruled as well as reigned deceived few; in fact, it emphasized the king's lack of fitness for his hereditary burden. By 1458 the situation was so tense that magnates never came to Council without troops at their backs. The mayor of London maintained 5,000 soldiers to keep the peace against them. All efforts to reconcile the Percies and Nevilles failed, chiefly because their struggles now were inseparable from those dividing York and the queen. Duke Richard added to the crisis by giving rise to stories of an alliance between his family and the Burgundian duchy. The queen was a French princess and could not mistake any such overtures: her house and Burgundy were linked in a struggle that would end only in the supremacy of France in continental Europe's north-western corner. She countered by issuing a call to the country against York. At the same time she cast Warwick out of his several offices. He withdrew to Calais. Within a few months York and the Nevilles were in the field in force; they were defeated at Ludlow on September 23, 1459. Parliament affirmed the decision of arms by attainting the duke and his followers of treason, a judgment from which York and Warwick saved themselves by flight—the duke to Ireland and Warwick to Calais. The Commons were packed with men favorable to Margaret by the simple expediency of giving the sheriffs lists of suitable M.P.s.

When Margaret's agents moved Parliament to declare the estates and offices of York and his followers forfeit, they made a grave error. This step drove York from a policy of controlling the Lancastrian monarchy to one of ending it. The duke's political liabilities in the country at large were turned into credits. Society was based on the premise of the sacredness of property. If the rights of the greatest magnates could be so easily extinguished, then no man was safe. Lancaster, in fact, had forgotten its own history, and Margaret had provided York with the same pretext of "legitimacy of inheritance" used by Henry of Lancaster to justify the usurpation of Richard II's throne. On November 19, 1399, it was Bolingbroke who had announced, "it was not [his] will . . . to disinherit anybody from his heritage, franchise or other right. . . ."

Within a year of the attainder, most of the exiles had returned to England. York himself watched warily from Ireland, but his son Edward of March and Warwick defeated the royalists at Northampton. The king was captured; Beaufort, Buckingham, and Shrewsbury were killed. It was 1455 revisited, with York's heir proclaiming no wish to depose Henry. York himself had already decided on usurpation, however. The evidence indicates that in this he deceived even his closest supporters, for they were startled by his procession to London and his display of the royal arms guarded by the naked sword of state. Contemporaries reported that at Westminster he "sore dismayed" the lords by putting his hand on the empty throne. His boldness frightened his allies, for he followed the gesture with an exposition of the superiority of his own descent from Clarence and Mortimer to Henry VI's descent from John of Gaunt. The judges refused to adjudicate the issue, and the lords rejected the claim. York answered with a carefully prepared rebuttal of Lancastrian legitimacy and primacy of inheritance. What resulted from this impasse was a parliamentary compromise: Henry should remain king for his natural life, but York should be his successor. The king accepted the disinheritance of Prince Edward. Margaret did not, appealing against the verdict of Westminster at Wakefield, where her forces slew Richard of York in 1460, and at St. Albans, where she defeated Warwick in 1461. While she triumphed in the field, Edward of March showed superior insight by marching to London, where, on March 4, 1461, he was acclaimed as King Edward IV, just as Lancaster was within reach of victory.

Both the rejection of Duke Richard in 1460 and the acceptance of his son in 1461 show how little of "Yorkist" conspiracy and legitimacy there was before 1460 and how it failed to move the magnates in that year. Why, then, did they elevate Edward a few months later? On pragmatic grounds. Margaret's savagery in her triumph of 1460 gave them scant hope of a gracious pardon in the event of her complete vindication. She had executed the earl of Salisbury at Wakefield. Three times in six years she had cast York and other magnates from power and restored courtier government, using power to humiliate a large segment of the nobility. Few magnates could hope to outlive Henry VI and his son. Hence the compromise in York's favor made sense; it was an utterly conservative decision. Only their own act in reconstituting the monarchy could guarantee their place in society and government. They knew that no baronial faction had successfully controlled a king by machinations at one remove from power—not in the time of John, Henry III, or Richard II. The failure of Henry VI's government threatened them all; in their pockets, in their standing in society, in place and power. The misuse of prerogative gave rise to persecution by factions more than to lawful prosecution. The paramount influence of magnates in Council had been replaced by courtier-political forces, which unsettled in property and family every lord, gentleman, and prosperous burgess. The magnates wanted law and order. But the central lessons of the 1450s were that they could neither have law and order nor gain and keep power without replacing Henry VI. While there was still hope of working with and controlling Henry VI, they had not thought of usurpation. But when the queen's ambition made it clear that the problem went deeper even than the king's incapacity and unfitness, the magnates accepted Edward IV.

That this was their motivation became clear in the 1460s. Edward IV at times seemed as great a threat to baronial survival as had Henry VI. The nobility then struggled to return king Henry to power in the Lancastrian "readeptation" of 1470. Warwick, the so-called Yorkist kingmaker, went over to Margaret. The nature of the struggles—small campaigns, exiles, and anarchy, which appeared often between 1464 and 1470—closely resembles that of the 1450s. There was the same nonideological polarization of 'ins" and "outs," the same changing of sides, the same efforts to control a king and then to replace him. Finally, the politically articulate elements of English society opted for a government responsive to the need for better law-enforcement, financial retrenchment, and monarchy "regale and political." After Edward IVs decisive emergence as an effective king, there was no issue left to join. And the people could not have cared less about the labels Lancaster, York, or Tudor.[1]

For more than thirty years, the political weakness of the crown had threatened the collapse of public order. Feuds had escalated into civil wars. Neither dynastic principle nor legitimacy nor "bastard feudalism" had caused this to happen—nor had bankrupt magnates made civil war in the hope of recouping fortunes lost elsewhere. The most bellicose peers in 1455–61 and 1464–71 were men richer than their fathers had been. Between 1450 and 1460 no question of legitimacy was raised by York. Both Lancaster and York came to power on the strength of aristocratic self-interest against a ruling king. The Wars of the Roses took place because there was no other cure for Henry VI's regime. The men who made the Yorkist revolution had no liking for it, but they could not stand apart. Opportunism and necessity demanded their participation on one side of the struggle or the other, with changes of sides being so regular as to be the rule. The *final* overthrow of Lancastrian government resulted not from a conspiracy against it but from the judgment of the country. Englishmen had learned that a man who had no order in him could not spread it about him. They had discovered there was no policy apart from that reality.

---

[1] The interpretation that follows relies chiefly on Storey. I find his views more congenial to the broader social history of the century than the narrow, dynastic, and legalistic ones championed by S. B. Chrimes, *Lancastrians, Yorkists and Henry VII* (London: Macmillan, 1964); or the one long championed by the late K. B. McFarlane, that the Yorkists acted solely to rescue the kingdom, as a matter of principle, coupled with a denial that the spread of disorder was the seedbed of the Wars of the Roses: K. B. McFarlane, "England: The Lancastrian Kings," *Cambridge Medieval History*, vol. VIII (Cambridge: Cambridge University Press, 1936); "Bastard Feudalism," *BIHR* (1943–5), XX, pp. 161–80; "The English Nobility in the Later Middle Ages," *Rapports* (Vienna, 1965), I, pp. 337–45.

Feudalism and Bastard Feudalism

The problems of social order and lawlessness in society thus derived in large measure from the nature of royal government in a personal monarchy. The system required a fit king who was on good terms with his nobility and with the larger aristocracy, which embraced the gentry. Beginning with the Angevin use of the shire to do the work of the crown, it had been vital that the men of the countryside be friendly to the king. Self-government might otherwise degenerate into a series of local squabbles and conspiracies in defeat of the royal will. In exchange for service and cooperation, the crown had distributed fiefs, franchises, and the fruits of the prerogative. The ancient feudal arrangements whereby land was given in exchange for allegiance and homage had created a social system in which privilege was justified by political service. Feudalism was thus never "opposed" to royal government; it was but an extension of it. The holder of franchises and fiefs was an official whose office endured as long as he exercised his powers in the crown's interest. Strong kings managed their vassals and officials in what was, in effect, a multi-tiered system of power spreading out from the king in ever-wider circles. If the king was weak or perverse, however, his dependents in theory and in fact could oppose him on the grounds of broken contracts. If land and privilege entailed "a great and continual labor" for the aristocrat, as Disraeli once said, then it was also true that men were tied to the king only because he truly governed them. That alone enhanced their power to govern locally.

One special feature of the system was therefore the standing of the aristocrat *in loco regis*—that is, his role as a *vice-roy*. The good use of privilege was rightly treasured, as when a fifteenth-century monk of Bury St. Edmunds wrote: "What time this rule[2] was kept, it was noted and holden for the most honorable franchise of good rule in the land." It must be stressed again that feudalism was a method of organizing political life and administration for a government far too poor to maintain all services directly by salaried servants and too limited by technology either to overawe the country or to govern well at a distance. Even the Stuart King James I was more witty than wise in thinking he could govern Scotland by the stroke of his pen in London.

It was crucial, too, that the man at the center of power be well ordered. When he was not, as in the case of Henry VI, the theory of privilege in exchange for service might yield to another: no obligation where there was neither royal peace nor justice. In the event of general insecurity caused by ineffective kingship, the fabric of local power and interest became the court of last resort. Since local magnates maintained their influence and rewarded their followers

[2] The franchise of the monastery to rule in East Anglia.

out of the profits of estates and office, peace, stability, and the absence of monopolistic courtier influences were essential to them. Henry VI's government threatened their "good lordship" and thus weakened their allegiance to the monarchy. The decline of royal government into rule by faction produced the failure of the centuries-old policy of ruling by transforming privilege into administration.

Of course, this failure had historical roots of a more general character than Henry VI's personality and that of Suffolk, Somerset, and others who shared their politics. Throughout the 1300s, both the numbers and powers of territorial lords had increased. A 1347 Commons petition protested the policy of enfranchisement. Between 1378 and 1394 it was often noted that fiscal privileges added to the burdens of the taxable. All three Edwards had rewarded suitors and supporters by lavish grants of liberties and offices. Men already enjoying franchises added to their holdings. In 1377 the County Palatine of Lancaster gained the right to have its own chancery, a concession that became the pattern for the fifteenth-century appanages that devolved upon the heirs of Edward III's sons. By 1414 it was a common complaint that the North was so enfranchised as to defeat the ends of government and make murder and robbery a better law than the king's.

The emphasis on the North reminds us that the problem of the overmighty subject had geographical as well as fiscal roots. Deep in the mist of Northumbrian history we cannot go. We can, however, touch on the accumulation of local power in that region. The Scottish wars waged between 1295 and 1547 kept the borders in a state of confusion. War-readiness was what the crown wanted there. And to ensure this, successive kings had divided the North into wardenships, which were vice-royalties. Thus the Percies were "kings of the North" and the Nevilles their rivals, each governing areas that were recruiting grounds. On the Welsh Marches there were more than one hundred "marcher lordships" with small armed forces and private secretariats. After 1284 Edward I had abandoned efforts to control them effectively, and the situation there was less ordered than that in the North. Disputes in both regions were either arbitrated by strong kings or left to private warfare by weak ones. Since the area between the Marches and the border was made up chiefly of the Palatine of Chester and the Duchy of Lancaster, in effect the entire western region of England stretching from Cornwall to Westmoreland was linked in disorder and resistance to central control even in the best of times. In East Anglia, where Suffolk held sway, a series of ancient ecclesiastical liberties (Bury, Ramsey, Peterborough, St. Albans, and Ely) made effective what Maitland called "the abbatical government" there.

Wherever they were, men holding vast lands and franchises faced challenges similar to those of the crown: to organize councils, to administer estates in new economic conditions, to make the law work and office profitable. To do all this after 1350 required genius and restraint. With the breakdown of tenurial relationships and the transformation of the social and economic bases of lordship, the permanence of land gave way to fluid money contracts, which became the link between masters and men. This change from feudal relationships to contractual ones that were quasifeudal in character has been variously styled "bastard feudalism" and "neo-feudalism." It has also been widely blamed for the disorder in the middle decades of the 1400s.

Whatever we call it, the system of lordship that employed money wages in contracts of indenture found its way into the arrangements of local government prevailing in England—on the estates and in the franchises. It also continued a notable feature of feudal society: landed classes and franchise-holders were agents of administration doubling as warriors. The crown allowed this development in its own interest. In fact, a case can be made for the fact that ever since Edward I, the crown itself led the way in making indentures do the work once done under the feudal contract based on land. In practice, knights and squires who were retained for the king's wars by great captains became the permanent "feed men" of a lord's retinue. In exchange for wages and patronage of every sort, they served in peacetime as grooms, clerks, councillors, and bailiffs. They wore the liveries and badges of their lords, bound by uniforms in a brotherhood of arms, an implicit recognition of the psychological rewards inherent in such group identification. No wonder the M.P.s in 1433 sought from all magnates an oath that they would cease the practice and its consequences in the courts of law:

No lord, by color nor occasion of feoffment, or of any gifts of movable goods, shall take any other men's causes or quarrels in favor . . . or maintenance, as by word, by writ, or by message to officer, judge, jury, or party, by the gift of his clothing or livery . . . nor conceive against any judge or officer indignation or displeasure for doing of his office in form of law. . . .

This new feudalism did lack the security of landed ties. But that did not mean it could no longer operate as an aid to a coherent system of government. The contract itself did not promote factions or drive desperate men to take the law into their own hands. Lordship had always meant the exercise of local power to protect clients and local interests—sometimes through the intimidation of juries or the corruption of officials, sometimes by the direct use of force and fraud. Vassals were as much committed to their lords' right as was any indentured retainer ready to judge in his master's case—*addicti jurari in verbis magistri!* Franchises and fiefs had always given rise to some illegal manipulation —inside the liberty by delegated power, beyond it through the subservient loyalty of lesser men to greater. But these abuses of feudalism and bastard feudalism could be controlled by a strong king who was supported by the major part of the aristocracy.

What made bastard feudalism parasitic and inimical to government was the failure of the central government. When the kingship itself was rootless and remote from loyalty and faith, so too were its dependents and agents. Fortescue grasped this when he commented on the socioeconomic bases of political power—the crown's and the aristocracy's. He advocated redressing the balance between the government and its natural agents in the countryside, partly by the policy of resumptions. But more than anything else he stressed the need for strong kingship in the personal sense of kingcraft. He did not propose the destruction of the aristocracy. He proposed only its transformation, a reduction in scale relative to the crown's power. This would enable the crown to reward and punish condignly, to suppress feuds and reconcile factions through evenhanded justice in Council and in the court of law. Failing that, aristocratic disorder was a symptom of the crown's failure and a stimulant of general lawlessness. Fortescue did not make the mistake of some modern historians and treat bastard feudalism as a prime mover or an uncaused cause. Agreements that once had provided stability could do so again. If the abuses of royal finance and aristocratic privileges could be curbed, even the "debased imitation" of feudalism might be made to work. In the conditions of the fifteenth century, controlling the aristocracy and channeling its energies was the most important task of the monarchy. Henry VI lacked the will and the wealth to attempt it. Edward IV and his Tudor successors compensated for past failures and rebuilt the strength of government, and recognition of this achievement is vital to any understanding of the Tudor Century.

Chapter Three
THE RESTORATION OF ORDER

For what is he they follow? Truly, gentlemen,
A bloody tyrant and a homicide;
One raised in blood and one in blood established;
One that made means to come by what he hath,
And slaughtered those that were the means to help him;
A base foul stone, made precious by the foil
of England's chair . . . .

SHAKESPEARE
Richard III, Act V, Scene iii

Thus spoke Henry Tudor before God and his soldiers in defiance of King Richard. Offering his life in battle, he held out the prospect of "smooth-faced peace" as every man's prize. Proclaiming pardon for rebels, Richmond in his hour of victory thanked the God of Battle. This was fitting. For despite his denunciation of King Richard as one "raised in blood," Richmond's own title to the throne had been earned by battle. Nor was this claim a novelty of York or Tudor or the peculiar legacy of the fifteenth century. Since the day Harold fell at Hastings in a hail of Norman arrows, the God of War had been the arbiter of kings in England. Edward IV's publicists had elevated the accident of victory into a claim to the throne when, after Barnet but before Tewkesbury, they proclaimed no more evident sign of God's will and royal right than "by reson, auctoritie and victorie in batailles . . . ."

This reminder of what York and Tudor shared with Normans and Plantagenets and with Lancaster may serve to introduce an account of other achievements common to York and Tudor: the resurrection of the late medieval monarchy, the start of the process by which the aristocracy was restored to its natural place as the party of law and order, the gradual restitution of royal finances to a level adequate for governance, the renewal of the slow process of integration that was to knit together the regions and the center and finally sweep away the great lay and ecclesiastical franchises, and the emergence of a foreign policy that looked askance at the old dreams of empire in Europe. These elements of restoration and renewal cannot be severed from one another. Without the reorganization of finances it is inconceivable that law and order could have been vigorously enforced or the aristocracy domesticated. And it is as unlikely that a wild, rude, and disordered kingdom would have proved attractive as an ally for the great powers of Europe. Finally, the whole style of kingship and its celebration, which engaged the attention of Edward IV and

Henry Tudor, rested safely on the twin pillars of money and the promise of justice.

Monarchy Restored: Kingship and Kingcraft

Let us begin with the center of the government. There the chief accomplishments were certainly the emergence from shadows of the dignity of kingship, the ordering of good counsel in an effective Council, and the elaboration of a body of law that had as its central motif the tightening of control over far-flung regions and local sentiments. We cannot stress too much that these were not *Tudor* achievements only. Two Tudor apologists, Thomas More and Polydore Vergil, gave Edward IV high marks in kingcraft. They agreed about his diligence, the effectiveness of his justice, his popularity, and the growth of prosperity in his reign. Their view was not widely accepted by later Tudor writers or even by the scientific historians of the nineteenth century, however. These historians stressed Edward's cruelty, self-indulgence, and arrogance, and his neglect of administration. It is closer to the truth to see in York "a king of iron will and fixity of purpose."[1] He was famous in his time for the suppression of piracy and criminal gangs; appearances with the justices in eyre in every corner of his kingdom; the strong use of provincial councils in the West and North; a steady stream of instruments of government and orders, which trained men to order and obedience to law; and a steady decline in public and private royal indebtedness.

His brother Richard of Gloucester has also suffered from a bad press. Henry VII was especially sensitive about Richard III's stories concerning his own house and the legitimacy of his queen, Elizabeth of York. This worry he showed in the first statute of his reign, wherein he commanded that certain of Richard's acts be taken out of the Parliament roll and burnt, and all copies likewise destroyed, "so that all things said and remembered . . . may be forever out of remembrance and also forgot. . . ." Despite his desire to obliterate the past and rewrite it to ensure his own future, Henry could not erase altogether the contemporary evidence about Gloucester. Richard had been a vigorous and loyal Edwardian governor in the North. He was able in battle, religious in his habits, zealous for England's trade, a promoter of justice, and a repressor of usurped privileges. He facilitated the petitions of poor men in his Council, reduced taxation, and followed the path of Edward IV's financial reforms. He also earned the gratitude of churchmen for his patronage and his defense of clerical privileges. A stern popular moralist and patron of learning, he lacked vindicators after his fall, especially among the powerful gentry. So

[1] See J. R. Green, *History* (1887 ed.), II, v. 27–8. For his reputation among historians, see Lander, "Edward IV: The Modern Legend and a Revision," *History* (1956), XLI, pp. 38–52.

he is known chiefly as a paranoid peacetime warrior and as the slayer of his nephews. But even this measure of the Tudor triumph did not silence the rebellious Londoners in 1525 when, in arms against Wolsey's forced loans, they appealed for the contrary practices and good laws of Richard III.[2]

Both Yorkist kings elevated respect for kingship. Through sumptuary legislation, minstrel shows, pageantry, and heraldic developments, they sought to show this policy in the outward forms of political life. They showed their awareness of the "iconography of kingship"[3] in identical ways. Their titles were proclaimed at Paul's Cross in London; they gathered noblemen in council at Baynard Castle—the ancestral home of the Plantagenets; they assumed the role of ruler publicly, through appearances in the king's bench— the marble chair in Westminster where judgment was, by fiction usually, always in the king's presence. They also appealed to the political nation in Parliament; made distinctions between de facto and de jure kings, that is, between kings in deed but not of right; put forward again the notion of legitimacy and the crown as property; sought acclamation by the people, thus translating possession of the crown into an acknowledgment of right; and got from churchmen the chanted lauds of majesty in the Abbey at Westminster.

In all of these things, Henry VII imitated his Yorkist enemies, except that he never personally dispensed justice in the king's bench. There is no Henrician example to match that of Edward IV who, in 1462, joined the chancellor in hearing the suit of a distressed widow, thus showing to all the might of the king as a righteous judge. The Yorkists developed anew the style of kingship perfected by the first Tudors. It was kingship with popular, autocratic, and aristocratic elements: in the notions and practices of acclamation, the submissions made to the newly crowned king, and the parliamentary cooperation in the possession of the realm.

But beyond the show of kingship lay the substance of it. Here, too, the continuity of York and Tudor is remarkable. From the perspective of the historian of government, the period 1300–1640 often appears to be made up of a series of postfeudal reigns that contributed to the centralization of government. This "era of kings"[4] was not without its grave crises and lapses. But, as Professor Powicke has argued in an earlier volume of this history,[5] from the early fourteenth century there was agreement that the monarchy in England was politically limited. The consent of prelates, earls, barons, knights, and the "community of the realm" in Parliament was necessary for vigorous govern-

[2] M. Levine, "Richard III—Usurper or Lawful King," *Speculum* (1959), XXXIV, pp. 391–401.
[3] C. A. J. Armstrong, "The Inauguration Ceremonies of the Yorkist Kings and their Title to the Throne," *RHST* (1948), XXX, pp. 51–73.
[4] See B. P. Wolfe, *Yorkist and Early Tudor Government* (London: Historical Association, 1966).
[5] See M. Powicke, *The Community of the Realm*, Volume II in this History.

ment. Neither 1461 nor 1485 marks a divide in this history, separating medieval from modern; nor does the Reformation legislative program of the 1530s, although the changes in administration within that decade did dig the deepest trench across the unity of the period.[6] After Edward I's death in 1307, the principle of primogeniture had been subordinated to that of "election"— through the effective usurpation of the crown by the ablest male members of the whole royal family. This motif can be traced in ancient German law and is much in evidence in Anglo-Saxon times. In this sense Edward IV stands in the tradition of Henry IV; and the fertile early Tudor theories of kingship merely sought to make sense of the residual notions of birthright and election. More to the point, however, is the fact that the Yorkists and Tudors did what the Henrys of Lancaster had not done: they restored finance, built an effective Council, grasped the significance of public opinion, and secured European support for their houses. They ruled as well as reigned.

This they did through established institutions rather than through any "constitutional" experiments or through the mystical effects of unction. In 1506 John Stokesley, who later became a bishop, baptized a cat, a collegiate prank that did not make the animal a Christian. Nor could the royal character stem from ceremonies. Princes gained their reputations by maintaining themselves in power and their governments in order. Toward that end, nothing was more vital than good counsel made effective in the king's Council. The function of counsel and Council—thought and executive action—was to enable the king to do what he ought to do.

Henry VII's reputation in this respect is secure. His use of the protean Council and its "committee" offshoots included a court sitting in Star Chamber,[7] the surveyors of land revenue (1493), the council "learned in the law" (1500), the special committee to study foreign treaties (1504), and the infamous group that audited the forced loans and benevolences in 1507. Despite a relative lack of evidence, which has led in the past to an underestimation of the Yorkist Council, it is clear that Edward IV and Richard III reshaped the Council from the magnate board it had become under Henry VI. While many things formerly done by the factions of magnates using the Council's seal (the privy seal) were done after 1461 by seals directly controlled by the king and his secretaries, there is compelling military, diplomatic, and fiscal evidence of conciliar actions over the years before 1485. Some of it derives from the needs of defense—against the French in 1461, 1468, and 1475; the Lancastrians in 1463-4; and the Scots in 1480. The finances of the garrison at Calais and trade expedients occupied the Council's attention in 1462 and again in 1467-8. Numerous orders illustrate the Council's key position in estate

[6] See the discussion in Chapter Four.

[7] Not founded in 1487, by the so-called Star Chamber Act of that year.

administration, in raising and disbursing money, and in paying officers of the crown. Seven orders survive from 1462–71; these were renewed in 1483 by Richard III, and a draft in Edward V's name survives from 1483. Scrutiny of finances by the Council was especially critical when civil war threatened in 1464. By various names, which were less definitive than descriptive, less adjectival than adverbial,[8] under Yorkists and the Tudor Henrys, the Council met in "the White Hall," "the starred Chamber," the "court of requests," or "wherever the king was."

The king often presided in person, in sharp contrast to Henry VI's nearly perpetual absence. Councillors derived their power from his confidence, and their jurisdiction in legal matters from the fact that he was the fountain of justice. Leftover parliamentary business came to the Council; judicial matters touching the crown came on referral from ordinary judges; aliens lay outside the common law and so sought its shield and remedy; foreign affairs and internal security came before it as royal concerns. And in order to avoid being drowned in routine legal casework, it became increasingly necessary for the Council to refer cases to its own judicial committees or to the civil and common law courts. Thus, although the great fines for illegal retaining had conciliar scrutiny, cases were settled at common law, either in the king's bench or before assize justices in the countryside.

But it is not the Council's capacity for work that was the central issue. Lancastrian Councils were just as voracious and competent. Rather it was the identity of the councillors that was critical, especially when set against the backdrop of magnate-faction rule in the 1440s and 1450s. Between 1461 and 1483, 124 men were styled "councillors." Nineteen gave only casual or diplomatic service, leaving 105 sworn oathtakers during the whole reign of Edward IV. During the troubled decade of the 1460s, when York struggled to consolidate his power, 60 names were recorded: 20 noblemen, 25 clerics (11 bishops), 11 crown officials, and 4 who defy classification. For the more settled years from 1471 to 1483, we possess the names of 88 councillors: 21 nobles, 35 clerics (22 bishops), 23 officials, and 9 "others."[9] These figures may be set alongside similar ones for Henry VII's reign, for which we know the names of 179 councillors distributed occupationally and by social groups in nearly identical ways.

The large number of bishops and nobles makes it impossible to support the old myth of a policy that deliberately excluded either group. The number of peers receiving parliamentary summonses c. 1461–1509 varied from a low of 39

[8] K. Pickthorn, *Early Tudor Government, Henry VII* (Cambridge: Cambridge University Press, 1934), p. 32.

[9] See J. R. Lander, "Council, Administration and Councillors, 1461–1485," *BIHR* (1959), XXXII, 138–80, and the analysis based on the data.

to a high of 45. Over 50 percent of them became councillors! This was because Edward IV and Henry VII were equally in need of local magnate support. Retainment and maintenance contributed as much to the restoration of government as they had to its breakdown. The difference was chiefly that strong kings built up clients in critical districts to strengthen government, whereas under weak kings magnates built factions, which impaired law, order, and royal authority. This has been shown to be true of Lord Hastings' indentured retainers in the 1470s and 1480s.[1] Tudor policy continued this system of control and connivance, under which councillors were allowed to consolidate carefully selected territorial properties in exchange for audited services. Loyalty and ability governed in principle and in fact among members of the traditional elites of the church, nobility, and officialdom. Far from a policy of replacing these elites—although there was a steady growth of lay professionalism in the administration—or a system of building crown power in alliance with the bourgeoisie, the restoration of government rested on a species of political expediency that lacked ideology and made a moral principle out of astutely turning one's coat. Bishop Morton, who rose to the cardinalate under Henry VII, grasped this in his remarks to the duke of Buckingham about his conduct during the Wars of the Roses:

But aftre God had ordered hym [H. VI] to lese it, and King Edward to reigne, I was never so mad, that I would with a dead man strive against the quicke. So was I to King Edwarde faithful chapeleyn and glad would have bene yf his childe had succeded him Howbeit, yf the secrete jugement of God has otherwyse provyded: I purpose not to spurne against a prick, nor labor to set up that God pulleth doan.[2]

English kings from Edward IV onward drew on the resources of their Councils and their committees for executive efficiency and parliamentary management. They found the institution ready for their purpose. It could use its power to deal fearlessly with any question or any person. Procedure in Council cases was swift and suited to extracting the facts in those cases in which good government required celerity and existing law did not authorize other modes of action. Council could control litigation and avoid ensnarement in its details. It could choose to act secretly, out of the privilege of those sworn to the king's business. Or it could act publicly, in Star Chamber or elsewhere, bringing home the king's justice to malefactors and good subjects alike. Its composition and policy depended on the will of a vigorous monarch. Hence,

---

[1] On the development of this practice in the Midlands, see W. H. Dunham, Jr., *Lord Hastings' Indentured Retainers, 1461–1483: The Lawfulness of Livery and Retaining under the Yorkists and Tudors* (New Haven: Connecticut Academy for Arts and Sciences, 1955), especially Chap. 5.

[2] W. E. Campbell, *Thomas More's English Works*, I, p. 70.

it could be said that never was an organ of government under a strong king better suited to facilitate the administration of a kingdom.

Perhaps this can be illustrated best by looking in turn at each of three related issues: how the aristocracy was domesticated and regions brought under the control of the center; how the phrase "law and order" was given substance; and how finance was put on a new footing. Then we may look closely at Henry VII's rule, in order to see how in practice these achievements were always inseparable and sometimes were regarded with suspicion and loathing.

The Crown and the Aristocracy

We have already stated one conclusion drawn from our understanding of the composition of the Council between 1461 and 1509. York and Tudor built on the strength of established elites through certain techniques of control and through the landowners' natural interest in stable regimes. What was true of Lord Hastings' retainers in the Midlands in the 1480s was true of the Herberts in the Southwest, the Howards and the Ryvers in East Anglia, and, two generations later, of Lord Wharton in the North, Sir Ralph Sadler in Hertfordshire, and the Russells in Devon.[3] No political test was applied, apart from that of the scrutiny of loyalty. Where earlier the giving of a badge and livery was regarded as a sign of lawlessness and anarchy, it came to be viewed increasingly as a protective device in sixteenth-century society. Elizabethan lords who gave their players badges sought thereby to shield them from popular hostility. This we may use as one measure of the Yorkist and Tudor achievement. By Shakespeare's time livery had become a convenient fiction to shield actors from the pugnacity of respectable society, for "playing" was as bad an occupation for a man in 1600 as rebellion in livery had been in 1500.

Castles had lost their fearsome aspect as well. These had always been bastions of baronial power, in much the same way that monasteries had represented abbatial strength. It is thus odd that we celebrate Henry VIII's destruction of the one institution while passing by without a notice that his father won a kingdom without one castle siege. Henry VII faced rebellions in 1485–6, 1487, 1489, 1491, 1495, and 1497—from Lambert Simnel, the Lovels, Yorkshiremen resisting taxes, Perkin Warbeck's impostures, the earl of Lincoln, and Cornishmen. Yet he neither laid sieges nor resisted them. Although external defenses continued to rely on castle guards and artillery forts, such things were obsolete in domestic broils. This was not because great men had no money to spend on

---

[3] See M. E. James, *Change and Continuity in the Tudor North* (York: St. Anthony's Press, 1965); H. P. R. Finsberg, *Tavistock Abbey* (Cambridge: Cambridge University Press, 1951); A. J. Slavin, *Politics and Profit* (Cambridge: Cambridge University Press, 1966); and J. Youings, "The Terms of the Disposition of Devon Monastic Lands," *EHR* (1954), LXIX, p. 23.

castles in 1500 (although James I did find most English strong-forts in ruins a century later). Rather it was because the castles had undergone a century of neglect and because the Tudor policy was to bring under crown control every place that could become a repository of feudal violence.

Edward IV began the practice of confiscation, not as an independent policy but as a by-product of the forfeitures that were the "fallout" of civil wars. Henry VII and his son took possession of most of the great fortresses, adding to the forty that were part of the crown's estate from York and Lancaster in 1485. By 1503, Henry Tudor obtained the Berkeley castles in return for a marquisate given to the incumbent earl. The execution of Buckingham in 1521 brought Henry VIII twelve great castles, all but two of which went in grants to reliable courtier-gentry and loyal officials. The policy was most successful in the Southwest and in the Welsh Marches by the 1520s. In the North, however, Percy and Neville influence survived well into the 1530s and, in some cases, the 1540s, only to be brought to an end by the confiscations that followed the Pilgrimage of Grace and later satellite risings.[4]

Once made, these acquisitions were not maintained for military purposes. They were converted into residences and stopping-off points for royal perambulations. Often they were allowed to decay; a few were pulled down. So, in 1561, in a list prepared for Queen Elizabeth by a commissioner of inspection, remaining castles were described as "superfluous buildings." The Exchequer refused requests for repair until, in 1609, over sixty were "ruined and decadent." Their use by rebels in the 1640s—when siege warfare and the crossbow found exponents in the allegedly "modern revolution" of the Saints—finally led to a policy of deliberate destruction.[5]

Thus both the domestication of retainers and the confiscation of castles were policies and accidents in a larger struggle to harness aristocratic power, reduce that of franchise-holders (lay and clerical), and bring outlying regions under control.

By 1485, the aristocracy was curbed not so much by decimation in war as by the accidents of birth, death, and inheritance. There was no duke of York; that title and the earldom of March were united in the crown that Derby gave to Henry VII at Bosworth. The earl of Warwick had no heirs; the Mowbray dukes of Norfolk were extinct and their Howard cousins defeated; Richard III had executed the Stafford duke of Buckingham. And the Tudor claimant was the residual legatee of several Lancastrian titles and more lands. Despite these noble disasters, a close inspection of attainders and forfeitures between 1453

---

[4] The Westmorland Nevilles lost their castles in the 1569 rebellion; the Palatine of Durham forts came to the crown by various exchanges and forfeitures c. 1536–59.

[5] On this question, see H. M. Colvin, "Castles and Government in Tudor England," EHR (1968), LXXXIII, pp. 225–34.

and 1509 forces us to dispel yet another myth: the notion that the Tudor peace resulted from aristocratic self-destruction in wars or the bloody-minded vengeance of the Yorkists or Tudor Henrys.

Attainder was a legal process used frequently against rebels, supposedly with vital political and financial consequences.[6] Historians have conjectured or stated that the nobility came close to extinction as a result of attainders and that the crown was vastly enriched by the consequent forfeitures. Yet of the 397 known attainders c. 1453–1509, 256 were reversed (64 percent). Among peers, the rate of reversal was 84 percent; for knights and squires the figures are 79 percent and 76 percent, respectively. Reversals were made ex gratia by letters patent or by acts of Parliament. The latter restored lands as well as legal life, while patents restored only legal life.

Close analysis of the data shows how clearly Edward IV and Henry VII grasped the realities of political life and avoided permanently alienating their aristocracies. Sir Henry Bellingham had treason in his blood, but he secured four successive reversals of attainders. Henry VII reversed twenty of twenty-eight attainders against prominent "Yorkists." The ascending curve of numbers of attainders in his reign stands in contrast to the descent of the curve for Edward IV. But the difference lies in the repeated anti-Henry plots c. 1489–1503, rather than in Tudor caprice. What was striking about Henry VII's practice was the harsh terms arranged for most of the 140 men who were attainted in his time. There is evidence that both Tudor Henrys compounded beforehand the prices to be obtained for reversals, using them to pay official salaries, reward courtiers, and put the fear of royal power into potential rebels. All but one of their reversals called for restorations beneficial to the crown. Restoration often took the form of a forced sale of manors to a royal official. The most famous instance of this involved John Lord Zouche, numerous Tudor courtiers, and at least one bishop. The Howard attainder was pointedly used as a technique of social control. Reversal was by slow stages, and only after the earl of Surrey won a great victory in 1513 over the Scots at Flodden was the Howard title to the Norfolk dukedom revived. Nineteen years of service and the loss of certain manors were required before the Tudors found the Howards worthy of complete freedom!

The treatment of nobles as a class resembled that given Zouche and the Howards. Reversals were obtainable on terms and under the conditions of careful political scrutiny extending to deeds rather than ideas. The further

[6] Attainder was a common-law penalty. For treason it decreed a savage individual death and the legal death of the family through the doctrine of "corruption of blood," or perpetual forfeiture. From 1398 on, it embraced all lands of the attainted, not merely those held in feudal tenure. In the 1400s it was often imposed by acts of Parliament, either after common-law judgment in king's bench or before special commissioners. Henry VII used the commission process regularly.

removed men were from noble status the less likely they were to gain reversals and the more difficult it was for them to pry loose lost lands from the grasp of powerful courtiers. Again, the evidence runs counter to any notion of a monarchy tied to the middle classes or in any way significantly "new" in its modes of government.[7] As for the alleged decimation of aristocrats by attainder, these figures bear stressing. Only nine of twenty-two men of front rank failed to reverse attainders between 1461 and 1509. Five of these were peers, but of that number three titles had lapsed because of biological failure to provide heirs. Under both York and Tudor, the constant resort to attainder was part of a royal policy of mortgaging noble futures in order to build support for the crown. However, vengeance was mitigated by political necessity. Contemporary opinion among the landed classes as a whole would scarcely tolerate huge abridgments of rights of property. What was wanted was not the ruin of the aristocracy or the clergy but their conversion to the will of the monarchy in restoring law and order and reconstituting English society. In the early Tudor period especially, this policy resolved the fifteenth-century aristocratic crisis by tying aristocratic interests to those of the crown. Not the class, but their territorial independence and old bases of power against the monarchy were being destroyed.

The revival of effective monarchy in cooperation with the aristocracy may also be illustrated by the history of the law that regulated common royal and aristocratic interests in land. The story touches on both royal power and royal income and may usefully link the crown's financial recovery to the fate of the aristocracy.

The enlargement of royal power depended in large measure on what contemporaries called the royal prerogative. *Prerogativa regis* is a term difficult to

---

[7] *Attainders and Reversals, 1453–1509* (Lander, *op. cit.*, p. 149).

Attainders,	by ranks	Reversals	Unreversed	% of Reversals
Dukes	4 ⎫	3 ⎫	1 ⎫	75 ⎫
Marquesses	1 ⎪	1 ⎪	0 ⎪	100 ⎪
Earls	12 ⎬ 34	10 ⎬ 29	2 ⎬ 5	83 ⎬ 84
Viscounts	2 ⎪	1 ⎪	1 ⎪	50 ⎪
Barons	15 ⎭	14 ⎭	1 ⎭	93 ⎭
Knights	84	67	17	77
Squires	170	115	55	67
Yeomen	65	32	33	47
Clerics	18	6	12	36
Merchants	17	5	12	29
Others	9	2	7	22
	—	—	—	—
Totals	397	256	141	64

define precisely. Yet the concept clearly embraced the powers and attributes of kingship grounded in common law, statutes, and customary usage, without being clearly limited by them. As we shall see, Henry VII was zealous in expanding his prerogatives through practical applications. This expansion was not always popular, especially among aristocrats and lawyers. Nathaniel Bacon put the matter this way:

Then casting his eye upon the government, and finding it of mixt temper, wherein if royalty prevails not, popularity will; like a good soldier, whilst his strength is full . . . he taught the people to dance more often and better to the tune of prerogative and allegiance, than all his predecessors had done. . . .[8]

Theoretically, what Bacon distrusted was the lack of definition inherent in royal sovereign rights and those of the king as feudal suzerain. Edward IV had made use of special commissioners to survey his rights where crimes against the crown were concerned, especially arson, extortion by officials, rape, the concealment of crown lands, treasure-trove, wards, and the destruction of forests or illegal sales of woods. His ministers quickly focused their attention on the feudal rights of wardship, marriage, and escheats in lands of the crown held in military tenure. Henry VII sharpened this practice and by 1508 had organized an office to survey the royal prerogative. Obtaining accurate information about his rights in lands was both difficult and unpopular, however. Great landowners did not like inquisitions *post mortem* made by feodaries and escheators, which sought to discover the king's prerogative to act as guardian over the minor heirs of deceased aristocrats. Such wardship included the right to take the profits of the heirs' estates and the right to manage their marriages until they reached the legal age at which they could take into their own custody their lands and destinies. The establishment of the survey office in 1508 proved an abortive act. In 1513 it lapsed. But in 1540 the Court of Wards was established by statute and it incorporated features of the prerogative survey and the Office of Wards. This court firmly asserted the ancient rights of the crown, especially in wardship; and wardship had vast social and economic implications in late medieval society. No longer vital in guaranteeing to the king successive generations of military service in return for land, or in educating minors to their tasks in the absence of their fathers, this feudal arrangement took on another significance. It became an irregular but considerable source of crown revenue. By the thirteenth century "fiscal feudalism" was well established, as we know from the regular sale of wardships under King John. Wardship and marriage rights had become a land tax on men holding an anachronistic tenure.

---

[8] *The Laws and Government of England*, II, p. 114 (4th ed., 1739).

The crown's incentive to take fixed "reliefs" by directly tapping the lands of its tenants grew with the fall in the value of money and the erosion of royal assets. The crown was not the only beneficiary of this process, of course; its tenants exacted from their tenants the same incidents of feudal tenure. But the crown was the greatest beneficiary as lord of all the greatest landed men. The statute of *Quia emptores* (1290) had made all purchasers of military tenures tenants of the king, the superior lord, and not of the seller. Moreover, the right of prerogative wardship gave the crown a primary claim, as a royal tenant-in-chief, over all the lands of a man who held only a small parcel. By 1500, the chances of a lord's getting a wardship had declined, while royal claims constantly expanded.

Not surprisingly, aristocrats who suffered the tax sought the means to evade it. That it was onerous was clear from the fact that Edward IV, Henry VII, and Henry VIII exempted from it men who died in the crown's wars. Here again, loyalty had its reward, and conflicting interests were compromised in a policy that sought to subordinate the aristocracy rather than to eliminate it. A similar compromise had been made in the fourteenth century, when the crown gave licenses to sell land held *in capite* exempt from the provisions of *Quia emptores*.

An even more fundamental adjustment of competitive interests took the form of evasions of the statutes and prerogatives through the doctrine of uses. The use was the simple but ingenious legal device of "land by will." One landholder conveyed to another the use of a third's lands that were normally subject to feudal incidents. The bargain or conveyance was accompanied by a will requesting the new owner to yield the "use" of the lands to a specified heir after the seller's death. Thus, if A wished his son, B, to have his inheritance free of the feudal taxes on it, he granted it to C, a group of people who were the feoffees. The grant established a corporation, which could not die as A had to. When A did die and the king's agents made their inquisition, they were told that the king had no rights. A did not have the land. C was alive and was using the land as a trustee for B, the rightful heir. The feudal dues of the overlord were thus evaded; A had freely alienated land in the face of the law and without license from the crown.[9]

The motives for following this procedure were certainly more complex than tax evasion. One could in this way meet family obligations, pay debts or evade them, or preserve social and political independence in the local centers of power. Hence, the crown, which was the greatest winner in the old law, stood to be the greatest loser if uses were allowed to go unchallenged. The maker of the

[9] On all technical points and legal history, see J. Hurstfield, "The Revival of Feudalism in Early Tudor England," *History* (1952), XXXVII, pp. 131–45; and J. M. W. Bean, *The Decline of English Feudalism, 1215–1540* (Manchester: Manchester University Press, 1968), *passim*.

use also faced one very great risk. His feoffees might prove to be evil men who defeated his will by not performing its crucial clause—using the land as trustees for the rightful heir. Thus the crown and the aristocracy had vested interests in what happened to the use.

By Edward III's reign, the use had become an accepted part of the practice of landownership. When Edward was near death in 1377, he placed his own lands in the custody of feoffees to use. Since the courts recognized the feoffees as the real owners under common law, there was little chance for the crown to retaliate. Licenses to enfeoff lands "in use" multiplied, even as Edward IV, Henry VII, and Henry VIII sought to check the practice and enhance their revenues and control over the aristocracy. Edward IV allowed uses, even where they were plainly collusive and aimed wholly at evading crown rights. On the other side, the intended beneficiaries found that the common law would protect their interests only when the trustee provisions were contemporary with grant or conveyance itself. They resorted to the Council and the equity side of the Chancery court for relief from frauds. Gradually they gained this protection, and it is especially worth pondering, when we consider the rule of law in England's history, that the very courts closest to the crown helped to defeat its interests.[1] The casual revenues of the crown steadily eroded after 1350.

It is against the preceding backdrop that we must understand Henry VII's counterattack and the final settlement made by Henry VIII. Elaborating on an experiment first tried under Edward IV in 1483, Henry VII extended from Duchy of Lancaster lands to all crown estates the practice of seeking escheats on lands where he presumably faced the defeat of other feudal rights. Lacking legal and administrative tools for otherwise preventing certain erosions of rights, he extended the royal prerogative.[2] Personal intervention by the monarch alone promised to fulfill his aim. Edward IV had shown this in a negative way; while he struggled for control of the kingdom, twelve tenants-in-chief escaped wardship entirely. Great earls—Arundel and Northumberland—defied him in like manner with impunity. Feudal tenures were on the verge of oblivion if the occupancy of land implied no real ties between men and their lord. Moreover, the aristocratic campaign of evasion was itself a prime factor contributing to the transformation of the social position and character of the class. How significant this transformation was to the crown we

---

[1] The lords wanted it both ways, however. This we can see from the pressure they used to ensure that uses did not apply to lands held by bondsmen or other peasants in nonfree tenures. A statute of 1504 gathered the case law, providing that no use made by a peasant could defeat the manorial lord's right to enter such lands and take his dues as if the original tenant were still in possession.

[2] That is, he questioned the existence of the heirs in law. Lands in feudal tenure escheated when the tenant lacked heirs.

can grasp from one example. Henry Percy, the fifth earl of Northumberland, was in wardship. But £1,575 of the annual value of his lands was enfeoffed to use, thus representing a loss to the crown of £14,200 over the period 1489–98.

No king or government between about 1399 and 1470 had been secure enough politically to reverse such leakage. Both Edward IV and Henry VII showed a clear determination to do so, but York was tentative in his approach, and the first Tudor so plagued by rebellion that he was forced into a policy of concessions. This explains Henry Tudor's constant resort to heavy fines for technical offenses and the noxious use of escheats. The abolition of uses was not really feasible before the 1530s, when Henry VIII, under Thomas Cromwell's guidance, launched a full-scale attack on them. In a move that profoundly shocked the landholding classes, Cromwell managed an action in which the courts dramatically reversed the case law of 150 years, proclaiming a use to be of no effect in law. This action was quickly followed by the Statute of Uses of 1536, bringing victory to efforts of 1529 and 1532, which had failed, and sweeping away the prerogative practices of hated crown agents as well as royal concessions. Naturally the statute, which reestablished the crown's full feudal claims and destroyed the tenants' powers of bequesting land, was resisted by the propertied classes and the lawyers, since the connivances of lawyers and the tax evasions facilitated by them profited all but the crown. Yet even the statute made concessions. Uses were recognized at common law, thus allowing the lawyer's business and conveyancing while disallowing the consequences, especially the evasion of wardship.

What allowed the victory? Probably the destruction of ecclesiastical franchises and Roman power, which so enhanced the strength of the crown, as well as the intimidating impact of the case of Lord Dacre. Also, the destruction of the great northern lords and the Percy surrender of estates to the crown in 1537 had been foreshadowed by other developments between 1500 and 1536, as we shall soon see.[3] The aristocracy had been domesticated.

Royal Finances Revived

If this account illuminates the history of the conversion of the nobility into a dependent aristocracy, it is also vital in explaining the revival of royal finances. Long before the Cromwellian reforms of the 1530s brought the wealth of the church into Henry VIII's hands and created new agencies to administer it, York and Tudor had begun the resolution of the monarchy's financial woes. They created a new revenue administration; vastly increased land revenues, feudal dues, customs, and the profits of justice; expanded the

[3] This victory was undone in 1540, when Cromwell's fall brought in its wake a retreat, for which see Chapter Five.

range of direct taxation; and in other ways brought solvency to a bankrupt regime.

This success in finance is vital to an understanding of how the scope of government was extended over large areas. For the money problem then and now is central to government. Finance tells us more than what administrative measures were in effect. As we have noted in our consideration of the aristocracy, finance provides clues as to the character of the central government itself. The absence of an adequate financial base in the Lancastrian monarchy goes far to explain its failures, especially its inability to realize the reforms that from time to time activated Henry VI's government. No discussion of how control at a distance was made effective after 1461 can be secure unless it makes sense of the means and the uses to which those means were put. Even rich governments could establish bad priorities and fail to govern well and effectively. But poor ones resorted to prayer, apologetics, and deceptions. And in a time of price inflation, which radically increased the cost of war, debts accrued and even sound revenue systems faltered. Hence the achievements we associate with the "Tudor peace" must be set in the perspective of the revolution in the crown's economy. Money was the nerve and sinew of government, of the ability to control magnates and bring to peasants the benefits of law and order.

Had reforms and confiscations not enlarged the monarchy's pocket, it is unlikely that the Tudor dynasty would be remembered favorably today. Consider the increases in the scale of its expenses shown in these comparisons. Henry VII spent £1,200 a year on his guard, £2,500 to watch the northern Marches, £10,000 to garrison Calais, and a mere £2,461 on the Navy and Ireland in 1500. His French wars (1491–1500) cost £107,600. The same item cost Henry VIII £2,134,000 between 1541 and 1547 (including the costs of the Scottish campaigns). In three years (1547–50), Edward VI spent £1,386,000 for wars. Elizabeth I's campaigns in Ireland, the Netherlands, and France cost over £4,000,000, c. 1591–1600. Charles I spent £570,000 on the single Scottish war of 1640. Peacetime costs had no holding power. In 1600, Elizabeth's government spent £4,000 for palace guards, another £4,500 for pensioners, £10,000 for ordnance, £5,000 to garrison Berwick, an additional £5,000 on other border stations, £40,000 in naval maintenance, and over £95,000 for normal provisions for Ireland and contingents in the Netherlands. The royal household was a grasshopper that literally ate its way through money. Annuities to courtiers and officials rose from £1,534 a year in 1506 to £102,000 by 1638. The annual costs for the royal household were £13,000 in 1505, £25,000 in 1538, £50,000 by 1545, and over £70,000 in James I's time.

These costs were already rocketing upward in Edward IV's time. Yet there was a demand that he "live on his own"—that is, out of ordinary crown revenues and not on taxes—as we know from the extraordinary promise he made in 1467:

> John Say, and ye Sirs, comyn to this my Courte of Parlement. . . . The cause why I have called . . . thys my present Parlement is, that I purpose to lyve upon myn owne, and not to charge my Subgettes but in grete and urgent causes, concernyng more the wele of theym self, and also the defence of theym and thys my Realme, rather than myn owne pleasir. . . .[4]

Edward's pledge to finance ordinary government out of his endowed lands must in fact be put in the context of his traditional efforts to increase revenues and the major innovations he made in managing the royal estates.

Among his traditional efforts we may put these clear measures, all of them in use by 1464: levies on patent holders, acts of resumption, and special commissions to survey lands and improve their administration. Some of his innovations date from early in his reign: the institution of a "council" of professional administrators in charge of Duchy of Cornwall lands (1461) and the removal of farms and ancient fee-farms from Exchequer control (1462). The latter measure included the setting-up of eight "receivers and approvers" of revenues on a regional basis. These men were drawn from men with experience in financial administration and were soon paying in £2,000 annually to the treasurer of the royal household, where the money was immediately available to the king.

Edward's way of by-passing the Exchequer was in fact an ancient technique used by kings who needed ready cash and could ill afford the slow and cumbersome routine of the bureaucratized central treasury. From 1461 onward, lands coming into Edward's hands for the first time were kept out of Exchequer control. This tended to create a new system of royal estate management, the actual purpose of which was to supply the king with ready cash.

The model for the practice lay in contemporary, large-scale techniques for the management of private estates, by which a combination of surveyors, receivers, and auditors maintained a fluid money supply under the headship of a receiver-general. The receiver-general collected revenues, disbursed money for bills, and kept a working balance that reflected actual cash flow rather than traditional obligations, arrears, or elaborate fiscal fictions. The best example was that of the Duchy of Lancaster, which from 1399 had been part of the crown's holdings. But the system had not been extended to other crown estates before 1461. In that year Edward began to extend it to his own earldom of March, to the Buckingham wardship, and to land in ten counties. Soon forfeitures, as well as new wardships, were added to the revenues thus administered. By the 1470s, exclusion from Exchequer control was normal in new

---

[4] *Rotuli parliamentorum*, V, p. 572.

holdings, and in 1478 the system was dramatically enlarged by the lands of the king's brother Clarence, who suffered an attainder. Over £3,500 passed through the household treasury from such sources in that year.

The consequences of this systematic feeding of the king's own "chamber system" were far-reaching. The exchequer of receipt was no longer the main treasury for ready cash. The exchequer of audit lost its power over certain revenues. The personal manipulation of income by the king's most trusted men tended to promote the use of the signet as well as other secret seals in financial matters, where the great "departmental" seals had before been the only normal warrants. Thus the revival of the chamber treasury had an effect on administration in general. Long waits on Exchequer assignments, tallies, and receipts were no part of chamber routine. And by 1471 the Exchequer records reflected this fact in the discontinuation of the old issue-rolls, which did not reappear until 1556, when the long experiment in more effective royal finance yielded to the reestablishment of bureaucratic supremacy in 1566. The receipt and issue of the king's money were simply facets of the operation of a staff amenable to his control, whenever he had need of them.[5] By 1478, Exchequer clerks made note of a whole series of "foreign auditors," men who declared accounts there but whose income went elsewhere.

So successful was the chamber system that Richard III could tap £25,000 a year from it in 1483, after meeting charges for collection of over £10,000. Thus Edward IV's promise of 1467 was not a mere shopworn political promise but a gloss on the increasing effectiveness of financial management under York.

This fact bears emphasizing, if for no other reason than that the chamber system is often hailed as a Tudor achievement. When Henry VII won at Bosworth, he was in no position to continue Edward's effective administration or that of Richard III. In a personal monarchy, Bosworth changed the personnel at the center. Henry Tudor knew little about the English administration. His young life had been spent chiefly in custody or exile. The evidence from 1485 suggests how much of a setback government suffered, since Yorkist receivers who survived the revolution began paying into the Exchequer again. The "chamber" had vanished with York! It was not until 1491, after six hard and lean years of experiment, that Henry VII, using converted Yorkists and some agents trained by them in York's practices, began to reconsolidate royal finances in his own chamber.[6] Henry's earlier preoccupation with rebels witnessed the collapse of York's achievement. Only his emergence as a strong king

[5] The Exchequer or other treasuries (the hanaper of Chancery) still paid the civil service; but in 1478 the chamber had to transfer money to the Exchequer to enable it to do so!

[6] For these developments, see B. P. Wolfe, "The Management of English Royal Estates under the Yorkist Kings," *EHR* (1956), LXXI, pp. 1–27 and "Henry VII's Land Revenues and Chamber Finance," *EHR* (1964), LXXIX, pp. 225–54. Despite Wolfe's criticisms, W. C. Richardson's

enabled him to revive the effectiveness of chamber government. Even as late as 1495, his chamber handled less revenue than York's had in 1480.

After that year, however, Henry achieved what neither Edward nor Richard had. Almost the whole royal revenue, exclusive of taxes, passed under chamber control. The rate of change was tremendous—from £17,000 in 1489 to £27,000 in 1495 to £105,000 in 1505. Richard III's annual land revenues had been about £29,999; his customs were about £33,000. By 1509, these figures were £42,000 and £40,000, respectively, increases of 45 percent and 20 percent. The tightening of administration thus helped increase revenues significantly. So did Henry VII's vigorous pursuit of feudal dues: annual wardship income rose from £350 in 1489 to £1,500 in 1494. In 1507, wardships yielded £6,000 to the crown! In that year the Exchequer handled less than £13,000, out of a total crown revenue of about £113,000.

The achievement in raising customs, casual income, and land revenues was no more impressive, however, than the early Tudor revision of direct taxation. Since 1334, the basic parliamentary tax had been the 1/15 and 1/10, a levy on movable property. It yielded about £30,000 under Edward III. Henry VII's use of it on several occasions in the 1490s brought in about £29,000 for each fifteenth and tenth granted.[7] Clearly this tax had become a fixed compromise between the crown and the community and bore no relationship to a real assessment of changing taxable wealth. Besides this fourteenth-century tax, the crown from time to time experimented with poll taxes (1377–80), taxes on parishes (1371 and 1428), and various income taxes (1404, 1411, 1431, 1435, 1450, 1472, and 1489). The income tax was extremely unpopular and difficult to assess; evasion was pronounced (it yielded only £571 in 1489), and the level of exemption was often set by the crown's political strength—as high as 500 marks in 1411!

It was not until early in Henry VIII's reign that the rising genius of Thomas Wolsey fashioned a new basis for direct taxation. In a remarkable series of statutes enacted between 1512 and 1515, prompted by the costs of the campaigns in France and Scotland, Wolsey created the Tudor subsidy.[8] This was a complex tax that combined features of the fourteenth-century taxes on

Tudor Chamber Administration, 1485–1547 (Baton Rouge: Louisiana State University Press, 1952), is still the best account of the system. Richardson, Elton, and Dietz erred in crediting the creation of the system to the first Tudor: see *Tudor Revolution in Government* (Cambridge: Cambridge University Press, 1953) and *English Public Finance, 1485–1558* (London: Frank Cass, 1964).

[7] Parliament could, of course, grant multiple 1/15s and 1/10s in various combinations. The traditional parliamentary tax was the fifteenth and the tenth, which was a levy on movable property respectively rural and urban.

[8] See the unpublished Cambridge Ph.D. thesis of Roger Schofield, "Parliamentary Lay Taxation, 1485–1547" (1963).

movables and the Lancastrian income tax. It fell on every person in the country initially, and three categories of wealth were assessed: all annual income from lands, annuities, fees and corodies, and net of expenses; the capital value of movable goods, including debts owed to the taxpayer but allowing deduction for those the taxpayer owed to others; and wages and the profits from wages. Each category was separately assessed, although in the end men paid only the tax on the class of wealth that promised most to the crown.

The subsidy was a tax of enormous sophistication, even for 1513. Changes introduced by 1525 determined its character until well into the Stuart period, including the progressive nature of its rates and the policy of exemptions for the truly poor. The rate itself varied from a low of one shilling per pound to a high of six shillings per pound and reflected the crown's skill in Parliament and also the popular acceptance (or resentment) of policy. The subsidy of 1514 raised about £100,000, and between 1540 and 1547 Henry VIII raised over £650,000 in direct, parliamentary taxes. There is perhaps no better comment on the consolidation of crown power and prestige achieved by the Tudor Henrys than this staggering burden successfully imposed!

Coupled with loans and so-called benevolences ("love-money" gifts),[9] taxation showed the success with which the crown pursued its interests and expressed them in a way acceptable to the community of the realm. Henry VI had owed the Staplers £37,000 in 1460. That debt had been liquidated by 1485. The crown's sources of regular income were yielding about £140,000 a year in 1520, up from about £52,000 in 1460. The subsidy enabled Henry VIII's government to spend money on a scale altogether without precedent in English history, as government restlessly expanded its scope in an age of great inflation and revolutions in church and polity. Not until the wars of the 1540s were crown finances again exposed as inadequate. And then, even the wealth of the monasteries could not support them.

Great as this achievement was, however, it was by no means welcomed by all classes in society. Henry VII particularly suffered a reputation for avarice and cunning, which historians have stressed perhaps too much. But this reputation and the story of his rapacity and remorse—his exactions from his subjects and his later contrition over having employed men as odious as Empson and Dudley to get money from them—allow us a final gloss on the importance of royal finance and lead us conveniently into the subject of the rescue of law and order.

---

[9] That of 1497 cost Englishmen £120,000! Those imposed by Wolsey in the 1520s were fiercely resisted, to the point of rebellion in the Southeast.

Power and the Reconciliation of Interests

Lord Bacon wrote of Henry VII that "he was a little poor in admiring riches."[1] The king's policy regarding attainders and his scrupulous use of the chamber were parts of a policy of establishing legitimate rights, even if grasping or pressed very hard. From early in his reign he used special commissions to push claims that reached into rich men's pockets. By 1495, at a time when Henry was groping his way toward a "prerogative office," the prerogative had become important enough to attract a "reading" by Robert Constable that fell heavily upon the ears of a great number of men whose holdings had been drawn into the crown's scrutiny.[2] The scrutiny itself was no abuse of the law, but it was being put on a new footing by new methods of inquiry, accounting, and administration of the thirteenth-century notion of prerogative. An anachronistic and unpopular legal doctrine had come to serve the expanding financial requirements of a nascent "state" still doing its business in medieval ways. The infusion of vigor into feeble feudal institutions made a mark on the law. It also helped undermine certain aspects of aristocratic ascendancy. And insofar as it helped make the early Tudors less dependent on taxation, it postponed the great issue of who controlled the legislative process and on what grounds.

The more immediate reaction was not to these weighty implications, however. Hard-pressed landowners made traverses against the king's cases, especially after 1503, when the government was triumphant over its rebels and fully equipped with machinery to enforce what seemed an oppressive policy. Empson and Dudley were the legal agents of Henry VII's methods who gained most in evil reputation; they ran special commissions and captained the council "learned in the law." As success followed success, the scope of operations expanded: to hunting laws, usury, and lending; to the export of coin; to the making of silk cloth or its import; and to countless other items of the penal law. Doubtless these vigorous signs of enforcement of often dormant laws were resented. But it is an odd position for historians to take, as some have done, to find it outside a councillor's or lawyer's office to vigorously champion the law! It is true that Henry VII's procedures often involved techniques outside the common law. But common law was not England's only law, and using old laws was not the same as inventing new ones with which to tyrannize one's subjects. In fact, descriptions of Henry's methods, often taken from City

---

[1] *Henry VII* (Cambridge: Cambridge University Press, 1885), p. 213.

[2] That is, a series of explicative law lectures given at Lincoln's Inn; Thomas Frowyk also chose that subject at Inner Temple in 1495, when he too was called to the rank of sergeant-at-law. See S. E. Thorne, ed., *Prerogativa Regis* (New Haven, Conn.: Yale University Press, 1949), pp. i–li.

chronicles or Polydore Vergil, reveal more about oligarchic and aristocratic attitudes toward the invasion of privileges than about either what government was really doing or in what manner. These attitudes were fed by Henry VIII, who early in his reign practiced "scapegoatism" and the politics of reversal, sacrificing his father's ministers to appease popular disapproval of their policies. Yet by 1515 Wolsey was using the Council, Chancery, and Star Chamber in much the same way, and his Domesday of Enclosers was neither less legal nor more unpopular than other inquiries touching landed wealth had been.[3]

These facts necessarily raise questions. How could the interests of the monarchy and of the propertied, politically articulate classes be reconciled? How could the landed classes and the prosperous mercantile interests support a vigorous government in its campaign to bring order to the country, when, as the price of effective government, that campaign touched them in their pockets?

Certainly we can point to immediate benefits of effective government: England's initial overseas explorations in the New World, commercial advantages apparent in certain treaties that show the responsiveness of the government to the trading and shipping lobbies in the Commons, and the government's willingness to draw a veil across the past on the matter of enclosures. Or we can point to the fact that by 1524 fourteen English counties had aggregate incomes in which towns constituted 30 percent of the total; in 1334 this had been true in only two counties. The church in England found great comfort under the York and early Tudor kings, at least until the 1530s. The monarchy upheld its privileges, its tithes and dues, and enabled twelve English bishops to rank among the forty wealthiest prelates in Christendom. Henry VII especially used his patronage to nominate a distinguished episcopate, and, contrary to reports that still flourish, he conferred temporalities on twenty of his twenty-seven appointees before their institution.[4]

Moreover, diplomacy after 1461 brought profit and glory to the monarchy and to Englishmen without the resort to war in Europe that had so distressed the country under Lancaster. France's victory in 1453 had made her the greatest power in Europe. By 1477 Burgundy had been brought into France, and in 1492 Brittany followed. Thus England lost her traditional anti-French allies and the buffers that guarded England's coast. Tudor diplomacy before 1540 recognized this fact. Henry VII clearly abandoned hopes of a continental empire. He and his son began the insular sea-power policy on which another

---

[3] The whole controversy about intentions and methods may be followed in G. R. Elton, "Henry VII: Rapacity and Last Years Reconsidered," *HJ* (1959), II, pp. 104–29; and Elton, "Henry VII: A Restatement," *HJ* (1961), IV, pp. 1–29.

[4] On all these points of prosperity among laymen and clerics, see R. L. Storey, *The Reign of Henry VII* (London: Barrie and Rockliff, 1968).

empire was to stand. The Habsburg expansion into Spain and the Netherlands was not complete until 1519, but it had begun much earlier, in what Garrett Mattingly once called "the filling up of the interstices" in Europe.[5] These developments promoted the policy of peace in Britain and rapprochement with the Scots, despite repeated breakdowns (in 1512 and 1542–8) of amity. And it encouraged Englishmen to see in the Italian struggles of Valois and Habsburg (1494–1559) an opportunity. English support of the French might close off from Spain the sea route to the Netherlands while English alliances with Spain threatened France with a land-sea encirclement. The strong monarchy proved invaluable in establishing alliances through marriage in both countries, and it also provided the momentum behind a generation of treaties that consolidated old markets and opened new ones to English merchants and shippers.[6]

Something very much like a trade policy slowly emerged from the welter of negotiations not in themselves oriented to questions of economics. Ship bounties and navigation acts were passed. Hansa privileges were curbed and new fisheries were opened by treaties with Denmark (1491–9). Commercial depressions in 1494 and 1495 reflected a recognition that trade wars defeated the prospects of good Anglo-Dutch relations; and between 1496 and 1504 the *Intercursus Magnus* and other trade treaties had consolidated the English position in the North Sea. To the south and east, the treaty of Medina del Campo brought the prestige of a Spanish alliance and the lucre of Iberian trade; a 1490 negotiation established the Florentine satellite city of Pisa as a staple for English wool, and a 1491 statute made Venetian trade in Greek wines expensive enough to spur a direct commerce with the Greek Islands that by 1510 was worth £10,000 per year.

Law, Order, Justice

The prosperity of towns, the indulgence shown enclosers, the privileges of merchants, and the wealth of the church were not the best measures of what York and Tudor brought to Englishmen through their kingcraft; nor was England's growing stature in European affairs. Their supreme achievement was the resurrection of law and order and the restoration of confidence in the justice of the king's courts. These ends were accomplished in diverse ways, but nothing was more important in training men to order than the king's Council. Yet the conciliar courts were aided in their struggles by

---

[5] *Renaissance Diplomacy* (London: Jonathan Cape, 1955), p. 77.
[6] On the general movements of diplomacy and dynastic and foreign policy, see R. B. Wernham, *Before the Armada: The Growth of English Foreign Policy, 1485–1558* (London: Jonathan Cape, 1966).

common informers, by Parliaments that made new statutes touching public order and refurbished old ones, and by a measure of success in using the J.P.s as agents whose loyalty withstood most tests.

Freedom and the concrete liberties of which it consists are everywhere dependent on authority for vindication. More often than not in civilized societies, this authority takes on the forms of law. In England under York, and still more under the Tudors, Parliament made laws to bridge the gap between government as something external and imposed on man and something inherent in the nature of social order itself. Even a casual examination of most statutes passed between about 1450 and 1540 will show that they set forth what no one doubted was already law. Even when the most startling innovations were at hand—as in Henry VIII's Reformation legislation—customary right was adduced to warrant what was enacted. When lesser matters were involved, this was always the casè. Thus were procedures made stronger, penalties augmented, police work directed, and economic action regulated by old social principles in the name of the community. This reference to old ways was especially fitting in a country where common law was ancient and organic, where Parliament was more in theory and practice the supreme court than a modern legislature.

People readily accepted legislation aimed at preventing the disruption of order when it was couched in terms that suggested the guarding of liberties. Sometimes acts were especially designed to safeguard royal rights, as was the case with Henry VII's Collusions Act, the Riot and Unlawful Assemblies Act, the Household Offenses Act, the Star Chamber Act of 1487, the various acts regulating indictment procedures and the verdicts of juries, and those against the unlawful retention of armed men.[7] But the majority of subjects kept in mind that their security was also at issue. The law needed new weapons to fight forces that had obstructed justice and dethroned its majesty. Ordinary men had experienced the lack of governance under Lancaster as an evil rather than a relief. They grasped eagerly at whatever promised to make law real and order an achievement rather than an aspiration. They were thus apt to allow expansions in the government's scope and methods, offering resistance only when rules accepted by the government seemed to strangle rights and offend against the order of local communities. This meant that between 1461 and the Reformation Parliament there was little organized resistance in Parliament. The Commons had not yet thought of promoting bills to restrict royal rights or even of a legislative check on the royal prerogative. Henry VII never had to veto a bill, although two generations later Elizabeth often instructed her councillors to suppress noxious legislation.

[7] See the following acts: 3 H. VII, c. 4; 4 H. VII, c. 20; 11 H. VII, cc. 7, 24–6; 12 H. VII, c. 2; 19 H. VII, cc. 13 and 14.

The reason for so little resistance to the crown was doubtless that the bulk of the 120 statutes passed in seven Parliaments (which sat for sixty-nine weeks) embraced interests common to the crown and the community. This was especially true of the laws that settled the title to the crown (1485 and 1495); strengthened the executive (1487, 1495, 1497, and 1504); provided justice for poor men and redress of grievances against officials (1489 and 1495); regulated powerful corporations, whether municipal or guild (1497 and 1504); standard-ized weights and measures or otherwise promoted trade (1489, 1495, and 1504); or sought norms of social discipline in controlling wages and conditions of labor (1495).

Once made, laws required enforcement. Enforcement in turn depended on two different levels or tiers of government: the Council, its courts, and those of the common law; and the work of local officials, especially the justices of the peace. Only artificial emphases can be given to their respective roles. But in looking more closely at law and order in this context the conciliar courts bear special interest. For it is there that we see evidence of why the landed classes ought to be styled "the party of law and order."[8]

The court of Star Chamber has left few orders or decrees from the early Tudor period among its records. Surviving manuscripts seem to indicate that plaintiffs believed justice there would be fairer than in other courts. About 128 cases from c. 1485–1509 survive. They are from widely scattered areas, but there are more from London, the southwest, East Anglia, and the north than elsewhere. None are from the years 1485–9! Looked at by types of complaint, eighty-four cases allege riot. If the figure stood unimpeached, it would be hard to base on it any brief for the restoration of law and order under York and Tudor. But, as S. E. Lehmberg has shown, riot was often alleged in order to get cases before the conciliar court. The real matters at issue were usually determinable at common law, as we know from defendants' demurs, which often sought common-law trials. Land was the basic issue, not maintenance, and the cases mostly involved broken leases, debts, disputed property rights, unlawful arrests, contempts of court process, and official corruption. Twenty-three of the cases involved clergymen and show a decided anticlerical force in society. There is much less material on corrupt juries, livery men, or extortion by aristocratic bullies. Subjects looked to Star Chamber for swift justice, not for protection against overmighty subjects. The evidence here is decisive: of the four cases that did involve maintenance, none was brought by a govern-ment official.

[8] For what follows, see especially: R. L. Storey and K. Pickthorn in their books on Henry VII; Thorne's "Introduction" to Constable; and these articles: S. E. Lehmberg, "Star-Chamber, 1485–1509," *HLQ* (1960–1), XXIV, pp. 189–214; D. C. Somerville, "Henry VII's Council Learned in the Law," *EHR* (1939), LIV, pp. 427–42; and A. F. Pollard, "The Growth of the Court of Requests," *EHR* (1941), LVI, pp. 300–303.

In fact, private-party suits dominated the work of this court. And in these suits the court often played a useful role in litigations involving unequal parties. In this respect it was similar to the nascent Court of Requests, where poor men found aid in litigation against more powerful members of society. Star Chamber, far from being an instrument used by government to repress powerful subjects, was the place where propertied men looked to find fair hearings of their grievances. Together with Requests, and long before its alleged "creation" in 1487, Star Chamber was a committee of the Council hearing cases on the king's authority and too strong to be misused by either plaintiff or defendant with impunity.

The same was true of the council learned in the law, another committee of the king's Council. Its entry books for certain terms between 1500 and 1509 show clearly the resemblance of its function to Star Chamber, Chancery, and Requests. Its proceedings began with English bills rather than the Latin writs of the common-law courts. Orders to appear came under the privy seal, an instrument particularly associated with the Council, and had the same force as a *sub poena* writ. Stiff fines of £100 or more grew out of disobeying orders publicly delivered. Men gave bonds (obligations and recognizances), which were forfeited upon failure to come to court. Proceedings of contempt and attachments of property often followed. Men so summoned did not know the charges against them until they came to make their answer. Then, answers, rejoinders, and replies were allowed, often coupled with denials of jurisdiction and appeals to the common law. Often these were really appeals to the security of the technicalities of the common law or the known friendliness of juries of peers, and it is surprising that historians still see in them appeals from despotism to liberty.

The conciliar courts were taking cases often not determinable elsewhere or ones in which powerful interests interrupted the processes of common law. Yet even in the "council learned," private-party actions over property were the most usual cases. And remissions to other courts were by no means rare in reply to defendants' denials of jurisdiction. The king's councillors were in fact addressing themselves there to the king's business in judicial form. This was especially true in those matters in which detection of crimes was a public concern, and there government initiative can be found.

Cases touching the evasion of regulations of every sort abound in records of the Council and its offshoots: the export of wool; the shearing of worsteds; coinage frauds; lands unlawfully given to the church in mortmain; the sale of wares forbidden by statutes against engrossers and forestallers; false returns by juries; the numerous invasions of royal rights of treasure, fisheries, and forests; and the more serious crimes of perjury and murder.

When economic regulations or penal statutes were broken, the crown often had to rely on common informers to begin enforcement actions. This was because the absence of police forces made it difficult to bring matters before the courts. The danger from common informers was that the law made them the beneficiaries of actions begun and successfully prosecuted; half of the profits went to the crown and half to the informer. This danger was perhaps outweighed by the advantages. Information to the Council allowed it to avoid cumbersome common-law proceedings. These involved citizens directly in law enforcement, brought offenders otherwise immune to the bar of justice, and encouraged public-spiritedness in an age that needed it. Yet serious informers questioned these benefits when balanced with the misuse of the courts by other informers for blackmail, for the pursuit of private quarrels, and for the conversion of matters over community welfare between the crown and its subjects into something less wholesome.

Whatever one's judgment of that question—and in 1534 Thomas Cromwell sought to abolish by statute this "malice of private ends"—the common informer was then necessary for enforcement.[9] The entire system of government suffered from a lack of effective police work. Collusion between officials and informing citizens was not rare. Nor were false verdicts by local juries. And by 1530 both presented a danger to public order more real than that of the overmighty subject. Too many jurors ranked perjury lower on the ladder of crime than the conviction of their friends or neighbors. In a time when respect for law needed saving, the flouting of it was common and injurious. There is perhaps no comment more apt and telling against the idea of a despotic "new monarchy" in the age of York and Tudor than the common informer and the way in which ordinary men could match themselves successfully against the powers of government. That Star Chamber concerned itself with petty perjuries is more a measure of how difficult it was to govern and how fragile respect for law was than of anything else.

And yet Englishmen were being made more lawful as the fifteenth century gave way to the sixteenth. Where an adequate police force was lacking, the J.P.s multiplied in number and in powers. Much of what there was of local law and order was due to their adherence to Council orders interpreting law and policy at the center. Just as the extensive use of the prerogative gave rise to the interpretations of Constable and Frowyck, so the rise of the J.P.s promoted the writing and printing of treatises on the office and duties of the justice of the peace. The manuscript tradition began in 1422, roughly the time at which the rule of federations of feudal potentates endowed with boroughs and manors drew to a close. And in the sixteenth century the stream of treatises ranged from the 1506 *Boke of Justyces of Peas* to William Lambarde's famous

---

[9] See PRO, S.P. 1/28/24–41, for the draft legislation to promote police. The final abolition of the practice came only in 1951!

Eirenarcha (1581), with Fitzherbert's 1538 version bridging the gap.[1] These early works were characteristic of efforts to spread the burdens of the restoration of social order from the crown to the gentry. Between 1506 and 1599, fifty-seven editions or versions were printed: thirty-two of the *Boke* of 1506; twelve of Fitzherbert; four of Crompton's revision of Fitzherbert; and nine of Lambarde. The readings from which they derived span the years in which the Year Books of the medieval courts decayed and the Law Reports had not yet appeared (1480–1520). And they constitute yet another evidence that magnate power of a feudal or quasifeudal sort was yielding rapidly to the class rule of an aristocracy, among whom the gentry came to dominate judicial and administrative functions.

We have already studied some early signs of this domination: the exclusion of peers from the commissions, the barring of manorial seneschals and stewards, and the requirement that J.P.s clear £20 a year.[2] Now we can look at the laws that concentrated in their hands powers to deal with heresies, felonies, and trespasses.

The Yorkist and Tudor kings greatly enlarged the duties of the justices. By 1430 their charge included headings occasioned by many great medieval statutes: Winchester (1285, robberies), Northampton (1328, felonies), Westminster (1361, keeping of the peace), Cambridge (1388, wages), Westminster (1399 and 1401, giving liveries to unauthorized persons), Leicester (1414, detecting Lollards), and Westminster (1414, forging money). They were also responsible for the whole body of the common law, including felonies other than treason. Their "Quarter Sessions" were the chief origin of government at the local level and were central in every effort to replace feudal jurisdictions and communal law with regal power.

This effort was well established before 1461, 1485, or any other date that supposedly marks the end of the Middle Ages. A host of statutes passed between 1389 and 1461 thrust the justices into social and economic regulation of every type, from the profits of victualers to the powers of guilds, the guarding of rivers from pollution, and the watch on the coast against the French.[3] Yet there is clear evidence of a dramatic surge in their usefulness under Edward IV, who, in this respect as in so many others, anticipated Henry VII's fame and works. This surge was signaled in 1461 by the act that ended forever the sheriff's *tourn*—the tour of his county on which he took indictments—which Henry VII reinforced in legislation regarding juries and indictments in 1495. Another

---

[1] Lambarde, however, drew directly on the 1503 Inner Temple readings of Marowe, for which see Bertha Putnam, *Early Treatises on the Practice of the Justices of the Peace in the Fifteenth and Sixteenth Centuries* (Oxford: Clarendon Press, 1924), vol. VII of *Studies in Legal and Social History.*

[2] See *Statutes of the Realm*, 13 R. II, c. 7; 14 R. II, c. 11; and 18 Henry VI, c. 11.

[3] See especially 12 R. II, c. 10; 17 R. II, c. 9; 5 H. IV, c. 3; 15 H. VI, c. 6; and 23 H. VI, cc. 10–11.

indication of the J.P.s' growing significance in transmitting the will of the center was the frequency with which Edward IV reconstituted the commissions, a measure to ensure obedience and maintain the good will of locally powerful men who wanted the dignity and power of the office.

But perhaps the best indicator that points the way upward for the justices and toward sound local order for the countryside is Edward's Act of 1468. In it he abolished all maintenance effected by giving liveries. A fine of £5 per month was imposed for each man so retained. When the crown turned a blind eye to the practice—as it did in the case of the sixty-four contracts Lord Hastings made between 1469 and 1482—the reason showed in the event. Hastings' men were vital to York's recovery of power in 1470. Henry VII continued this policy of discrimination with regard to Northumberland's men in 1486 and the armies raised in 1492. There was a spate of statutes aimed at public recognition of the fact that military services belonged to the crown alone.[4] Enforcement rested with the J.P.s—at least until 1504, when trials of aristocratic clients passed over to the Council and the king's bench.[5]

The year 1495 (11 Henry VII) was in fact the *anno mirabilis* for the J.P.s. At least eleven chapters in the Parliament roll added regulatory, investigative, or punitive powers to those already in their charge and reinforced already existing powers. Complemented by the acts of 1504 (19 Henry VII), these new burdens prompted Lambarde's anxious, retrospective comment:

If Hussey[6] did think it was enough to load all the Justices . . . of those days, with the execution, only of the Statutes of Westminster and Winchester for robberies and felonies . . . Labourers, Vagabonds, Liveries, Maintenance, Embracery, and Sheriffs: then how many Justices (think you) may now suffice (without breaking their backs) to bear so many, not Loads, but Stacks of Statutes, that have since that time been laid upon them?[7]

Royal policy and Lambarde's opinion call to mind John of Gaunt's indictment of those peers "bound in with shame/with inky blots and rotten parchment bonds." It also reminds us that sheriffs as well as magnates were objects of keen scrutiny. The sheriffs had long enjoyed vast powers in county society and government. Throughout the medieval centuries they delivered writs, began prosecutions, concluded legal actions, summoned defendants to the king's courts, made attachments of property, selected jurors in civil and criminal

---

[4] See especially 3 H. VII, c. 4; 4 H. VII, c. 20; 11 H. VII, cc. 7, 24–6; 12 H. VII, c. 2; and 19 H. VII, cc. 13 and 14.

[5] The case of Lord Abergavenny (1506) is justly celebrated. For illegally retaining 471 men, he drew a penalty of £70,650 after his plea of guilty.

[6] Chief-justice, on 1 Henry VII, c. 3, touching the burdens of the justices, in a case before him.

[7] *Eirenarcha* (ed. 1610), Bk. II, c. 6, p. 188; see Chapter Ten for the late Tudor burdens of the J.P.s.

actions, enforced verdicts, supervised police work, made arrests, published proclamations, collected the shire revenues of the crown, and arranged the elections of members of Parliament. The abuse of these powers, which thrived *c.* 1440–60, resulted in a restrictive act of 1461, by which sheriffs lost certain powers. This clipping was made more effective by the supervisory role given the justices who in 1495 were empowered to audit shrieval accounts, examine the sheriffs' conduct, and institute proceedings against malefactors at Quarter Sessions.[8] This did not mean the total eclipse of the sheriffs. What it did mean was a dimming of their luster, an assertion of royal control over them—with the help of other landed men. And, as if to show awareness that new justices might be old sheriffs writ large, 4 H. VII, c. 12, provided for redress of grievance against J.P.s who abused their power, to take place before the full bench of their colleagues or, when that did not suffice, before assize justices, the Lord Chancellor, or the king's Council itself.

All of this illustrates the crown's dedication to the central task it faced in 1461 and in 1509—that of showing a vigorous will to govern and finding the means and techniques with which to do so. The task required little invention, since both means and techniques lay ready to hand in the tradition of finance and government already developed in the great age of kings in the medieval monarchy. The success of York and Henry VII is perhaps shown in the powerful aristocratic reaction of 1509–12, which cast down Empson and Dudley. Northumberland, Abergavenny, and Surrey (Howard) were especially active in calling for the restoration of a magnate Council. The absence of a mature king aided their resurgence. But while Henry VIII grew to know his strength, he found in Cardinal Wolsey a governing genius more than adequate to the challenge of keeping order and more than willing to use the power of Council and church to continue the policy of integrating the kingdom and making it responsive to the king's will.

---

[8] There was a 1455 precedent for this act.

Chapter Four
THE REFORMATION

Until they become conscious they will never rebel,
and until they have rebelled they cannot become conscious.

GEORGE ORWELL
1984

The English Reformation was in many respects the culmination of the crown's drive to subordinate to itself the most privileged communities in the realm. (The church was the greatest franchised power in England, with its own monarch, princes, territories, courts, and laws. Hence the history of the Reformation is in one sense the history of a great revolution that swept away Roman jurisdiction and ecclesiastical liberties) Yet any view of the 1530s limited to constitutional history will frustrate understanding of why the revolution in government even came about. For the church was not only a judge and governor of men, contesting with kings for their loyalties; it was a great landlord and the motivating force in a vast educational system. And the church was also a religious institution to which men looked for the keys to open the gates of heaven.

The history of its reformation is a history of how inertia and tradition were overcome. Men, when they had the opportunity to do so, changed by their conscious acts institutions and religious life that had evolved over a period of centuries. In their actions lay the thrust of their hope—the renewal of a fondly imagined golden age of Christian life—and also the sum of their achievement— changes that transformed politics and government, shifted the control of vast landed estates from clerical to lay hands, swept away the class of regular religious men and women, wrenched old social structures from their moorings, and began the creation of a Protestant society in which new myths of justice and social order took form.

This break from Rome and old religious traditions was of course part of a movement that was European in its extension and global in its significance. Yet its circumstances were peculiarly English. It began with Henry VIII's change of mind and heart about Queen Catherine of Aragon. This fact is important, because the king's grievances determined that reform took place

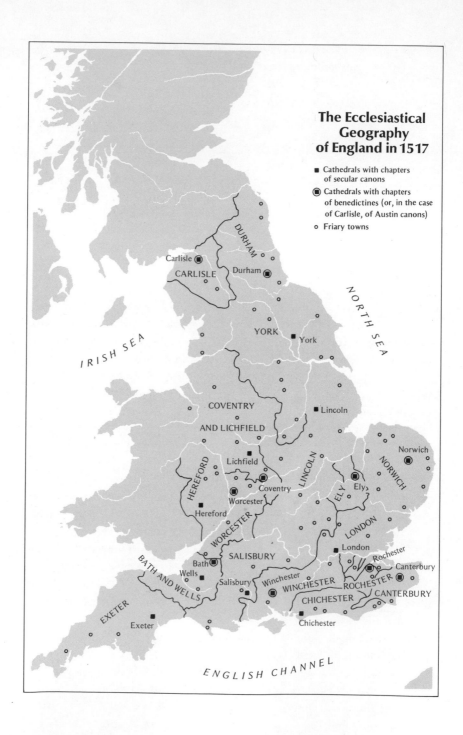

The Ecclesiastical Geography of England in 1517

■ Cathedrals with chapters of secular canons

◉ Cathedrals with chapters of benedictines (or, in the case of Carlisle, of Austin canons)

○ Friary towns

NORTH SEA

IRISH SEA

ENGLISH CHANNEL

Carlisle

CARLISLE

Durham

DURHAM

YORK

York

COVENTRY

AND LICHFIELD

Lincoln

LINCOLN

Lichfield

Coventry

Norwich

NORWICH

HEREFORD

Worcester

Ely

ELY

Hereford

WORCESTER

LONDON

London

Rochester

Canterbury

Bath

Wells

SALISBURY

Salisbury

Winchester

WINCHESTER

ROCHESTER

CANTERBURY

BATH AND WELLS

CHICHESTER

EXETER

Exeter

Chichester

not in communion with Rome but in schism. The rebellious royal conscience, however, merely gave a focus to forces of dissent and criticism whose origins lay deep in the fabric of English society. The social, economic, political, and spiritual grievances of ordinary Englishmen were already dissolving loyalties in the parishes long before the gospel light shined in Anne Boleyn's eyes, before Henry VIII thought to complete the creation of a royal sovereignty that knew no superior in England. Thus Englishmen supported the royal revolutionary for many reasons, some inscrutable, but for all it was *their Reformation*, their crisis, and their choice. Unless we address ourselves directly to the character of that popular crisis, we shall never understand why Henry VIII's revolt led his people where he had not intended to go—toward Protestantism in worship and doctrine.

Our approach lies, therefore, in an attempt to grasp why some men eagerly dedicated their strength to the task of changing their lives with respect to religion. This requires attention to the social conditions in which people met their priests, worldly and cloistered, and to the various plaintiffs who spoke against the church. There were in that chorus men of every shade of religious opinion and some of none at all, men made malignant by greed and others with the courage and forbearance of saints. Many had in common alienation profound enough to promote the view that the church could not heal itself. Some held that only the power of the crown was adequate to the task. In 1529 their force, combined with Henry's wrath, severed England's ties with Rome and set the English church adrift in seas only provisionally charted until the Reformation ministry of Thomas Cromwell marked a course. Then, between 1532 and 1540, his work and that of Thomas Cranmer directed Englishmen toward a reformed commonwealth. The result of that often heroic craftsmanship was the infant Anglican Church, which assumed in the decade of the 1530s the shape it was to have for centuries.[1]

Temporal Dominion: The Church in Society

The church in England was a part of the mystical body of Christ, the communion of the faithful in Christ. It was also a "possessioner" church, rich in lands and wielding a wide secular lordship. Thus the consciousness that bound the faithful to it was shaped not only by doctrine and worship but by ties of a wholly worldly nature. The church had shared in the expansion

---

[1] The best general histories of the Reformation in England are by A. G. Dickens, *The English Reformation* (London: Batsford, 1964); G. Constant, *The Reformation in England, I, The English Schism (1509–1547)*, tr. R. E. Scantlebury (London: Sheed and Ward, 1934); F. M. Powicke, *The Reformation in England* (London: Oxford University Press, 1941); and P. Hughes, *The Reformation in England*, 3 vols. (London: Hollis and Carter, 1951–4).

of agriculture that marked the boom before 1300. This expansion had fostered interdependence between the church and the groups in rural society that collected and husbanded its resources and enforced its laws. Lay aristocrats and professional men owed services and thanks to churchmen from whom they received leases, offices, and gifts. The profits from their work and agriculture itself were basic to the expansion of the parochial system and church administration in response to the pressure of population. The era of prosperity gave a color of mutuality to the interests of lay and clerical elites and helped mitigate what there was of competition. The church was thus fully implicated before 1300 in the defense of the distribution of wealth and power in feudal society.

After the year 1300, there was increasing evidence of conflict and strain among laymen and clergy as the waning of prosperity took hold. And in the aftermath of the Black Death the temptation to pursue purely economic considerations struck the church heavily. Lawyers, merchants, jailers, and gentry-officials were immediately affected by the depression. The terrible toll of death and famine threatened the traditional system of demesne cultivation and the social relations of peasants and clergy as well. After 1348 the church underwent the same involuntary conversion from seigneurial lordship to *rentier* economy that characterized the life of so many landlords.

This conversion was especially painful to abbots and bishops, for they never forgot how futile it was to separate the cure of souls from the payment of bills. Religious authority and discipline were too tightly tied to the land for such forgetfulness. Fixed obligations and social relations based on land tenures were disappearing and being replaced by the more fluid money contracts typical of rural capitalism. The alienation of the demesne and other economic adjustments disrupted what managers had come to think of as their rights rather than their rewards for serving the church.[2]

The Post-Plague Unrest

The entire fabric of the church was thus struck a serious blow by the economic and social dislocations that followed in the wake of plague. This was of grave concern to the monarchy, since the bonds of rural society were secured as much by what the church did as by the direct action of royal officials. Wherever clerics alienated laymen, they also endangered the social bond itself. The characteristic reaction to this threat was the series of repressive statutes that spelled out the policy we earlier called "the seigneurial reaction."

Evidence of the conflict and the challenge to religious authority is plentiful. On Canterbury estates, bailiffs ceased to record entries of homage and alle-

[2] See the bibliography for Chapter One, especially the studies by Hilton and Raftis.

giance about 1350. The gentry who dominated county society after 1400 demanded more equivalent relations with clerical elites. This we know from court records in which laymen insistently sought recognition of their titles of distinction, thereby reflecting both a changing social order and a corresponding shift in initiative. Struggles arose out of customary exercise of clerical jurisdiction over laymen in church courts.[3]

Many such cases grew out of rents and dues in kind or money. Before the Black Death, a whole structure of these had formed, over and above the basic *gabulum*, or acre rent. Some new levies reflected popular thinking in their names; they often were *mala*—the bad rent! Without right, some abbots and bishops enclosed what was common land. Others forcibly evicted tenants. And in every such case churchmen played an unseemly oppressor's role. This undoubtedly devalued the priest's reputation. Old norms of hospitality and charity seemed to be discarded. Churchmen often considered temporal acts of resistance to such traditional dues to be affronts to God. Attacks prompted by strong passions were sometimes tried as sacrilege—for example, if an irate man invaded the altar to strike his priest. Had not the Lord said, "Touch not mine anointed?"

Merely putting a man on notice in the church courts opened the abyss of persecution as well as the prospect of just prosecution. The secular interests of clerics threatened men in their property. The Christian courts rose alongside the secular court system. In them the affairs of the clergy were protected from laymen. If these courts regulated clerical behavior, they also exercised jurisdiction over lay religion, morals, and testamentary causes. To look at these causes is to grasp in detail their potential to provoke conflict. In church courts, men found themselves charged with riotous conduct in church, failure to pay tithes and spiritual dues, sexual misconduct, matrimonial matters, and faults in the testamentary disposition of their goods. The law administered in these courts was Rome's canon law. The penalties imposed ranged from minor penances to excommunication; all of them tended to damage a man's reputation and his credit with his neighbors. And relapsed heretics might be remitted to the king's officers for execution.

The bitter anticlerical sentiment that flourished in Henry VII's reign is particularly clear in the proceedings of Star Chamber.[4] In *Appliard v. Johnson*

---

[3] See I. Churchill, *Canterbury Administration*, 2 vols. (London: Society for Promoting Christian Knowledge, 1933); Felix Makower, *The Constitutional History and Constitution of the Church of England* (New York: Macmillan, 1895); W. A. Pantin, *The English Church in the Fourteenth Century* (London: Cambridge University Press, 1958); and A. Hamilton Thompson, *The English Clergy and Their Organization in the Later Middle Ages* (Oxford: Clarendon Press, 1949).

[4] See S. E. Lehmberg, "Star Chamber: 1485–1509," *HLQ* (1960–1), XXIV, especially pp. 196–205, for all examples cited here. On Hunne's case, see A. Ogle, *The Tragedy of the Lollards' Tower*

et al., the Principal of Furnivall's Inn complained about attacks on law students by servants of the bishop of London. The prior of St. John of Jerusalem charged riot against a gentleman—falsely, if we can trust the defendant's rejoinder. The abbot of Clyffe, Somerset, enclosed a part of the highway there. Twenty-three of 128 cases so far studied by Professor Lehmberg involve clergymen in an atmosphere of marked anticlerical feeling: threats of murder directed at priests; riots by townsmen of Dunster, Somerset, against Bath Abbey. Refusals to pay tithes figure prominently in these cases, one of which has thirty-eight pages of testimony relevant to what tithes were due the abbot of Eynsham from the people of Dernforth, Oxfordshire.

But none of these cases tells us as much about such hostilities as does the case of Richard Hunne of London, in which a mortuary due was denied to a priest by a layman in 1511. Hunne, a citizen and tailor, argued that his dead infant son had no property in the burial sheet that the priest could claim. The rector, Thomas Dryffeld, despised Hunne's bourgeois reason to the point of making suit for the sheet in a church court at Lambeth some thirteen months later.[5] The immediate background to the case was a rising tide of heterodox opinion in London, where clerical privileges, as well as the ways of prelates and priests in general, were under sharp attack in the king's courts. Both Parliament and the convocation of Canterbury archdiocese had discussed the problems. So had popular dissenters and nonconformists—the Lollards—who were just then under sharp attack in London diocese. Thus Hunne's case in 1512 seemed to test the will of the London hierarchy.

When the decision at Lambeth went against him, Hunne countered early in 1513 by citing Henry Marshall in the king's bench on a charge of malicious slander, alleging that the priest had refused to hold services in Hunne's presence on the grounds that Hunne was "accursed." This refusal was alleged to have damaged Hunne's business. While the case was pending, Hunne, again in the king's bench, charged Dryffeld, his proctor, his doctor-advocate, Marshall, Charles Joseph, and all witnesses in the Lambeth suit with the exercise of papal jurisdiction contrary to the fourteenth-century statute regulating royal licenses to convoke courts Christian.[6] These charges against Thomas Dryffeld and his abettors escalated the war sharply. What was at issue was no longer an isolated charge for church rites but the juridical basis of ecclesiastical courts in England.

(Oxford: Clarendon Press, 1948), where the facts of the praemunire and its chronology are scrambled badly; for the chronology given here, see "S.F.C. Milsom, "Richard Hunne's *Praemunire*," *EHR* (1961), LXXVI, pp. 80–2.

[5] April 4, 1512, in the person of his chaplain, Henry Marshall.

[6] The praemunire was in reality not one statute but a complex of laws passed between 1352 and 1393; they were intended to protect the king's rights against interference by foreign courts.

Bishop Fitzjames of London correctly construed the new charges by Hunne as intolerable, especially when account was made of the agitation from other quarters. He ordered Hunne arrested and made a search of his home, where a forbidden Lollard Bible was discovered. Hunne was put in Lollards' Tower, where he was found hanged in his cell late in 1514. London jurors refused to find a verdict of suicide. Instead, they ruled that Hunne had been the victim of an act of willful murder. They then moved an indictment of the bishop's chancellor, jailer, and bellringer. The jailer—Charles Joseph, Dryffeld's summoner—confessed to the charge of murder. At that point, Fitzjames intervened decisively. He sought the aid of Henry VIII and Wolsey, arguing that to prevent the trial at common law was in the interest of civil order and the privileges of the church. The young king supported this view. He himself was orthodox beyond mere belief and saw only trouble in the prospect of giving anticlericalism new scope.

Londoners in the streets said that Hunne had been the victim of clerical revenge. But they misjudged the length to which their bishop would go. Fitzjames presided over a posthumous heresy trial in which Hunne was declared guilty; the body was burned at Smithfield. Contumacious heresy meant the living would suffer with the dead, by law, so Hunne's estates were forfeited to the crown and his family ruined. The London annalist Charles Wriothesley wrote that Hunne "was made a heretic for suing a praemunire." His more famous contemporary, the chronicler Hall, repeated the charge, adding to it this judgment of the clergy: they were men "more of wit to prefer the bishop's jurisdiction . . . than the truth of the Gospel. . . ."

Thus the courts Christian tightened more than ever the thongs throttling the amity of priest and layman. Men who saw in acts of disobedience the stuff of heresy escalated the potential for violent anticlerical resentment. The Hunne case showed how little dissent from below was tolerated by governors in church and commonwealth. Clergy and crown agreed that common men, given scope and encouragement, might shake the order of things. Strife over tithes and manorial dues was already widespread; now spiritual dues were under attack in the kingdom's densest urban parishes. And churchmen reacted as if the vigorous use of force might rescue society and again infuse authority with its ancient legitimacy. Some men were clearly seeking new ideas for social order and the distribution of power and wealth. Others were questioning clerical powers. And still others were asking about the rectitude of traditional religion itself. Hunne's protest was thus a measure of clerical compassion and of clerical statesmanship, or the lack of those qualities. For that reason, it also was a measure of the alienation that stood dammed up in 1514 by Henry VIII's piety and traditionalism.

Prelates and Priests

Many contemporary critics placed the source of bad govern-
ment and alienation in the church at the top, in the alleged independence of a
vicious hierarchy. This view finds scant support in the evidence left by Henry
VIII's dealings with the church. Since the reign of Edward III, popes had
acknowledged the kings' rights, even without formal concords of the sort
that made royal supremacy a fact in France and Spain. The legislation touching
papal provisions and praemunire was sufficiently definitive. Moreover, Henry
VII had used it to impose fines on some clerics and to prevent others from lodging appeals in Roman courts. Thus he maintained good relations with Rome
and control over the English church.

Even more significant as an indicator of church vitality in his reign is the
evidence of the appointees themselves. Henry "appointed" or translated
twenty-seven bishops; in fact, he merely nominated men who then gained
papal appointments. Of these, eight were translated once again, four were
moved twice, and Richard Fox was thrice promoted. Every translation expressed the pattern of careerism; in each case the migration took place to a
wealthier see or to one of the two archbishoprics. All beneficiaries were in
royal service, as chaplains, diplomats, or great officers of state. Their collective
biographies make an impressive chapter in English church history, with only
the appointment of Bishop Stanley of Ely (1506) being of dubious merit. But
he was the earl of Derby's son, the only baronial nominee of the reign! There
were few regular clergy in the English sees, although some quite distinguished
monks and friars served in Wales. The majority of bishops were secular priests
of gentry or burgess origins. All were graduates, chiefly in canon and civil
law. These bishops were well qualified for their offices and several were scholars
of great distinction in humanist circles (Fox, Morton, Bainbridge, and Ruthal).
Some were notable preachers (Fisher, Alcock, and Fitzjames). Only two,
Fitzjames and Smith, can rightly be said to have been set against change or
reform. This bench was able, profound in learning, and worthy of respect for
repeated benefactions, cathedral repairs, and endowment of schools and
colleges.

This is not to say that the bench of bishops sitting at the time of Hunne's
troubles and after was above criticism, but merely to warn against supposing
that the ways of prelates or their bad reputation in Henry VIII's time explain
the roots of the radical anticlericalism that then flourished. We must also
beware of historians who choose to highlight only the most scandalous events,
while suggesting that they have shown the whole truth, thus drawing our
attention away from the social history of religion and into the shallow depths

of conventional vilification. More of the church's failure may be seen in the mass of humble and often impoverished parish clergy than in the lives of Wolsey and his colleagues. Yet it is true to say that the parish priests were not helped by the popular inferences of literate laymen about prelates.

The secular clergy were guided by two archbishops and seventeen bishops who were themselves helped by hundreds of members of the clerical elites of law, diplomacy, finance, and theology. Above them all, in the fifteen years that separated Hunne's death from the Reformation Parliament, stood Thomas Wolsey. He was Henry VIII's wheel horse, a careerist in government who had first come to notice as an Oxford don. He rose slowly in Tudor service until 1512–13, when his priestly talents found an unlikely outlet: he became a great war minister, the guiding genius of the French campaigns. And he was well rewarded. Perhaps only Becket or Henry Cardinal Beaufort had in the past equaled Wolsey's accumulation of offices, wealth, and power. For this son of an Ipswich butcher was by 1515 a cardinal; over the next four years he established his mastery in the kingdom and in Europe's diplomacy. In 1519 he added to the ordinary legatine powers of metropolitan bishops the special powers of a *legate a latere*. This title he secured for life. It gave him the final leverage to elevate himself over Canterbury (William Warham) and the lay aristocracy.[7]

Wolsey proved himself a stern disciplinarian. He used his powers to the dismay of other bishops, whose jurisdiction he often usurped. Cloaked in his special powers, he hoped to effect a general reformation of the church in England. This he did not in fact do. But he showed Henry VIII how clerical wealth and power could add to the authority of the monarchy, especially through the majesty he brought to the prerogative courts and the operation of special commissions. The cardinal-archbishop-factotum was also Lord Chancellor, the king's chief councillor—some said his only one—and at various times bishop of Durham, Winchester, and Bath and Wells in plurality, while farming the income of livings in the hands of nonresident, Italian bishops: Salisbury, Worcester, and Llandaff. His net income from these preferments alone was at least £10,000 a year.

Wolsey used his wealth and offices to live with the pomp and authority peculiar to a Renaissance prince. He converted the courts of bishops into legatine courts; he intimidated local officials and exercised control over lay and clerical patronage; he showed himself unsympathetic to Parliament and

[7] On Wolsey and the bishops dominant in the church *c*. 1515–40 see A. F. Pollard, *Wolsey* (London: Longmans, 1905); J. A. Muller, *Stephen Gardiner* (Cambridge: Cambridge University Press, 1926); Charles Sturge, *Cuthbert Tunstall* (London: Longmans, 1938); L. B. Smith, *Tudor Prelates and Politics* (Princeton: Princeton University Press, 1953); and R. L. Storey, *Diocesan Administration in the Fifteenth Century* (York: St. Anthony's Press, 1959).

the convocations of York and Canterbury; and he gave preferments worth £3,000 a year to his bastard son, Thomas Winter. Yet this side of the great cardinal was not all there was to see. He championed clerical privilege and resolutely defended the dignity and independence of the church in an age that threatened both. He used his offices to extend royal protection to some of England's poorest and most rejected men, and he built on a great scale at Hampton Court and York Place (Whitehall). The funds gathered from the suppression of some two dozen monasteries, which he deemed a disgrace to religion, he applied to St. Mary's Grammar School in Ipswich and to the erection of Cardinal's College at Oxford. Wolsey also planned to redress the unbalanced distribution of dioceses—which favored the South and East, reflecting early population patterns—through the creation of thirteen new bishoprics. He drew reform-minded men to court; Thomas More dedicated *Utopia* to him in 1516. And he absolutely refused to launch a general persecution of alleged heretics. Finally, as far from the least of his contributions to government, he taught Thomas Cromwell the business of church and commonwealth.

Had his ambition in politics not matched his king's, he might have deflected Henry VIII into a program of reform. As it was, he left no impression on English religion in a career marked by self-interest. Moreover, his career spurred the lust for wealth, pomp, and power inherent in so many who sought clerical work. His ministry encouraged palace sycophants and widened the scope of clerical careerism. No other member of the hierarchy matched Wolsey, but some were imperfect copies. Warham of Canterbury was an undistinguished diplomat whose services were not only well rewarded but also the occasion of great distress in his province.[8] Fitzjames we have already observed as a mighty persecutor in London. Fox had retired to his diocese in 1517. Other bishops who might have served the church through reform were in Wolsey's era caught up in the royal ambition for power at home and influence abroad. Their often permanent absences from their dioceses gave impetus to hundreds of middle-rank careerists, who swarmed over the body of the church. These lesser members of the clerical elite accumulated benefices in plurality, emulating the cardinal. The pattern of careerism they followed bears careful scrutiny, since it very directly weakened the reputation of the clergy at the parish level and also sharpened the sense of divided interests that separated the humbler curates from the lawyers, accountants, and theologians who grew fat in God's employ.

[8] See pp. 136–7.

The Church on the Local Level

Parish priests served Englishmen in about 8,500 units. The parish was the basic cell of church life. The character of the parochial clergy was therefore critical to the health of the church, since those thousands of men could mitigate or reinforce popular views of corruption, nepotism, and worldliness. A pastor's failings were immediate and familiar to ordinary people. And if these were many, or even few, but were blown out of proportion by egregious scandals, then the problems of prelates would seem significant only because they were the problems of the parish writ large.[9]

The priest charged with the cure of souls bore a great burden. He had to bring the young up in a knowledge of the faith, give warnings against deadly sins, praise the cardinal virtues, catechize men and women, reveal the sacraments as effective channels of grace in the economy of salvation, and preach God's word. His chief aids in these tasks were whatever education he had and manuals of devotion or books of sermons mined for his own speeches. Many of the faithful were rude and illiterate. This made the maintenance of the whole church fabric important, since wall paintings and images revealed God's grace to all, whatever their skill in reading.

To support the spiritual burdens, there were spiritual dues payable at christenings, marriages, confirmations, and burials. There was also the temporal endowment of the parish—the great tithe of grain and the small tithes of local produce. This is a reminder that the priest was also often a neighboring farmer, working his own land (glebe) and getting from the community part of its product. Hence the relations between priest and parishioners were often competitive; there was no idealized, fantasy scene of the good shepherd tending his flock.

Thus some important questions arise. If men did not demand sanctity from their priest, did they find in him neighborly qualities and the orderly provision of guidance? What in fact was the collective character of the English parish clergy on the eve of the Reformation? Was this chief link between Christ and the Christian likely to produce dissent and disquiet? Were most priests diligent, competent, and moral? Were they sufficiently educated for their office? Were they falling short of the mark because of ordination abuses, indiscriminate patronage, grinding clerical poverty, the vice of avarice, and the plague of pluralism? How conscious were the faithful of their curates as com-

[9] See Margaret Bowker, *The Secular Clergy in Lincoln Diocese, 1495–1520* (Cambridge: Cambridge University Press, 1968); E. L. Cutts, *Parish Priests and their People* (London, 1898); and Peter Heath, *The English Parish Clergy on the Eve of the Reformation* (Toronto: University of Toronto Press, 1969).

petitors in social and economic matters? Was the alienation that exploded so violently after 1529 explicable at all in parochial terms?

Recent studies of the parochial clergy do not always lend support to the worst tirades of Tudor anticlericals or their sometimes more moderate reformist contemporaries. But they do in some significant ways supplement conclusions drawn from traditional accounts that rely chiefly on literary sources.[1]

The complaints of advocates of reform were often persuasively and cleverly made. This we may readily see in William Tyndale's *Practice of Prelates*, which shows that the sins of the hierarchy set a pattern for the lower clergy to follow. Tyndale's parish priests run from one benefice to another, often holding cures of souls in plurality. They neglect preaching, exploit their people financially, lead corrupt lives, and disrupt the peace of their parishes. Thomas More bitterly opposed Tyndale's heretical, Lutheran doctrines. He also wished remedies other than those Tyndale proposed. But his own writings exposed priestly ways just as relentlessly. *Utopia* made priests laudable only because they were few in number. John Colet, More's close friend and London associate in reform circles, preached the ways of clerical wickedness in the teeth of the assembled Canterbury convocation in his 1512 sermon opening their meeting. The list in his wholesale indictment included heresy-hunting, ignorance of the Bible, the avaricious motives of pluralists, moral laxity—especially incontinence— and a score of failings in sacramental administration and parochial work. He especially singled out the overzealous application of canon law in the courts Christian. William Melton, the humanist chancellor of York diocese, had said much the same thing in 1510 in an exhortation to new ordinates. Where men as diverse in their views and fates as Colet, Melton, Tyndale, and More agreed, radicals followed readily. And that is reason enough for us to look closely at the corporate image of parochial clergy as reflected in the records of the church itself.

Parish and Cloister: The Roots of Alienation

Priests were daily commanded to offer their hearts to God, their intellects to Holy Scripture, and their bodily strength to their flock. These things they had to do in a social context of great violence and rude passions. Often their parishes were dominated by men like Richard Richard, a lecher

---

[1] Examinations of various kinds of criticism of the clergy may be found in J. K. McConica, *English Humanists and Reformation Politics* (Oxford: Oxford University Press, 1965); Arthur B. Ferguson, *The Articulate Citizen of the English Renaissance* (Durham, N.C.: Duke University Press, 1965); F. Seebohm, *The Oxford Reformers* (London: Longmans, 1867); and W. A. Clebsch, *England's Earliest Protestants* (New Haven: Yale University Press, 1964).

and gangster of Oxnead, Norfolk; or the men of Tenterden in Kent, who in Cade's time had advocated killing all priests; or those who had assaulted John Baker, a priest, in a public house at Bowers Gifford, Essex. To face such lives, most priests had gone through the canonical eight stages that led from lay to priestly life. Before the final steps of ordination, fitness tests were given, touching their age, moral worth, and educational level. But surviving evidence suggests that examination was perfunctory in Henry VIII's reign, as it had been in 1450, when Thomas Gascoigne, Chancellor of Oxford, complained that unworthy men were regularly ordained. Colet and Melton agreed; and so did More, who prayed for fewer priests and better ones, especially in "their living." Certain places—York and Lichfield—earned reputations as "ordination mills."

Why this should be so is not obvious. Melton stressed "pressures and deceit" rather than cynicism or carelessness, and in this view may be found a valuable clue. Pressure sometimes took the form of letters from powerful patrons. There are instances of impersonation at examinations. Still more serious was the collusion centering on yet another test: each ordinand was required to have a "title"—a guaranteed income of £5 a year net—to support him until he obtained a benefice or permanent clerical work. Bishops who ordained men without titles became liable for their support. The diocese records show clearly that most ordinands gave as "title" the guarantee of some monastery. Yet most houses making this promise neither delivered the income nor later provided a benefice.[2]

The evidence suggests that very large numbers of would-be priests connived with such houses, sometimes in the hope of avoiding beggary, more often in the knowledge that overcoming the "title" obstacle opened the way to public service or the undemanding ease of a household chaplaincy. And in order to avoid tests based on local knowledge, such men got letters dismissory, which allowed them to seek ordination in a diocese other than that in which they lived. In the period 1510–11, 265 priests were ordained in York; a further 544 became deacons or subdeacons. The diocese provided no useful employment for such numbers. Lincoln diocese possessed about 20 percent of all English parochial cures. Yet only 2,609 men took final vows there between 1495 and 1520.[3]

The apparent racket in titles and the problem of York's excessive ordinations signify not only redundant vocations and the ambitions of men with no real calling. They emphasize yet another contemporary problem of a structural nature; namely, that of *appropriations*—acts by which persons or corporations acquired permanent patronage of a parish church. Patronage gave the

[2] See the Appendix, Figure 6.

[3] See the Appendix, Figure 7, for other comparisons.

power to nominate incumbents and to take the great tithe (rectorial tithe). Appropriating the tithe for a rector's support made it necessary to endow a vicarage in lieu of the rectory and so give income to the man who did the priest's work. This was necessary because monastic corporations were the greatest appropriators, followed by the royal estate and those of the lay aristocrats, with municipal corporations close behind.[4]

Throughout the fifteenth century, rectories were converted into vicarages. Even the vicarages were sometimes appropriated, with the result that mere curacies were left. This trend depressed the income of many parish cures. What was provided was often not enough to maintain the poor chaplain or stipendiary priest. Again, monasteries were the worst offenders, drawing off the funds nominally given to support a well-educated and endowed parochial ministry.

Thus, in Lincoln diocese around the year 1500, there no longer was any real relationship between titles to livings, numbers of ordinands, vacant benefices to be filled, and the ability of a parish to attract or support a priest. Half of the parish churches in the diocese were victims of appropriation. The crown had 123, and great houses of religion—Ramsey, Peterborough, Groyland, and Osney—held over 200 among them. Appropriators manipulated parish endowments in their own interests to support administrators, endow pluralists, reward friends, or for other reasons that made of Christ's patrimony an article of commerce.

The consequences were dire. The means by which benefices were traded and secured were an obstacle to securing incumbents with genuine vocations. There was an abundance of priests. The shortage of benefices made the advowson, or patron-right, marketable. Those who found no benefice swelled the ranks of chaplains. Monks who traded in them corrupted the churches they had sworn to serve. In many cases, assistants to beneficed clerks were not receiving the statutory minimum wages in a time of great inflation. Deputies for absentee rectors and vicars lacked security of tenure. This often undermined their authority in the parish. Where serious erosion took place—especially where a rectory had been converted into a vicarage, which was in turn further degraded—the priest of the parish was hired by the real benefice-holder, or else the curate was hired by the vicar, who was himself nonresident. The impoverished curate then would hire assistants, where the cure was a large one. Thus economic pressures, personal insecurity, and social subservience promoted frantic competition for benefices and encouraged "benefice agents"

---

[4] Bowker and Heath are valuable on tithes and appropriations; these works can be supplemented with N. A. Adams, "The Judicial Conflict over Tithes," *EHR* (1937), LIII, pp. 1–22; R. A. R. Hartridge, *A History of Vicarages in the Later Middle Ages* (Cambridge: Cambridge University Press, 1930); and A. G. Little, "Personal Tithes," *EHR* (1945), Lx, pp. 67–88.

to ply a cruel trade inimical to the life of religion and the vigor of the church. The bishop charged with the welfare of a diocese was rarely, if ever, the chief patron of benefices. Lay and royal interests conflicted with monastic ones, and all along the line the interests of the parish were made subordinate to those of clerical elitists in some superior service.

Simony was rife, though by its very nature it defies exact measurement. One example will suffice. John Spynney, chaplain of the chantry of St. Katherine in Bridport, made a pact to pay John Kyrkeby, a priest, twenty shillings a year until £50 had been paid, for advancement to a benefice worth 20 marks a year. If the benefice obtained was worth £20 per annum, the fee was to be £5 a year!

Proxy Priests

These practices were closely connected with absenteeism, an abuse attacked over the centuries by statute, canon law, and convocations.[5] The reason is not obscure. Absenteeism was common among the clergy of the later Middle Ages. While its exact extent will never be known because of inexact evidence, it seems clear that in some dioceses there was less of it than contemporaries assumed or historians today believe. In Norwich diocese in 1499, there were forty-eight cases in 489 parishes. When Warham visited 266 Canterbury parishes in 1511, he found seventeen vicars and twenty rectors to be absentees. Yet in Lincoln diocese the scandal was huge; in 1518, 25 percent of all incumbents were nonresidents. Thus it is less important what the numerical measure was than that between 1450 and 1530 every church lacked a resident incumbent at some time in the life cycle of most parishioners. This fact and that of prolonged individual instances of absenteeism gave a notoriety to the practice perhaps slightly out of keeping with its total incidence.[6]

Absence from the cure of souls was licensed by popes, nuncios, and legates. Since the 1200s, the indiscriminate granting of papal licenses had facilitated pluralism. Not all nonresidence was for this reason, of course. Some priests sought leave to study, to make pilgrimages, or because they were called to episcopal or royal administration, and in all such cases only episcopal license was required. Nonresidence was most pronounced in combination with pluralism in the richest benefices. In Lincoln diocese, there was little of either

[5] On absenteeism and pluralism in the later Middle Ages, see V. F. M. Garlick, "The Provision of Vicars in the Early Fourteenth Century," *History* (1949), XXXIV, pp. 15–27; H. M. Smith, *Pre-Reformation England* (London: Macmillan, 1938); A. H. Thompson, "Ecclesiastical Benefices and their Incumbents," *Transactions Leicestershire Archaeological Society* (1945), XXII, pp. 1–32; and "Pluralism in the Medieval Church," *Associated Architectural Societies Reports* (1916), XXXIII, pp. 35–73, as well as Bowker and Heath.

[6] In 1827, 5,000 of 10,000 incumbents were nonresidents!

?

in livings worth less than £5 a year. But 22 percent of all livings worth £15 or more reported a nonresident. Among them, thirty-five of every hundred were university graduates, although these were only 15 percent of the total priests in the diocese.

And it is this conjunction that underscores the importance of absenteeism and pluralism. The men best suited by education to an active, preaching ministry were the least likely to live that life! Kings, bishops, abbots, and lay aristocrats competed for the services of learned clerks. Their competition encouraged the abuses—from fraudulent titles and appropriations to simony and pluralism. The result was to siphon off men and money from the parishes where these were needed and where the potential for alienation was enormous. Curates without benefices occupied cures stripped of income. This often forced them into competition with their parishioners, contests that promised no good service in return. By 1535, 87 percent of all Coventry diocese parishes were worth less than £20 a year, 77 percent less than £15, 60 percent less than £10, and at least 10 percent worth less than £5. The pattern in other dioceses was not much different.

These figures give the color of truth to Hugh Latimer's complaint that the line between priestly penury and mild affluence stood at £10 a year. In a time of rapid inflation, no smaller sum could keep a priest in books and allow him to keep a good house for his neighbors. Latimer and Edward Lee, the reforming archbishop of York (1535–44), agreed on a further point: the fall of parish incomes, accelerated by inflation, promoted immorality and ignorance in the clergy. Worldly careerism was blamed by them for pushing down parochial educational levels, despite the vast expansion of educational facilities in the 1400s and early 1500s. The number of graduates had steadily risen, and printing had radically increased the pastoral preparation of men. Cranmer gave an average of fifty-three licenses for absenteeism with pluralities each year between 1534 and 1549. This was a figure greater than the annual average granted by Wolsey or by the Roman curia in the years 1450–1530. It cannot be put down to lack of zeal for reform. The abuses were structural, in the fabric of the society itself.

The single fact was that pluralism and nonresidence were as essential to society as they were to the church. Churchmen could neither stop them nor control them, at least not until the church found an alternative to using priests in its own civil service and the monarchy was rich enough to hire all of its servants on its own income. Until then, the church would continue to grapple with the effects of abuses. Perhaps these had best be illustrated before they are commented on or put in general terms.

In 1514, the faithful of Thundersley in London witnessed the absence and incontinence of their rector. Miles Hogeson stayed away from his cure for most of the winter and spring. No deputy had blessed the fount in which babes were baptized, and this perturbed the parishioners. Moreover, during Lent no one was on hand to hear confessions. A chaplain did appear to bless ashes a week after Ash Wednesday, but only through the parishioners' benevolence, since they were out of pocket for his hire. The church fabrics were so ruined that cheap labor had to be hired before the Eucharist was decently housed. The reason for all this was simple enough. Hogeson kept a whore at the home of one Pettigrew.

In 1520, in the parish of Braughing, Hertfordshire, the men were forced to hire "Chekemaisters" to tally the absences and celebrations of Robert Phelipson, vicar. Nor were such watch committees unknown in other parishes. In the parish of South Ockendon, between 1504 and 1515, Domenic Civi, rector, had never been seen following his induction. Rumors that he was at a university went the route from time to time, but the parishioners assumed Civi was dead. Even the farmer[7] of the parish, the chaplain Thomas Goodwyn, had never seen him. Meanwhile, the church was dilapidated, the books and lectern were ruined, and the foundations were decayed. Goodwyn, who was the pluralist rector of West Thurrock, was specifically relieved of fabric maintenance in his bargain with the ghostly Civi. Otherwise, Goodwyn served the parish's needs well enough.

It was not often the case that absentees' replacements served the parish that well. The bulk of the evidence supports a different hypothesis: scandal figured more prominently in the disciplinary history of parishes with nonbeneficed incumbents than those with resident, beneficed clergy. Such statistics as we possess do not make the difference huge; and the orderly curate is not recorded in visitations of the parish. But there are enough complaints to balance some apparently healthy pictures. Norwich diocese in 1499 reported forty-eight cases of nonresidence; only two parishes reported gross negligence or corruption in the vicars and curates there. Or consider York, where one court book kept from 1453 to 1491 shows that there were fewer than ninety-three adulteries attributed to priests in fifty urban and thirty-six rural parishes. It seems more to the point to recall that among the more than ninety priests charged only seven were rectors; forty-four were chaplains and thirty-one were curates.[8]

At Didcot, the priest had gone to Oxford, apparently permanently. There

---

[7] That is, the man who paid the rector to be able to collect the tithes of the parish, offering a fixed sum and hoping to make a profit.

[8] Heath's apologia rather naively asks what else we should expect, given the numerical preponderance of chaplains over vicars and vicars over rectors! Moreover, the same parishes over the same years reported only 284 cases of adultery by laymen, a suspect figure or a remarkable comment on the virtue of Yorkshiremen or the looks of their women!

were no services in the parish and "grete unease." The vicar of Wrangle had never resided there, nor had the chaplain. The rector of Mixbury lived in London, while the resident curate merely lived in sin! A Leicestershire vicar claimed a poor man's tenth son as a tithe. In many parishes curates pilfered the alms box, or were suspected of the crime. Priests were often cited for taking a poor woman's last cow as a spiritual due. At Quadring, the pastor was a farmer who sold grain at prices that undermined the local market. The parson at Fleckley went about without a tonsure and in sporty clothing. The Surfleet curate stole sheep and the vicar at Wooten stalled horses in the confessionals. Some learned men complained of their curates' ignorance, noting that they alleged the gospel out of place, knew not the Fathers, or mumbled the canon of the Mass because they did not know the Latin. In Lincoln diocese, these were common complaints.[9]

Sources of Scandal

Why this was so should now be easier to grasp. Priests, depressed economically and often spiritually, entertained themselves in unpriestly ways. These failures were social as well as moral. Propagandists exploited them mercilessly, perhaps out of proportion to their incidence. This can only mean that alienation was close enough to the surface to be easily tapped. Poor livings did not enlist well-educated men. Offenses touched the fabric of parish society as well as the church fabric. Compassion for men in Tudor society was never too evident, and for priests weighed down by the psychological and economic stresses of celibacy, it was scarcely noticeable. Poverty bred loneliness and ennui, especially among celibate proletarians of the church. And this gave to every dispute over chicken and eggs the quality of a morality play. Certainly in every case of priestly adultery, village solidarity and family integrity were at issue. Where the poverty was grinding enough, so too was subsistence and life itself. All suffered, and most knew—at least indirectly—of the opulence of the elites.

Thus, our image of the rural parson and his poor urban cousin is that of men victimized by the careerism of others and avid to have its lightning strike them. They were easy targets for scorn. Their lives touched the lives of laymen in ways that promoted alienation. The way they lived bore scant resemblance to Christ's life in chastity and obedience, regardless of the extent of their poverty. And the men who witnessed all this were ripe for an age of revolutionary criticism.

The reputation of the regular clergy did nothing to relax criticism. Their

[9] See the Appendix, Figure 8.

numbers had declined markedly between 1500 and the ecclesiastical census of 1535, but there were still about 11,000 monks and 1,600 nuns living in 825 houses in England and Wales. Their decline ran counter to the general rise of population, a fact that may reflect a loss of zeal in Christians who suspected the cloister or those who, like Erasmus, thought the need for walls against the world was no true test of vocation. Moreover, hostile critics castigated the wealth and luxurious lifestyle of the regular religious and the corodians and abbey-lubbers who surrounded them. Few could have guessed that the houses had a combined net worth of £135,000 in 1535. But most critics would have been aghast to discover that the poor in Christ had a greater combined annual revenue than the crown in England![1]

What men did know long before Thomas Cromwell's visitors combed the monasteries in the wet winter of 1535–6 was usually some example of abuse that others had experienced at first hand: venal sins of property ownership; great tables and fine apartments; the sight of an abbot, richly clothed and bejeweled, walking down a London street. Some men undoubtedly knew that monastic accounts disguised nepotism and that social bribery made local gentry wealthy in the management of monastic estates. Others no doubt had direct experience of the disorder, disobedience, and contentiousness that sometimes disrupted life in a particular house. For such disruptions often were followed by immorality, or at least by a lowering of morale to the point of scandal. Men and women entered cloisters when little more than infants, ignorant of their sexuality. Not a few women were put there because they violated social mores or because they were not marriageable—neither circumstance promising a sincere vocation.

Monastic life appeared to laymen to offer a pleasant release from economic insecurity. Monks and nuns thus seemed as bound to worldly patterns of society as did parish priests. But if this was so, laymen connived at the existing condition by fobbing off girls whom they regarded as ugly or sinful. They lived parasitically on monastic wealth, as we can see in too many letters and court cases that show aristocratic and professional ambitions taking root in squalid quarrels, drinking bouts, dances, hunts, gambling sessions, and the fixing of abbatial elections. Religious corporations also ranked high among those guilty of depopulating enclosers, rack-renting, and the arbitrary use of power

---

[1] The great work of David Knowles is basic in all questions touching regular religion: *The Religious Orders in England, III: The Tudor Age* (Cambridge: Cambridge University Press, 1959). See also Geoffrey Baskeville, *English Monks and the Suppression of the Monasteries* (London: Jonathan Cape, 1937); F. A. Gasquet, *Henry VIII and the English Monasteries*, 2 vols. (London: G. Bell, 1888–9); and some of the many specialized studies: J. P. Moorman, *The Grey Friars in Cambridge, 1225–1538* (Cambridge: Cambridge University Press, 1952); A. Savine, *English Monasteries on the Eve of the Dissolution* (Oxford: Clarendon Press, 1909), chiefly for their economics.

to oppress the poor. Thomas More placed certain holy abbots among the chief usurpers of common grazing rights.

These matters were less applicable to the women who lived in their 136 communities than to the men in their 690 houses. Many houses were very poor, especially the nunneries, which accounted for only £15,000 of the total annual monastic revenue. Near the city of York was the great house of St. Mary's, with revenue of nearly £2,000 a year. Less than 10 miles away, the women at Nunnerholme could raise less than £10 a year. The smaller houses—some 450 establishments in all—controlled only one-ninth of the monastic wealth. These also were often egregious in their failure to keep the rule of their particular order. In 205 houses, each worth less than £200 a year, there lived only 1,651 religious, fewer than 8 people in each community. There were instances in which a house had only one or two inhabitants. Clearly there was no rush of men or women to the pleasures of privation for Christ's sake. On the contrary, the rich houses drew more inhabitants than was necessary to maintain a cloistered life properly, whereas the poor establishments could not attract enough to maintain worship properly. At Rievaulx, 22 monks were served by 122 domestics and professionals; and the 12 canons of Butley Priory employed 2 chaplains, 11 body servants, 3 cooks, 6 laundresses, 34 common laborers, and at least 10 craftsmen. There was thus among the regular religious the same evidence of a radical social stratification and elitism, with the richer houses drawing particularly on the gentry classes for their vocations.

In return for great power and wealth and a collective life of great failure— when judged against the harsh standard of the rules of regular religion—the monasteries gave little to society. Less than three percent of the endowment was spent on charity or hospitality. There were no parallels to the German and Italian teaching orders, or those working in missions or nursing. Only the smallest congregations were distinguished for general piety and spirituality: the observant Franciscans, Carthusians, and Bridgettines. The monasteries and nunneries did not excel in educational work. Not surprisingly, therefore, the regular religious found few defenders against Henry VIII's wrath and Thomas Cromwell's dissolution of the monasteries. Most Englishmen agreed with the judgment their governors made in 1536: the regulars lacked the capacity for both reformation and self-government.

This was the face of the church so ruthlessly exposed by pamphleteers before 1529 and by royal commissioners after that year. Indeed, in the year of the Reformation Parliament's first session, the village of Hayes in Middlesex experienced in microcosm the whole burden of scandal and malfeasance that, though characteristic of only a minority of parishes, harmed the reputation of all.

St. Mary's at Hayes had a long record of trouble between shepherds and sheep. Tithe disputes were frequent, with the ministers complaining about arrears as a means of countering parochial views of clerical performance. The situation was complicated by the appropriation of the rectory by the archbishop of Canterbury. Generations of archbishops had milked the great tithes while endowing a vicarage to meet parochial needs. But population pressure after 1480 forced the incumbent vicar to add to his own efforts a staff of assistants. Eventually, the vicar had found the game not worth the stakes and he too had become nonresident—in the 1520s. This absentee vicar was in fact the namesake and cousin of Archbishop Warham, William the Younger. Warham senior had made his kinsman archdeacon of Canterbury diocese, drawing him into nonresidence and pluralism by way of Cathedral business.

This prompted the cousin to farm or lease his Hayes living. Farming was a common practice by which a third party—the rector and vicar being absentees —got the property rights, including the small tithes and the right to name the curate. One of the men who farmed Hayes was Thomas Gold, a grasping schemer who promptly named his brother, Henry, as curate. The brothers employed an assistant, Peter Lee, in the parish church and at North Wood, where a chapel had been added to house the growing faithful.

The Gold brothers and Peter Lee soon reduced Hayes to open warfare. In a season of bad harvests, they charged a wealthy parishioner with refusing to tithe. The man gathered his neighbors to aid him. Suits were pressed in church courts. A riot ensued. On one side stood the farmer, the curate, Lee, the keeper of the local bawdyhouse, and a few wealthy villagers. Against that motley crew came the four corners of the community, in arms. The result was tragic: Lee broke a man's head in church; he and the curate stood accused of murder, of adultery with a taverner's wife, and of frequenting a whore's house. The curate had disobeyed the archbishop's orders to fire Lee, who must have been very troublesome if he roused the somnolent Warham. Parishioners sought relief from vexatious suits and looked to private devices and other men for spiritual comfort.

At Hayes, the ruin of a parish was symbolic of the impending fall of Rome's power in England. When Henry loosed the forces of anticlericalism, the abyss that separated the whole clergy from the laity was wide and daily growing wider. It was in fact too wide a gap to be bridged by internal reform, for on the road that led from Pope Gregory VII (Hildebrand) to the Age of Reformation, the clergy misplaced their zeal and lost their way. A selfish king engrossed in his own dynastic problems made this abundantly clear. But he could not have done so had the five centuries since the Norman Conquest not put down deep roots of alienation and despair. The clergy had created a myth of their own Christian perfection, but to most laymen they seemed to suffer more the afflictions of this world's flesh than the wounds of Christ. Henry VIII's rebellion was merely the signal of the Reformation and not its cause.

Dissent and the Demand for Reform

Englishmen had for generations shaped movements protesting abuses and resisting church power. John Wycliffe's movement had been confined to aristocratic and university circles in the 1370s and 1380s.[2] But in the 1400s lay radicals called Lollards had questioned church teachings and the proprietary bases of its power. This, not unnaturally, was seen as a challenge to royal power also, especially when certain Lollard gentry raised the standard of revolt in 1415 and again in 1431. The crown gave its full support to repressive measures then, just as it had done in the 1404 legislation that renewed the death penalty for heresy. Thereafter, the Lollards, who drew their ideas from popular religious grievances rather than from Wycliffe's abstract teachings, went underground, drawing strength from homespun anticlericalism among wage laborers and petty craftsmen.

The successive waves of persecution after 1431 failed to uproot dissent. During the Hunne affair, and in the years 1509–12, London had witnessed the great persecution and abjuration of Lollards that had threatened even John Colet, dean of St. Paul's. Official sources in many dioceses show the persistence of popular dissent in the North, especially York diocese; in London where, as late as 1521, 350 Lollards were accused in church courts; in Kent, Essex, Lincoln, and the West Midlands. The Londoners showed an especially sharp appreciation for the support their own faith could draw from foreign ideas, especially Luther's, and in the 1520s they encouraged a notable trade in heretical books, along with the zealously propagated Lollard Bible.

The native dissent was characterized by a number of anticlerical and antisacramental notions. Lollards condemned Roman influence in England, the hierarchy's wealth and power, and church pretensions in secular business in general. They linked their stance to a general pacifism, which the crown disliked intensely. They often held up to ridicule religion that elevated the sacraments over the gospel. And they rejected as superstition saints' relics, the adoration of icons, prayers for the dead, and pilgrimages. Not a few spoke openly and decisively against baptism and the Eucharist. Many, if not all, believed passionately in the right to have Scriptures in English.

Early English Lutherans—friar Robert Barnes and Tyndale, for example— understood this hunger for vernacular Scriptures well and made gains in

[2] See especially: J. A. F. Thompson, *The Later Lollards, 1414–1520* (Oxford: Oxford University Press, 1965); A. G. Dickens, *Lollards and Protestants in the Diocese of York, 1509–1558* (Oxford: Oxford University Press, 1959); Erik Routley, *English Religious Dissent* (Cambridge: Cambridge University Press, 1960); and E. G. Rupp, *Studies in the Making of the English Protestant Tradition* (Cambridge: Cambridge University Press, 1947).

Lollard circles. Less sympathetic observers—Erasmus, More, Tunstal, and Bishop Fisher—feared that Lollard radicalism would endanger the more moderate reforms to which they had committed their own energies. Thus, despite their advocacy of English scriptures and devotional works, and in clear recognition of other points of compatibility, first-generation humanist-reformers looked for the means to end Lollard activities. It frightened them to see how eagerly the native "heretics" welcomed German ideas. It was their commonplace wisdom to say that Lollardy sparked the flower of Lutheranism.[3]

More and his friends preferred satire and elegance to rude Lollard dissent and Luther's attack on Rome. They put obstacles in the way of a united front of reformers, while giving to their own advocacy what both Lollardy and Lutheranism in England lacked: respectability built on status within the three power elites that governed England—church, court and aristocracy, and the universities. The humanists' emphasis on educational reform expressed their status as a power group in much the same way that clerical reformers looked to the curia or convocation and the lay elitists slowly turned toward Parliament. Reformation was a problem of power—and of this in the 1520s the radical reformers had none. Movements of reform from above might be of diverse motives and character, but they looked safe. And the moderates hoped to gain a hearing for their own views by helping to discredit the radicals—hence the enthusiasm with which the humanists of More's generation persecuted Lollard and Lutheran alike.

Herein lies the profound significance of Henry VIII's divorce.[4] His marriage to Catherine of Aragon had produced no male heir in a period of eighteen years. There had been at least six births and several miscarriages. The royal couple had had four sons either stillborn or dead soon after birth. Only Princess Mary (born 1516) had survived. And as early as 1514 Henry had thought his marriage ill-fated; there were rumors in that year of the king's intention to procure annulment from the pope on the dual grounds that Julius II had erred in issuing a dispensation for Henry to marry Prince Arthur's widow in 1503 and that the queen's "barrenness" was proof of the blight on his marriage. In this early report there was undoubtedly a hint of Henry's disenchantment with the Spanish alliance. But thirteen years passed before he found certain Old Testament texts—especially Leviticus XVIII—that denounced marriage between a man and his dead brother's widow. The deaths of so many sons was in Henry's mind God's judgment on his marriage.

---

[3] These conflicts are clearly presented in the works of McConica, Clebsch, and Ferguson, already cited. An interpretation of the dynamic interplay of Erasmians and Lutherans accompanied by documents is A. J. Slavin, *Humanism, Reform and Reformation* (New York: Wiley, 1969).

[4] The best book on Henry VIII is J. J. Scarisbrick's biography *Henry VIII* (London, 1967). See also A. F. Pollard, *Henry VIII* (London, 1905); and G. R. Elton, *Henry VIII* (London, 1962).

When Henry found a scruple about his marriage and a text—or a pretext—for acting on it, he altered the balance of power between opposed views of how reform should come about and what might be its content. As the king's scruple became a certainty, his desire for a divorce and for Anne Boleyn also grew. This conjunction drove him onto the shoals of diplomacy and papal courts in 1527, with the result that by the summer of 1529 a trial began in England under the jurisdiction of Wolsey and a special legate, Cardinal Campeggio. Suffice it to say that the tangled question of whether the Pope legally dispensed impediments to the marriage of Henry and his brother Arthur's widow was not finally settled by that court. Catherine refused its jurisdiction and appealed to Clement VII in Rome. Campeggio adjourned the case on July 31, 1529.

No papal court was ever again convened in England. Henry was enraged by a summons to Rome. He blamed his embarrassment on Wolsey. Thus the first consequence of the failure of the court was Wolsey's removal from power. Just as Henry VIII had sacrificed Empson and Dudley, so he allowed an aristocratic coup well larded with popular anticlericalism to cast down the greatest churchman in English history.

The other consequences of the king's anger were less immediately discerned but more momentous. There was a revolution in ecclesiastical polity that ended Roman power in England. The forces of anticlericalism had for decades needed the king; now he needed them. And his need ensured that the constitutional revolution would go forward. It also provided an opportunity for the men who wanted a revolution in the country's religious life. A profound revolution in society and in politics came about as the ministers of the crown took over and shaped the enthusiasm for reform—in the process making a Protestant commonwealth out of Rome's staunchest ally.

Onset of the Reformation

The chief thrust of the Reformation thus begun was threefold: against the abuse of ecclesiastical power and lordship; against the burden on society of church wealth and the church power that stood in the way of integrating the kingdom; and against religious practices that had provoked a surge of pietistic reform and criticism in Lollard, Lutheran, and Erasmian circles alike. Men such as More and Fisher hoped to achieve these ends in communion with Rome. Others—Thomas·Cromwell and the second-generation humanists, anticlericals, Lutherans, and religious radicals in his entourage—were willing to do it by whatever means were necessary. The king stood somewhere between them, as we shall see.[5]

[5] For this interpretation of the 1529–40 unfolding of the Reformation, the following are indispensable: G. R. Elton, *England under the Tudors* (London: Methuen, 1955), pp. 98–192; A. G. Dickens,

There was little initial disagreement in one area, however: the community of the realm sat in Parliament. It had not met for six years, yet it alone embodied the will of king, the lay aristocracy, the clergy, and the chief burgesses of England. Reformation on a large scale could not be achieved without the motive force of the whole community, for what touched all in consequence pertained to all in action. So Henry VIII convoked Parliament on November 3, 1529. Neither he nor anyone else could have anticipated that it would sit for seven years in six sessions, nor that its fame would make it the Reformation Parliament. By 1536, it had not only given Henry a new queen, it had legislated to reform society. It had enriched the crown with the spoils of the monasteries. And it had made clear three crucial tenets on which the Anglican Church rose and a revolutionary monarchy stood: the king was sole overlord of the English church; the church in England owed Rome no tutelage; the crown had a divine mission to reform and guard the cure of souls. It became the government's view that right order in a Christian monarchy depended on the realization of those tenets. In fact, the legislative history of the 1530s was to realize each of them in turn. Here we can concern ourselves with how this was done, leaving to another place a fuller examination of how the revolution of the 1530s generated the crisis of the mid-Tudor period, how the effort to resolve the crisis of religion and the succession of the dynasty in fact produced the "permanent crisis" in government and society.[6]

The revolution of the 1530s occurred in three stages: 1529–32, when Parliament gave scope to anticlericalism and circumscribed ecclesiastical independence; 1532–5, when the break with Rome was effected and the royal supremacy enacted; and 1535–40, when the monasteries were dissolved and the outlines of Protestant worship first appeared. We shall deal with the characteristics and legislation of each phase in turn before we arrive at an interpretation of the decade as a whole.

The Commons in Parliament quickly became the focus of anticlerical sentiments. Encouraged by Wolsey's submissiveness to the common law, and on his indictment in the king's bench on praemunire charges, members enacted statutes reducing the spiritual dues and scaling fees for proving wills to the means of the people. Clerks in minor orders lost the benefit of clergy in felony cases and were thus submitted to the mercy of the common law, as laymen had always been. Acts in 1529 and 1530 reformed abuses of nonresidence and

---

Thomas Cromwell and the English Reformation (London: Secker and Warburg, 1959); and A. J. Slavin, *Thomas Cromwell on Church and Commonwealth: Selected Letters, 1523–1540* (New York: Harper & Row, 1969). There is no study of Cromwell's ministry apart from Professor Elton's great book on *The Tudor Revolution in Government* (Cambridge: Cambridge University Press, 1953). I am at work on a study of Cromwell and the whole problem of the politics of the Reformation. *The Reformation Parliament*, by S. E. Lehmberg (Cambridge: Cambridge University Press, 1969), is also basic.

[6] See Chapters Five, Six, Nine, and Ten.

pluralities. In 1530, fifteen prelates received writs of praemunire for having aided Wolsey in exercising papal powers. This change was extended to the whole clergy in 1531, and they reacted like badly shaken men. The convocations of York and Canterbury paid £118,840 to the crown, by way of compounding for their crime. Next came Henry VIII's demand that he be acknowledged "Protector and Supreme Head" of the church, to which the clergy yielded.

These measures left clerical independence restricted but not abrogated. More, who was made chancellor in 1529, used his power to keep reform within the confines of doctrinal orthodoxy and communion with Rome. He feared heresy and schism equally. But the rise in influence of Thomas Cromwell in 1531 foreshadowed the defeat of the politics of amelioration and ecclesiastical independence. Cromwell's thoughts had taken shape in Wolsey's employment, where he managed the cardinal's monastic dissolutions and mastered many aspects of crown business, especially finance. Being a common lawyer, like More, this son of a Putney smith had had wide experience in commerce, had read law and given readings, and had acquired a direct knowledge of the politics and culture of the Italian Renaissance. He had also served in the 1523 Parliament, for which he prepared a brilliant speech in opposition to Henry VIII's French war. In 1529 he had survived his patron's fall and found a seat in Parliament.

His rise in Council thus derived from Henry VIII's direct experience of his utility and skill in government. But it is probably true that he had allied himself with the forces of popular religious dissent and anticlericalism well before 1529. There is evidence of his friendships in Lutheran circles as early as 1525. By 1529, his ideas were well enough developed for him to favor the radical *Supplication of the Commons Against the Ordinaries*. This document, which advocated the complete submission of the clergy and their power to the crown, survives in four drafts. Each bears Cromwell's hand in either text or emendations; when the *Supplication* failed to gain wide support in 1529, Cromwell seems to have kept it alive in court circles. In 1532 it was enacted over stout clerical opposition as their Submission.[7]

What had been an attack outside the orbit of the Council in 1529 became a radical fusion of unsatisfied anticlerical resentments and the needs of the king. Its indictment of the clergy required remedies that only the crown could administer. This fact the bishops correctly construed in their *Answer*, which so

---

[7] See Elton, "The Commons' Supplication of 1532: Parliamentary Manoeuvres in the Reign of Henry VIII," *EHR* (1951), LXVI, pp. 507–34; and the critique of J. P. Cooper, "The Supplication Against the Ordinaries Reconsidered," *EHR* (1957), LXXII, pp. 616–41; and M. Kelly, "The Submission of the Clergy," *TRHS* (1965), XV, pp. 97–119.

angered the king that he personally invited a Commons delegation to join their efforts to his own and so make the clergy more than "half his subjects." The *Supplication* became the main business of Parliament in the spring of 1532 and, after blunders and threats of praemunire against any cleric who maintained the independence of convocation or the courts Christian, the clergy made their Submission on May 15, 1532. This marked More's failure to keep the church independent. He resigned the next day. The first phase had ended.

Toward a New Church: Cromwell in Command

Cromwell now came to the fore and spelled out the implications of the Submission in a remarkable series of statutes enacted between 1532 and 1535.[8] The 1532 Act of Annates conditionally withheld from Rome certain taxes and forbade Roman bulls of consecration of bishops. It declared papal interdicts and excommunications of no effect. The 1533 Act in Restraint of Appeals abolished appeals from English courts to Roman ones, and its preamble proclaimed that England was a sovereign monarchy, a commonwealth in which laymen and clergy were equally subject to the laws of the realm and participant in their making. These acts were conditional, in the sense that final convocation of their clauses depended on Rome's actions and attitudes. When the Roman curia decided against Henry VIII, Cranmer used a clause of the appeals statute to give the king an English divorce from Queen Catherine.

In 1533 and 1534, the conditions attached to enforcing the restraint of Annates and appeals vanished. Episcopal elections were made by royal license only. The Dispensations Act gave to Canterbury the regulation of benefices and nonresidence. Another act provided that convocations of the clergy might legislate only with royal license. The Succession Act of 1534 declared Anne Boleyn to be Henry's only lawful wife and England's queen and made their children the only legitimate Tudor heirs, thus replacing Mary with Elizabeth. Another act of 1534 made it treasonous to defame Anne or her daughter or doubt their place in England's royal family. Oaths promising support of the Succession were taken from all officials.[9] The Act of Suprem-

---

[8] The studies of the legislation are chiefly by G. R. Elton. They are too numerous to be listed here but too important to be passed over: see items numbered 284–95, the critiques on 399–400 and 671–73, in Mortimer Levine, *Tudor England, 1485–1603* (Cambridge: Cambridge University Press, 1968), the Bibliographical Handbook compiled for the Conference on British Studies. Lehmberg's *The Reformation Parliament* is an able synthesis of this and other material.

[9] For the executions of More and Fisher and other consequences of the 1534 legislation, see Chapter Six.

acy then made perfectly manifest what the antecedent flurry of statutes was about:

Albeit the King's Majesty justly and rightfully is and oweth to be the supreme head of the Church of England, and so is recognized by the clergy of this realm in their convocations; yet . . . for corroboration and confirmation thereof, and for increase of virtue in Christ's religion within the realm of England, and to repress and extrip all heresies, errors, and other enormities. . . . Be it enacted by authority of this present Parliament that the King our Sovereign lord . . . shall be taken, accepted and reputed the only supreme head in earth of the Church of England called Anglicana Ecclesia . . . and shall have full power and authority from time to time to visit, repress, redress, reform, order, correct, restrain and amend all such errors . . . which ought or may lawfully be reformed. . . .[1]

This statute thus looked backward, to the constitutional revolution it capped and summarized, and forward, to the revolution not yet achieved. It quite explicitly promised the realization of the third tenet of Henry's Reformation, the reform of religious life and the royal responsibility for it. For it was an essential principle of the revolution that doctrinal and liturgical disputes were subject to the authority of the crown. The Act of Supremacy in fact took this as much for granted as it did the supreme headship itself. Parliament had not created these tenets; it had only recognized existing facts, which Henry VIII proved by his most significant consequent action.

He named Thomas Cromwell his vicegerent, giving him all the powers of the Supremacy and the authority to move from the break with Rome toward a reformed church. This commission was given not later than December 1534, although we do not know its exact date.[2] More vital is the fact that in it Cromwell and the agents he appointed were given full powers to reform the "lamentable corruption" of the church and its rules. In fact, the commission gave Cromwell powers to supplant the bishops and their courts, nominate prelates, visit all ecclesiastical institutions, punish offenders, make deprivations, fill vacancies, issue injunctions, and correct the manners and morals of clergy and laymen alike. Not even Wolsey's combined powers as chancellor and legate had been that broad. It is hard to discern how Cromwell's powers could have been made broader, or how he could have used them more vigorously than he did between 1535 and his execution for treason in 1540.

In September 1535, Cromwell sent orders to the bishops inhibiting them from exercising the powers delegated to the king's vicegerent. No action

---

[1] 26 Henry VIII, c. 1.

[2] It was not enrolled. Several drafts survive in the British Museum, as well as an instrument made under the powers given to Cromwell, dated December 19, 1534. See S. E. Lehmberg, "Supremacy and Vicegerency. A Re-examination," EHR (1961), LXXXI, pp. 225–35.

better illustrates his responsibility for reformation or better justifies our insistence on seeing his genius at work in the heroic days of the Reformation. He stamped his mark on the Anglican Church and the English commonwealth in the furnace itself, when the metal was at white heat, and paid the price of his labors in 1540. Before his fall, he began the process of religious revolution in at least four significant ways. He radically revised the finances of the crown and religious life by suppressing the monasteries. He visited the secular clergy and gave reform injunctions to them. He began the transformation of liturgy and worship. And he became the great patron of the English Bible. A sketch of these achievements closes this account of the onset of the Reformation in England.

Where the acts touching annates had converted a Roman tax into an English revenue, other measures attacking church wealth soon followed.[3] The Act of First Fruits and Tenths, in 1534, made over to the crown the first year's clear value of all benefices, while imposing an annual income tax of 10 percent of the clear value of any preferment. Special commissioners assessed clerical incomes under an order issued by Cromwell early in 1535. The crown was soon aware that Cromwell's statute added enormously to its annual income, since more than £25,000 in tenths alone was forthcoming. Existing agencies could not cope adequately with the new cash revenues along the lines adopted to deal, principally through the chamber, with earlier augmentations of its estates. The solution lay in the erection of a new treasury, with its own officers and jurisdiction. The Court of First Fruits and Tenths grew out of this office and received parliamentary recognition in a statute of 1540. Thus began Cromwell's revolutionary financial reforms. Between 1535 and 1540, the crown realized £406,415 in first fruits and tenths.

If Cromwell's actions in 1535 were clearly anticipated in a stream of memoranda calling for new fiscal agencies and economic retrenchment (1532–4), the importance of this first step pales when compared to the next one. In the last session of the Reformation Parliament, an act was passed to dissolve monasteries and another to set up a court to handle the rich resources of the religious houses. This was only the beginning of a policy of placing under the control of the Court of Augmentations all property, franchises, and jurisdictions held by religious corporations. In 1540 and 1545, further acts dealt with colleges, chapels, chantries, and hospitals. The resultant departmental proliferation

---

[3] For the creation of new agencies to handle ecclesiastical wealth coming to the crown, see W. C. Richardson, *Tudor Chamber Administration* and G. R. Elton, *The Tudor Revolution in Government*, as well as Richardson's *The History of the Court of Augmentations* (Baton Rouge: Louisiana State University Press, 1962). For the consolidation of the administration of feudal revenues on departmental lines, see Joel Hurstfield, *The Queen's Wards* (London: Jonathan Cape, 1958). Professor Richardson is at work on a history of the Court of First Fruits and Tenths.

transformed the economy of the crown and the system of revenue administration. It made obsolete the great achievements of chamber administration, just as the influx of lands and casual revenues had relegated the Exchequer to a subordinate role under York and Henry.

It also swept away a vast segment of the possessioner church. The process began when Cromwell was made vicegerent. Long devoted to the secularization of church property, Cromwell had appointed visitors to survey the monastic houses in 1535. Their reports, the infamous *comperta*, exposed to parliamentary scrutiny the "vicious, carnal, and abominable living" cited in the act, which gave to the king the property of all houses with annual income of less than £200 net expenses. Exemptions were given to sixty-seven of the 304 lesser houses covered in the 1536 statute, but by 1540 voluntary surrenders and a second suppressive statute ended regular religion in England. This was clearly the most visible aspect of the changes that overtook the church in the 1530s. The total suppression derived in part from the government's desire to add to its wealth. But the gentry and other groups in society were avid for this wealth as well, and few defenders of the religious sat in Parliament.

Yet in our present concerns these questions are less vital than two others: the constitutional consequences of the Dissolution and its fiscal effects. The 1535 inquiries and 1536 execution of decisions show decisively how Henry VIII's government was able to climax the process of centralizing the monarchy and reducing franchised power in England. In four years a transfer of about one-quarter of England's landed property was accomplished, and agencies to deal with resultant problems proliferated. There were surprisingly few problems, as Augmentations began immediately to govern real and movable property and the litigation growing out of the transfer. The chief agents of the court were Cromwellians, men he could rely on to wield their great powers to the advantage of the crown. The total net receipts of the new court in the first eight years of operation were £899,120, an average of about £112,400 a year.

The crown's victory was complete when it successfully put down the Pilgrimage of Grace in late 1536–7. The northern magnates saw their estates diminished and their franchises appropriated. The church disgorged a great part of its wealth, and monastic franchises vanished forever. The political power balance was radically altered by the disappearance of priors and abbots from Parliament. And the crown was suddenly wealthy beyond imagination after a history of relentless struggles against its pauper backgrounds. Yet, it is arguable that this profound revolution in the constitution, finances, landed wealth, and techniques of government was not the most significant of Cromwell's reformation measures.[4]

[4] On some consequences of this revolution, see Chapter Five.

He had the close support of a remarkable circle of Erasmian humanists, Lutherans, and radical anticlericals in carrying out a religious revolution. The Erasmian element included Richard Taverner, Richard Morison, Thomas Starkey, and Thomas Elyot. Among the secular-minded reformers were legal and social writers: John Hales, Clement Armstrong, Christopher St. German, and William Marshall. And then there were the leading English Lutherans— apart from the exile William Tyndale and the early martyrs, Frith, Roye, and Joye: Miles Coverdale, Sir Francis Bigod, John Hales, Robert Barnes, Hugh Latimer, John Hooper, William Jerome, and James Garrett, all of whom— except Hales—paid the martyr's price after 1540. But the chief prop of this work and of its continuation after 1540 was Cranmer, a donnish man who had enjoyed a quiet Cambridge career before Barnes led him toward Lutheran views and the king's divorce took him to court.

These friends and allies channeled ideas to the people through the press, where its revolutionary force could best harness the popular support for reform. Under the aegis of Cromwell, they wrote on ecclesiastical polity, welfare reforms, what to do with the monasteries and their wealth, iconoclasm, celibacy, popular devotion, superstitious abuses of religion, the hurt of sedition, and the reform of doctrine. Most of them exalted scriptures over tradition. All accepted the Supremacy and prompted its chief agent to use his powers widely. They thus gave further momentum to movements of popular opinion and helped reshape Christian religious life and social myths when it became certain that the Reformation would alter more than property relations and asymmetries in lay-clerical power.

In 1536, Cromwell and Cranmer began the stream of formularies of the faith on which later settlements rested.[5] *The Bishop's Book* (1537) rested on *The Ten Articles of 1536*. Both works bore a marked resemblance to the classic formulas of Lutheranism—the Augsburg Confession (1530) and Melanchthon's explication of it, the 1531 *Apologia*. Although ambiguous on many points, the 1536 articles demanded belief in only three sacraments: baptism, penance, and communion. There was no prescription in favor of transubstantiation or purgatory or prayers for the dead. The central Lutheran point of theology—justification by faith—was put forward in a delicate way that minimized the whole notion of good works as efficacious for salvation. There was a Protestant distinction between "true" Sacraments—those with a clear scrip-

---

[5] See C. Butterworth, *The English Primers, 1529–1545* (Philadelphia: Scribners, 1953); C. W. Dugmore, *The Mass and the English Reformers* (London: Macmillan, 1958); C. Hardwick, *A History of the Articles of Religion* (Cambridge: Cambridge University Press, 1859); Millar Maclure, *The Paul's Cross Sermons* (Toronto: Toronto University Press, 1958); H. R. Willoughby, *The First Authorized English Bible and the Cranmer Preface* (Chicago: University of Chicago Press, 1942); Horton Davies, *Worship and Theology in England*, I, 1534–1603 (Princeton: Princeton University Press, 1920); and Jasper Ridley, *Thomas Cranmer* (Oxford: Oxford University Press, 1962).

tural sign and a promise of grace—and merely "traditional" rites not so supported in the Bible.

These advanced propositions were to some extent compromised in 1537; and a reaction against them certainly set in with the *Six Articles* of 1539, in which the lost articles were found again. But as we shall see in the conflicts of the next thirty years, these "reactions" were unable to reverse what had been set in motion or stop at the halfway point the descent of Rome's power in England. Cranmer had begun to change Henry VIII's mind on oral confession, confirmation, the special grace conferred on priests at ordination, and even the Mass itself. Together with Cromwell, he began the downgrading of sacramental celebration and the uplifting of preaching the Word—in which consists the fundamental difference between Catholic and Protestant worship.

However, the intellectual revolution implied in formularies was nothing without power. And power Cromwell both had and used. Almost as soon as he had issued letters inhibiting the bishops in their supervision of the parishes, he showed the scope of his intentions. In 1535, he drafted a set of injunctions for the regular clergy that Dom David Knowles considered a radical call to return to the spirit of Gregorian reform. When bishops complained about his intentions, Cromwell answered that his work pertained to his office under God and the king. Moreover, it was manifest in his correspondence that he wanted to bring home the meaning of the Supremacy to prelates and parish priests:

If they had any jurisdiction, they must needs have received it either by the law of God, or by the bishop of Rome's authority, or else by the king's gracious permission.

So wrote two of Cromwell's agents to the vicegerent, discussing the right they had to visit and reform clergymen. They advised their master to show that no scripture allowed clerical jurisdiction and to permit those who would claim Rome's warrant to do so if they thought it convenient to take the consequences. What followed from the argument was a draft scheme according to which the vicegerent's power would first be shown in a far-reaching reform of the courts Christian and canon law. There is evidence of an immediate start in legal reform, although it never came to fruition in Cromwell's time. The agenda of reforms touched on lay grievances unredressed by statutes: removing tithe cases and the probate of wills from clerical courts, providing for a review of marriage law, and providing a civil lawyer to advise the vicegerent on such matters. This last reform was achieved when Dr. William Petre became Cromwell's deputy in 1536; he presided over the Canterbury convocation to settle any doubts about his role. So great became the power of the vicegerent that bishops had to get his permission to visit parishes in their diocese, even after the first inhibitions had succeeded in suspending and demonstrating the dependency of episcopal powers.

But the most conclusive demonstration of Cromwell's powers to reform the church took the form of two sets of "injunctions" to the clergy of England and Wales issued in 1536 and 1538. The first of these dealt with the *Ten Articles* and the banning of certain superstitious practices. There was great stress placed on the rudiments of Christian education and belief: the teaching of the creeds, paternoster, and the commandments in English. Priests were instructed to share this burden openly with laymen, especially parents and masters over apprentices. Priests were given the power to withhold the sacraments from persons unfit to receive them by virtue of their ignorance of the faith. Admonition against idols, relics, pilgrimages, and contrived "miracles" were common themes in 1536 and 1538.

The stress on education showed in other respects. A better-educated clergy was an object close to the heart of the reform intended in 1536 and 1538. Both sets of orders required that wealthy benefices contribute to the support of grammar-school pupils and university scholars. The tenths of colleges were to be remitted, provided that the funds were used to endow public lectures to advance worship and comprehension of the faith. These measures were combined with disciplinary ones, especially restrictions on nonresidence. Those who were able to gain licenses had to give 20 percent of their income for fabric maintenance, thus putting an end to some of the worst features of the careerism that drained parochial funds and scandalized the poorer parishes.

When the 1536 warnings against vain practices were not heeded, Cromwell licensed preachers to give quarterly sermons on Biblical religion; priests were ordered to lecture publicly on the vanity of old practices. Those who would not were heavily fined. And the vicegerent also commissioned men to pull down miracle-working statues and pilgrim shrines, an icon-smashing campaign that has yet to be properly studied as a force shaping Protestant worship in the 1530s. The 1538 injunctions also required every parish to begin recording baptisms, marriages, and deaths. These registers were to be admissible as evidence in law courts, partly to protect parishioners against the oppressive practice by which remote relatives who married each other were fined for marrying within degrees of kinship forbidden in church law. But it was also Cromwell's hope to put government on a better footing through the keeping of accurate records. The convenience of such records for governors and the governed, in a village society lacking them, is difficult for us to grasp, but even the registers helped to reduce tensions at the parish level. They did so by providing a record admissible in courts of common law, establishing the facts of marriages, divorces, legitimacy, and therefore questions of property and other material issues.

What was perhaps closest to Cromwell's central purpose as vicegerent was making the Bible available to Englishmen in their own tongue.[6] The laws of the realm had been Englished in his circle early in the 1530s. And from 1527 on, he had shown a keen interest in the work of Miles Coverdale and Tyndale, the two great Lutheran translators who pioneered vernacular scripture. The 1536 injunctions had implied the future licensing of an authorized version. Then, in 1538, the hints that the "spiritual food of man's soul" was to be distributed took concrete form. A circular letter was sent to all the bishops, ordering them to establish a date for setting up an English Bible in every parish church; the injunction of that year spelled this out to the clergy as a whole.

The orders meant little without an English Bible to distribute. So Cromwell set Miles Coverdale to work on a translation.[7] He was a graceful writer and familiar with Luther's work and Tyndale's prohibited, polemical versions. Later in 1536 there appeared an English version by Coverdale, and in 1537 a text sponsored by Cranmer—the so-called Matthew Bible. Although neither had royal support, Cromwell assumed the risk of licensing this frankly Lutheran translation. Cromwell resolved the situation in 1538 by arranging a Paris printing of a new text under the supervision of Coverdale and several English printers. The work went forward from June until December, when the French Inquisitor-General seized it. Cromwell, who had £400 of his own money invested, protested to no avail. Then, in one of the most mysterious episodes of the era, he apparently arranged to have part of the printing smuggled into England in wine kegs. Technical evidence shows beyond doubt that the "Great Bible" of 1539 was compiled from Parisian and London pages. A little later than expected, it was given to Englishmen in accordance with the 1538 injunctions.

The initiative, financing, political and diplomatic machinations, and motive force of the so-called Cranmer Bible were in fact the vicegerent's. Holbein's woodcut frontispiece represents the truth in that regard: Cranmer takes it from Cromwell and gives it to the king. The king gives it to a waiting people! Along with the printers, formularies, and injunctions, this Bible was Cromwell's legacy and the testimony to his pursuit of a reformed religion. His object was that of raising men up from clerical domination to the freedom of a reformed commonwealth. Whether he was a Lutheran or an Erasmian, a cynical

---

[6] T. W. Whitley, *The English Bible Under the Tudor Sovereigns* (London: Macmillan, 1937); S. L. Greenslade, *The Work of William Tyndale* (London: Blackie and Son, 1938); J. F. Mozley, *Coverdale and His Bibles* (London: Lutterworth Press, 1953); H. Guppy, "The Royal 'Injunctions' of 1538 and the 'Great Bible,'" *BJRL* (1938), XXII, pp. 31–71.

[7] Coverdale had been driven into exile, along with Tyndale, by Henry VIII. Tyndale's opposition to the divorce led Henry VIII to hunt him down and secure his execution in 1535. Cromwell interceded for Coverdale, as he had done earlier for Tyndale, this time successfully.

HENRY VII GIVING THE BIBLE TO HIS PEOPLE.

This Holbein woodcut was the frontispiece for the 1541 edition of the Great Bible. Courtesy the British Museum.

anticlerical or a radical reformer, is unimportant. The evidence and effect of his ministry transcend labels, as does his last great speech on reformation, which he gave in Parliament two months before his arrest for heresy and treason. In it he told the Lords and Commons of his wish to see a Biblical religion flourish, free of sectarian excess and the crushing weight of clerical persecutions.

He had used his power to link together popular dissent, humanist criticism, and Lutheran notions of worship and doctrine. His ministry founded the Anglican Church and set it on the road between Rome and Geneva. In its origins the church was comprehensive and tolerant, grounded on scripture, conservative of what was useful in tradition, yet harsh toward loyalties that extended beyond the waters that were England's "moat defensive." The processes of change he aided in the 1530s were irreversible, once men had learned Coverdale's lovely cadences and Cranmer's liturgies, once they had heard the evangels in their mother tongue and knew by heart Paul's letters. Thus it made little difference that Henry VIII put "paid" to the account by executing Cromwell in 1540. The Reformation was well launched, and in its wake revolutionary crisis was the normal condition of the mid–Tudor polity. The forces of reaction, however, could no more prevail against it than could Rome against the Hell within its own gates.

Chapter Five
THE WALL
OF AUTHORITY
BROKEN

The heavens themselves, the planets and this center
Observe degree, priority and place. . . .
Take but degree away, untune that string,
and hark! what discord follows.

SHAKESPEARE

Troilus and Cressida, Act I

The specter of rebellion haunted England for four decades. It wore the cloak of religion. It filled the heads of Englishmen with the dread of anarchy and the presses with a vast literature on the virtues of obedience. Where rebels were lacking, plotters thrived, weaving together the threads of a tapestry whose central theme was the permanent crisis created in society by the newfangled royal supremacy and all its works. Englishmen were denied the chance to enlarge in peace the compact Reformation of the 1530s. Magistrates saw in every dark corner of the kingdom the ghost of the German Peasants' War, in which the commoners had risen hydra-headed from every defeat and skirmish.

The 1525 riots of tax-resisters in Kent and East Anglia were said to be linked with the spread of German heresies. From that time until the late 1560s, English writers of every religious opinion shared the notion that heresy and rebellion were twins spawned by new religious ideas and by the resentments of the poor. Sir Thomas More had said so in 1523, when his *Responsio ad Lutherum* warned against perverters of the gospel. Henry VIII himself had insisted to his princely Saxon "cousin," Duke George, that heretics lied "to incite the people against their princes." John Fisher had preached and printed great sermons denouncing those murderous commons whose victims "numbered above 100,000, as credably and faythfully reported." Ten years later, Thomas Starkey hoped the German horror would be an example to the English and would minister to them "no small instruction" on the danger of diverse sects in one commonwealth. His *Exhortation to the People* fell on deaf ears north of the Trent, however, for in the year 1536, while visitors were beginning to execute the suppression orders in monasteries of Lincoln and York, riot grew into rebellion, threatening a revolution.[1]

---

[1] On the actual course of the great revolts *c.* 1536–53 and the prevailing doctrines of obedience, see:

The Pilgrimage of Grace brought home the German experience, so vividly as to overshadow it completely. Minor revolts followed in 1538, 1541, and 1543. And then, in 1549, the whole country was shaken by the wave of revolts known as the Prayer Book Rising and Ket's Rebellion. Bishop Stephan Gardiner, echoing More's grim warning of 1523, prophesied to Archbishop Cranmer that "if the wall of authority . . . be once broken, and new water let in at a little gap, the vehemence of novelty will flow further than your grace would admit." Where common men thought they could prevail in religion, he warned, civil wars of peasants and the old English curse of noble factions were likely to triumph.[2] Whatever contemporaries thought of the bishop's analysis, the Somerset and Northumberland coups in Edward VI's reign, the Dudley and Wyatt revolts against Mary Tudor, and the related risings of the northern earls against Elizabeth prevented the issue from being moot for three decades running.

Even the mere recital of this sequence of blows to the alleged Tudor peace raises the question: What, if anything, links the repeated crises? This question prompts others. If between 1536 and 1570 social order was nearly overthrown by a concatenation of religious, political, and economic ills, how can we account for the appearance of stability in the silver age of Elizabeth I's middle years? To what extent did government and society live again in that precarious balance upset by Henry VIII's Reformation policies?

The declaration of independence from Rome in 1533 was as fundamental in the shaping of England's history as the Declaration of Independence was in American history and the Declaration of the Rights of Man was in French history. From it derived those measures that transformed the business of the king's government and made politics something they had never been before. Before the Reformation there had been only a blurred distinction between government and politics. The "politicians" were the body of persons charged by the king to run the government. No notion of legitimate opposition existed. But there were no remedies for bad government except revolt or urgent appeals to the crown to let go the corrupt politicians and make the stream of justice pure again. These were means enough to reconcile the formal elements of government and the stuff of government, the legal order and that ready war of patrons and clients, in service to the crown.

Robert P. Adams, *The Better Part of Valor* (Seattle: Washington University Press, 1952); Franklin L. V. Baumer, *The Early Tudor Theory of Kingship* (New Haven: Yale University Press, 1940); A. B. Ferguson, *The Articulate Citizen of the English Renaissance* (Durham, North Carolina: Duke University Press, 1965); A. Fletcher, *Tudor Rebellions* (London: Longmans, 1968); Ruth and Madeleine Dodds, *The Pilgrimage of Grace . . . and the Exeter Conspiracy*, 2 vols. (Cambridge: Cambridge University Press, 1915); S. T. Bindoff, *Ket's Rebellion* (London: Smith, Elder & Co., 1949); F. Rose-Troup, *The Western Rebellion of 1549* (London: Longmans, 1913).

[2] Gardiner noted that course of events in Germany: *de bello civili rusticorum . . . in bello civili nobilium.*

We have stressed the success of Yorkist and Tudor efforts to convert political energy into a steady source of governmental power. Now we must stress how events between about 1530 and 1570 promoted a shift in power from the monarch to his aristocracy, at the same time augmenting the corporate power of the crown. For the most important of the unintended consequences of the Henrician Reformation was the completion of a parliamentary aristocracy with a political will and power of its own. The meaning of the transformation was not readily visible before 1570. But the facts behind the profound change in political life lay scattered about the kingdom like pearls on a queen's gown—especially in the northern shires.

Revolt in the North: Pilgrims of Grace

Cromwell had sent three government commissions into Lincolnshire in September 1536: one to dissolve the smaller monasteries; another to assess and collect a parliamentary subsidy; and a third to inquire into the fitness of the secular clergy. Men of the shire viewed with alarm too much government in the best of times. In that season, rumors about Cromwell's intentions regarding religion, bad harvests, drought, and questions of a more local nature caused many to think they "should be endone forever." On October 3, some reacted by beating to death the bishop's chancellor at a place he had come to for the purpose of visiting the local clergy. They followed Captain Cobbler and the shoemaker Nicholas Melton. Their outburst signaled a general rising. By the fifth of the month, over 10,000 were in arms; the commons were forcing gentry and monks to run with them in fear for their lives and goods. At Horncastle, the rebels took from the church an old banner of the five wounds of Christ, the chalice, and the Host, proclaiming their cause was Christ's. To these they added a plow and a horn, the one certainly a reminder of hurtful enclosures, the other a mark of either their civic pride or their resentment over a rumored tax on cattle.

The king sent the duke of Suffolk to receive the Lincoln rebels' grievances. Meanwhile, Robert Aske heard of the events in Lincolnshire. He soon took the rebels' oath, abandoned his plans to attend the Michaelmas law term in London, and began to organize the commons at Beverley, in Yorkshire. Aske sent letters throughout his native shire, recruiting men to the cause of God, king, and commonwealth. His messages and proclamations spoke of the rising as a pilgrimage. Men from the Yorkshire Ridings and textile towns joined. York City yielded in mid-October. This made it apparent in London that both the regime and the dynasty were in jeopardy.

Articles and plans skillfully drawn up by Aske and other captains helped spread the revolt. Nuns were restored in the York house of St. Clements. The North Riding groups spoiled the bishop of Durham's palace and besieged the loyal earl of Cumberland at Skipton Castle. The revolt spread to Lancashire, where the crown received loyal support from the earl of Derby. Elsewhere, Hull surrendered, and Carlisle was menaced by popular leaders, captains Faith, Charity, Poverty, and Pity. Suffolk was kept busy in Lincolnshire. Lord Darcy, the key to the far North, lay helpless in Pontefract Castle. Royal forces under the earl of Shrewsbury had not moved from Nottingham. Only three towns east of the Pennines (Skipton, Newcastle, and Scarborough) were in royalist hands!

By October 20, the government had evolved a strategy for dealing with the rebels. This involved sending agents to Doncaster for negotiations, thus dividing the pilgrim camps on the question of whether or not to give up the initiative that lay with their disciplined force of 30,000 and posing a choice between the pilgrim's oath and the allegiance men owed their king. The effect was to divide the gentry and the commons. On November 20, Henry VIII made a harsh reply to the pilgrims' petitions, blaming their rising on rumors and false grounds. The duke of Norfolk urged him to take a conciliatory stand, saying that promises so made could be slenderly kept. The Pontefract council committed the rebels to negotiations, the commons, clergy, and gentry having assembled in what was in effect a rebel parliament. They sent to the colloquy at Doncaster ten knights, ten squires, and twenty "commons"; there the king's lieutenant promised pardons, a free Parliament, reconsideration of the Dissolution, and the preservation of religion.

Henry's policy had succeeded. Despite new risings in the East Riding under the Protestant Sir Francis Bigod and widespread disorder in the Northumbrian shires, the royal forces put into effect the king's vengeance. Martial law was established. Some 216 men were executed, among them Aske and other "pardoned" leaders and many gentry, especially Sir Thomas Percy, Sir Stephen Hammerton, Lord Darcy, and Sir Francis Bigod. The North had been tamed, at least temporarily.

Yet the question remains: What had motivated the risings? Aske said the gentry feared that the suppression of monasteries would destroy "the whole religion" in England. Others—Percy, for example—had mainly secular motives, hidden in the monk's cowl. The popular rebel ballads failed to distinguish causes, voicing instead the fears of men who saw in the threat to the church a threat to poor men who looked to the abbeys for relief. Wealthy officials mourned the loss of a much-exploited social institution.

Thus the Suppression seemed the chief cause of the "pilgrimage." Every set of rebel articles demanded a repeal of the Suppression Act of 1536. Sixteen of fifty-five houses were reoccupied by monks and nuns during the risings, despite the frightened apathy of many regulars. Moreover, rebels burned the English New Testament, listened readily to clerical condemnations of novel doctrines at Pontefract, castigated "Protestant" bishops and their lay patrons (Cromwell especially), grumbled over the suspension of old rituals and saints' days, and in many other ways gave evidence of their concern for religion. Widespread clerical attacks on the Supremacy found an echo in the Pontefract articles: "It is in all men's mouths that the Supremacy should sound to be a measure of a division from the unity of the Catholic church." In fact, there had already been over 300 prosecutions under the 1534 Treasons Act, chiefly for words against the Supremacy.

Nor were secular complaints few. The rebels disliked taxes about as much as the priests disliked royal visitations. The subsidy act in 1534 was revolutionary; it had extended to peacetime the experiments Wolsey had justified by French wars, arguing the novel basis of the civil benefits conferred by a newly vigorous government. The Yorkshire marshes and dales of the West Riding knew little of such benefits and much of poverty, however. Their resistance met with support among the commons from Holland in Lincolnshire and from the border shires as well. Since less than 1.4 percent of the northern population was liable for taxation under the assessment of 1534, popular resistance there appears to reflect a general hostility to southern interference in northern society. Rumor had it that Henry VIII was richer than Croesus. Riot had doubled his fortune, rebellion had trebled it, and the force of resentment had made it into a peerless treasure. Yet tax piled on tax.

The admixture of religious and economic grievances among the commons had its counterpart among their social superiors. The gentry resented the trial of a whole Yorkshire grand jury for wrongful acquittal of a murderer. They heard of the alleged rapacity of the royal visitors. They were in arms over the Statute of Uses. The shabby treatment of Princess Mary had confused the succession. It even was rumored that Henry would bring Cromwell into the line. More earthbound was Aske's fear that, should Mary not succeed, Henry might invite the Scottish claimants descended from his sister Margaret. The very stones in the streets of border villages would rise on that note.

These grievances were political in character, as were others reflecting northern particularism. There were demands for judicial decentralization, as well as charges that Cromwell muzzled and misled Parliament and that the community of the realm was being made to dance, puppetlike, to an upstart's tune.[3] What the Percies and Tempests disliked was the threat to their good lordship inherent in old policies now brought to ripeness in the great Reformation

[3] Cromwell's policies, their background, and their impact on northern society are fully examined in W. Gordon Zeeveld, *Foundations of Tudor Policy* (London: Methuen, 1948); A. J. Slavin, *Thomas Cromwell on Church and Commonwealth* (New York: Harper & Row, 1969); M. E. James, *Change and Continuity in the Tudor North* (York: St. Anthony's Press, 1965); and James's *A Tudor Magnate and the Tudor State* (York: Borthwick Institute, 1966).

statutes. This threat was a deep, festering sore in the aristocratic body politic, and it was the spot at which gentry and commons solidarity weakened. It also showed the political nature of the crisis most clearly.

The upper aristocracy of lords and great gentry in Yorkshire's West Riding, Northumberland, and Cumberland were the most ruthless and oppressive landlords of the North. The Percies and the Cliffords levied the heaviest fines on new entries and made changes in tenancies to augment the profits of estate management. The earl of Cumberland was a notorious rack-renter. In the West Riding, tax records testify to deep peasant poverty and also show the dominance of ecclesiastical and aristocratic lordship. The duke of Norfolk, a man unmoved by the hardship of peasant life on his own East Anglian estates, reported in 1537 how desperately poor the lake counties were (an observation with the ring of truth even in 1937[4]). The area had declined steadily in wealth since the fourteenth century.

Hence there was talk in the lake country of killing priests and gentry. The commons of Westmorland petitioned to abolish the tithe, and they seemed strongly anticlerical in other matters. The cloth towns resented legislation that tightened London's grip on England's commerce. From west of the Pennines, peasant petitioners constantly sought royal protection from noble enclosers, a reminder that the menace of enclosure had lingered somewhat longer in the North. These causes undermined rebel solidarity. They pitted commons against lords, as can be seen in article nine of the Pontefract Manifesto, which held that tenant rights should be allowed and that peasants should have the right of succession in family lands without unreasonable fines.

Whatever the religious occasions of the risings, it takes no profound social sense to see that the various classes of men met the Supremacy on different grounds. Lord Darcy brought with him the banners left over from his 1511 campaign against the Moors in Spain—a real pilgrim's crusade—and Sir Francis Bigod had enjoyed Cromwell's patronage and had advocated putting down the religious houses. The Pilgrimage of Grace was the greatest challenge to the Tudor dynasty, but only because it represented more than a crisis of conscience for conservative men. What was at stake in the winter of 1536–7 was the crown's drive to centralize power and to subordinate the regions to the center. That the risings assumed a special character in the North was not, however, an accident. For the Supremacy was bound to dismay most those whose positions were least comprehended in the traditional administrative arrangements of the South.

Despite the largely successful struggle of the crown with its rivals in the North, the traditional ethos of "good lordship" still linked the gentry and

---

[4] See the moving descriptions in Melvyn Bragg's autobiographical novel, *A Place in England* (New York: Knopf, 1970).

the magnates there. The crown appeared less as the upholder of the rule of law against feudal anarchy than as a power seeking to advance its own interests by attracting to its service exactly the sort of violent men patronized and supported by the Percies and Cliffords. This policy had encouraged faction, since it disrupted relationships between lords and their fee'd men and violated the ethos of service in return for support, protection, and rewards—the essence of good lordship.

What Henry VIII had sought in the North in the time of Wolsey was the substitution of crown lordship for that of the earls. Men who had participated in Percy's authority had done so because that authority was the keystone of the structure of order in provinces that were distantly "under the king." Such service was natural, sanctioned by time, motivated by accustomed fees and duties. The "Tudor peace" had neither displaced this relationship nor entirely discredited it, despite efforts to depict as anarchists those lords who were out of favor with the crown. In the North, the humanist doctrines of an order reaching down from God in heaven to the king on his throne seemed remote. The border shires especially were still rude and archaic; there, men like the Percy dependent Sir William Lisle, threatened by Wolsey with a seizure of property, swore, "By God's Blood, there is neither king nor his officers that shall make any distress on my ground. . . ."

Sir William's case in the 1520s had reminded London how dependent it was on the earl of Northumberland. Both Wolsey and Cromwell learned a lesson from it: the center would not prevail fully against the region unless the crown's resources there were fully mobilized to demonstrate the dispensability of the magnates. Moreover, the earls were able to lead the North against the South, as they had done in 1215 and 1460. If government was not to remain a dialogue between regional powers and the crown, the estates and dignity of the earls had to be degraded. Hence the necessity of those underground struggles of the 1520s and 1530s. Hence, also, the fury with which they came to light in 1536. Henry VIII was pursuing contradictory policies: an adventuresome foreign policy of French and Scottish wars, which thrust forward the militant earls, and a campaign to reduce the influence of those same earls!

The conflicts of Tudor and Percy or Tudor and Clifford—with the alignments of dependent families and the internal rivalries of the aristocracy— provided the main motifs of change and continuity in northern society. The wardens were recruited from the heads of great families (Percy, Clifford, Dacre), and they in turn ruled "graynes," or clans of feuding dependents. Loyalty was introverted. The great lords had strong ties with the upland clans and were also influential in monasteries and cathedrals. To break these circles, Wolsey had initiated the policy of securing Percy lands. Cromwell continued it with steady purpose in the West March, whetting the appetites of the men of small standing who stood to flourish on the ruins of Percy's power. Elsewhere, the Dacres and Cliffords were played off against each other. The Dissolution served the same ends.

Perhaps the success of this policy can best be seen in the case of Sir Thomas Wharton, a Percy lieutenant and steward of the minor gentry who rose in estate management. Although Wharton remained personally faithful to the sixth earl of Northumberland, he also was in league with other gentry who had come up the same way. They had arraigned Lord Dacre on charges of treason in 1534. The Curwens, Musgraves, Carnabys, and Lowthers, together with the Whartons, were supported by the crown as challengers to the lords. The half-dozen years before the Pilgrimage were thus a time of great changes in the pattern of power in the Marches.

Among the greater lords, Dacre and Clifford emerged from the rebellion with a reputation for loyalty and with their power intact. The Percies, on the other hand, were deeply implicated in the rebels' cause. Wharton managed to refuse the pilgrims' requests for help while keeping faith with Northumberland, despite the earl's support of Aske. The Eures, Carnabys, Lowthers, and Musgraves were staunchly loyalist.

Cromwell had aided the second rank of northern aristocrats in the power game. When peace was restored, he urged the king to take advantage of the Percy disgrace and the strains among peasants, gentry, and earls. Clifford was thus made a court dependent, honored with the Garter and with marriage to Henry VIII's niece. But his wardenship of the West March was weakened by the appointment of Wharton as his deputy. The gentry who had fees were specifically placed under Wharton's command. Meanwhile, the duke of Norfolk saw in Percy's disgrace and death on July 2, 1537, the chance to carve out a northern base equal to his native East Anglian one. He drew a rebuke from Cromwell and the Council, however, as it became obvious that king and minister were determined to reconstruct the North and its council with gentry rather than the lords. Wharton knew he owed his deputyship to Cromwell's determination to use the rebellion to advance the crown's strength. This he stated clearly, by contrasting the days before the rebellion with those afterward: it had been "A Dacre, a Dacre, a Clifford, a Clifford," and now it was only "A king, a king." When the childless Percy made Henry VIII the legatee of his lands, the slow revolution in favor of royal power was completed. Seven years later, in 1544, Wharton and Eure were made wardens of the Marches in their own right, with peerages to boot.

The events of 1536–7 were thus linked to the old campaign to break the secular and religious franchises and bind the regions to the center. They were also linked to the new men whose titles of nobility signaled their rise and the crown's successful ambition to rule through men of its own making. The

Whartons became a great political dynasty. Interest, inclination, and religion drew them toward careers of service. A single lifetime had been enough to accumulate a vast fortune, a peerage, high office, great lands—largely crown gifts out of dissolved monasteries—and a network of important marriage alliances. These enabled Sir Thomas to found a free school at Kirkby Stephen, formerly a parcel of St. Mary's Abbey, York, where Erasmian and Protestant ideas flowed into the culture of a region once swayed by monks.

Wharton's success was thus an omen in his society. Other families rose to affluence on monastic spoils. In fact, the Dissolution allowed some reconstruction of the landed classes in that conservative area; and this was done to advance those who gave loyal service to the crown. The avenues thus opened were broader than those paved by magnates.[5] The great houses could regard Wharton as a parvenu—as indeed the Dacres did—seeing in him the radical upstart who had overthrown the traditions of good lordship.

This success merely personalized a social movement that was larger than the northern rivalries and tumults. In mid-Tudor society, the ongoing crisis appeared in other regions and with different actors. We can see how the Pilgrimage and Wharton's career merely represented a shift in power within the traditional governing class and the rise of new elements within it. Changes in religion, culture, the economy, and politics had joined together in a way that had allowed striking enterprises, but had also nearly dissolved society. In the crisis some leaped the barriers of traditional society. Others manned them against the consequences of the Tudor Supremacy.

The Last Years of Henry VIII

If the Pilgrimage was in part a response to what some thought to be an attack on the old religion, its consequences must have been even more unwelcome. The prominent part taken by the heads of houses at Bridlington, Whalley, Barlings, and Jervaulx provided the crown with ammunition for a general campaign against the remaining great houses. From 1537 to 1540, there was a steady stream of voluntary surrenders to the crown—188 in all, made under pressure. This process was transformed in 1539 by the final Act of Dissolution, which gave legal recognition to the surrenders and provided for the suppression of standing houses. When Waltham Abbey—the last of 825 houses—was dissolved on March 23, 1540, regular religion had ceased. There would be no monks to preserve saints' cults or the Mass. An institution incompatible with the realization of a Protestant commonwealth had been destroyed, either by design or by accident.

[5] See the analysis in Chapter Ten.

The consequences for society were many. The ex-religious were pensioned, sometimes lavishly. The nuns did less well than the monks in every respect. Although the men could make their way as secular priests, the women could not. Moreover, all who had professed a vow of celibacy were barred from marrying until the law was changed in Edward VI's reign. Many who did marry were then forced to resume single status during the reaction of Mary's reign. The emotional strain on women who became mothers was often profound, as we know from some court cases. The friars, though not pensioned because they were nonpossessioners, were as a group successful in gaining parochial work. Preaching curates were increasingly in demand as reforms took religion toward Protestantism, where the pulpit was more central than the altar. The large crowds of lay servants did not fare badly: they were in demand as tenants and domestics in the regimes established by the new lay owners.

The banishment of the mitered abbots from the Lords gave Parliament a new complexion. Lay peers now had a clear majority for the first time in one hundred years. There were less desirable consequences, however. The harm to scholarship was immense. Libraries were lost or dispersed, despite the efforts of John Leland, the famed antiquarian who gathered 250 choice items from over fifty monastic catalogues and preserved them for the Royal Library (which is now in the British Museum). Vandalism and insensitivity doomed vast treasures of medieval plastic art, a desecration obvious to all who visit the lovely, fractured ruins of the abbeys of Fountains, Peterborough, or Beaulieu. Six new bishoprics—Peterborough, Gloucester, Oxford, Chester, Bristol, and Westminster—were endowed from the profits of the Dissolution. In the universities, the spoils helped to enlarge Cardinal's College—renamed Christ Church—at Oxford and Trinity at Cambridge. In both universities, Regius chairs in Greek, Hebrew, civil law, medicine, and theology were established on the same basis in 1540. Many grammar schools were founded or reendowed on the proceeds of dissolved monasteries, chantries, and chapels.

Among the generality of men and the bishops and divines close to government, it was clear in 1540 that the Supremacy touched Englishmen in both their mental and material interests. What was not clear at Cromwell's death in 1540 was how the king would use the Supremacy. One group of his councillors was headed by Bishop Gardiner of Winchester, who advocated a halt to innovation and retrenchment. He had the support of the more conservative Henricians—Stokesley, Heath, Bonner, Tunstal, and Day—men made cautious by training in law and experience as administrators. They were humanists by education but bureaucrats by choice. Their reactions to the crisis of the Pilgrimage and its episodic aftermath (the Exeter Conspiracy of 1538 and the Wakefield Plot of 1541) were those of men concerned more about human prudence than divine wisdom. It was their belief that further innovations would upset the fixity of faith. The Bible in English had put explosives in the hands of fools. The Six Articles had helped to restore balance. To men trained in law, diplomacy, and other arts of compromise, the apparent need was for outward unity and solidarity in a dangerously split country.[6]

John Parkyn, the "fool of Oxford," was a case in point. He had moved from a career of advocating law reform in search of royal patronage to that of *agent provocateur*. He offered himself as a political means for entrapping rebels and would-be rebels *sub colore amicicie et cum fidei vultu* (under the guise of friendship and with a true face). Having baited the trap, he could then lead raids in which the menfolk would be burned, the women and children simply murdered! At least some of his effort stemmed from animus against the abbot of Osney.

But not every threat of disorder concealed blackmail by a deranged, disappointed careerist. Nor could Cromwell endorse every information thus: "It was but a babbling matter." There were 537 indictments for treason in Henry VIII's reign, of which 517 occurred in the 1530s. About 300 indictments were for armed rebellion. Yet the crown obtained fewer than 175 convictions. Nearly half of those convicted were pardoned. Even where treason lurked, the government knew that its power lay in the good will of its people. The problem was similar to that of the trial of felonies by local juries: the petty juries often failed to find for the crown. In the new circumstances in which treasons occurred, this ancient defect of the Quarter Sessions in dealing with rapes, arsons, robberies, and murders was crippling. Though still enabled by 34 Edward III, c. 1, to exact the death penalty, J.P.s in sessions often were unable to do so. No move to alter this situation was made until 1590, when new commissions encouraged the J.P.s to set capital cases before the more majestic assize judges. The taking of serious felonies from the local justices' scope was yet a long way off in 1536, however; even in the 1630s, Somerset records show J.P.s hearing capital cases and obtaining eight death sentences.

Wherever the crown and its ministers turned, they faced such limitations of power. In Sussex, from 1534 to 1547, a slow revolution in local politics shifted power from entrenched territorial lords to courtier gentry. Sir John Gage fell heir to the mantle of leadership once worn there by the Fitzwilliam earl of Southampton, the Howard dukes of Norfolk, and Lord Dacre of the South, Thomas Fiennes. In Kent, good will toward the crown was severely strained

---

[6] The 1540s have not benefited from intensive study, especially with regard to the politics of reform. The works of Lacey Smith already cited are useful, as well as my own *Politics and Profit*. But much of what is said here rests on the draft of my book about Sir Thomas Wriothesley (*Politics and Power*) and on the research of my students—Joseph Block, Peter Lowber, and Michael Zell. See also G. R. Elton's *Star Chamber Stories* and his *Policy and Police* (New York: Cambridge University Press, 1972).

in the early 1540s, especially by gentry plots against Archbishop Cranmer, whose forward religious politics in Canterbury diocese made the jobs of conservators of the peace difficult. Heterodoxy bred tumult; it upset the natural principles of deference in local government. And it led, in 1543, to a plot against the archbishop in which certain gentry allied with a group of prebendaries. Such broils and stirs wakened the memory of the Pilgrimage and nourished the determination of the cautious councillors.

Cranmer's hopes for further reformation had been dealt a tremendous blow by the death of Cromwell and the resignations or deprivations of the ardent bishops Ridley, Latimer, and Hooper. These bishops were typical of the theologically trained bachelors and doctors of divinity and the group of ex-monks and contemplatives who formed the core of the advocates of further reform. Before 1529, their careers were academic and pastoral rather than legal and bureaucratic. Only Henry VIII's need of the "new learning" in the divorce crisis had opened the way to their episcopal careers; it had also confused and divided the bishop's bench between men whose art was expediency in government and those citizens of the *civitas dei* who would later die martyrs' deaths under Mary I.

Holgate, Salcot, Hilsey, Holbeach, Latimer, Ridley, Hooper, and Cranmer were in fact anxious to maintain order. But to them this meant realizing the implications of the reforms made under Cromwell's aegis before 1540. Not one of the eleven late Henrician bishops who were lawyers joined them in this. Hence the so-called reaction of Henry VIII's last seven years was less a struggle of rival ideologies—of Catholicism versus Protestantism—than a contest of parties widely agreeing in doctrine and utterly divided as to tactics and timing. John Ponet, the future bishop, could thus rebuke Bonner:

Thou allowest nothing to be well done except it is lawful, nothing that is not canon nor custom to be lawful—but our master Christ said: "I am the way, the Truth, the Light"—not "I am custom, I am the law."

The abyss between Cranmer and Gardiner separated men whose lives were spent in books of divinity from those learned in the law. Against Cranmer's schemes, men like Gardiner, with wide experience of the king's foreign wars and his domestic problems, stood as a barrier.

Policy between 1540 and 1547 thus oscillated between two poles of opinion and temperament. Those whose chief strength was a capacity to tolerate fools in a world less than wise temporized. The king instinctively turned to them for the business of government. And they used this political leverage to ensure that gospelers would have nothing but half-opportunities to do a thorough housecleaning in the church. The party of governance had what amounted to an almost aristocratic commitment to order. They could little understand Latimer's mind when, in 1538, he had urged Cromwell to launch the iconoclastic campaign that swept away the shrines of Becket and Our Lady of Walsingham.

Yet even in the face of a lack of kingly enthusiasm and divided conciliar opinion, Cranmer pressed on.[7] While the Canterbury prebendaries plotted against him in 1543, the archbishop was hard at work on new liturgical texts. He and his friends managed in 1545 to publish from Richard Grafton's press an English litany omitting petitions to the saints in behalf of the dead. That same year, Parliament passed an act suppressing the chantries—chapels in which "Mass priests" were endowed, in the belief that their prayers and sacrifices were efficacious works contributing to the freeing of souls from the toils of purgatory. This act was not enforced until its reenactment early in Edward VI's reign. But the Henrician act of 1545 had clearly stated in its preamble the religious reasons for dissolving chantries. It alleged that the errors and superstition afflicting Christ's church derived from common ignorance "of the very true and perfect salvation [worked] through the death of Jesus Christ." The result was that people devised "phantasing vain opinions of purgatory and masses satisfactory to be done for them which departed. . . ." Resources so vainly used would be better dedicated to building grammar schools, strengthening the universities, and providing for the poor.

It was a strange reaction that moved so boldly in the direction of destroying perpetual-Mass chantries and much dubious, sterile doctrine. Moreover, this move had the support of the conservatives, even Gardiner, who once remarked that "putting away the chantries" and the abbeys was no injury to either faith or the Mass itself, which "consisted not in multitudes but in the thing itself." A year later, Francis Van der Delft, Charles V's ambassador in London, reported that Henry VIII was considering the abolition of the Mass itself, and in 1546 he also commented that two other movements at court pointed to a Protestant future. The king had entrusted his son's education to Erasmians and some markedly Protestant tutors. The Council increasingly seemed motivated by men of the "advanced party"—Sir Edward Seymour, the earl of Hertford, Sir John Dudley, Lord Lisle, and Sir William Paget.

---

[7] On religious changes in the 1540s before Edward VI's accession, the works cited in Chapter 4 remain basic. To these may be added these works on Cranmer: G. W. Bromiley, *Thomas Cranmer, Theologian* (New York: Church Book Room Press, 1956); F. E. Hutchinson, *Cranmer and the English Reformation* (London: Home University Library, 1951); and Jasper Ridley, *Thomas Cranmer* (Oxford: Oxford University Press, 1962). The transition of power in 1546–7 may best be followed in W. K. Jordan, *Edward VI: The Young King* (Cambridge, Mass.: Harvard University Press, 1968), the first of two volumes [see also Volume II, *The Threshold of Power* (1970)]. This book and its detailed bibliography are indispensable.

This does not mean that late in life Henry VIII had begun a Protestant grand design. It does mean that careful and graduated change was possible, even after the supposedly conservative triumphs of 1539–40. The whole momentum of events after 1533 had loosed in the kingdom forces not easily fettered again. Evangelical and radical Protestant sentiments flourished. Against them, Henry's arrogant belief that he could utterly control them proved wrong. Men close to court wondered whether the king knew his own mind, or at least they found it hard to know "what religion the king was of." Great Lutheran protégés of Cromwell—among them Winiam Jerome, Robert Barnes, and Thomas Gerard—were burned for attacking the Eucharistic doctrines believed by the king. Anne Askewe suffered for holding a view of the sacrament essentially the same as Cranmer's, and even Katherine Parr, the king's last queen, was queried on her faith. In 1546, Henry savagely attacked the leading conservative peers, executing the earl of Surrey. Surrey's father (the duke of Norfolk, great Howard) was saved only by the king's death on January 28, 1547, which voided the warrant for his own. Before Henry died, the arrangements he made for the council of regency excluded Bishop Gardiner from power. Events perhaps set in motion long before were putting power in the hands of men ready to press for further reformation.

Far from the center of power, ordinary Englishmen spoke against the persecution of Anne Askewe. Secretary Paget shielded a number of Protestants. Hertford patronized some others once he was large in Cromwell's books. In the remote North—in Yorkshire and Nottinghamshire, supposedly frozen in thoughtless love of the old religion—the proportion of men making their wills with "nontraditional confessions of faith" grew from 25 percent in 1545 to 40 percent in 1547! This trend continued despite statutes in 1543 and 1545 that forbade the open Bible to all but gentlemen and the nobility. The Word of God, as the king himself admitted in a moving speech to Parliament (December 7, 1545), "is disputed, rhymed, sung, and jongled in every alehouse and tavern. . . ." By this admission, Henry had recognized that he had failed to control his own revolution; from 1544 on, he had failed to maintain a balance between the factions of his Council. Maneuvers then complete ensured that the transition of power from the old king to his nine-year-old son would mark the advance of Protestantism.

Protector Somerset's Regime

Keeping the king's death secret for three days, the lords of the Council also kept Parliament illegally in session. They had agreed among themselves to breach the king's regency device, which he had incorporated in his will.[8] According to that device, power was given to sixteen councillors collectively; excluded were Gardiner, the Howards, and certain ministers not weighty enough for inclusion. The sixteen executors were under the eye of another body of twelve enforcers. Paget, and most of the *politique* and Protestant regents, speedily worked to abrogate the will and lodge power in a protector, the new king's uncle Sir Edward Seymour, the old king's brother-in-law. The Lord Chancellor, Wriothesley, demurred at first, but then acceded to the scheme agreed on by Paget and Seymour. None of the conspiring sixteen bore a title of nobility more than a decade old. Power thus passed to new men. The new government consisted in fact of men whose rise followed the course of the Henrician Reformation, of which they had been agents and defenders and were now beneficiaries. Within a few days of this coup, proceedings were initiated to deprive Wriothesley of the Great Seal, on charges that mocked justice but enabled the newly created duke of Somerset (Hertford) to dispatch from power his weightiest remaining opponent. The other conservatives who had initially been privy to the coup were soon expelled by force or the accident of death.

The conspirators had anticipated that Somerset would act only with their advice and consent, since he had inspired confidence by his early decisive actions, by his great military reputation, and by the genial face he had shown.

The import of these political events was made clearer in Cranmer's coronation sermon. In it, he made a strong defense of the Supremacy and bade Edward VI to make a further reformation of the church. The king's ministers took up the challenge in the boy's name, as the duke of Somerset and his confidants grasped the full power of Tudor kingship. This they used to support the actions and plans of Protestant divines and of those humanist-oriented social reformers who became famous as the "commonwealth men." The roots of their advocacy lay deep in the program of the late 1530s, from which Hooper, Hugh Latimer, Nicholas Ridley, Holgate, Barlow, John Hales, John Mason, Richard Taverner, Richard Morison, Stephen Vaughan, and their political leaders derived continuity.

The need for religious reform was as pressing as ever. Most of the parish clergy were not well-informed preachers. Only 14 percent of Lincoln priests in 1550 willed books or left inventories testifying to decently stocked studies. The Edwardian clergy were in fact holdover Henrician clerks—poor, perplexed by change, not yet profoundly permeated by Protestant ideas, and anxious lest new doctrines force on them the choice of whether or not to serve.

Bewildered they might well have been, for one of the first of Somerset's

[8] The will was drawn up on December 30, 1546, and was apparently signed on January 27. There is controversy as to whether Henry signed his will manually or whether his signature stamp was applied by a clerk ordered to do so by Council. The king died on the twenty-eighth.

policies to bear fruit was freedom of the press. The period 1547–9 was one of striking propaganda. Well into 1548, the new regime gave no clear direction to doctrine. Laymen debated the Articles of the Faith. A steady stream of influential foreign preachers and teachers—Peter Martyr, Bullinger, Ochino, Martin Butzer—brought to bear Zwinglian and Calvinist ideas as well as Lutheran ones. The collective force of this advocacy was to demand a full Protestant Reformation.

The government cautiously felt its way in that direction. While iconoclasm raged in London and in the ports of the provinces, parishes in scattered villages took the initiative in selling church ornaments. Gardiner advised that the law told against preachers of false wisdom, as indeed it did in the form of the Henrician statutes. The answer to his objections to popular innovation came in the opening round of Edwardian reforms. On July 31, 1547, new injunctions were issued to the clergy. These were in the main restatements of those of 1536 and 1538, defining the practice of religion rather than doctrine. A book of homilies had earlier been printed. Their use was enjoined on pain of deprivation, the fate Gardiner suffered for his refusal to preach the homilies and for his attack on the injunctions, which he refused to put into effect in Winchester diocese. Elsewhere, the commissioners sent to see to the use of the homilies had been nominated by Cranmer. They were dominated by strong Protestants like Richard Cox and John Hales, and they found in each of the six circuits a mixture of Catholic practice, indifference, and ardent Protestantism. Where resistance was met, the Council ordered the reconstruction of cathedral staffs. This meant jail for Bonner and Gardiner. The government also moved quickly to ensure the open-Bible policy of 1538, aided by libraries containing the books of recommended Fathers of the church. This insistence on the Bible and the Fathers was characteristic of the reformers. So was their view that the Fathers were not in themselves an absolute standard of Christian truth, but had weight (*auctoritas*) because they had been Biblical, historical, and exegetical in their concerns.

Such government use of prerogative measures clearly pointed toward the consolidation of a Protestant ministry. So, too, did the general visitation of the clergy, which inquired closely into popish superstitions. While the doctrine of the Mass was not touched in 1547, the Chantries Act of Edward VI's first Parliament convinced conservatives that the full revolution could not be far off. This Parliament was frequently divided over bills concerning religion. Yet it soon repealed Henry VIII's treason legislation and allowed laymen communion under both species. It swept away the punitive heresy legislation of 5 Richard II and 2 Henry V, as well as Henry VIII's prohibitions of certain Protestant books and the infamous Six Articles establishing conformity of opinion. The apparatus of religious repression was gone.

The floodgate of the Reformation stood open to the full. It was still not lawful to doubt Christ's real presence in the sacrifice of the altar. But the entire area of ceremonies—vestments, the authority of bishops, the endowment of the church, redemptive merit and good works; justification by faith, altars versus plain tables for communion, the communion of saints, relics, and the authority of the scriptures—was akin to a free-fire zone in warfare.

Cranmer, who had encouraged disputes, soon recognized the need for a minimal clarification of doctrine. The Council supported him and soon produced the draft bill of the first Edwardian Act of Uniformity. A poll of the bishops revealed great disagreements on nearly every important article of faith, liturgy, and worship. Throughout January and February of 1549, in both Lords and Commons, debate raged. The Lords' debate revealed clearly the fissure in episcopal ranks, for when the bill became law on February 19, 1549, eight bishops, joined by four temporal peers, voted no. The majority of the bishops had previously indicated their doubts about many facets of the first Prayer Book (Book of Common Prayer), drafted by Cranmer and attached to the bill as a schedule.

The passage of the act had immediate and radical implications. It furthered the conversion of a priesthood into a ministry, displacing the altar and giving an unfamiliar primacy to the pulpit. The Word was to become more important than the Sacrifice. The Act of Uniformity violated ancient customs and threatened certain strongly rooted local liturgical traditions (e.g., the Sarum Use in Wiltshire), by making the Prayer Book the only authorized liturgy. Parliament thus gave voice to the Supremacy in an unmistakable manner, bringing the new faith to the people in Cranmer's hauntingly beautiful English. Every man could now grasp that the canon of the Mass no longer conveyed the notion of sacrifice; it was forbidden to elevate the wafer or the chalice. While to Protestants the rubric touching the Mass seemed a compromise resulting from "the infirmity of the present age" and good only until the English were ready for further reformation, to the English the Book was revolutionary.

If the 1549 acts involving religion assuaged the sensibilities of some who had urged further reformation, they assaulted the consciences of others. There were some Protestants in England who wanted a Calvinist settlement derived from the radical doctrines. Calvin had then an unrivaled authority in the Protestant world. Many who had left England in the reverses of 1539–40 had studied his methods at first hand. They liked his special brand of biblical theology with its insistence on God's terrible predestination, whereby men were from eternity damned or saved by His perfect foresight of their merits. Calvin had not shrunk from God's absolute sovereignty, His incomparable power. He had instead glorified God's crushing omnipotence. Never mind

[handwritten margin note: I don't think Calvin taught that,]

that this idea negated the freedom of human will and committed men to a life of anxiety and uncertainty. This they could escape by their commitment to a godly ministry working in a reformed commonwealth. The direct Calvinist influence on Cranmer was small. His formularies mixed his residual Catholicism and Luther's ideas in a strange way. But through his genius, the Prayer Book and the Act of Uniformity settled tricky questions ambiguously, using phrases that suggested both the abolition and the retention of transubstantiation.

Cranmer freely said that his own convictions went beyond the Book. He knew there were court elements and citizens of London whose predilections worked nearer to Calvin's or Zwingli's. Hence much of the pamphleteering of 1547–9 was decidedly "Swiss" in character. Cranmer thus took the measure of the radical opponents of the Act of Uniformity; he knew their resentment as well as their optimism, and he knew that half-measures led to whole ones. The Church of England was now at least wholly Protestant, even if conservatively so. No matter that in his own diocese the archbishop scrutinized closely those who taught wild opinions about magistrates, gentlemen, or bishops. Meanwhile, he was already at work on revisions of the Book to bring English practices and doctrine closer to the "apostolic church" (reformed usage on the Continent). What mattered for the moment was not the small cliques of "Swiss," but the large masses of cautious country priests in Devon, Cornwall, Dorset, Oxfordshire, and the North. There were not yet enough reformed preachers to carry a missionary faith into the dark corners of the realm. The Reformation had not so much to "tarry for the magistrate," as Elizabethans would complain, as to wait for a revolution in clerical education that had not yet happened.

A Summer of Discontents: 1549

This cautiousness had other bases. Between 1547 and the summer of 1549, Somerset's regime had failed to keep under control either its foreign policy or the program of domestic reforms championed by the men of the "commonwealth party." Excessive concern for domestic affairs had led the government into a fundamental error about its strength. The Protector had made his reputation chiefly in the wars against Scotland and France in 1542–5. He rashly used his authority to renew both struggles at a time of great domestic unrest. This move had dreadful consequences, and Somerset's dream of a Union of England and Scotland fell to pieces when France intervened against the English. Treasure and blood were spent to no end, and in 1549 war-weariness at home forced a steady deterioration of both the will and capacity to continue. France's declaration of war in midsummer of that year found

England without allies, near bankruptcy, and amid danger signals of discontent in every shire.[9]

These domestic broils were in no little part the product of Somerset's support for social and economic reforms. His first domestic measure had been the savagely repressive statute of 1547 (I Edward VI, c. 3) "for the punishment of vagabonds" and the relief of the impotent poor. Persons refusing work were, upon conviction before two J.P.s, branded and adjudged slaves of their masters for two years. Should they attempt escape, their fate was to be legally the slave of their lord for life; a second escape was punishable by death. More characteristic of the duke's drift in domestic matters, however, were charitable acts. One such act, to relieve the poor and their children within the parish, signaled the campaign then being waged outside Parliament by men such as John Hales, Richard Taverner, Robert Crowley, and Hugh Latimer.

Despite the failure of the government in 1547 to bring before the county omnibus social reform, the idea of securing a community of interest transcending diversities of status and function thrived in Somerset's entourage. The welfare of the body politic was assumed to be a duty of government. We have already studied at length the degree to which the precarious social and economic balance achieved late in the 1400s had been upset by 1520, owing to a combination of causes: enclosures, inflation, the redistribution of church lands, intrusions upon customary relationships by market mechanisms, a new spurt of population growth, and the decline of workers' real wages.

In combination, these things had proved false the old moral truths about the identity of community and society. The Reformation had quickened the pace of social change and questioned the direction whence certain social sanctions ordinarily derived. Moreover, the bellicose policies of Henry VIII in the 1540s had seriously increased the strain on royal finance and thus enlarged the crown's demands for taxation. Attempts at reforming social and economic practices in such circumstances laid bare the nature of the crisis in Edwardian society and its consequences for government. For in dealing with the root problems of poverty in mid-Tudor society, Somerset led where other men possessed of power would not follow.

The commonwealth reformers were Protestant in opinion, country people rather than Londoners, and truly conservative in their attack on poverty. But the center of their case rested on undoing harmful enclosures and so ensuring

[9] Jordan's first volume is virtually a book on Somerset's regime. It follows A. F. Pollard's *Protector Somerset* (London: Longmans, 1902) in its general overview. R. D. Whitney-Jones, *The Tudor Commonwealth Men* (London: Athlone Press, London University, 1969) is useful on the circle of reformers and their social writings, while C. S. L. Davies' articles on military administration and the issue of slavery, in volume XVII, pp. 238–48 and volume XIX, 533–49, of the *EcHR*, cast another light, as does M. L. Bush, "The Lisle-Seymour Land Disputes," *Historical Journal*, IX (1966), 255–74.

the commodity of peasant life and prosperity for yeomen. They believed that the old imbalance of grain and grass—so favorable to pasture, sheep, wool, and textiles—was becoming progressively worse. In fact, by 1549 it is nearer the truth to say that the balance was better than it had been in 1520. Grain prices were up, even though the volume of exported textiles rose steeply after 1545, at least partly in response to the debasements undertaken in England to help pay for the wars of Henry VIII. Somerset supported the reformers' demand that strict checks be made against new enclosures and that inquiries be made into old ones. Excessive grazing had forced the poor below the level of sub-sistence, they alleged, by making necessities scarce and thereby rocketing prices upward. Their moralism found in covetousness the root of poverty. And the Protector encouraged them, licensing Latimer to preach against en-closures and to condemn usury, forestalling, and the evil practices of gentlemen and lords: "It may not be lawful for every man to use his own as he listeth, but . . . to the most benefit of his country."[1] Sir William Cecil confided that gentlemen feared to touch the commons, because "that Common wealth called Latimer hath gotten the pardon" of them for their usurpations of right order.

It was not only Latimer, however. Somerset had disparked the royal deer chases at Hampton Court. He had seen to the passage of a bill protecting copy-holders on his own estates. He had given Hales a commission to disforest and dispark certain crown lands and had used the prerogative of proclamations to warn lawbreakers not to make novel enclosures. A powerful general com-mission was appointed to inquire into abuses in the Midland open-field areas. The duke had done worse things. The Subsidy Act (2 and 3 Edward VI, c. 36) of 1549 placed a new levy on sheep, allowing a special schedule of collections to accomplish social reform through the taxing power. This act had met heavy opposition in the Commons, where landlords had the dominant voice. Great sheeprunners like the Spensers of Althorp stood to lose too much if reform went unchallenged. They also may well have sensed what we know: that Hales' claim of 400–500 villages newly suppressed in the Midlands was non-sense. The 1517 inquest had shown less than one-half of 1 percent of land had been enclosed at the peak of depopulating enclosures in the twenty-four counties hardest hit. Yet the Imperial ambassador reported Somerset preaching Latimer's gospel to an angry Council of skeptics. They knew that only three of seventy-eight radical bills concerning social, economic, and educational re-forms had survived the scrutiny of the worried gentry and nobles in 1548 and early 1549. They also understood that among the 118 public measures passed since 1547 were forty-nine acts regulating the economy or social relations. There was too much meddling!

[1] From Latimer's *Sermon on the Plow*.

Somerset's appeal to "the great multitudes" to carry out these purposes had by 1549 alienated him from his fellow conspirators of 1547. They looked at England's palpable ills more closely than they did at the poverty-stricken million at the bottom of the social ladder. The country's political classes gaped at reports of the cost of the wars: £2,100,000 under Henry VIII since 1542, and £1,356,000 upon their renewal. They did not know the figures. But they did know that the crown had financed the wars by forced loans, huge sales of land, and a disastrous debasement of coinage. While the government realized about £2,000,000 from capital sales and £367,000 from silver taken out of coins that were then restruck at the old face values, the royal debt, which had stood at £152,180 in 1546, had edged steadily upward. The economy was engulfed in a false boom, with foreigners taking over textile production, since the goods paid for in sound marks and guilders looked cheap in continental markets. The pattern of industrial expansion, vagabondage, religious disputes, crown borrowings, coinage clipping, and ruinous foreign policy was weakening the government's grasp on power. A disastrous drought in the early summer of 1549 promised a bad harvest. There was sporadic rioting over much of the country among men aware that prices had risen by about 250 percent since 1510, while real wages had been halved.

In fact, the nervousness of the Council merely reflected the near-anarchy of the countryside. Somerset's answers to the disorders seemed to promise more of the same—the Midlands Commission, new propaganda, further religious changes, and a determination to debase the coinage again. In August 1548, Hales' appearance in Buckinghamshire had coincided with riots against landowners. Discontent among the commons was spreading, with reports of riots reaching the Council in mounting numbers in June 1549—from Kent, Warwickshire, Leicestershire, Cornwall, Norfolk, Devon, Yorkshire, and many cities. The earl of Warwick led the councillors who laid the blame at the feet of irresponsible reformers. By July, it seemed as if all of England south of the Midlands was on the verge of social and economic collapse. There were, in fact, tumults in the Midlands and full-scale rebellions in the Southwest and East Anglia. The Spanish ambassador thought the monarchy was breaking up!

However, the revolutionary movements of 1549—the Prayer Book Rising in Devon and Cornwall and Ket's Rebellion in Norfolk— failed. The reasons were many: the failure to develop common objectives, the lack of support of the commons among nobility and gentry, and the ultimate defection of most of the Council because of the Protector's reluctance to use armies against the king's subjects. Yet the revolts doomed Somerset's rule and once again dramatized the crises inherent in the Supremacy.

In Devon and Cornwall, the motive for rebellion was conservatism in religion and economics. Many commoners spent their strength in furious attacks on authority simply because they were victims of wounds whose causes were beyond their grasp and that of the statesmen in London: scarcity, inflation, and general social dislocation. There was also a deep dislike of the religious changes of 1549. Men who had endowed a tiny obit for a mother's soul rebelled against its confiscation. Others were driven to despair by the hunger of their children or the sharp practices of their landlords. For others, the failure of the hopes inspired by Somerset's promises was enough to make them cross the line of obedience. In the peninsula and in Oxfordshire, Catholic clergy were deeply involved before the suppression effected there and in Berkshire, Northamptonshire, and Buckinghamshire by Lord Grey of Wilton. The southwestern rebels marched under banners of the five wounds of Christ, often led by expelled chantry priests and curates who refused to use the new Prayer Book. At least ten priests played leadership roles.

When the rebels sent grievances to London, they were for the most part manifestoes of Catholic reaction: they asked for the Six Articles, the Mass, the ancient Latin ritual, the Latin Bible, and the restoration of chantries. Yet such complaints only masked the disorder produced by economic dislocation and the political collapse of the Courtenay earls of Devonshire. The crown's attempt to establish the Russell family on monastic lands (as president of the Council of the West) failed, largely because the head of that family preferred to remain at the center of power—in London. Bedford was as yet no match for the great local gentry—the Pollards, Grenvilles, and Carews—who gave sporadic leadership to the rebels. Only the loyalty of the city of Exeter saved the area for the crown. When the rising was over, nearly 4,000 men had died, a demographic disaster in the thinly peopled Southwest.

During July and August, the Council could not concentrate the resources it had in Cornwall and Devon. Small forces were required to suppress riots in Essex, Surrey, Lincolnshire, Rutland, Hampshire, Sussex, Yorkshire, and Wiltshire, as well as in counties and shires already mentioned. The threat in Hampshire was especially grave, for there the dissident earl of Southampton was one power and Bishop Gardiner was another. Both remained quiet, however. So did the ranking gentry of the county, though they were conservative in religion. The commons, however, were disaffected and there was much lewd talk in the shire. In August, when the fates of East Anglia and Cornwall were in doubt, a Winchester carpenter and his accomplices plotted to raise thousands of men, march westward through Salisbury, and join their cause to that of the peninsula rebels.

The greatest threat to the regime came from Norfolk. Unlike the rebels in Devon and Cornwall, those who rallied about Robert Ket at Mousehold Heath, near Norwich, were strong supporters of Protestantism. Yet their aspirations were wholly secular, their grievances social and economic in character. There existed in East Anglia a political power vacuum, which was the result of the fall of Thomas Howard, duke of Norfolk, late in 1546. The duke had been the focal point of the crown's influence in the region. His influence at Westminster, like that of other magnates, brought home to the countryside the shadow of the throne. Prestige in Council was one of the twin pillars of Norfolk's power in the county, the other being his broad acreage, which allowed him to dominate rural society. Wealth and status caused lesser men to defer to the duke and, through him, to the monarchy. By casting down this tower of Tudor strength, the crown's hold on many burgesses and gentry suffered in proportion to the crash. This devastation was complete, because of the turpitude and incompetence of Rugg, the bishop of Norwich. Lacking leadership, the gentry of the area made no move to inhibit the rioters as they swelled to make a rebel army between June 20 and July 20, 1549. Behind the imposing façade of Tudor power lay the hollowness of self-interested misrule by courtiers. The waning power and responsibility in the counties reminded men of Henry VI's minority.

This was the case in Norfolk, despite the fact that of fifty-six J.P.s commissioned in the county forty-six resided there and had a stake in preserving order. As the rebel force increased, the Council recruited mercenaries to combat it. Meanwhile, Norwich and the central and eastern parts of the county were in rebel control. The earl of Warwick, John Dudley, commanded the recruited Germans and some shire levies—perhaps 7,500 in all—and defeated the rebels between August 17 and 27. Ket was captured and executed on December 7, 1549, and his body was displayed at the gate of Norwich Castle as a warning to the discontented. Some 300 of his followers were also hanged.

The government was shaken by the investigations conducted after the rebellion and by the articles signed by Ket and representatives of twenty-two out of thirty-three Norfolk hundreds and some from Suffolk. What had begun with a local riot—when some commoners threw down the hedges of Robert Flowerdew and Robert Ket—had ended in the slaughter of some 4,000 men on the rebel side, about 1 percent of the population of the small kingdom. Landlord-tenant relations had promoted the local conflicts, but then Flowerdew and Ket had joined the rioters, perhaps merely to save their property. Grievances of a wider character had quickly appeared. These had touched on the relationship between the governors in London and those they governed in East Anglia, with the focal point of unrest clearly the lodging of royal power in the hands of local agents who were deemed unsuitable. This unrest had opened the door to the general attack made by the rebels on the fabric of national politics.

Riots over land utilization had been common in the area since Wolsey's inquest of 1517. Norfolk enjoyed a prosperous wheat, barley, and wool economy. The county possessed a prosperous peasantry in the central, northern, and eastern areas, where there thrived a larger proportion of freeholders and men under minimum tenurial obligations than elsewhere. The density of population was high, and holdings were therefore small. The increase in pastoral farming and sheep-enclosed areas had engendered conflict, especially where flocks were accommodated on commons. Thirteen of twenty-seven rebel articles demanded the redressing of agrarian wrongs: lords were not to pasture sheep on commons, copyholds were to be rented as in 1485, no new rents were to be imposed, there were to be no conversions of freehold to copyhold, no 40-shilling freeholders (the county electorate!) were to keep sheep beyond the subsistence level, weights and measures were to be honest, dovecotes and rabbit warrens were to be restricted. This list constituted a broad indictment of local agrarian capitalism.

The role of religion in the East Anglian tumults is harder to assess. The Prayer Book had been put into use on June 9. In the Cornwall-Devon area, this event had triggered the insurgency. In Norfolk, the Ket-Flowerdew feud had religious overtones, including disputes about the parish church. Princess Mary was in residence at Kenninghall, two miles away. But the Council rightly concluded that she gave no impetus to reactionary forces. Ket himself used the Prayer Book, and the preachers of the rebel encampments were Protestants— even radical ones—rather than conservatives. The grievances cited in the rebel articles show no trace of theological concern, and the clergy of the locale generally remained aloof from the risings. Where religion entered, it was the force of anticlericalism that dominated Ket's articles. Priests were not to purchase land. Present holdings of the church were to be let to laymen. Incompetent preachers were to be dismissed and parishes allowed to choose their ministers. All priests were to be resident. Benefices were to be raised to at least £10 in order to attract men who would teach the Primer and properly catechize children. Tithes were not to be more than eight pence out of every five shillings, and the Council's orders despoiling churches were to be withdrawn. In their one deeply religious complaint, rebels cited Calvary as a general act of manumission for men. How, then, were villeins still in England?

What fused agrarian and anticlerical sentiments was good leadership along with the fact that local law and order was in a state of collapse. Sixty years of Tudor rule had weakened the role of magnates. Yet they were not dispensable when it came to controlling the shires. In Norfolk's absence, good lordship was lacking in the county. His power had pacified the county in 1525, during the revolt against Wolsey's amicable loan. His influence had been critical, in 1536-7, in keeping the East Anglian risings from linking up with the Pilgrimage of Grace. In 1545, he had been made the first lord lieutenant of the shire, a Tudor creation set up to transfer military power from the sheriffs to the great aristocrats. His dependents comprised—with the duke—the triarchy of county magistracy: lieutenant, J.P.s, and sheriff.

Norfolk's fall stimulated rivalries for power he would earlier have checked. The wealth provided by the Cromwellian revolution had stirred ambitions in a hierarchical society. Without the deference paid the duke, these raged unchecked in the county. To the rebels, the local contests among gentry seemed only an echo of the disorder at the center produced by factions of noblemen contesting for the rule of a boy-king.

A few malcontent gentry were no threat to Tudor government, however. The crown's power in the sixteenth century derived from no mere mechanical balance of its personal assets and those of the gentry. There was instead the old system by which the great aristocrats saw mutual interest in their own hold on the loyalties of the provincial elites. But to make the system work in 1549 as it had worked in 1450, effective rule in the country was as indispensable as good order at the center. In his last year, Henry VIII had weakened both. Somerset had failed to make good the loss. The consequence was that county factions discredited the machinery of justice. Not only were Flowerdew and Ket at odds; there were powerful feuds between Lestrange and Townshend, Knyvet and Townshend, Drury and Woodhouse, and Paston and Clare. The rise of a powerful group of lawyers in county society had promoted legal racketeering. The best lawyers went to London. But the others practiced locally, and they became the special bane of the rebels in 1549. Nearly all the lawyer-J.P.s were taken prisoner. A whole series of rebel articles attacked their covetous, self-interested use of both the law and local office. These heirs of ducal and episcopal powers had squandered their trust and thus weakened respect for all government. Government seemed to be a conspiracy of rich men seeking their own commodity.

That the problem lay in the ungoverned expansion of the ruling elites in the prosperous areas of Norfolk seems clearer with the help of an instructive comparison. The poor region in the county's southwest corner attracted neither sheeprunners nor lawyers. Seven of its eight hundreds were not represented on Ket's rebel council at Norwich. It was in the most prosperous areas that the competition was fiercest and the political order most disrupted. Ket's soldiers were no jacquerie; they were the yeoman-artisan classes who stood to lose most from a revival of unfettered ambitions.

What had happened in the rebel coup before its defeat must remind us of the Doncaster "parliament" of 1536. Ket had not wanted to make war on the Protector's regime. But he had wanted to *restore* government, unlike the hostile forces of the westerners, who had sought to overthrow it. The local rulers needed correction. London had not done it. Perhaps two men from each of Norfolk's twenty-four risen hundreds could. Along with a Suffolk contingent, the delegates in fact established a government at Mousehold Heath. They held a parliament, issued writs, negotiated, appointed a "secretary of state" (the son of a royal signet clerk), and appealed to the king to put down evil councillors and appoint good ones. The husbandmen, butchers, tailors, and innkeepers wanted good government, some relief from the decline of the local cloth trade, better wages, stable rents, and less taxation. Their wants were not masks of anarchy but the stuff of order. The Protector's intentions they thought laudable. He had picked up the tattered flag of reform carried earlier by Wolsey and Cromwell. Then he had lost his way. Ironically, when the rebels sought to put the duke back on the straight path, his fellow councillors had decided on another road entirely. William Paget, Russell, and John Dudley were decreeing a bloody end to social reform.

It was this change of policy, made on July 8 in London, that transformed the humble petitions of a rude colloquy into the grievances of rebels. The decision to give command to the stern Dudley also ensured that Somerset would not survive in power much longer than the coup at Norwich. The two premises of the rebel council—that London had aims identical with their own and that London would welcome their restoration of order in East Anglia—were no longer true.

Northumberland's Rule: The Other Duke

Almost immediately following their victory over Ket, the lords of the Council took steps to see that the centripetal forces of that summer would not again try to rule the center. Somerset had planned a new Parliament to deal with the country's grievances. Warwick planned a coup to deal with Somerset! Late in September and early in October, he brought over to his side the important councillors and their assistants, the twelve enforcers. War- wick recruited the conservative peers Wriothesley, Arundell, and Shrews- bury, as well as the support of Bishops Gardiner and Tunstal. They seemed to believe Somerset's fall would lead to a Catholic restoration, or at least to the repeal of his reforms.

They were quickly put right. Between October 10, 1549, and his abortive attempt in June 1553 to prevent Mary Tudor from succeeding Edward VI, the newly named duke of Northumberland pursued a mixed policy of radical Reformation and savage domestic repression.

The coup against Somerset worried the Protestants. The apparent return to authority of Dudley's conservative allies alarmed even the young king, who noted this in his diary. On Christmas Day, however, Dudley enforced the use of the Prayer Book. Those who had aided in the league against Somerset in October were cast aside. The duke himself was restored to the Council and his adherents released from arrest in January 1550. But adherents to Dudley's interests were raised in rank and power. Parliament was convoked, and it proved to be socially conservative in its mood, alarmed by the summer rebellions of 1549 and intent on repealing the dangerous social experiments of Somerset while letting religious changes stand.

In this determination, the members of Parliament were at one with Dudley's followers. The Council was one of landlords. Their dislike for the common-wealth men and economic reformism was only slightly less great than their distaste for challenges to social hierarchy. These shared sentiments, rather than a desire to roll back the Reformation, had inspired them. And in the 1550 Parliament, such sentiments obtained a clear majority, despite the presence of a still-numerous group of articulate reformers. The commonwealth partisans fought again on the subjects of sheep, enclosures, and the relief of the poor. But the signal act of the session made it treason for twelve or more men to assemble for the purpose of taking or killing a privy councillor, altering the law, or for refusing to disband when ordered. The infamous sheep and cloth taxes were repealed; 3 and 4 Edward VI, c. 3, went further and had the effect of repealing antienclosure legislation back to the great statute of 1488. A sop to popular opinion came in the repeal of the "slavery" statute of 1547, al-though the penal code against the able-bodied poor who would not work was maintained. More telling were the requirements that men accept offered work, that they be returned to their native parish for relief, and that children of the poor be taken from their parents by J.P.s and put to "useful service." It was a landlord's Parliament, bent on restoring order, degree, and gentry rule. Fifty-two reform bills more favorable to the common people failed to pass into law.

In the realm of religion, Northumberland's policy was so bold as to alarm even ardent reformers. Butzer urged the young king, then only thirteen (1550), to avoid thrusting on men "the religion of Christ . . . by proclamations and laws." He addressed the king but not the power. Despite the fact that the country was far from quiet between 1550 and 1552—and for good causes—the duke carried England along the road to Switzerland.

The King's Book (1543) contained the little-noted clause that prayers were good only for the generality of men. The act of 1545 that slated the chantries for destruction did the deed when reenacted in 1547. The reform of 1549 admitted a host of truly Protestant practices and doctrines. Conservatives lamented all of this, sometimes in verse:

. . . we have one faith
And all trod right one ancient path.
The time is now that each man may
see new religions coined each day.

Yet no quarter was given. Edward VI told his sister Mary that she could not practice Catholicism, even in her private chapel. Her retort to the Council—

that her father had made "the most part of you out of nothing"—did not deter the 1550 acts against Romish books or delay the use by Cranmer and Bucer of the new ordinal, a book markedly Lutheran in tone. The radical Bishop Hooper denounced the ordinal as "popish," since it invoked the saints and seemed to preserve the Mass. But by December, his puritan conscience was appeased by orders to remove altars and erect plain communion boards: altars were for magic sacrifices, tables were for simple community meals! There was resistance to the substitution in some areas, despite the work of preachers licensed to amble through the countryside in the train of royal commissioners. But in 1551, the Venetian ambassador Barbero could write that while Romanism in the provinces survived, most Englishmen were moved to hatred of the pope. There was in fact a remarkable domestic missionary force at work, even in the northern region, where Bernard Gilpin won his fame as the "Apostle of the North."[2]

The more ardent spirits could say openly in 1552 that England had moved fully into the light of God's grace and out of the shadow of His wrath. The fourth session of King Edward's first Parliament enacted the second Book of Common Prayer. Under the prodding of Hooper and Knox, Cranmer made bold revisions. Every crucial clause struck at the doctrine of the Mass, which now became the Lord's Supper. This completed the Protestant structure of worship and also the conversion of the priesthood into a ministry of the Word. Holy water, chrism, the sign of the cross, prayers for the dead, the old burial rite itself—all were forbidden. The new Act of Uniformity incorporating the Prayer Book (5 and 6 Edward VI, c. 1) made of the sacrifice on the altar a congregational communion. Priests were not allowed to "celebrate" in their accustomed vestments. The altar gave way to the table by law. The doctrine of the real presence was allowed only in a Zwinglian sense; there was no miracle of transubstantiation, but Christ was present to the believing communicant. When Cranmer stopped short of banning kneeling in the presence of the sacrament, the Council added to the Book the famous Black Rubric forbidding the practice. A short Catechism was put forth in support of these changes.

That the evangelicals prevailed in the Council was even clearer in 1553, when the Articles of the Faith (forty-two of them) became law. Cranmer had hesitated to burden the Church of England with explicit doctrine, realizing how divisive this might be. The Council treated him brusquely, however, and set out to replace the old canon law with a code fully as intrusive in marriage, wills, adultery, sorcery, blasphemy, and fornication.

The result was a transformation in the tenor of theology and faith. The allowance of clerical marriage pointed up how much the clergy were removed

---

[2] Among the other noted preachers were Latimer, Lever, Hooper, Ridley, Bradford, Knox, Coverdale, and the future archbishops Parker and Grindal.

from their old status as a special estate in Christian society. Zwinglian and Calvinist teachings on the Mass, predestination, purgatory, and baptism had been established. Every later English confession of faith—Elizabeth's Thirty-Nine Articles, especially—pointed back to the 1552 acts. Further attacks on Church endowments were also made, chiefly against the bishops, deans, and cathedral chapters deprived of part of their "princely and lordly estates." The great county palatine of Durham was annexed to the crown in April 1553. Plate and the ornaments of the parishes were expropriated for being incompatible with the new doctrine of the Lord's Supper.

What happened in the countryside bore small promise that a new Jerusalem was at hand. The government was weak in the resources of true power. There were serious plots in 1550. Somerset's second fall and subsequent execution in 1551 provoked other plots. English power in Europe was at its nadir. The French were bidding to end England's independence, since Mary Stuart's regime in Scotland made England's neighbor into a French province. The spending of £3,500,000 on war since 1542 had produced a disaster in diplomacy and domestic politics.

The disarray of the Antwerp exchange in 1551 had ruined the textile trade and deepened the depression at home. The king's finances were in complete collapse, as a special commission to survey them made clear in 1552. One official of the Mint had embezzled over £10,000. The crown in 1551 had an income of £271,192, and ordinary expenditures of £235,339. War costs added some £200,000 a year to deficit finance. This was chiefly in an external debt to German bankers, mostly in short-term notes constantly in need of payment or refinancing. There was £240,000 due early in 1553. Even the daily expenses of government could not be met at the Exchequer or in the newer revenue courts. In August 1552, payment on royal warrants had stopped. Crown lands worth £144,259 were sold between January and June 1553. The mood produced by the evidence of economic disintegration was darkened by terrible outbreaks of a new epidemic disease, the sweating sickness, which was characterized by profuse sweating and was frequently fatal in a few hours. Throughout the country there was also great famine. Death rates not unlike those of the days of the Black Death combined with a poverty beyond remedy. The price of corn had more than doubled between 1548 and 1552. Church wardens defied the crown's expropriation of their parish goods and sold off the stuff for local purposes. In eighty-nine of 106 London parishes this cost the crown nearly £10,000. The pattern was nationwide.

Chapter Six
THE MONSTROUS REGIMENT OF WOMEN

*If . . . the regiment were such as all hanged upon . . . the queen's
will and not upon the laws . . . if she might dispense alone of war
and peace; if, to be short, she were a mere monarch and not a
mixed ruler, you might peradventure make me to fear the matter
more.*

JOHN AYLMER, in his *Reply* to JOHN KNOX's
First Blast of the Trumpet (1558)

It was Edward VI's failing health that proved the heaviest blow
to England's stability. His doctors gave no hope that the young king might
survive the summer of 1553. The courtiers and politicians joined prelates and
propagandists who could see Mary Tudor, Henry's daughter by Catherine of
Aragon, beyond Henry's only son. It was not only that she was a "Spanish"
princess. Mary was in her thirties, as yet unmarried and childless. Her spirit
dwelled on the hope of succession and the use to which she would put the
Supremacy—a Catholic restoration. The future thus promised not a king but
a queen, not a family equal to the challenge of dynastic stability, but a woman,
an innovation in government—excluding, of course, the contested rule of
Matilda in the twelfth century. Remembering the anarchy of that time, men
who cared little about whether hell was Protestant and heaven Catholic considered what might be the results of a regiment of women. Nor was this mere
chauvinism on their part. The social and family structure of England was
patrilinear in nature. Only in scattered cases had titles passed through female
lines on the extinction of male heirs.[1]

The Succession Struggle of 1553

To contemplate that event under the circumstances seemed
madness to many. The regime of Edward was as feeble as the blood-spitting,

---

[1] To the works on Edward's reign already cited, these may be added: F. G. Emmison, *Tudor
Secretary: Sir William Petre* (Cambridge, Mass.: Harvard University Press, 1961); H. Chapman,
Lady Jane Grey (Boston: Little, Brown, 1962); B. L. Beer, "The Rise of John Dudley," *History
Today* (1965), XV, pp. 269–77; S. T. Bindoff, "A Kingdom at Stake, 1553," *ibid.* (1953), III,
pp. 642–8; M. Levine, "The Last Will and Testament of Henry VIII," *Historian* (1964), XXVI,
pp. 471–85, which is a critique of L. B. Smith's paper, "The Last Will and Testament of Henry
VIII," *JBS* (1962), II, pp. 14–27.

expiring boy. Its head, Dudley, was himself a sick and tired man. The Council was in disarray. Somerset had been executed, Arundel shunted aside, Paget discredited. Lesser men busily calculated what tomorrow's fortune might be, were Mary crowned. Certain councillors had mercilessly browbeaten the princess about her religion. Sir William Cecil, later the master of Elizabethan politics, in 1553 had withdrawn from court, perhaps to keep clear of the guilt that could arise from plots to deny Mary the succession. He even prepared for her eyes an apology for his role in discomforting her worship after 1550. Hearing of the news of the plot to set aside Mary's rights, he went so far as to plan a flight into exile.

The nerve of the parliamentary classes similarly failed. They went home early in the spring, having given a subsidy and passed administrative reforms in the briefest of all Tudor sessions. In the Church, even so ardent and precise a Protestant as Hooper of Gloucester could be forgiven for supposing God's plantation in England poorly seeded. His 1552 visitation of the diocese yielded 311 clergy in need of correction—among them sixty-two absentees, 171 unable to recite the commandments, ten ignorant of the Our Father, twenty-seven who did not know its author, and thirty who could not tell its place in Holy Scripture! The faith and suitability of ministers could scarcely be controlled by a bishop who had only fifty-six advowsons in his own gift, in a diocese in which we know the patrons of 286 livings.

A kingdom was at stake in terrible circumstances. Neither the political classes nor the reform leaders seemed to have the determination to protect the Reformation from the threatened Marian reaction—or perhaps they lacked the wit and motivation to do so. The duke of Northumberland, however, was possessed of all three. And he acted vigorously.

On May 21, 1553, Dudley married his son Guildford to Lady Jane Grey, a descendant of Henry VIII in the female line of Mary Tudor, the French queen. Although it seems that Dudley then had no plan to usurp the crown for his new family connections, the course of events brought him to that resolution. On June 12, he prevailed on Edward VI to alter the succession. When the judges called to do the legal work refused, on the good grounds that altering the succession was treason against Henry VIII's statutes and his royal will, the duke bade the king command it again, on June 15. The duke reminded them that to refuse their sovereign's command was manifest treason. The intimidated judges prepared a "device" still further changing the line of succession, and on June 21 this received the assent of the privy council, twenty-two peers, a scattering of bishops, the London City magistrates, and some powerful merchants. This new device had the effect of bringing into the succession not only any male heirs Lady Jane might have by Guildford Dudley but Lady Jane herself.

The diagram on page 190 shows more fully the direction taken by Edward VI at Dudley's urging.

Henry VIII's statutory provisions had drawn the line of succession through his children, and his testament added the granddaughters of his younger sister's line. Edward's first will adhered to this plan in that it barred the senior line by female descent of the Scottish queen. But this Tudor break with seniority had the healthy motivation of excluding a foreign and Catholic influence, the Guise-bred infant queen of Scots. The exclusion of Henry VIII's two daughters was, however, another matter. This was part of the original scheme of June 12, aimed at excluding female succession. The Protestant Grey line was to succeed by virtue of male heirs born to Jane, Catherine, and Mary Grey. But Edward was dying before the hoped-for births were achieved. Indeed, none of the Grey girls was known to be pregnant. Hence the second device, by which the duke's daughter-in-law was brought directly into the title, which was willed "to Lady Jane and her heirs male."

Guildford Dudley's young wife was thus made queen. For the duke of Northumberland this was an effective way to keep his power. What its portent was in the politics of religion was less clear. Nor did it matter. The country would not accept the coup.

Northumberland found he could not set aside the Tudor line, the patina of legitimacy it carried, and the hope for peace inherent in its seeming permanence. While Jane was crowned in London, Mary proclaimed herself queen and by letter told the Council of their treason in setting aside Henry VIII's will and the Succession Act. Mary seized the initiative and made a royal tour of East Anglia. The gentry there decided for her cause. They supported her. The earl of Derby came southward, and from the Channel coast came the earl of Sussex. Lord Hastings raised Buckinghamshire for her. Sir Peter Carew proclaimed Mary queen in Devon. England's ruling classes preferred gambling on a Catholic Supremacy to risking a revival of the civil wars Mary's house had finally ended. The radical Protestant politician Sir Nicholas Throckmorton put their reason in doggerel:

And, though I liked not the religion
Which all her life Queen Mary had professed,
Yet in my mind that wicked notion
Right heirs for to displace I did detest.

Dudley's support in the Council melted away when it was clear he had none in the country. All confessed they had been wrongly persuaded about the succession. They urged him to spare the country this alteration in the succession and the bloody campaigns it might mean. London proclaimed Mary. On

THE PLAN TO ALTER THE SUCCESSION, 1553.

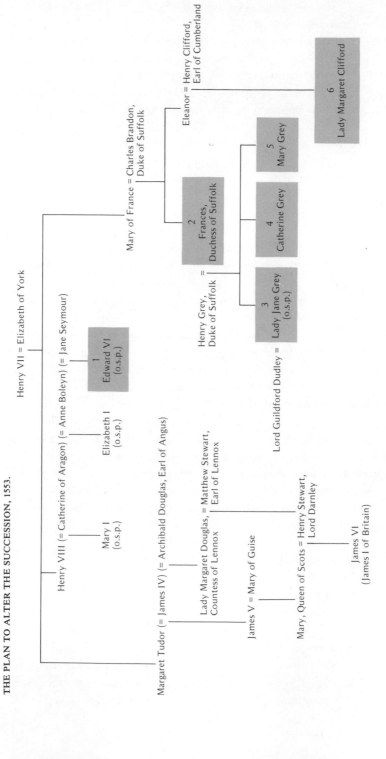

Henry VII = Elizabeth of York

Henry VIII (= Catherine of Aragon) (= Anne Boleyn) (= Jane Seymour)

Mary I (o.s.p.)

Elizabeth I (o.s.p.)

1 Edward VI (o.s.p.)

Margaret Tudor (= James IV) (= Archibald Douglas, Earl of Angus)

Lady Margaret Douglas, = Matthew Stewart, Countess of Lennox   Earl of Lennox

James V = Mary of Guise

Mary, Queen of Scots = Henry Stewart, Lord Darnley

James VI (James I of Britain)

Mary of France = Charles Brandon, Duke of Suffolk

Eleanor = Henry Clifford, Earl of Cumberland

2 Frances, Duchess of Suffolk

Henry Grey, Duke of Suffolk =

3 Lady Jane Grey (o.s.p.)

Lord Guildford Dudley =

4 Catherine Grey

5 Mary Grey

6 Lady Margaret Clifford

(o.s.p.) = died without heirs (*obit sine proles*).

190

July 24, the duke surrendered at Cambridge. No blood had been shed, although he and his blameless sixteen-year-old daughter-in-law and her silly husband were soon to pay the price of his vaulting ambition.

The moral is hard to point out. If legitimism and the sense of Tudor order had won the day in 1553, this did not mean that Mary Tudor's rule would be a love affair with her people. There were vital questions of policy yet at issue. How would Mary use the loyalty of her subjects? To what use would the fourth Tudor actually put the Supremacy?

Wyatt's Rebellion: Disaffection in the South

The answers were not long in coming. Although it is patently wrong to represent Mary I's reign in wholly negative terms—under her aegis the revenue system reforms studied by Edward's commissioners were pursued, important statutes began the removal of the more serious felonies from Quarter Sessions, the parish was made responsible for maintaining roads in a manner fruitful for Elizabethan poor-law reforms, and the lieutenancy system was made more responsible to the Council[2]—it remains true that the reaction in religion was the dominant motif of the years 1553–8. The most salient notes of this motif were the Spanish marriage, the various statutory stages of repeal, a reenforcement of Roman practices, some subsequent persecutions, and the political consequences of these campaigns.[3]

As Mary's government began to work, the issues facing it were formidable. Would her marriage to Philip, Charles V's son, divert foreign policy into channels inimical to independence? Could she allay the fears of the landed classes, who believed reunion with Rome might mean an attempt to confiscate their monastic lands? Would war with France necessarily follow a Hapsburg marriage? English statesmen were naturally anxious that the nation's resources not be used to advance Spain's struggles with the Valois. They were equally concerned that Spanish officials should not usurp the profits of office while Cardinal Pole led an attack on their landed wealth. Place and profit were the stuff of politics and order in the counties. If to these worries a repressive religious policy were added, would fear and distrust make for treasons?

The marriage of Mary and Philip proved disastrous. The Hapsburg purpose

[2] See *Statutes of the Realm*, 1 & 2 Philip & Mary, c. 13; 2 and 3 P & M, c. 10; *ibid.*, c. 8; 4 & 5 P & M, c. 2.

[3] Mary's reign is less adequately studied than that of any other Tudor. The best general works are: Hilda Prescott, *A Spanish Tudor* (New York: Constable, 1940); J. M. Stone, *The History of Mary I* (London: Sards, 1901); D. M. Loades, *Two Tudor Conspiracies* (Cambridge: Cambridge University Press, 1965); and H. E. Harbison, *Rival Ambassadors at the Court of Queen Mary* (Princeton: Princeton University Press, 1940).

was to outflank France and to gain the English throne for Philip's son, if such there were, or for Philip in his own right. Pressures to put Philip in the succession increased in 1555, when it became clear that Mary's "pregnancy" was false, perhaps truly hysterical, and likely the onset of symptoms of the cancer that took her life within three years. The radical preacher John Bradford appealed openly against the queen's right to so devise the crown. His published *Letter* (1556) to the earls of Derby, Arundel, Pembroke, and Shrewsbury touched a grave constitutional matter: "whether ye may lawfully consent, contrary to the discretion of the whole nation of Englishmen . . . to give away the crown. . . ." Bradford argued that the crown belonged only to Henry VIII's children, the last of whom was Princess Elizabeth. More stinging was his rebuke that to defeat her claim would be to do what Northumberland had attempted. Why should the queen who ruled because of her people's commitment to Tudor power suppose they would be less vigilant in her sister's behalf?

The question was not moot. As early as November 1553, a group of prominent Edwardian aristocrats and officials had met to consider the consequences of the failure of their petition against the Spanish marriage.[4] They had the adherence of a few noblemen, the chief being the self-interested duke of Suffolk. As a group they were indifferent to doctrine, very antipapal but outwardly conforming, fearful for their offices and lands, and willing to take steps to avoid unwanted foreign influences. Thus motivated, they conspired to raise their widely scattered counties in rebellion, setting Palm Sunday 1554 as the day for their drive toward London. Although their strategy aborted, the threat implicit in it was real. They had arranged for French sea power to aid their own command of coastal areas. Unlike the Ket rising and that in the West for the defeat of the Prayer Book, their plan was to drive to the center, avoiding centripetal forces capable of isolation and defeat in detail. What they could not plan for was the successful intelligence work of the Council. The knowledge that the government knew their plans forced the rising to occur in January, a full two months premature.

The French aid failed to materialize. Huntingdon held Suffolk in check in the Midlands, as the now-settled Russell power contained Carew's friends. The leading elements of the Tudor aristocracy were loyal and able to fill the local power vacuums that were so central to rebel successes in 1549. The commons were often aloof, inclined toward suspicion of mere magnate tussles, and distrustful of leaders whose *politique* cause was not the popular concern. Plain folk could be just as indifferent to gospel shouts as aristocrats, in the wake of three violent alterations in religion since 1535. But they were

[4] E.g., Sir Peter Carew (Devon), the duke of Suffolk (Leicestershire and East Anglia), Sir James Crofts (Hertfordshire), and Sir Thomas Wyatt (Kent).

not yet indifferent to the issues of peace, law, and order. And these seemed more disturbed than settled by the risings.

The true measure of the situation lay in Wyatt's thrust through Kent. Sir Thomas was the heir of an official family somewhat in financial straits. He was also an experienced soldier and diplomat. His estates lay near London, but his connections were also strong in the Channel port areas. Kent had always been of great concern to the crown on just that account. Successive dynasties had taken pains to populate the county with courtiers and officials of known loyalty.[5] This made for a social distribution of power inimical to magnate control and tended to reduce the chance of holding the area by mechanisms of control used in the North, the West, East Anglia, and the Welsh Marches. A numerous free peasantry had also made Kent turbulent in every major medieval revolt. Among Kentish men, Wyatt's appeal was well chosen. He raised no cry of religion, calling instead on Englishmen to rescue their queen from bad councillors and Spanish influence. His articles enshrined Tudor legitimacy. The "avoidance of strangers" was an argument that engaged men of all classes and opinions. Thirty gentry joined the rising, while only fifteen actively supported the crown in a county specially managed in its interest. The greater part stayed to one side, perhaps exhibiting again the indifference bred by too many changes. The army Wyatt raised was no larger than 4,000 men. Yet it passed on the road to London virtually unopposed. If most people did not fight for Wyatt, neither did they rally to Mary. They were torn between disciplined loyalty and passive dislike for policy, between fear of the hangman and fear of losing their worldly goods to foreign plunderers.

The Council in London negotiated with the rebels, while the queen and her Spanish adviser, Simon Renard, secretly advocated savaging traitors and heretics. Mary also duped them, by promising to marry beyond the realm only by good counsel and the advice of Parliament. What proved vital, however, was the loyalty of London's magistrates. This was assured by their fear of a sack of the City, and not without reason, since the rebels camped on the south bank of the Thames, in sight of St. Paul's. Fighting of a skirmishing nature lasted for nearly three weeks before Wyatt despaired of gaining the capital and surrendered.

Even in defeat, the nature of the rebel force proved significant. We now know the names of about 750 rebels, 560 of whom came from Kent, the remainder from London or its suburbs. Their indictments (and pardons) often tell us

[5] Among famous Tudor instances: the Southwells, Bakers, Brookes, and Wyatts. The pattern held in Charles I's reign. G. E. Aylmer has shown that in a sample of 172 Caroline officeholders, ten claimed Kent as their county of origin, while fourteen made it their destination. Only London gave more sons to Charles' government, and only Surrey and Essex claimed more among its settlers, apart from the metropolis.

their status and occupation, as well as their home parish. Hence we know that 103 of Kent's 124 parishes supplied rebels, usually concentrated in the areas supplying gentry leaders. In Kent, then, local mechanisms of deference clearly worked against the crown, underscoring the fragility of social order and its dependence on local elites. Both Canterbury, tightly held in check by the archbishop, and the coastal towns under admiralty interests were conspicuously loyal. The eastern section was also pacific, chiefly because of the location there of the mansions of the three chief loyalist gentry, Abergavenny, Southwell, and Cheyney. But where local causes of unrest promoted gentry discontent, there was a resonant cry among the commons. Over thirty different trades are represented among them. There is evidence of unemployment and population pressure in the most unquiet areas. Yet the dominant fact is that local social coherence derived from the attitude of the gentry rather than from any broad unity of material interests.

Unlike the Devon-Cornwall area, where coherence was inhibited by sharp differences of ideology between known Protestant gentry and the largely Catholic commons, the religion of Kent was widely Protestant and not likely to divide leaders and followers. There were neither clearly defined parties nor issues, but merely a general unease about how local and national politics would mesh. No one liked the marriage. Yet few were willing to risk much to defeat it. Though the government assumed religion was the vital factor, not one of Kent's 560 rebels is among the forty-eight Kentish Marian martyrs for Protestantism found in Foxe's *Book of Martyrs*. Only one rebel was accused as a nonconformist, whereas forty-three were notable parish church members and church wardens. These facts must have irritated John Bradford in 1554, for he reproachfully complained: "Do we not see some to die shamefully as rebels, which refuse to die for God's cause?"

The preacher glossed resistance to Mary correctly. It was primarily secular and political in nature. The lesson of conspiracies against her was that rebellion, to be effective, required gentry-commons solidarity. Such solidarity had been lacking in 1536–7 and again in 1549. It existed to a degree in Kent in 1554. The question was thus raised: What if such solidarity became widespread? What if the gentry of the kingdom became alienated from the goals of government in a direction appealing also to the ordinary folk? Religion had not figured in the great 1554 plots, at least not overtly. Yet clearly the political issue in 1553 and 1554 had become inseparable from religion. The Council in 1554 was kept busy investigating plots, rumors of coups, subversion, and riot. Its energies were distracted from ordinary good government. Exiles streamed to Europe. Executions cast a dark pall over native hopes of peace. There seemed to be a general, permanent crisis of the constitution.

The Marian Reaction

Mary's policies deepened the crisis.[6] The religious settlement of her reign rested on royal authority. It took the form of a compromise between the view that Mary might personally effect a general absolution from heresy and reunion and another that saw in reunion a political tinderbox. The Spanish resident ambassador wanted a "gentle policy" of expelling foreigners, restoring the Mass, and then seeing what to do about the Church lands. He knew that Catholics held as much spoils as Protestants. Hence reconciliation was of necessity a political bargain concerning property as well as popery. The first Marian Parliament repealed religious legislation made since 1547 and acted to curb radical preachers. These moves restored Henricianism. Then, in the 1554 Parliament, certain bills were hotly debated, touching as they did the creation of an "inquisition." This legislation against heresy in time produced the long list of martyrs made famous by Foxe. Then, in the third Parliament, the first held after Philip's arrival as consort, 1 & 2 Philip and Mary, c. 8, repealed all laws made since 1529 concerning the Church. The ensuing talks concerning Church lands touched off a parliamentary furor pacified only by the queen's agreement to rest content with freedom to settle doctrine. For those bold enough to assert spiritual jurisdiction over secularized lands, Parliament unsheathed the sword of praemunire.

The Marian reaction in fact maintained the Henrician royal Supremacy, despite appearances of a surrender to Rome. The Church was dependent on the monarchy for power. It was Catholic in doctrine to the extent that English statute allowed; and the queen could make no law without Parliament. There was no return of the great wealth that had made prelates independent powers in politics. Te Deums could be sung as absolution for twenty years of error, but Englishmen clearly did not love the Mass enough to disgorge wealth in return for its treasury of divine merit. Cardinal Pole's legatine visitation to Canterbury province in 1556 did not reveal a clergy of heroic, militant Protestant resisters. Yet there were 120 vacant parishes to witness the hardiness of some who suffered deprivation rather than subscribe to popery. Hundreds of laymen and scores of ministers chose exile in the Swiss cantons and German states.

[6] The reaction of the reign is the main concern of some very good articles and brief monographs, especially: S. R. Gammon, "Mary Tudor's Tragedy of Conscience," *Emory Univ. Q.* (1953), IX, pp. 39–47; P. Hughes, "A Hierarchy that Fought," *Clergy Review* (1940), XVIII, pp. 25–39; D. M. Loades, "The Enforcement of Reaction," *JEccH* (1965), XVI, pp. 54–66; C. H. Garrett, *The Marian Exiles* (Cambridge: Cambridge University Press, 1938); two works by A. G. Dickens, *The Marian Reaction in the Diocese of York* (York: Borthwick Institute, 1957): Part I (*The Clergy*) and Part II (*The Laity*); and W. Schenk, *Reginald Pole* (London: Longmans, 1950).

This resentment of the Marian enforcement of late medieval acts *adversos haereses* was duly noted by Renard, who testified to the passive resistance of the English. Some churches stood empty; others had meager congregations. The nominally Catholic ministry in command of restored altars was lacking in zeal and also in the support of many peace officers, who shied away from the repressive statutes. They were more interested in local ties and neighborliness. Despite repeated orders by Gardiner, now Lord Chancellor, at least thirty London parishes refused to restore the Mass. And anticlericalism was everywhere reviving.

Persecution nourished this renaissance. The vast majority of serious Protestants gave outward conformity to Mary's laws. Yet, in the five years of her reign, 275 Englishmen were burned alive at Mary's command. This number need not be exaggerated; nor should it be interpreted only in the context of religious devotion. In the single county of Essex, in the five Elizabethan years 1579–84, the assize justices found forty-nine persons guilty of black witchcraft out of eighty-nine presented. The penalty for a second offense was death by burning. Thus the sentence for heretics was like that for other practices deemed dangerously superstitious.[7] Few men supposed that men ought to have the liberty to believe or disbelieve at will. Certainly the most fervent Protestants did not, as Catholics were to discover in the 1570s and 1580s. There was wide acceptance of an often harsh and barbaric legal code.

Yet even this acceptance could be expedient. Protestants came to look on the martyrs as being witnesses to God's truth, truly Christ-bearing men. They learned of them in John Foxe's 1563 *Book of Martyrs*, where over 1,400 pages of text vied with grotesque, painful renderings of executions. The effect was to provide a genealogy of heroes whose torment in the 1550s gave continuity to the line leading from Wycliffe's poor bones to the quick flesh of Latimer, Ridley, Hooper, and Cranmer. Foxe's book was second in influence only to the Geneva Bible. And it is an open question whether his tales or the returned exiles exercised greater influence on successive generations of Elizabethan Protestants.

Returning exiles found comfort in the deaths of those too stern to take flight. Providence had clearly meant them to survive. Only their later zeal would make certain the earlier witness of martyrs was not given in vain. Their preservation was the guarantee that Truth would banish Roman error from England, with the Book and the discipline of exile combining to brighten the glory of men long dead. Those who had suffered separation from the nourishing native soil would keep bright the legendary stream that ran from Oldcastle to little Bilney and from him through Anne Askewe to Mary's catch of bishops

---

[7] Only relapsed, contumacious heretics were burned!

burned at Oxford. God had mixed in that stream the blood of martyrs to water the tree of liberty!

This was, however, but one way in which Mary's concentration on persecution had unintended results. Professor Dickens has shown with startling clarity how Mary's rule substituted the effort to suppress the new faith for a campaign to rebuild the old one. This was especially true in the very North-Country society reached by Bernard Gilpin in his desperate apostolate and allegedly conservative and receptive to the reaction. The court books of York diocese show the officials there struggling less to uproot a well-planted Edwardian Prayer Book than the more ancient popular contempt for censing altars, holy water, elements of the Eucharist, and contrived miracles. The force of "survivalism" could be made to work for Marian orthodoxy as well as for popular heterodoxy. Not every Marian dissenter was a Protestant. The memory of an ancient faith was present in the North, as Grindal was to discover during his term as archbishop there, when he complained that York diocese seemed part of another church. But the Marian missionaries never came to the distant places. And the force of survivalism went unharnessed in the 1550s, despite its being strong enough to make credible in the 1580s the mistaken notion that the North was largely Catholic and recusant.

Perhaps the most pathetic evidence of the error in direction made by Marian churchmen is that of the small group of nuns compelled to give up their husbands. The fractured life of one of them, Meg Basforth of Moxby, symbolized both the frustration of Mary's maternal drive and the broken monument of her policy. Meg Basforth had in the end "no marriage, no pension, no monastic community, but . . . compulsory permission to live outside the disused buildings of her dissolved nunnery."[8] In that land where the Pilgrims of Grace had restored monasteries, Mary could not rebuild chantries or restore church ornaments. Some altars were put back. Wills resumed the praise of saints and the Virgin. Priests said Mass with their backs to the faithful again.

The big campaign, however, was against the married clergy. Roughly 10 percent of the northern clergy had married in Edward's reign. This proportion was perhaps common elsewhere, although in Essex eighty-eight of 319 beneficed clerks were deprived because of marriage. It was especially significant that the eighty-seven married priests in Yorkshire were rarely presented for errors in faith; only one of the number was deprived for nonconformity. The clergy who were forcibly divorced from their wives and made to abandon sons and daughters as the price of their benefice were no match in zeal for the fifty-three earnest Protestant ministers of the diocese, led by their archbishop, Robert Holgate, who were forced from office on account of doctrine. Men of

[8] Dickens, *The Marian Reaction in the Diocese of York*, II, p. 17.

every religious opinion may well have wondered at the energy spent in breaking social bonds that could have been used to fashion spiritual ones. And they could be pardoned their curiosity as to why married priests who kept families intact were deprived whereas adulterous whoremasters were merely put to penance.

The local fabric of northern society had doubtless been altered by the dispersal of monastic wealth. And the structure of local interests was by 1555 perhaps inimical to a theocratic reaction. Certainly this must have been true of the many men of property. For in one sample of 330 wills proved in York's probate court, fully 25 percent used Protestant formularies, and 18 were adamant about salvation by faith alone. Yet few Yorkshiremen were then zealous enough to choose exile—only twenty-two men among a carefully analyzed sample of 472 studied by C. H. Garrett![9] But there was widespread, if superficial, acceptance of the Mass. Men easily believed one day in the sacrifice of the Mass even though the day before there had been only a memorial communion table. The old paraphernalia of bells and public processions was alive. There were men and women who remembered the gorgeous days of the great Wolsey. But only an active effort could transform the echo of the bells and the fading glimmer of Wolsey's age into an intense devotion to the restored religion.

The papacy was a distant thing in the North, even though daily life there could not have been a close approximation to the fervent Protestant sacrifice of the Southeast. Had there been a Marian campaign of Jesuits in the 1550s, or the social work of the teaching and healing orders so characteristic of continental Counter-Reformation efforts, laymen might have been moved toward active loyalty. Instead, there were only sporadic efforts to unseat heretical university divines and others that inflicted individual suffering. Officials seemed zealous enough to execute orders that revived their power in the courts Christian. This was no substitute for good preaching, however. And in the end it merited the measure of love given cynically in an order of the York city magistrates on the day of reconciliation with Rome:

That men should make bonfires to be lit to show themselves true children of the Church. . . .

This was weary advice to a tired people from perplexed men. England had become a kingdom more full of changes than the moon was of phases. Mary's death in November 1558 promised yet another. The future of the nation danced between the wiles of domestic plotters and foreign powers. There

[9] C. H. Garrett, *op. cit.*

were religious and social ills enough to make the wearing of the crown dangerous for even the most gifted of kings. Yet in England there was no dynasty of David and Solomon. Elizabeth stood to succeed her sister at a time when some leaders seemed willing to make war on the crown and others seemed ready to give it to France or Spain. The trimmers seemed in the majority at home, and it did not help their tempers to be hectored by the exiles' presses in Emden, Geneva, and Frankfurt. Monarchy and faith had been united in the Henrician marriage of the Supremacy. The fruit of that union was failing. Mary's childlessness was the epitaph of her reaction and also a sentence of doom on Spanish schemes. This realization opened yet another fault in the political landscape, since it was by no means certain that Spain would abandon the expansion of its English encirclement of the French enemy.

Thus the contest to determine the meaning of the Supremacy began again in circumstances as inauspicious as those of 1547 and 1553. There were as yet neither settled ideas of constitutional responsibility nor any agreement on the fundamental nature of the community, socially, politically, or religiously. The crises of Edward's reign had made that much clear. But could the nation survive if some means short of civil war were not found to limit the arbitrary use of the Supremacy? Members of Parliament had begun a revolution, *within* the framework of old institutions, by refusing to allow Mary to alienate the crown to Spain or disinherit Elizabeth by statute. But in turning against the history of Henry VIII's settlements and Dudley's revisions of them, they had not necessarily escaped the full burden of their past acquiescence. Henry had made the political classes his partners in ruining Rome; he had also excluded them from any share in making his royal Supremacy. Reformation was not yet the business of the realm in theory, even if practice had encroached some- what on the prerogatives of kings. What the Commons had done was merely to indicate the limits of the crown's coercive power—which stood on the consent given to its acts by the parliamentary aristocracy. But this was a matter of reaction rather than initiative. And Mary had repeatedly shown her readi- ness to try cases with them.

Elizabeth's Regime Takes Shape

When Elizabeth first acceded to the throne on November 17, 1558, the conventions of the monarchy gave her great flexibility. She could choose her councillors and friends at will. She could call Parliament and dis- solve it as she thought meet, or control its sessions by adjournments and other devices. There was nothing in the law requiring her to share the making of policy with peers or commons. Conceivably, she could have decided to shape her regime more like the "Turkish despotisms" of France and Spain. In religion, the last Tudor could carry forward the movement begun by her sister's strong Catholicism, pursue a course neither Roman nor Calvinist, or give free rein to returning ardent exiles and their domestic allies, the Puritans. Her foreign policy, like her religion, was her own to make, whether it took England toward the Hapsburgs or the Protestant monarchies of the North and the restless French and Dutch Calvinists. In economic matters, the queen could choose advisers hostile to industrial change or men devoted to commercial expansion. She could select those who wanted to continue the old controls over wages, prices, and every condition of labor or those who thought it best to allow unrestricted urban development and a consequent loosening of the framework of the social order and landed power.[1]

Whatever choices were made in Whitehall and Westminster, they impinged on English hearts and pockets. How the early Elizabethans helped Elizabeth choose went far toward determining the inheritance of the Stuarts as well as the deep-grained attitudes toward government among Englishmen. It will therefore be our object in what follows to set in perspective some of the major features of the Elizabethan political landscape. To do so, we shall look closely at the first fifteen years of Elizabeth's reign. That span witnessed the end of the instability of the previous two decades, although few at the time thought the queen's reign "glorious" or pacifying in its youth. Then we will survey broadly her consolidation of both secular and ecclesiastical government.

We will show the compromises by which she ruled. For her regime's beginning was marked by vast public contests. Papists struggled to find a place in the emerging Anglican world. Puritans showed themselves of mixed minds. Most sought to live in the new Anglican world while changing it by degrees. Some sought to remake it wholesale, chiefly along the Calvinist lines dictated by the Book and the discipline. Strife about religion and church polity remained endemic. We must be content to defer temporarily certain problems of religion as well as the work of the continuing effort to stabilize the economy. We must also defer consideration of questions touching the ways by which government was financed and ways in which such policies molded the fabric of society. These will be included in the last part of this

---

[1] The best treatment of Elizabeth's accession and early history is in Wallace MacCaffrey, *The Shaping of the Elizabethan Regime* (Princeton, N.J.: Princeton University Press, 1968). Also valuable are many books in a vast literature, among them: Sir John Neale, *Elizabeth I* (London: Jonathan Cape, 1934); M. Levine, *The Early Elizabethan Succession Question* (Stanford, Calif.: Stanford University Press, 1966); and volume one of Neale's *Elizabeth I and Her Parliaments* (London: Jonathan Cape, 1953). The best general study of the whole reign is J. B. Black, *The Reign of Elizabeth* (Oxford: Oxford University Press, 1952). Much light on domestic as well as foreign policy is also shed by Conyers Read, *Mr. Secretary Cecil and Queen Elizabeth* (New York: Knopf, 1955).

history. It is enough now to consider the initial shape of the regime fashioned by Elizabeth and her advisers.

The setting of Elizabeth's accession made a mockery of the vaunted liberty of the crown. England was divided by religious upheavals, schism, and heresy stretching back nearly thirty years. The Reformation called into being a European geography of faith. Ideology played an unaccustomed role in politics, making the medieval notion of the commonwealth more difficult to realize. Everywhere fanatics had their dreams, ". . . wherein/They weave a Paradise for their sect."[2]

The international Counter-Reformation had begun to develop, and the 1540s and 1550s saw the rise of the Jesuits and the debates that shaped the decrees of Trent's great church council. At home, Mary's reign had left a legacy of terror. The ardent Protestants wanted a new revolution against Rome and they had, in their minds, shaped a New Jerusalem.

Elizabeth, to whom they had assigned the Biblical role of Deborah, was her father's daughter by Anne Boleyn, whom Londoners had once called "that Protestant whore." Her education at the hands of Roger Ascham and Sir John Cheke had been humanistic, moderately Protestant, and godly. As the "second person," she had stayed free from implication in the Marian conspiracies. This circumspection had saved her life. It had also permanently influenced her ideas and garnered Spanish support. Yet she resented any suggestion by De Feria, Philip's ambassador, that she owed her throne to the Hapsburgs. That, she said, was her people's gift, by which she must have meant the lack of support for Mary's policy. In any event, the Spaniard found her an admirer of her father—whose wisdom was to burn his cap if he thought it knew his mind!

Her people, strong in their welcome to her, were materially weak and anxious about their ability to survive new broils. The politician Sir Thomas Smith had remarked that the loss of Calais to the French in 1558 cast soldiers homeward "with looks hanging down. . . . And what marvel of it? Here was nothing but fining, heading, hanging . . . and burning, taxing, levying . . . and loosing our strongholds. . . ." Yet the people were Elizabeth's chief asset. Other assets existed partly by design and partly by accident. Ten of twenty-six bishoprics were vacant shortly after her accession. This allowed her to go toward whatever religious direction she willed, with men of her choice. Leading gentry had sent their pledges of support should the Catholics make a stir along the unsecured Scottish Marches. Others came forward with advice—perhaps unwanted—about selecting her Council or with offers to serve. Among them was Sir William Cecil. He hailed Elizabeth at Hatfield on November 17,

[2] John Keats, *The Fall of Hyperion.*

became her secretary of state soon after, and remained her weightiest minister until 1598. Londoners welcomed her with dazzling shows of love and loyalty, their pageants proclaiming her role as their deliverer.

With the dumb-shows hailing her as Deborah (or Judith) fresh in her mind, the queen saw running before her also the tides bearing the Marian exiles homeward. She began to frame her policy with new councillors. They agreed on a Parliament, mindful that those who today welcomed her planned to build "the walls of Jerusalem . . . that the blood of martyrs, so largely shed, may not be in vain." What became clear in that first Elizabethan Commons was that her policy was not the only one. For in many minds the queen was slated to be titular head of a revolutionary movement skilled in the use of adversity, master of the press and pulpit, and steeled by the discipline of exile.

The policy Elizabeth and her councillors carried to Westminster on January 25, 1559, was one of moderation. It was informed by her view of Henry VIII's statesmanship. And it looked toward a religious settlement as comprehensive as possible, wholly untouched by sectarian enthusiasm. She knew how uneasily poised her father's revolution had been. She knew also how war debts had mounted, how trade was stagnant, unemployment wide-spread, discontent and war-weariness prolific. Hence it seemed necessary in her policy to harness the ardor of the Protestants without discouraging her Catholic subjects. Could she but do so, then the Puritans might watch over her throne as the Pillar of Fire had guarded Israel in the desert. Papists abroad would thus have no cause to launch a religious war to save England. The unity of England would guarantee her independence. But to manage this the queen needed the support of the political classes.

This she hoped to win by the regime formed in 1558. She managed to build a Council of politicians and officials broadly based and willing to carry her program to the country. Among the lords, Arundel, Clinton, Pembroke, Derby, and Shrewsbury were successful courtiers, able advisers, and great county magnates. The secretariats and higher administrative cadres were com-posed of Edwardians such as Cecil, Mildmay, Sadler, and the new Lord Keeper, Sir Nicholas Bacon; but she maintained the middle reaches of officialdom that had served Mary. She strove to have the best of both worlds—a strong anti-Marian cast among the policymakers, and continuity of personnel not set aside by dynastic accidents. This combination of neuters, Protestants, and Marians gave the government of 1558–9 a tone of political Protestantism devoid of evangelical fervor and moderately anti-Catholic yet wholly anti-papal. An observer might have been pardoned for thinking it Henrician. Only the hard-core Marian Catholics were purged from the Council board and the new Parliament. The local magistracy was left alone, at least initially.

Thus buttressed, Elizabeth's bill for a new religious settlement appeared. It was confined to the following matters: a new act of Supremacy, communion in both species, and a continuation of the Marian order of worship. This was to return to the point of political separation from Rome with very little advance from the Henrician settlement in worship or faith. Further reform might come later.

The queen's political education began with dissent on two sides. The Marian bishops did not cooperate in the Lords. Much more vital was the thunder on the left. The radical Protestants were undeceived by the apparent Protestant partisanship of the regime. They had organized public opinion and a faction in the Commons. They served notice that their clerical and lay sympathizers had their own notion of right religion. They brought to bear an informed body of opinion, from within the country, as to what policy should be. They proposed a series of amendments to the Supremacy bill, the effect of which was to add a new act of uniformity. The government found the Commons demanding the radical 1552 Prayer Book as an acceptable minimum reformation. Both the queen and the Council appeared stunned by this concerted invasion of the crown's prerogative touching religion. By Easter Week (March 26), an impasse had been reached. The queen wished to dissolve her first Parliament, the Commons having reluctantly agreed to little more than an act of Supremacy. The Catholic bishops in Convocation openly called their queen a schismatic, despite her moderation.

Signing the bill would perhaps have suited Elizabeth's own religious views. But politically it was undesirable. It seemed to alienate all but the indifferent and the *politiques*. Yet to do more with the war with the French unsettled and the Spanish–Papal axis threatening to withdraw their benign patronage, she needed more than advice and an empty treasury. It appears that her hesitancy sprang from a desire to have better international circumstances. These would allow a purge of rigid papists who opposed even the Supremacy in Lords and Convocation. She was also intent on guarding her rule against the pretensions of the Commons, especially of such as dared ask her, "How long halt ye between two opinions?" Elijahs abounded.

What probably changed her mind and brought about the Settlement of 1559 was a stroke of luck. On March 19, news of the peace of Cateau-Cambrésis had reached London. The treaty, signed in early April, ending the war with France coincided with, if it did not cause, the decision not to dissolve Parliament but to adjourn until after Easter. No doubt the vigor and exactness of Protestant advocacy also had moved Elizabeth toward compromise, since it was abundantly clear that Henricianism was now a useless formula. Moreover, the intransigence of the Catholics in Convocation implied that sooner or later Parliament, rather than the Church assembly, would have to be the theater of change. Bishop Scot and Abbot Feckenham had defended papal supremacy.

Free now of excessive reliance on Spain, and also provoked by the Marian bishops' blow to government solidarity, the queen moved in the sessions after Easter toward the dominant Protestantism of the Commons. Nearly one hundred of its 400 members looked for leadership to the dozen or more "exiles" there. The number of such godly gentlemen, who were returned under the patronage of reform-minded aristocrats like Francis Russell, earl of Bedford, was vital. The exiles also influenced a rigged conference on liturgical change held at Westminster, discrediting the Catholic bishops. In the Commons, a new government bill for the Supremacy, and another concerning uniformity, based on the 1552 worship, subordinated Elizabeth's preference for the more moderate 1549 Prayer Book. Only then did she gain agreement on modest changes in the words of administration and in the striking of the Black Rubric.

This essentially Zwinglian compromise admitted some conservative departures, a few inroads on an essentially radical bill. Catholic hopes were ended. Yet the Act of Uniformity allowed much that was abhorrent to nearly all who returned from Geneva and Frankfurt: private baptism, confirmation, kneeling at the communion, the sign of the cross, and Romish vestments—"that comical dress," as some soon styled it. The administration of communion contained both memorialist phrases and some implying the real presence. The allowance of the "scenic apparatus" of priests—that is what John Jewel called vestments—provided as many bones of contention as did the sacramental definitions.

The fact was that few expected this settlement of religion to survive as the force modeling a distinctively reformed but English church. The record of three decades made that outcome cause for neither reasonable hope nor optimism—then as now the luxury of fools. Moreover, unlike the Supremacy of Henry VIII, both the queen's title and the new Act of Uniformity bore the marks of rude joinery. She was ambiguously styled "Supreme Governor, etc.," but this was not a choice she had made alone, as Henry had done in 1534. She had been forced toward the settlement by a strong radicalism in the ruling classes. Wallace MacCaffrey has rightly insisted that the Elizabethan regime was shaped both by the sovereign's initiative and "a powerful, determined, and organized party of her own subjects."[3] The new political and religious order was being molded by the opinions of a mass of the queen's subjects. A great decision of state depended on political accommodations between ruler and ruled.

[3] *The Shaping of the Elizabethan Regime*, p. 62.

The Permanent Crisis Eases

This fact was even more evident in the other efforts made to define the faith and settle the polity of the Church, just as it was in the two greatest secular matters of the next dozen years: the succession question and the queen's marriage. Both determined the choice of a subsequent foreign policy.

The 1559 legislation had left untouched the structure of ecclesiastical government. This left aside discipline—how in fact the Church courts and the Supreme Governor would enforce the 1559 Acts. The Supremacy statute required an oath of temporal officers—those who took holy orders, studied at the universities, or held land in feudal tenures. Those who refused it were to suffer deprivation and disability for life. The Act of Uniformity required key men to commit themselves fully and the masses to conform outwardly. There were penalties of deprivation for clergy who refused to use the Prayer Book and for anyone encouraging any other form of service. These promised the forfeiture of all goods and life imprisonment for a third offense. Absence from Sunday and holy-day services incurred the fine of 12 pence and sometimes censure. Although mild compared to Mary's penalties for not conforming, these were nonetheless harsh, especially for men influenced after 1560 by new religious texts.[4]

Before these texts appeared, the 1559 visitations concentrated chiefly on rooting out Roman practices and any resistance to the Prayer Book. The most important result was the deprivation of the Marian bishops. The enforcement of sentences given on lower levels was left to local notables and was usually uneven. There was, therefore, early disagreement on what subscription to the 1559 Settlement meant. And this was to remain a center of contention until the Subscription Act of 1571 made it clear how "final" the earlier settlement had been.

While Elizabeth was filling the two-dozen vacant sees, the Royal Injunctions of 1559 revived those of 1552. They were in fact restatements of them. There was in the new ones, however, a significant move toward checking Protestant excesses. Vestments were prescribed. Altars still standing were to be preserved. Communion wafers were to be of the Roman style. And printing was carefully checked. The crucifix and candles reappeared in the royal chapel. Between 1561 and 1563, several formularies defined the theological foundations of this parti-colored Protestantism. The Bishops drew up eleven articles in 1561, before the fuller Thirty-Nine Articles of Religion passed Convocation in 1563.

[4] For example, William Whittingham's version of the Geneva Bible (1560), the 1561 Genevan *Forme of Prayer*, and Thomas Norton's 1561 version in English of Calvin's *Institutes*.

These constituted a statement close to the prevailing doctrine of 1553 and were made explicitly Protestant by radicals in the clerical assembly. Meanwhile, the government printed official expositions of doctrine: Archbishop Matthew Parker's *Book of Homilies* (1562) and John Jewel's famous *Apology* of the same year.

Resistance to published doctrine steadily mounted until 1571, when the queen finally gave statutory assent to this array of statements. The advantage to the crown lay in the legal sanctions, which were better than those deriving from mere proclamations and injunctions. The necessity of these bills can easily be grasped if we consider the subscription question. Some 200 conserva-tive beneficed clergy had been deprived in the 1559 enforcement campaign. Radical Protestants were of course not inclined to lament those "dumb dogs" and their Romish ways. They did worry, however, over what subscription meant to them.

The background of the 1571 bills had made this clear. In 1563 the reformers in the Church and the Commons had tried to secure an act confirming the Articles of the Faith. The queen had stopped the bill in the Lords, however. The 1563 Parliament's zealous Protestants had opposed forcing general sub-scriptions to the Articles. So had their allies in the 1566 Convocation. They wanted the Articles of Faith but not the ceremonies. The royal faith agreed well enough with their "true Christian faith and the doctrine of the sacraments." They thus favored measures for a minimum oath. This would catch the pro-Marian clergy, while sparing "precise" Protestants who found the ceremonies obnoxious. When the government bills of 1571 seemed to require subscription even of those stalwarts ordained under Edward's and Elizabeth's ordinals, the radicals balked and amended the bills. They weakened them enough to win a royal veto. The queen would not admit their right to "mutilate the Book" or to accept what articles they deemed convenient. That amounted to a Commons censorship of the established Church.

The question was compromised by providing a general subscription only for clerks ordained by the Marian ordinal and those taking cures in the future. The words of Parker, "you will refer yourselfs wholly to us [bishops]," had met an ominous rebuke from the Puritan Peter Wentworth: ". . . we will pass nothing before we understand what it is [i.e., how concordant with scripture], for that were but to make you Popes. . . ." The dispute was typical of many at the heart of Puritan rejection of the Settlement.[5]

The politics of religion had yielded the outline of a settlement. Other events since the 1550s, however, had made it clear that politics also involved two domestic issues closely related to those of faith and discipline: the marriage of

---

[5] See the long section on Puritanism in Chapter Nine.

the queen and the succession. Both trenched on foreign policy. Their impact was reciprocal.

The experience of religious revolutions clearly had made faith an annex of sovereignty. Supremacy and uniformity depended on the heir to the crown. Elizabeth was unmarried in 1558; before 1563 she had come perilously close to letting her infatuation with Sir Robert Dudley degenerate into a marriage opposed strongly by most magnates and the lesser elites.[6] Perhaps this opposition was less important than her own deep psychological inhibitions to marriage, even marriage with Leicester. She repeatedly said she would have no competitor for power, no king to her queen. The fact that any marriage, whether at home or abroad, would diminish the flexibility of her foreign policy, conveniently fitted her mental makeup. A French marriage would alarm the Hapsburgs; a Spanish or Imperial one the French; a Protestant one, whether German or Scandinavian, the Papacy and the Catholic powers. Since Elizabeth saw the maintenance of dialogue with Rome and Spain as essential to England's security in the 1560s, her view of policy marched in step with the nation's needs.

The basic elements of the "permanent crisis" still prevailed, however. There was no heir apparent. Elizabeth was exceedingly reluctant to create a "second person," because of either her own inner security or that of the realm, or both. She would react with rage to any suggestion that she either marry and produce an heir or, failing that, designate a successor among the various lines close to the Tudor blood—Scottish or English. Her advisers pointedly asked her how the country could escape a new wave of dynastic wars if her resolve to remain a virgin queen hardened. She was the last of the Tudors. The question being thus tossed, some of her councillors wanted to bring in the Grey heiress, Lady Catherine. Others favored the nearest Protestant male, the earl of Huntingdon, Henry Hastings. There was also a scheme to bring back the Scottish line, the best claim by Tudor blood. If Mary Queen of Scots renounced either her religion or any title during Elizabeth's life, she would remove at one stroke the danger inherent in Catholic dynasticism and French threats. So bizarre was Elizabeth's thinking on the Scottish claim and its dangers that she once proposed her own Dudley as a husband for Mary. The three would then live in one household at Elizabeth's charge![7]

---

[6] Dudley was raised to the earldom of Leicester.

[7] Elizabeth's psychosexual configurations may have derived from a bizarre, traumatic childhood in which her allegedly adulterous mother was beheaded and successive stepmothers suffered death—Jane Seymour in childbirth and Catherine Howard because of her treasonable adulteries. Henry VIII also put away a fifth wife, Anne of Cleves. Elizabeth's earliest socialization (and awareness of sexuality) was steeped in murder, adultery, and rebellion. Moreover, she was examined by Edward VI's privy councillors, regarding her virginity, at the age of fifteen, in the context of Admiral

Public opinion would never let the matter rest, in or out of Parliament. The queen protested that her marriage was private business and told Dean Nowell of St. Paul's that she would "not in so deep a matter wade with so shallow a wit." The Dean, however, shot back: "If your parents had been of your mind, where had you been then?" A serious illness in 1562 had raised to fever pitch fears of a succession struggle. The Commons in 1563 urged her to declare a successor. She told them "it would cost much blood to England." Before the next session of Parliament, pamphleteers waged a vehement campaign to urge the queen to marry. Her reaction was to tell the Commons they were not to meddle with marriage or the succession. This raised the question of free speech, causing Elizabeth to retreat and promise to marry, but not without giving a sly rebuff:

God forbid that your liberty should make my bondage, or that your lawfull liberties should any ways have been infringed. . . .

Earlier she had played the patriot:

Was I not born in this realm? [Were] my parents born in any foreign country? Is there any cause that should alienate myself from being careful over this country? . . . What turmoil have I made to this common wealth that I should be suspected to have no regard of the same?

Yet the furor would not die down. The political elite had too much at stake to put aside either marriage or succession. The increasingly Protestant nation knew Foxe's book.[8] Its leaders could not contemplate a Catholic succession calmly, even if Catholic nobles such as the duke of Norfolk and the earl of Sussex wanted the Scottish queen. The flight of Mary into England in 1568 had heated the issue to a boil. The Earls' Rising in the North (1569), the Ridolfi Plot, and other conspiracies—especially the abortive rising of the duke of Norfolk—kept before the Protestants the idea that there was an international Catholic conspiracy against Elizabeth and England. Tumults had revived the notion that rebellion with foreign assistance might best determine the succession. Hence, the Parliament of 1571, besides ruling on the queen's marriage, insisted on excluding Mary Queen of Scots from the royal line, made harsh measures against Catholics, and risked stormy debates on the forbidden subject of succession. In the exclusion clause of the Treasons Act of 1571, Elizabeth

---

Seymour's treason. Finally, Seymour, who sought to marry Elizabeth, did marry her last stepmother, Catherine Parr! Mary's marital failure and history of delusive pregnancy pointed up the lesson of how worthless and dangerous a consort might be.

[8] See William Haller, Foxe's " Book of Martyrs" and the Elect Nation (London: Jonathan Cape, 1963).

was made to reconcile her prohibitions with the Commons' strong political opinion, amply supported in the Lords.

No little part was played by the politically inept issuance of a papal bull of deposition against Elizabeth in 1570. The stupid papal fulminations stressed the close connections among religion, the succession, and the general issues of foreign policy. Elizabeth shared with her future antagonist, Philip of Spain, a cautious and devious diplomatic tactic. She preferred to keep all foreign parties optimistic regarding religion and the succession. Yet her real weakness required Spanish patronage against the French preponderance in Scotland. It therefore was apparent to some of her ministers that a Protestant power in Scotland would neutralize the threat in the North, allow scope to pursue an independent line on the Continent, and perhaps put England squarely in the circle of Protestant forces arrayed against an expansive Counter-Reformation. The first great move in that direction was Cecil's daring, successful gamble pitting the queen's money, and then troops, against the French efforts to suppress the Protestant lords. When the queen herself considered a similar intervention and a campaign on French soil in order to recover Calais, her more cautious councillors rightly warned against the risk.

The two schemes of 1560 were symptomatic of the future. Elizabeth's politicians had for the moment edged her toward a policy inimical to France in Scotland but dissuaded her from overseas adventurism. Yet in 1562, when civil war broke out in France and the Huguenots fared badly, the weight of her Council was for aiding the cause of religion. Just as her caution in doctrine had been forced to the left by political pressure, so by 1563 had the queen been tied to the expansive foreign policies of her more radical politicians. In this respect, nothing was more vital than the movement to consolidate opinion, which saw the favorite Dudley join Cecil and reverse his earlier stance favoring the Hapsburgs. The intervention in France in 1562 had been an ignominious failure. But the balance struck had been one in which English power was being committed to the cause of the Protestant states.

Throughout the decades of the 1560s and 1570s, this commitment was enlarged. Elizabeth consistently supported the Protestant lords north of the Tweed. In 1568, the earlier raids of sea captains on Portuguese and Spanish territories and ships in America were capped by the English siege of San Juan de Ulua, on the Gulf of Mexico. Elizabeth also approved the capture of a fleet with a cargo of silver intended to supply the duke of Alva in his repression of Dutch Protestants. Marriage negotiations with the Hapsburg archduke were broken off on the grounds of infringement of England's statutory religion. The Catholic conspiracies against the throne (1569–72)[9] and the papal sentence of 1570

[9] See Chapter Nine for the government's policy toward Catholics.

simply clarified the logic of past events. There was an increasingly bold anti-Spanish policy, coupled with one of reserve toward France.

What finally forced a full commitment to a Protestant internationalism that would match the religious settlement of 1571 was the fate of the Netherlands and France. England's economy had been geared for generations to the good trade centers of Burgundy and its environs. The disturbances in Flanders clearly meant a strain in Anglo-Hapsburg amity. The effort to crush Protestantism in the provinces had produced a wave of emigration across the North Sea. Meanwhile, the Huguenots had won La Rochelle and were raiding commerce from the Pyrenees to the Zuider Zee. So were the Dutch, sometimes using English bases. When the Spanish seized English ships—or were alleged to have done so—Cecil had ordered seizures of Flemish and Spanish property. Cecil had been saying for some time that the moment was ripe for bold strokes. Spain was distracted by the Turks in the Levant. The wars of religion in France weakened that enemy. Waiting would only mean facing Spain when she was no longer so preoccupied and the French Protestants had been defeated. That would ruin the Protestant cause and threaten both England's commerce and her very independence. To drive home the point, the Merchant Adventurers planned to move their main bases to Hamburg or Emden.

By 1572, the decisions that shaped the English politics of Protestantism were made. The enemies at home had been weakened or struck down. The precarious position of the Dutch rebels and the slaughter of French Protestants (the St. Bartholomew's Massacre) in 1572 made clear the choice: either go actively to the aid of the Protestant rebels, as England had done in Scotland years before, or be prepared to see them defeated and to fight alone. This realization was borne home by Spanish support for the Irish Catholics and by the French intervention against Spain in the Netherlands. If France won Dutch independence or became the patron there, thus establishing a French hold on the Atlantic, the Channel, and parts of the North Sea, English commerce would be inhibited or ruined.

Economic needs were central in determining the tortured course of trying to preserve Dutch freedom under a weak Spanish rule. This option ended in 1584 with the assassination of William the Silent. A Spanish victory was as much a dagger aimed at England's heart as any French success. A year later, English faces and subsidies were there. For the foreseeable future, England's foreign policy would be rooted in her Protestantism, and the country would make future sovereigns pay dearly for deciding otherwise. The Armada was already on the horizon in 1572![1]

Men did not perceive at once that the sum of these compromises in religion

[1] Garrett Mattingly, *The Armada* (Boston: Houghton Mifflin, 1959).

and politics had ended the permanent crisis. But in retrospect we may say that the threats to England's independence between 1558 and 1572, at home and abroad, had unified the nation's political classes. The Catholics at home were a sullen and defeated remnant. The radical Protestants were critical but loyal. The Anglican Church had been set on a course promising broad support. The Papacy's bull went unenforced. The Scottish threat seemed over, and Mary was in English custody. When the Armada did come, the French monarchy was weak and had Protestant prospects; half the Netherlands had been saved from Spain; and there had been a span of two decades of internal peace, unprecedented since the middle of Henry VIII's reign. The furious social-reform advocacy of the Commonwealth Men had burnt itself out in the 1550s. Court preachers now made hierarchy, humility, and obedience the "popular" themes. The future of the regime seemed less precarious, even if the succession still grieved many. A hybrid political system had come into being, with a consolidated political elite taking initiatives in its strange new role of cooperating in policy with a still-powerful monarchy.

Before we consider more fully the shape of this religious and political system and make any analysis of its structure, it will help to turn to the developments at large in the economy and the impact these had on the English social system.

Chapter Seven
THE REVOLUTION IN AGRICULTURE

As England emerged from the four decades of crisis that marked the transition between two societies, her economy exhibited signs of expansion in both its agricultural and industrial-commercial sectors. Rising population inflated food prices and broke the back of permanent pasture conversions. In agriculture the era of Elizabeth and the early Stuarts was one of revolution. The expansion of English industry and commerce rested on the changing shape of agrarian life and agriculture. The natural boundary lines of society shifted constantly and rarely coincided with either the administrative divisions of the English nation or the linguistic lines that separated Wales, England, and Scotland from one another. But the boundaries of the richly varied regional societies were slowly yielding to political and cultural integration as the pressure of a growing people demanded new ways of life.[1]

Our knowledge of population growth after 1500 is uncertain as to degree but indisputable as to trend. Various tax data and ecclesiastical surveys between 1547 and 1650 suggest a rise to about four million in 1603 from a base of about 2.5 million in 1500, followed by a further increase, at a slower rate, to about 4.5 million in 1650. The rise in population was itself subject to local and regional variations. A Leicestershire study shows a 58 percent rise between 1563 and 1603. One Cambridgeshire village grew little before 1550 but doubled its size in the century after 1563. Between 1550 and 1670 the population of Wales and Northwest England increased by 50 percent. The growth of London was wholly disproportionate to that of the kingdom generally. Immigration helped to swell the metropolis from 60,000 inhabitants in 1500 to at least 250,000 in 1640, a mushroom growth that had a seriously distorting impact on production and prices in the Thames basin, as we shall see.

[1] See G. S. L. Tucker, "English Pre-Industrial Population Trends," *EcHR* (1963), XVI, pp. 205–18; and E. A. Wrigley, "Family Limitation in Pre-Industrial England," *EcHR* (1966), XIX, pp. 82–109.

This raises the questions: what was the character of agriculture and how did existing practices accommodate themselves to demographic pressure?

Englishmen in the late sixteenth century thought of their country as a rich, open farmland somewhat pockmarked with poverty. Travelers from Europe noticed more the green than the gold, more the riches than the hardship. They encountered pasture, sheep, and cattle more often than fields groaning under the burden of corn. Foreigners especially noticed landscapes other than the common fields[2] of the East Midlands and the richness of East Anglian grain, stressing in their comments that no other place in Europe used so much land in pasture. Friedrich, duke of Württemberg, on a trip between London and Oxford in 1592, was amazed by the numbers of cattle and the immense flocks of sheep. Some voyagers recorded colorful and seemingly pagan celebrations of the harvest of corn. Most observers noted forest and pasture, not only in the wild and thinly populated parts of northern and western England, but all along the road from London to Bristol and from Oxford to Southampton. Plowed fields appeared as oases in the desert, and the barren slopes of the Pennine ridges and the southwest uplands impressed most observers by their inhospitable look.

The farming systems of England reveal the general astuteness of foreign comments on land use. While these systems are too diverse to be discussed here in great detail, either in the geographical or the topographical-agricultural sense, farming in different regions (Fen, Cheese Country, Butter Country, Midland Plain) showed the rich variety of ways in which men worked the land and lived in the societies formed by its features.[3]

[2] The common-field system was but one of many arrangements for agricultural purposes. In common-field districts, the arable, pasture, and waste were not permanently divided among the local peasantry. Instead, the land was privately owned but under the management of the community. The peasants practiced cooperative husbandry on plots allotted with the arable fields. All men could "common" their cattle on the pasture and take such from the waste; they were "commoners." The social framework of common-field England was related to the farming arrangements, with nuclear villages and small hamlets a natural reflection of common work. The contrast was marked, when we consider the patterns of isolated farms in "severalty," or personal management, by lessees and proprietors. Common-field England, based on strong communities and customs of work, was in contrast to the simple management of enclosed fields.

[3] The indispensable work of topography and historical geography is H. C. Darby, *An Historical Geography of England before A.D. 1800* (Cambridge: Cambridge University Press, 1948). Professor Eric Kerridge, *The Agricultural Revolution* (London: Allen & Unwin, 1967), describes forty-one topographical-agricultural regions lying within the ten geographical ones used by Joan Thirsk in her essay on farming regions in Joan Thirsk, ed., *The Agrarian History of England and Wales, Vol. IV: 1500–1640* (Cambridge: Cambridge University Press, 1967). These books are basic to the account given here, supplemented by the works cited for particular regions, as well as H. L. Gray, *English Field Systems* (Cambridge: Cambridge University Press, 1915) and R. E. Ernle, *English Farming Past and Present* (London: Longmans, 1961).

The Farming Regions of England

Mixed
Wood pasture
Open pasture

NORTH SEA

IRISH SEA

Cumberland
Durham
Westmorland
Lancashire
Yorkshire
YORK
Lincolnshire
Cheshire
Derbyshire
Nottinghamshire
LINCOLN
Norfolk
Staffordshire
Shropshire
Leicestershire
Cambridgeshire
Suffolk
Herefordshire
Worcestershire
Warwickshire
Northamptonshire
Bedfordshire
Essex
Gloucestershire
Oxfordshire
Buckinghamshire
Hertfordshire
LONDON
Berkshire
Somerset
Wiltshire
Surrey
Kent
Sussex
Devon
Dorset
Cornwall

ENGLISH CHANNEL

The structure of farming depended on gross physical characteristics. Men modified these significantly by clearing woods, draining swamps, and cultivating moors. But nature herself had made divisions between the North and West of England, where moors and mountains dominated, and the South and East, where valleys and broad plains with mild climates were common. Where men found cold, stony, and thin soils, they had to admit the supremacy of grass. Animal production necessarily dominated these regions. In the softer, warmer, and deeper soils, farmers had a greater range of choices. The South and the East were areas of mixed farming, where cattle and sheep helped to fertilize and work the soil. In the uplands, stock raising, dairying, pig farming, and horse breeding were practiced in varying proportions, although food production was mostly for domestic consumption rather than the market. In the flatlands of the South and East, corn was produced for the towns. Animals were kept mainly as manure sources to maintain field fertility. Elsewhere, farmers cropped arable land to fatten cattle for the butcher and kept only marginal supplies for the market. In valleys, plains, fens, and marshlands there was a great variety of mixed-husbandry enterprises.

England's Farming Regions

The general boundary between the pastoral zone and the counties of mixed husbandry stretched from Teesmouth in the northeast to Weymouth in the southwest. Into the pastoral zone fell Cornwall, Devon, Somerset, West Dorset, Gloucestershire, Herefordshire, Worcester, Shropshire, Staffordshire, Derbyshire, Cheshire, Lancashire, West Yorkshire, Durham, Northumberland, Cumberland, and Westmorland. All other counties fell into the other zone.

The northern region of the pastoral zone embraced Cumberland, Westmorland, Durham, Northumberland, and Furness.[4] The entire area possessed

---

[4] For the description and analysis of regional farming, I have relied on Thirsk and Kerridge, as well as Gray, Fussell, and Ernle. These more specialized studies were helpful: C. M. L. Bonch and G. P. Jones, *The Lake Counties, 1500–1830* (Manchester: Manchester University Press, 1961); G. E. Fussell, *Farming Systems in the North and East Ridings of Yorkshire* (York: City of York, Castle Museum, 1944); H. C. Darby, *The Draining of the Fens* (Cambridge: Cambridge University Press, 1940); J. Thirsk, *English Peasant Farming* (London: Routledge & Kegan Paul, 1957) and *Fenland Farming in the Sixteenth Century* (Leicester: Leicester University Press, 1953); K. J. Allison, "The Sheep-Corn Husbandry of Norfolk," *AgHR* (1957), V, pp. 12–30; E. C. K. Gonner, *Common Land and Enclosure* (London: Macmillan, 1912); M. Havinden, *The Rural Economy of Oxfordshire* (Oxford, 1961; unpublished B. Litt. thesis); A. L. Rowse, *Tudor Cornwall* (London: Jonathan Cape, 1957); W. G. Hoskins, *Devon* (London: Collins, 1954); H. P. R. Finberg, *Gloucestershire Studies* (Leicester: Leicester University Press, 1957); W. G. Hoskins, *The Midland Peasant* (London: MacMillan, 1957) and *Essays in Leicestershire History* (Liverpool: Liverpool University Press, 1950); C. S. Orwin, *The Open Fields* (Oxford: Clarendon Press, 1954).

a few scattered highland communities, infrequent villages where peasants practiced mixed husbandry in common fields. The area was remote, not easily accessible to travelers or the government, not much concerned with industry and commerce, and was generally regarded as wild, even savage, by the southerners. Its farmers were dispersed among secluded farms; there were few hamlets. As in many other frontier societies, war (against the Scots) and clan loyalties influenced the tenor of life. The hills were a refuge for outlaws, and the crown itself was often helpless when faced with the resistance of the solitary, stubborn men in this region. The most influential landowners often did not reside on their estates, a fact that contributed to lawlessness. Between the violence of society and that of nature, poverty spawned.

Those who lived there did not see their country as others did, of course, as we know from the novels by Walter Scott that celebrated the fruitful plains below craggy mountains. There was in truth relatively little plowland—and what there was was confined to low-lying areas. There a mixed husbandry prevailed. The people of the area counted their wealth in cattle; hunting grounds; good fishing lakes; sheep, with coarse wool and fine; and sweet mutton. Barley was the chief grain, along with oats, and both were used for bread and cakes and for brewing. Wheat was scarce. Poor harvests necessitated additional means of support, so the men mined coal, quarried rock, and maintained cottage handicraft industries. Coarse woolen cloth was manufactured. Between the mountain fells and the villages, differences in farming methods abounded. In all the lower valleys, villages took the place of hamlets. Common fields with large arable tracts dominated meadowland. The bulk of the field crops was used as fodder for livestock and not as market produce. Store cattle and sheep were driven to markets, which often were far to the South. Beef and mutton ruled the economy, supported by dairying and horse breeding. By the early seventeenth century, enclosure was making rapid progress, however, as part of the process of agricultural improvement. Between the mountains and dales of these counties there were as many differences in patterns of living and farming as there were between the whole area and the champion[5] areas of the South.

Yorkshire and Lincolnshire constituted another region, which comprised a variety of subregions. Yorkshire had highland valleys in which cloth manufacture was prominent—a reflection of the dominance of pastoral farming. Many farms grew small amounts of oats and rye, and some barley. But arable constituted as little as 7 percent of the land, while meadow took up 55 percent and pasture 37 percent. Holdings were small in the dales, where dairying and sheep breeding held sway. Graziers on a large scale controlled the slopes, often causing alarm among those who noted a growing shortage of grass in what

---

[5] Open-field country, from the French *champagne*, through corruption into *champaigne* ("flat, level, or open fields"); derived ultimately from the Latin *campania* ("open country").

was a poor pasture-farming country. The lowland areas of both counties consisted of mixed-husbandry areas in which southern-type scenes were common: open fields of arable; good pasture and meadow lands; nucleated villages; and crops of wheat, barley, peas, and rye. Stock was more profitable than crops, a strong manorial society prevailed, and manor and village were often synonymous. There were also chalk and limestone uplands fit for little but sheep running and the raising of coarse barley. Wool went to the clothiers of West Riding and East Anglia. Barley was the cash crop, a source of income supplemented by a growing cattle industry. Large-scale capitalist farming thrived, as the small local population facilitated enclosures for sheep walks. Mixed farming was also characteristic of the marshland of both counties; most attention went to sheep and cattle, but hemp, fishing, and fowling also were much in evidence.

The region had much forest and fenland, of which most of the forest was in Yorkshire. Forest and fen regions had distinctive economies and personalities. Royal forest law discouraged improvement of arable; consequently, pasture farming—both dairying and meat production—was more important than arable production of any sort. Numerous pigs foraged in the woods, as we know from the fame of Yorkshire ham and bacon. As the population grew rapidly after 1500 and forest law enforcement abated, these districts had land to spare. Nevertheless, a large part of the population lived in poverty, and the Yorkshire forests were infamous for the wretchedness of life therein. By contrast, the chief danger to subsistence in the fenland system of pastoral farming was flooding. The fenland social structure was similar to that of forest regions and lowland village communities. Where drainage had reclaimed fertile land, villages spread. There were large populations. Commons yielded peat fuel; reed thatching and wildfowl added to the income of a large population of low-ranking peasants who were relatively comfortable. The country did not attract gentlemen. Village communities were largely self-governing, with the obstinacy that came from an active role in planning the husbandry practiced there. The few high-ranking peasants benefited from a rich and abundant grassland. Cows yielded good milk; cattle could be fattened for slaughter, along with sheep; fish were plentiful. Hence, while holdings were small and many peasants had no land of their own, the region produced enough corn and animal calories for all, with some surplus for marketing.

One of the centers of greatest prosperity was East Anglia, in which the main counties—Norfolk and Suffolk—made up three farming regions. On the loamy and sandy soils, there was a mixed sheep-corn husbandry; the heavier clays of the central parts of Suffolk and southeast Norfolk were chiefly grassland; and there was a large fenland area in west Norfolk and northwest Suffolk. The lords in most light soil areas had sole sheep-grazing rights, which forced the tenants to keep cattle; there they were also allowed to graze with the lord's sheep, mostly for dairying purposes. Areas with sandy soil were used for cattle fattening, pig production, and small corn crops. Because the area as a whole was a sheep-corn region, arable usage dictated that sheep be run primarily for their manure rather than for either mutton or wool. Poultry was also raised on a large scale. Society was of the village-manorial kind. Lords of great wealth were the "natural leaders" of society. Norfolk had a flourishing cloth industry. The coastal waters provided a ready source of additional seasonal employment in net making, boat repairing, and fishing, and in houses where salt was gathered by evaporation of sea water.

On the heavier clays of the wood-pasture soils, ash, oak, and hazel trees grew in profusion around the small hamlets and scattered farms. Pheasants and partridges attracted hunters who wanted sport as a relief from commercial dairying and cattle fattening. There was timber working. Cheese, butter, and milk were market enterprises, and the breeding of Norfolk ponies and Suffolk Punches[6] were more important livestock activities than sheep running. Barley was the largest cereal crop, with wheat a poor second. Early in the 1630s, carrots and turnips were grown for feeding cows and bullocks; this enabled butter making to continue throughout the winter months. Thus the clay soil regions resembled other dairying areas: they were peopled thickly with family farms and landless peasants. The manor was not a significant institution. Cloth making took up the slack in employment during the winter months. Human enterprise was shaped by nature; such shaping governed the society as well. Except for the lands dominated by a few rich upland graziers and capitalist grain farmers, these were regions of small family farms, few rich men, many prosperous peasants, an even distribution of wealth, gently blending social classes, and little profound poverty.

The same could not be said of four home counties that composed another "country": Buckinghamshire, Bedfordshire, Hertfordshire, and Essex. Their economies were shaped largely by London demands. Most local farmers dealt directly with the drovers and merchants whose custom took them to the central London markets. Yet the soil bases of these counties were so diverse that it is misleading to say only that the metropolis determined their husbandry. Bedfordshire had areas of mixed husbandry in common fields that typified the Midlands. Buckingham was dotted with small, dispersed woodland settlements, where Chiltern Lollards once ran pigs, worked cloth, and raised some cattle. Hertfordshire and Essex had sheep-corn countries like those of the upland chalk regions, as well as marsh meadows that were ideal for fattening cattle. But the most significant factor was common to the four counties: a large

---

[6] Suffolk Punches are draft horses, with short legs and thick bodies.

amount of enclosed land, which facilitated improvement and commercial agriculture geared to urban needs.

Hertfordshire and Essex had a high degree of specialization. Wheat was an important cash crop in Hertfordshire, and a large variety of grains and vetches was sown to provide fodder for the thousands of horses that were stabled about London or were bred in the region. Oats grown elsewhere for human consumption took the largest share of arable intended as feed lands. Pigs went to market, as did geese, chickens, and bullocks. Most crops were for fattening, except the several wheat varieties and the best barley, which went to brewsters. The chalk hills of the north of the region were especially provident for maltsters. These facts give credit where it is due, for in the *Domesday Book* Hertfordshire was still chiefly woodland and pasture. Only energetic reclamation of the land had since converted it to market uses. Although some dairy farming in woodland and pasture survived, most of the land was being plowed by 1500 and had been enclosed long before the Tudor era.

One consequence of this specialization for the market was full employment, which made it hard for the nascent cloth industry to take hold, since idle hands were few. The same can be said of Essex. Although it had once been dense forest, Essex in Tudor and Stuart times contained scattered farmsteads and hamlets, which thrived on mixed husbandry in association with common fields, as well as on enclosed pasture farming. Grazing grass and cornland dominated the marshland, with dairying having much the same hold as it did in the marshes of Lincolnshire and Yorkshire. On the lighter northern clays corn grew, while in the woodland-pasture areas of the south men raised stock of every sort.

Further to the southeast, Kent, Surrey, and Sussex experienced London's influence no less profoundly. It was a market for all the grain farmers could grow, and what could not be sold there could be sold in the coastal trade or exported from dozens of seaports. Thus, corn production flourished in the North and South Downs, abetted by large flocks of sheep whose manure was necessary on the thin soil. Wool and meat were secondary. Wheat, barley or oats, peas, and tares were common crops. Dairy was for local consumption only. Farms were large, dependent peasants few, and social mobility very marked. By contrast, the Weald of Kent and Sussex was densely populated, holdings were small, the land was tough, and crops were grown mostly for fattening cattle and pigs. Dairy houses and cheese chambers served only local needs. Employment at more than one job was vital in a land where incomes were low and people plentiful. The charcoal and iron industries of this woodland area flourished, along with cloth working. By 1550 such bi-employment was essential to the survival of a large and growing population. People migrated into the area because there was more work to be found there than existed in the plains or open countryside. The manor was a weak institution, and the prevalence of gavelkind[7] promised young people a share of the land. This encouraged early marriage.

Kent and Sussex also had good marshland in abundance. For centuries this had been pasture, almost to the exclusion of crops. By 1550, however, much of this lush pasture was plowed up from time to time and put to crops, which were alternated with grass. Especially in the Kent marshes, this practice promoted cattle fattening and the growth of wheat, barley, and fruit for sale. Kent was already achieving its modern status as one of England's great orchard and hop regions. The family farm dominated the weak manor, and enclosed land was the rule in an area where not much ground had ever been held in common. Thus specialization here was the result of the pull of London and the push of natural and social conditions that had already existed for centuries when William the Conqueror tried to impose the manor and feudalism on the regions around Canterbury. When James I ruled in England, Kent and Sussex were already centers of capitalist farming.

The South and West of England formed another distinct region; it consisted of six counties: Gloucestershire, Wiltshire, Dorset, Oxfordshire, Berkshire, and Hampshire. Over so large a region there were marked soil and climate differences: vales with good clays for grass and dairying; forests suitable for rearing stock; the limestone hills of the Cotswolds and Chilterns, where corn supported huge flocks of sheep; and the downs, which also gave a good base for mixed husbandry, dairying, and the generally successful sheep-corn farming common on chalk land.

The Cotswolds were especially convenient for sheep-corn husbandry, as were other upland regions in lowland England. Common fields, nucleated villages, and great commons for grazing characterized these districts. Plowland was used for pasture in order to feed sheep. Sheep manured the arable, where fodder crops were grown and where market crops of barley and wheat were the major object of farming. Again, wool and lamb were of secondary value in these areas. Society was manorial and hierarchical. Farms tended to be large, as amalgamation increased efficiency and ensured prosperity. Thus the family farm slowly vanished in the Cotswolds, while it flourished in the dairying regions of Wiltshire and in the valleys, where the growing cloth industry gave ready employment on the side and helped small-scale arable farming. This was especially true in the vale of Oxford and parts of Berkshire, where barley was the first market crop and wheat the second. There was little dairying, but a good deal of cattle fattening and not much sheep running.

The pastoral vales of Gloucester and northern Oxford ran to the same land

[7] A custom in Kent also used in scattered locations elsewhere, by which "partible" inheritance divided land equally among heirs.

use as did the southeast of Hampshire, Wiltshire around the Salisbury Plain, and the heart of Dorset. There open pasture and woodland supported dairying on a large scale, sheep for wool and mutton, and beef cattle. Plowing the heaviest clays was unrewarding; hence cheese chambers were often the most prominent farm buildings, while arable crops were generally for home use. The woodland was often orchard, however, and apples and pears were sent in commercial quantities to Devon, Cornwall, and Wales. Social structure apparently was similar to that of other dairy areas reclaimed from forest: small farms, generally weak manorial organization, a free market in land, and an ability to absorb a large population with the supplemental employment provided on spinning wheels. In the more rugged, strictly forest regions of Dean, Kingswood, Bernwood, New Forest, and Savernake, cattle raising shared the farmer's attention with corn. Sheep in large numbers maintained soil fertility; pigs and horses were also raised for sale. Unlike some forest areas, these woods had an important cash crop of corn. They were similar to other forest areas in that they provided ready employment on the side in iron making, coal mining, glove making, and even lace manufacture.

To the far southwest lay Somerset, Devon, and Cornwall. These were mainly pastoral counties. Cornwall was a series of oases. Small farms alternated with hilly, moorish, barren ground. Only along the coast was there much fertile land. Consequently, the population was small and widely scattered, villages were few, and manorial society did not exist. Farming was for subsistence. On the coasts, fishing and trade with Wales, France, and Spain saved Cornwall from abject poverty. Somerset, on the other hand, was heavily populated, dairy farming and clothiers made for real prosperity, and the mining of tin, lead, zinc, iron, and coal supplemented agricultural work. Devon was not so well peopled as Somerset but was more hospitable than Cornwall. Cattle rearing and sheep running for beef and mutton prospered. On the south coast, corn and fruits grew in abundance.

The southwest was obviously a land of stark contrasts. There were strong manorial villages and the nearly desolate reaches of Blackmoor and Dartmoor. As the sixteenth century gave way to the seventeenth, the steady rise in population and London's magnetic pull stimulated imaginative farming. Even Cornwall made progress through enclosure, consolidation, and the use of fertilizers. Rents rose very sharply, and by 1603 Cornwall was exporting corn and providing for the fleet. The valleys and the coasts thus came to give as much wealth as the pastoral moors and the rich grass marshes. Somerset cattle and mutton ran to London along with Cornish and Devon dairy products, especially cream and cream cheeses. In the fenlands, stock breeding of every sort flourished, and fowl and eels went to local and distant towns. The forest regions sheltered many small farmers, dairying, cattle for beef, and the numerous poor, who sought work spinning, tucking, weaving cloth, and making clothes. Despite complaints of poverty by local justices of the peace, by the 1650s this region had experienced an agricultural revolution and justified later encomiums of its dairy chambers and weaving looms.

Cheshire and Lancashire were equally pastoral counties, with chiefly clay and sandy soils suited to grass. Land was plowed only to feed stock and the household. Lancashire had several distinct zones in which land under the plow sometimes dominated pasture. But even in those zones field crops were used as fodder. Efforts at land improvement were striking in both counties, where heath and moor were turned into good pasture. Estate surveys made after 1560 show this development clearly. Plowing up grassland and putting down crops became a defense against exhaustion, as well as against wild moss and bracken. In both counties there were also numerous common fields in the process of enclosure by agreement. These measures helped the growth of grass rather than capitalist crop farming. Where mixed husbandry ruled, its purpose was to feed animals; the barley, rye, oats, wheat, vetches, peas, and beans that were grown do not necessarily imply market gardens.

Cheese was the pride of Cheshire, and where land was converted to arable use, it was ultimately to feed stock and thus benefit dairies. Much the same is true of pastoral Lancashire, where cattle rearing and fattening were the object of agriculture. Much of the land there was cold, stony, and barren. Yet by 1600, farmers were dairying profitably, as improvements took hold. Both counties had other enterprises. The Cheshire forests developed a mixed-stock husbandry of pigs, horses, sheep, and cattle—what we already know from other forest regions. Lancashire had good lowland zones of mixed farming, in which between 55 and 62 percent of the land was plowed. Sheep flocks were numerous. Arable crops of barley and wheat were good. Farms were very large, and a vast separation existed between the prosperous freeholders and the struggling customary tenants who had on the average fewer than eight acres under crops.

Coal mining played its part also. The combination of arable and industrial activity was quite different from the mixture of woodland–pasture and mining elsewhere. Manorial administration was neglected, with the result that holdings were frequently divided and sublet until they could not support a peasant family. Hence poverty drove men into the mines in the summer and to begging in the cold seasons. Subletting had encouraged immigration, early marriage, and natural increase and had in this way made more traumatic to many the already difficult transition from pastoral to mixed husbandry. This transition produced serious dislocations in Lancashire society in the Tudor period and early in the seventeenth century, giving rise to poverty and the alienating life of the pit.

It remains for us to cover the Midlands, East and West, where we find both the classic landscape of common-field England and also the most pronounced changes in land use, which ushered in a revolution in agriculture. The East Midlands embraced the shires of Nottingham, Warwick, Leicester, Northampton, and the county of Rutland. There, in the mixed-farming champion areas, men fought against intakes of common fields and commons, struggles that in 1607 enlarged and became the Midland Revolt. It was in the East Midlands that the contest between improvement and tradition was sharpest. Apart from forest belts, which occur in all of these counties, and a small margin of fenland in some, the East Midlands was "fielden country," in which mixed husbandry prevailed. Common-field England was manorial England, while in fen and forest, as we have seen repeatedly, the large population often lived entirely outside the ordinary social structures of nucleated, manorial villages.

Nottinghamshire best illustrates the agrarian system of this region. Its soil was ideal for arable use; and between 1500 and the era of the civil war (1642) farmers there kept cattle for stud and market, bred horses for every sort of work, and raised poultry and pigs and fed them on huge crops of domestic peas. Sheep were few. After peas, barley was the main crop of the prosperous freeholders. The main difference in Leicestershire and Rutland was the prominence of beans and bacon and the larger flocks of sheep. Thus John Moore's comment of 1653 well describes the three counties: " We breed multitudes of hearty men for the service of the Commonwealth if need be; whereby we also send forth abundance of all manner of corn and grain . . . to the city . . . our ships at sea and to countries round about us; all fed with the plough in the common fields."[8] Very large crops also fed people and stock in Warwickshire. Dairying played a greater role there, however. Northamptonshire grew more wheat than was ordinary elsewhere, along with sheep in sufficient numbers to raise the claim in 1620 that wool was the major cash crop there.

Throughout the fielden counties, nucleated villages under seigneurial rule nestled in the common fields. Each showed several faces. The squire at the top often competed with a few solid, yeoman freeholders, who had perhaps sixty acres. Below them, mere husbandmen managed well on farms half that size. But as many as one-third of the villagers were cottagers and laborers with no land of their own and no hope of getting any. Inequality was the rule. Even in nonseigneurial villages there was often a very large group of landless men eager for framework knitting or other employment on the side. Mixed farming was more efficient on large holdings, and this fact threw the classes associated with the land into pitiless competition throughout the sixteenth and early seventeenth centuries. Especially when the manor was weak or deficient and

---

[8] Quoted in Thirsk, *Agrarian History*, IV, p. 91.

immigration heavy, tenant lands showed a tendency toward eviction and con-centration of population. The absence of partible inheritance thus sharply dis-tinguishes fielden areas from most pastoral ones, where population pressure was also unchecked by strong manors. Where landless men nurtured griev-ances in the common-field country, the pastoral area peasants lived in poverty on their *own* land.

But fielden society and agriculture were absent from about one-third of the East Midlands. Forests were numerous and lacked large common fields. In-deed, agriculture in the forest areas ran to grassland and enclosures. The abun-dance of grass made stinting stock unnecessary in some places; and where there were stints these were often very large. What common fields there were underwent enclosure by agreement in the interest of grazing, beef and veal production, and sheep rearing. Meat production dominated until the early 1600s, but by the 1630s dairy specialization was ascendant. The arable that survived grew the ordinary East-Midlands crops, along with flax, hemp, and fruits.

Unlike the Arden, Sherwood forest had very thin soil. Only rye, oats, and poor barley grew there; even for these, large flocks of sheep were needed for manure. As improvements took hold in the sixteenth century, grass was plowed up, and land was cropped for a few years and then returned to pasture, to help support the large numbers of small farmers and immigrants in every forest area. Not unnaturally, then, where there was little waste to recover—as in Northamptonshire—depopulating enclosures drove men into the forests and into the collective memory of fairy tales and *fabliaux* in which their griev-ances against the rich took shape. Some forest villages tripled in size between 1524 and 1670. Squatting was a problem, as were poaching and invasions of the king's rights. There flourished also the peculiar resentment that rich enclosing landlords had of the poor, whose poverty they blamed on natural unthriftiness and improvidence. Only knitting and weaving provided marginal relief in the early 1600s, as cottage industrialists took advantage of overabundant peasant labor. Hence prosperity lived cheek-by-jowl with poverty, as did rich farmers and proletarians throughout the East Midlands' common fields.

It is in the last of our regions that we meet with the beginnings of the most profound change in agriculture in the period from 1520 to 1650. Before 1500, much of Derbyshire, Staffordshire, Shropshire, Worcestershire, and Hereford-shire was forest. Even in the 1500s, clearance in the West Midlands was in-complete. Under the pressure of population growth in cities and villages, however, intensive improvement began to build an area of good farms and market gardens scattered throughout the pasture and woodland that domi-nated this part of highland England. We must not exaggerate this development, for in 1597 a Shropshire man noted that his country was "all dairy and oxen," and in 1636 a Staffordshire commission of the peace reported chases, parks, heath, and waste, but little farming.

Yet the area under the plow grew steadily. Herefordshire was a good granary for its neighbors in the depression of 1597. The increase of tillage throughout the West Midlands was constantly commented upon. Commons were plowed by agreement, and what had been permanent pasture became for a few years temporary arable. In any account of this region, this "shifting cultivation" stands out, as does evidence of enthusiasm for "improvement" through marling, liming, manuring, the "floating of water meadows," and other peaceful arts that generated meat, butter, and cheese. Throughout the region, therefore, an agricultural revolution was in progress: enclosure, techniques to put heart into poor soil, shifting cultivation, breed improvement, the floating of meadows to improve pasture, and what Joan Thirsk has called a "sweetly reasonable attitude" toward improvement. Grazing and fattening for the butcher, dairying, good corn crops—especially oats and rye—constituted the system in the moorlands, while in the forests typical animal production of a mixed sort prevailed. The face of the earth showed the impact of change, and the inventories of men's goods showed the result. At Penshore, John Gilbert died in July of 1617. He was not reckoned a rich man, but he had standing barley worth £80, 122 Welsh sheep, and 120 other good manurers!

Naturally, poverty and prosperity in this region participated in the general pattern of the distribution of wealth and the structure of society in woodland, moor, and fielden England as a whole. The pastoral woodland areas had isolated farms and small hamlets. The fielden areas favored the village and the manor. The moors were thinly populated at the higher levels. Population congestion was greatest in the woodlands, where local increase and immigration for work in lead and iron mines were common. These arrivals multiplied the number of poor cottagers in forest hovels, as well as the burden of poor relief on the prosperous. In fielden areas, poverty sprang mostly from the nature of improvement, which enlarged holdings and reduced tenant numbers. Local men recognized the problem of poverty in the region, but few did as much about it as Rowland Vaughan of Golden Valley. Noting the "want of employment" in Herefordshire, this successful agrarian improver prodded the growth of domestic handicrafts in a scheme to set up a "commonwealth of traders" in the valley. Others cursed the poor and the rates.

We may summarize the diversity we have reported. The largest contrast lay between areas of pasture farming and mixed husbandry. In pastoral areas, forests in the lowlands had land on which to place immigrants. In all areas, improvement went forward and changed the face of the countryside and the structure of society. Forest economies became pastoral when restrictions on clearance eased. Village communities began in areas where none had been. In many places, shifting cultivation had replaced older conditions of permanent pasture and tillage and in turn was giving way to an alternating use of the land. Pasture and plowland came into a more even relationship, as arable farming took hold as a result of improvements in technique. The frontiers separating regions and systems blurred somewhat, as forests with great commons and the more open pastoral areas increased their arable. They came to resemble places where fielden England tumbled grass to corn, reversing the pressures of the century after the Black Death. Throughout the country, but especially in the Lancashire Plain and the West Midlands, the change to mixed arable and pasture went forward.

Since farming specialization and social organization were closely associated, there was much evidence of strain coinciding with the change in agriculture. In part this was because old ways no longer suited the new facts. Hence the revolt of 1607, in which a corn-growing society resisted the change to pasture farming and the decline of manorial institutions. Between woodland and champion country, contemporaries grasped more than differences in appearance. The forest men were thought to be mean, stubborn, uncivil, lawless, independent, and resistant to government. In short, they were the stuff of dissent and political and religious nonconformity. Lord Burghley, Elizabeth's great minister, meant this when he said clothworkers and forest men were less governable than husbandmen. Bishop Fitzjames knew them to be prone to Lollardy, and Archbishop Parker saw in old Lollards new Puritans in the Chilterns. Charles I encountered the fenlanders and foresters as stout rebels opposed to his laws regarding experiments in drainage and taxation. And Kent was the primeval ground of sedition and heresy; its Weald was once called "the receptacle of all schism and rebellion."

Up-and-Down Husbandry

Especially in the period 1570–1650, the changes that were transforming the countryside and straining society deserve the designation Professor Kerridge recently gave them: the Agricultural Revolution.[9] It was

[9] The standard accounts attribute it to the period 1750–1850, chiefly because of the mechanization of production that took place then. For the analysis that follows, however, see Kerridge, *The Agricultural Revolution*, and Thirsk, *The Agrarian History*, as well as the following important articles: K. J. Allison, "Flock Management in the 16th and 17th Centuries," *EcHR* (1958), XI, pp. 98–112; G. E. Fussell, "Crop Nutrition in Tudor and Early Stuart England," *AgHR* (1955), III, pp. 95–106; W. G. Hoskins, "The Reclamation of the Waste, 1500–1800," *EcHR* (1943), XIII, pp. 80–92; E. Kneisel, "The Evolution of the English Corn Market," *J.EcH* (1954), XIV, pp. 46–52; Alan Simpson, "The East Anglian Foldcourse," *AgHR* (1958), VI, pp. 87–96; C. Skeel, "The Cattle Trade from the 15th to the 19th Centuries," *TRHS* (1926), XI, pp. 35–58; E. G. R. Taylor, "The Surveyor," *EcHR* (1947), XVII, pp. 121–33.

the means whereby the precarious balance between grass and corn was redressed in England and the nation became an exporter of grain.

It was once thought that this revolution's salient features were the wholesale discommuning of enclosures by the parliamentary classes, the replacement of bare fallow by root crops and artificial grasses, improvements in crop rotation, the use of drills and other improved implements, breed improvements, the large-scale draining of farmland, the use of horses in place of oxen for plowing, and mechanization. Suffice it to say here that these features either misrepresent or fail to explain the revolution that took place between 1500 and 1700.

Much open land in England had always been free of common rights, while in many enclosures common rights still prevailed. Furthermore, there is now no basis for the belief that open fields were backward and enclosed ones improved. The great disparking movement of 1560–1670 gave over enclosed land to largely conservative uses in which the extension of old techniques was typical. Nor was the use of fallow crops significant. There was no universal replacement of bare fallow. Bare fallow often was better for cleaning the soil than was cropping. Not all land took turning or rotation well. The supposed spread of the "Norfolk" four-course system is a myth; over most of the country hardly anything like a regular rotation prevailed, and even in lands adjacent to East Norfolk, clover would not "take" one year in four. Mechanization had no part in this early agricultural revolution. Plows varied from soil to soil and needed regional adaptability. This was inimical to standardization and hence to mechanization. Drills came to be used only after 1720. Similarly, the technology of drainage was not sufficiently developed before 1860 to contribute more than marginally to increasing England's food supplies. The changeover to horses was essentially complete by the 1520s. Neither this step nor breed improvement was central to the revolution, however.

Contemporary commentators understood their times. They stressed floated meadows and alternation of tillage and grass in their discussions of improvement. This usage had been established in certain places for centuries—in the Cheshire cheese country, for example. But elsewhere the substitution of alternate husbandry for permanent tillage and permanent grass was novel, and it revolutionized farming. It increased yields; changed soil structure with the use of temporary leys, which made the soil crumbly and loamy; cut production costs; and radically altered the ability of the land to provide winter feed for animals.

The floating of water meadows created new sources of grass and hay and thus also increased the number and size of livestock. The growing of winter hay had always depended on dry or upland meadows. Bottom meadows tripled the hay yield per acre, which gave a powerful incentive for damming up and forcing streams into irrigation trenches. Winter flooding preoccupied surveyors and exponents of improvement. "Drowning," as Norden called it, helped solve the problem of feeding stock over the winter. By bringing up spring hay as much as a month earlier, the floating of meadows crowned this advance in technique. This practice ended the March and April gap between hay and grass that had always sent sheep and cattle to the slaughterhouse. When animals lacking late winter food had to be killed, farmers lost their power, their dung, and thus the ability to grow more food for both animals and humans. The water meadow gave early grass and tripled production. Coupled with the new up-and-down husbandry, flooding—not drainage— revolutionized food production. And it is in this context alone that talk about new crops, selected grasses, manuring improvements, and stock breeding makes sense. Thus did "sheep-and-corn" husbandry give way to the lusher husbandry praised by late seventeenth-century travelers.

But what exactly was "up-and-down" husbandry? And what was its connection with the agrarian problems of this period? The cogency of these questions derives at least in part from traditions noted in R. H. Tawney's *Agrarian Problems of the Sixteenth Century*. Tawney tied "improvement" to the notion of class war. In his view, the rise of successful capitalist farming entailed the eviction of copyholders, the depopulation of the countryside, and wholesale enclosure by force and fraud. The earlier conversion of tillage to pasture, which was one adjustment to population decline, Tawney projected into the age of population growth. He conjured up an age in which a relentless agrarian capitalism flourished among England's landed aristocrats, chiefly because they engaged in a self-interested orgy of misgovernment. England had one law for the rich and another for the poor, and both secured the triumph of property over the peasantry.

No decent assessment of the agricultural revolution or Tawney's view of its implications is possible without grasping how up-and-down husbandry dominated this crucial development.

The system that replaced both patterns of permanency and shifting cultivation was called "ley farming." Land subjected to it was called "up-and-down" land. Everything depended on the arable fields, which were laid *down* to grass for a few years, after some years of being plowed *up* and tilled. They were then called *pastures*, because animals were grazed on the converted arable fields. All of the farmland, apart from the wet meadows and what was still permanent grass, was thus used. The grass was used for dairy heifers; the grazing of cows, ewes, and lambs was for the butcher; and the arable was under corn. Unlike medieval systems, however, arable, pasture, and meadow no longer have fixed meanings. Both tillage and grass leys were arable. Arable and pasture became synonymous in up-and-down farming, whereas in earlier systems "arable" and "tillage" always stood in the sharpest contrast, meaning permanent grass, permanent tillage.

Thus, in the years from 1520 to 1650,[1] behind the static language of legal documents, land use experienced a revolution. Time and again we encounter records of this kind: "In Kenilworth Old Park a close of pasture ground . . . being at present plowed, it being usual there to plow their ground a year or two . . . and then to let it lie again for pasture."[2] Clearly, a piece of enclosed ground—plowland in fact—was being plowed as if it were part of champion England, at least until it became pasture! Again, an account of some seventeenth-century glebe lands tells us "there are som enclosures plough'd up. But as much field land is layd down." In statutes of Henry VIII, Edward VI, and Elizabeth I, the new system is clearly reflected. Up-and-down land was known to be good for the commonwealth and was exempted from the laws governing depopulation. In court records, defendants charged with converting arable to pasture, contrary to statute and to the ruin of husbandry, showed their dealings to be otherwise. Since their land was in up-and-down use, enclosure entailed neither loss of tillage nor the destruction of houses. When Thomas Throgmorton pleaded to a charge of ruining husbandry, he answered that he had laid down to grass 200 acres at Weston Underwood. But he had also plowed up forty acres of pasture, and half of that laid down was but "for a short space only to the intent . . . that it may gain and gather to itself heart and strength, before being . . . very feeble, barren and out of heart. . . ." The agricultural writers from Anthony Fitzherbert (1535) to Walter Blith (1650) knew that the system had spread out of the Northwest, slowly at first, then rapidly after 1560, until between 1590 and 1660 it had conquered the system of permanency.

This beneficial use of the land often took over what had once been permanent parkland and grassland. But it was even more extensive in the common fields. Hence, Tawney was right to say that common-field England witnessed a new wave of enclosure. But he was wrong in the deductions he made from the facts. Where half the land had been permanent grass and the other half tillage, upon enclosure most tillage was laid down to grass. But the greensward was plowed up until between 50 and 80 percent of the area was in up-and-down husbandry. Where old, almost wholly enclosed grassland was brought into the system—and much of it was—the result was a manifest gain in arable. On balance, there was a loss in acreage in tillage only on old arable. This loss was countered by the conversion of permanent grassland, which necessarily augmented both arable and tillage. When up-and-down husbandry took over

---

[1] Eleanor Searle's soon-to-be-published study of the community and banlieu of Battle Abbey (Sussex) pushes the rise of ley farming back into the fourteenth century, under Flemish influence. The innovation failed to take hold in the circumstances of the disruptions associated with the Black Death. It is therefore not clear that Professor Searle's account, to which I am indebted for this note, will force back into the Middle Ages Professor Kerridge's "Agricultural Revolution."

[2] Kerridge, *The Agricultural Revolution*, p. 185.

from permanency and mere shifting cultivation, the arable[3] was extended and the amount actually in tillage was not reduced.

Furthermore, the choice of good "nurse crops" on the converted land brought the benefits of increased yield, lower labor cost, and the soil change noted above. The new husbandry also reduced the incidence of sheep disease and the impact of moss, moles, and ant hills. It was thus a great boon to live-stock; it gave better grass and more nutriment per acre, produced better milk, and raised the calorie production of an acre of land. More manure from the larger numbers of stock that managed to survive the winters made a permanent improvement in fertility. Growers noted that "one acre beareth the fruit of three," allowing two others to be preserved for grazing, dairying, and the sending to market of butter, cheese, milk, and every sort of meat. In the open fields, manuring was restricted by grass supplies. As fields were enclosed, they went to grass for more than a season and became high-quality pastures, which helped increase stock and thus the permanent manure supply.

Corn production on permanent tillage was about half that obtained on the up-and-down system. About 1640, a tenfold increase of seed was good on tillage in common fields; twentyfold increases were common in "plowed pastures." Tillage diminished, but not crops. It has been demonstrated in our own time that an acre of temporary ley produces more starch equivalent and thrice the amount of protein of an acre of permanent tillage. Had there been a halving of the area in corn, it would have meant no loss in production. And there was more milk and meat. Combined with the decline in production costs for grain because of soil changes—which made it four times as costly to produce a bushel on permanent tillage—this was a gain for every Englishman as the population soared. Furthermore, the output of industrial crops—flax, hemp, skins, hides, wool, and woad—greatly increased. It is hard to escape the conclusion that a rise in diet standards among Englishmen of all classes resulted from these often-misconstrued changes.

Up-and-down husbandry made much progress throughout the Midland Plain, in the fen country, in many highland areas between the wolds and the seas, and in numerous valleys in every geographical region. It also prospered in the famous cheese country, in the Wealden vales by inroads on woodland, in the Oxford Heights and the Cotswolds, in the chalk country, in the Saltings or fenland areas apart from Lincolnshire, and in the Lancashire Plain. The most spectacular change came in the northeastern lowlands, where there had never been any but a temporary cultivation of wilderness. There, up-and-down husbandry literally changed the appearance of the countryside between 1560 and 1670.

[3] That is, in the sense of the alternate use of *pasture* as tillage land—the crucial distinction. Tawney simply did not grasp the implication.

Peasants and Improvement: The Enclosure Problem

Enclosure was bound up with this revolution.[4] Common-field farms in peasant employ had for centuries made subsistence their goal. Engrossment of small holdings and the intake of commons and waste were necessary for the efficient use of the new system and its intensive use of capital for meat and dairy production. But this fact has little to do with the "problem" Tawney had in mind. It remains for us now to put the revolution in agriculture into the perspective of social history, especially with regard to enclosures and security of tenure.

Many complaints in the countryside between 1520 and the mid-seventeenth century were against depopulating enclosures in the fielden areas of manorial England. Aristocrats and gentry allegedly usurped the lands and rights of customary tenants, usually to enclose commons, waste, and common fields. Others created illegal manors and manorial courts in which they oppressed poor men. These practices made for a decay of tillage and the ruin of honest husbandry. Moreover, men so put upon had no redress of grievance and therefore lost their rights. For, as Maitland noted, "where there is no remedy, there is no right."

The legal formation of manors had ended in the thirteenth century. The manor was not primarily territory, although it usually had pasture, woodland, and arable on which there was demesne land. It was primarily legal and social, a bundle of services owed by tenants to the lord. Tenants could try to evade such services and lords could oppress them through forced increases. After 1300, some men tried to defeat the rights of others by erecting new manors in derogation of the rights of the lord and the king. Since setting up a feigned manor also meant creating a court-baron, lawyers for the crown and in private practice agreed that such erections might create a seignory but never a true manor.[5] For a manor had its heart in the court-baron, and only the crown could create that. This court-baron[6] (or court customary) was the place where

---

[4] The treatment given here rests throughout on Professor Eric Kerridge's careful critique of Tawney's arguments and those of other scholars in his *Agrarian Problems in the Sixteenth Century* (London: Allen & Unwin, 1969). His book makes clear the care that is necessary in using C. M. Gray, *Copyhold, Equity, and the Common Law* (Cambridge, Mass.: Harvard University Press, 1963) with regard to security of tenure. On technical questions of the land law, see S. F. C. Milsom, *Historical Foundations of the Common Law* (London: Lutterworth Press, 1969) and A. W. B. Simpson, *An Introduction to the History of the Land Law* (Oxford: Oxford University Press, 1961).

[5] That is, a lordship "in gross" over tenants with copyhold or lease agreements, extending to rents and services but devoid of manorial jurisdiction.

[6] The court "leet," on the other hand, was a delegation of royal authority in ordinary matters of local justice. A particular baron could conduct both leet sessions and his customary courts; the latter pertained to the manor, the former did not.

cases involving tenants of a manor were presented by a grand jury, investigated by a jury of inquest, and, when required, tried by a jury chosen from all the suitors who owed homage to the lord of the court. It should be stressed that process was by jury, since the lord was no more above the law of the manor than the king was above that of the land. The chief business of the court was to record land transfers and enforce the bylaws of the community. In it, the lord himself could be sued over infringements and trespasses. But in all cases of equity the lord himself was the judge, as he was in all appeals. This raises the question of security. Was the lord really limited in his power over his tenants, or did his position allow him to exploit them at will?

Within the legally constituted manors, tenants had more to fear from the decline of the manor than from its effective operation. The discontinuance of the court was detrimental to the tenants, especially copyholders, since it was the place where their rights and obligations were recorded and their bylaws were enforced. So well did they know this that they frequently got subpoenas from the Chancery to force the restoration of a valid but defunct court. Indeed, where manors were destroyed because of the absence of suitors in the court—which was common in the Midland Plain and the cheese country under the pressure of enclosure—a grievance existed. With the "memory" of the community destroyed, men were vulnerable. The bylaws lacked a forum. Land was sold to noncustomary proprietors. The obligations of copyhold customary tenants, once publicly recognized[7] in the manorial court, could be enlarged or altogether usurped, since stewards had the right to repossess tenements that were found to conceal peasant obligations. Examples of such self-serving fraud were numerous on crown estates under James I and Charles I. Surveyors were regarded as the instruments of oppressive power. These occurrences should not be magnified, however. Normally, the court-baron guarded the life of the countryside.

And beyond the court-baron lay other safeguards against oppression. This protection derived from the doctrine of estates, as opposed to that of tenures. As the law regarding land in England developed, it slowly came to reflect the facts of agrarian life. When tenure originated, farming for profit was largely unknown. Tenure meant the manner or condition of holding land; it expressed the *quality* of one's interest in land. Under common law, only the "free" or noble tenures were recognized. The best known of these was, of course,

---

[7] When legally constituted manors passed from one hand to another, or in times of acute economic stress and reevaluations of tenures, a survey of rights and obligations was made by the steward of the manor. He presented the results in a "court of recognition" to which all parties brought their records. Comparisons made before a jury of tenants yielded a final document, the official "survey of the manor." This signed accord preserved the public record or legal memory and from it derived the copies of obligations and rights of tenants who were copyholders (*tenantes per copiam*).

military tenure, or tenure by knight's fee.[8] But increasingly the most important was the freehold of common socage, in return for which holders of socage
owed little beyond nominal rents, homage, fealty, and suit of court. All other
tenures were deemed servile or customary and lay outside the scope of common law. These, however, were under the customary courts.

But when farming became a business for profit, it was not enough to talk of
tenures, which became a consideration secondary to estates. Estates applied to
both free and customary tenures and expressed the *quantity* of a man's interest
in land. In the doctrine of estates, "freehold" meant simply a continuous
interest of not less than the term of one life. Hence, a customary tenant or
copyholder might be a freeholder in his estate if he lived a life span roughly
equal to that of three people. Tawney never admitted this vital distinction
between legal realities and economic ones and thus was misled on the question
of security. He thought only of *tenures* unprotected by common law.

Numerous cases show that copyholders for life, several lives, and of inheritance, were in fact protected by decisions in the common-law courts and those
of equity, as well as in the judicial offspring of the king's Council. Thus we
find copyholders protected by common law against "arbitrary fines," even
when covenants specified that the lord could levy such fines. The courts held
that even arbitrary fines must be "reasonable," by which they meant compatible with the custom of inheritance. In cases where agreement between lord
and tenant was not reached, juries decided that fines of two years' net rent[9]
defeated the inheritance by making it too costly. From 1586 on, cases in several
courts show this decision.

Copyholders with freehold estates were as secure in law as holders of socage
were in freehold tenures. They had legal security against outrageous fines upon
entering their estates and against wrongful eviction. Even the mere annual
lessee was secure in his estate during his year. However, we cannot suppose
that courts gave security against a lord who did not wish to renew a lease.
Tenants for a term of years had no inalienable right to their holding. Nor did
laws provide guarantees against the ills of the economy, inflation, and the
movement toward larger holdings. And these engulfed many poor men. The
courts did admit that copyhold by custom was an estate "in the eyes of the
common law."[1] Customary tenants could thus take action at common law.
Law reports after 1500 abound with records of personal actions such as writs
of trespass against lords; to deprive a man of a freehold estate was a tort[2] even

---

[8] Among other tenures of a "free and noble" character were serjeanty (rendering specific services:
holding the king's cup, advising him in law, bearing his armor) and frankalmoign (the "free alms"
and prayers given by churchmen as the condition of their holdings).

[9] The net annual improved value of the land.

[1] Not *by common law*.

[2] A civil wrong or injury independent of the character of the relations between men.

in cases where the tenure was not free. Instances of this use of personal actions, which filled the gap left by the rule that only free tenures were actionable under the writs of real property, date from 1388. In 1467, Justice Danby noted that "a copyholder wrongfully ousted has suffered a tort."[3] Such wrongful ousters gave rise to cases barring actions of trespass, as Coke clearly stated:

If a copyholder be ousted by a stranger, he cannot implead him by the king's writ, but by plaint in the lord's court [-baron]. . . . If he be ousted by his lord, he cannot maintain an assize at the common law, because he wanteth a franktenement; but he may have an action of trespass . . . for it is against reason that the lord should be judge when he himself is the party. . . .

This doctrine did not, however, remove all threats to copyholders. While freehold tenures were protected by the writs of possession against illegal enclosures or other "intakes," no matter what the source, copyhold estates suffered a limitation revealed in Coke's dictum. Copyholders could not take a case against strangers to the common law, on the ground that the lord of the manor was the party at law rather than the tenant. This doctrine Coke challenged, saying that it was perverse and that it lent itself to collusive actions in which the lord might promote invasions by strangers, judge in their favor in the manor court, and then gain the tenement from the strawman. In an age when the lord was an "approvement maker" anxious to engross land for up-and-down husbandry, this often happened. Coke's view went to the heart of the matter; it proclaimed that one man should not lack rights at law merely because another had them. Yet, even in cases where common law was impotent, tenants could resort to courts of equity and frequently did so.

This does not mean that force and fraud were defeated, or that all enclosures took place by agreement or unity of possession (when leases expired). There are many allegations and denials of wrongful enclosure in the records of king's bench, common pleas, wards, Chancery, Exchequer, and Star Chamber. Some cases were proved, but William Finney's suit against his lord is typical of many that failed. The documents show that between 1547 and 1567 certain commoners sought enclosure with the lord's consent "for better tillage or corn." Finney, they said, masqueraded "as a true commonwealth man," of which he made a show. His real purpose, however, was that of a covetous grazier who wanted open range and permanent grass to rule, "to the destroying of tillage and the increase of corn. . . ."

Enclosure, then, was often a popular interest, and it is thus wrong to see lord and commoner in opposition, or to see in the struggle for improvement a plain and simple class struggle. Piecemeal peasant and yeoman enclosure was com-

---

[3] Danby's decision and that by Brian, CJ (1481), were incorporated in the 1530 edition of Littleton's *Tenures*, the first edition with references to case law.

mon. In 1549, the king's Enclosure Commission found yeomen and lesser gentry enclosing twenty to thirty acres at a time. Between 1550 and 1607, 19 percent of all known Leicestershire enclosures were carried out by small tenants, and after 1580 this practice was a common yeoman and peasant response to the market and self-interest. Peasant resistance to the practice had been a legacy of the age of depopulating enclosures (1350–1520), but such conservatism was largely overcome by 1550. It is thus ironic that so much is made of the literature of complaint, without regard to the new context. Enclosure by unity of possession was common in the northeast lowlands and in the Midland Plain. Where the lord had no farmers with estates and lacked freeholders on what had once been demesne, the year's end often brought him mere lease-parole tenancies. These he enclosed at will. The Elizabethan earl of Essex did this at Keyston, and so did Sir Edward Duncombe at Battlesden. Unity of possession also came through purchase. But there are cases that show pretended unity of possession and the eviction of tenants-at-will who were not subject to the protection of "estates." In still more cases, tenants enjoying such protection nominally were "weaned" by excessive fines. Robert Delavale enclosed 2,500 acres in the northeast lowlands in that way.

However, the worst instances of suffering from enclosures by unity of possession were not on manors. Rather, they occurred where men lacked the safeguard of the court-baron—in nonmanorial rural areas and in towns. In urban centers, the owners of land were often closed corporations of an oligarchic nature. Governments of commercial capitalists in free boroughs proved most dangerous to commoners who were wholly dependent on stints on a single small commons. In 1517, Southampton enclosed the salt marshes to help pay the costs for repairing the sea wall. These fences were repeatedly leveled over two generations. Leicester township leased the borough commons as a single farm after 1624, much to the disgust of an obscure local magistrate, Oliver Cromwell, who was taken into custody on account of his "disgraceful and unruly speeches." Earlier, in 1613, Malmesbury did the same thing; a baker, a blacksmith, and a strong waterman attacked the close and caused a riot.

Yet most enclosures came by agreement. The typical consent preserved common rights by incorporating a provision for "Lammas Close," according to which the field would be thrown open for common use at Lammas Tide (August 1). Another type of agreement was that of enclosure by commission. All consenting parties entered into commission, sometimes coercing a few dissidents, with the express purpose of enclosing whole tracts of waste and common fields. Such acts often had preambles alleging the improvements hoped for, such as that land unsuitable for corn and too wet and cold for sheep would become prosperous. Allotments were then made in the enclosed area, with a commutation of tithes and customary services. These practices also applied to lands that had not been in tillage earlier—wastes, forests, flooded lands, and old grassland. Cultivation and the "peopling of the countryside" were the great expectations, as the result of improvements flowing from intensive cultivation through up-and-down systems.

Too much attention has been paid to harmful enclosures, force and fraud, and the rhetoric of the dispossessed. There existed no simple relationship between enclosure in general and either depopulation or the decay of tillage. Both population and tillage increased in fen, heath, plain, and the chalky cheese counties. Examples of decline in the East Midlands should not engross our attention, especially since most conversion of arable to grass was complete before 1500. Norden's castigation of converters to grass as "cankers to the commonwealth," and "apish, woolvish men" whose avarice was the "apparent badge of atheism" might best be applied to those responsible for emparkment. But the movement of intakes for parks was largely early Tudor. Much emparking, like enclosure, was by agreement. Witness the practice of the earl of Arundel, Sir John Thynne, Edward IV, and many others who traded outland and meadow for inland common. This did not lessen resentment among some country folk who had deep loathing for "houses built alone like ravens' nests, no birds building near them. . . ." But disparking was ascendant after 1550.

Land Use and Living Standards

Most men in Elizabethan and Stuart England had been converted by the facts of life. They accepted as wise the suppression of permanent tillage and permanent grass. They grasped the benefits of up-and-down husbandry, which made it possible for a single horse to work eleven acres on a farm with improved capital, while on poor family farms and the better places of working farmers, the figure varied from seven to ten. They balanced the decline in small family farms against the profits in production, new crops, and cost reductions. And industrialists agreed with them, since they saw in the rural poor a good labor supply. In woad, flax, hemp, wool, and other animal products, they recognized what was vital to the expansion of industry. Hosiery making, metal working, and production of lace, nails, boots, and shoes were situated in the countryside, where labor was cheap and guild control absent. This fact may well have softened the stimulus to mechanization, but it was a main element in the early industrial revolution, which together with the revolution in agriculture made England a synonym for wealth in Europe. What had begun as an experiment among a few adventurous farmers and been praised by Fitzherbert in 1523 was common practice by the 1560s. By successive stages, the revolution went forward, especially in the 1580s, when up-and-down husbandry was widely combined with floating meadows, marling and liming, fen drainage, and breed improvement. By about 1615, the scale of activity had expanded enormously. By 1650, other innovations were common —chiefly in fertilization techniques and the growth of new grasses and root crops, especially carrots, cabbage, and turnips. The centuries-old habit of bowing before the cycle of poverty that limited flocks and food because grass and hay were scarce was not yet dead. It was dying, however.

What these developments meant among the various classes can be seen by looking at the movements of land, rents, prices, and living standards that accompanied them.

The reversal of trends in the conversion of arable to pasture derived from population pressure on food resources. Up-and-down husbandry helped to relieve the pressure, but it entailed enclosure and engrossing. Under the inducements offered by rising grain prices and soaring land values, few of the prospering possessing classes argued for the common fields and the community spirit fostered by common enterprises. Land use was becoming more efficient, and the demand for land was intense at every social level. Technical developments and the pressure of the market thus combined with other factors to ensure the triumph of commercial agriculture over subsistence farming. But this triumph meant the loss of peasant communities and an enormous increase in the number of agricultural wage earners, landless men in the truest sense, proletarians. It also meant a growing inequality of income among the classes of rural England.[4]

Thus, while it is true that our present state of knowledge about land ownership is one of "mitigated ignorance,"[5] we do know some things. The proportion of land held by lay peers continued the decline that was already marked by 1520. This was not because the peers were improvident and incapable of good estate management. It was the result of an inflation in their numbers— especially under James I and Charles I—out of proportion with the estates of their newest members. Hence the class as a whole held fewer manors in 1642 than in 1558. This fact, rather than the spectacular improvidence of the worst profligates, accounts for the literary laments about the decline of the landed nobility. Most noblemen, however, were in fact making profits from their estates between 1560 and 1640.

The gentry doubtless widened its lead in landed society. This was a natural consequence of their large numbers in a time of unparalleled prosperity among farming landlords. Beyond the exploitation of their estates, some gentry en-

---

[4] The sociopolitical consequences of economic developments affecting different social classes are dealt with in Chapters Four and Eight.

[5] Alan B. Simpson, *The Wealth of the Gentry* (Oxford: Oxford University Press, 1961), p. 21.

riched themselves and their class from the profits of office and business. Of the seventy-eight Sussex gentlemen who made Armada loans in 1588, the twenty-five richest included only four old landed gentry. But it is distorting to empha-size such sources of wealth beyond artificially excluding peers from the same enjoyment. The mass of the gentry were merely landowners making good profit out of the agricultural boom. After 1540, all landowners shared in the benefits of relatively stable labor costs and rising produce prices; it was a grower's and seller's market. Food prices doubled between 1500 and 1550 and again between 1550 and the great dearth of 1594–7. The tapering off of prices as a result of crop failure gave way to a slower rise after 1597, but by 1640 prices stood at six times the 1500 levels. A glance at the relevant data shows the favorable relations between costs and prices over the entire period from 1450 to 1640.[6]

These trends also favored the yeomen, that amorphous estate of Englishmen "living in the temperate zone between greatness and want," as Thomas Fuller wrote.[7] Such men often held copyhold lands and freeholds, along with good leases. Some were richer than most gentry, while others were as poor as Hugh Latimer's father and little better than wealthy peasants. But as direct producers, most tenant farmers benefited from rising prices and stable costs. The weakest members of this class, however, sometimes found natural disasters thrusting them from their "temperate zone" into the harsher climates of want. Crop failure could ruin them. So could too great a harvest, which might depress prices and cut into their living standards, a conclusion warranted by the data surviving for 1581–4, 1591–2, 1603–4, and 1619–20. It is quite possible that the depression in trade and the slowing of population growth after 1620 diminished their prosperity. Increased production as a consequence of im-provement affected farmers in an undesired way: it lowered prices for their profits. This conclusion is supported by the evidence of disinvestment in land in the latter part of the period 1600–1650.

The interests of the great landlords and those of their better-placed tenants thus coincided. They profited together for nearly a hundred years after 1540. Despite the currency given to contrary opinions, historians have demonstrated that the movement of rents between 1540 and 1640 kept pace with prices. Not all lords were encumbered with long leases and copyholds of inheritance. Contemporaries knew this and said so openly: Robert Crowley in 1550, William Harrison in 1587, and John Norden in 1613. Documentary evidence over areas of East Anglia, the Cotswolds, the Peak Forest district, and the Wiltshire chalk country supports them.

Most of the increase in rent derived from rising entry fines. But rentals per

[6] See the Appendix, Figure 9.
[7] Quoted in Thirsk, *Agrarian History*, IV, p. 301.

acre also rose commensurately, generally following the changes in food prices and running well ahead of industrial prices. Kerridge estimated that cereal prices rose over 400 percent *c*. 1540–1640, while wool rose 200 percent, with cattle and meat not far behind grain. Timber and wood rose somewhat less than 400 percent, building materials less than 300 percent, metal goods about 200 percent, and textiles somewhat less. Thus the price increases were beneficial for many proprietors and many tenant farmers. The greatest advantages lay with the largest operatives. Size provided a margin against short-term fluctuations, except on the crown estates, where land considered as patronage often went at less than market values. The other great exceptions to the rule of prosperity were the owners and farmers who had large numbers of copyholders for terms of life or lives and long-term leases. On such lands, the farmer had a steady income under the siege of inflation, while the subtenant derived the benefits of price augmentation. This arrangement doubtless tempted some men toward eviction and arbitrary fines of an unreasonable nature.

The obvious implication is that tenants-at-will and the most land-poor peasants paid the bill. It was of them that Robert Reyce spoke when he noted that "the rich cannot stand without the poor. . . ."[8] Many of the poor peasants lost what little land they had under the pressure of population, which subdivided small holdings—often to the vanishing point, unless some were disinherited to protect others. Either way, the number of landless men increased and swelled the ranks of agricultural wage earners. There is some evidence that the proportion of poor laborers in England grew from about 25 percent of the peasantry to as much as 33 percent between 1524 and 1660.[9] By the end of the seventeenth century, cottagers without land constituted perhaps 47 percent of the peasant population. Improvement thus swelled the ranks of a migrant labor army, as commercial farming and regional specialization combined to increase the demand for seasonal wage-labor, a feature of the English agrarian economy still visible in modern monocultures of cotton, sugar, tobacco, and tropical fruits. The disinheritance of peasants was thus a feature of capitalist farming, even though it is wrong to see enclosure or the predatory instincts of the gentry as the cause. For this disinheritance was common to most of Europe, regardless of the opportunities of politics, religious change, or the rise and fall of gentries or aristocracies, and it derived from real economic changes rather than the accidents of national history.

Whatever the explanation, the period after 1560 was one of rapidly shrinking peasant holdings. Peasants who migrated to forest and heath areas often preserved their independence by making a living out of limited stock and supplementary employment. But in the older villages small peasants had less

---

[8] *The Breviary of Suffolk* (1618), edited by Lord Hervey, p. 56.
[9] From tax records and occupational censuses of 1524, 1608, 1638, and 1660.

stock in 1640 than in 1560, and those without animals of any sort rose from 5 percent to 13 percent in that time. Since the better-off laborers increased their stock, as we know from probate inventories, the split that had always existed in the landed peasant classes grew among landless peasants as well. Many Hertfordshire laborers left goods worth between £10 and £15, whereas their brethren in the Midlands were destitute.

It is thus misleading to stress elements of agrarian prosperity, as we have done, without also emphasizing the growth of pauperism in an increasingly wealthy society. Landless peasants with stock and more than one form of employment invested between 40 percent and 50 percent of their wealth in domestic goods about 1640. This was a marked increase from the roughly 25 percent represented by nonstock and cottage investment c. 1560. It was also indicative of the rising standard of living among those who made an effective transition to the world of wage-labor from that of peasant landholding.

The volume of meat, dairy products, and grain produced by the revolution in agriculture more than matched the needs of the bulk of the rising population. This included more and larger Hereford cattle, more chalk country sheep, more good shire horses, and Suffolk Punches, more grass-fed lamb, mutton, and beef, and more winter-fed meat. There was also a startling increase in corn and grass nutrients for humans and fodder. Between 1500 and 1700, the yield increase was on the order of 500 percent, with some favored areas having tenfold increases—wheat and barley in the Cotswolds, common-field grain in the Midland Plain, and dramatic changes wherever up-and-down husbandry spread to what had once been waste and permanent grass.

The result was a diet improvement in even the lowest ranks of employed wage laborers, whose staples were bread, beef, beer, and cheese. Even rye, so vital in the diet of the poorest farm workers, had more protein than the milled white flour that is used in most bread today. Barley and oat bread were not as rich in protein; but the difference was not great. Increased wheat yields made wheat bread available to people who were quite poor. Calculations of the quantities of food available to the workers and servants of middling farmers are known from household books, and it has thus been possible to calculate the gram-calorie equivalents of their diets in protein, the B vitamins, fat, calcium, phosphorus, iron, and vitamins A and D. The conclusion reached is that the workingman's food in 1640 was somewhat better than his distant cousin's diet about 1450, the "golden age" of the laborer. Compared with modern "poverty" diets in industrial societies, especially in hard times, the food of servant classes in the seventeenth century had twice as much protein, a little more fat, seven times the calcium, four times the iron, and multiples of the necessary vitamins that varied from three to ten. More startling still, that servants' diet contained in almost every instance more of these nutrients than the diet of "middle-class" Englishmen in 1939![1]

But hundreds of thousands did not make the transition successfully. They were impoverished in an age of rising living costs. Their world was one of decay and utter hopelessness, as the mid–seventeenth century reproduced some of the features that had characterized English peasant society about 1300. Into that world there occasionally had burst the fury of a peasant rising. But the English revolution, terminated by Oliver Cromwell's rule, stopped short of embracing the commonwealth of the poor. Hence the radical Diggers, Ravers, Ranters, Levellers, and refugees from prosperity turned their eyes toward God, the City, and America, away from the inhospitable land. We may interpret their action as symbolic of the growing significance of commerce, industry, and England overseas—whatever we make of the connection with radical religion—and thus divert our attention to the growth of a mercantile economy.

[1] J. Drummond and A. Wilbraham, *The Englishman's Food* (London: Jonathan Cape, 1940), especially pp. 83–138, 301–2, 561–5.

Chapter Eight
THE GROWTH OF A MERCANTILE SOCIETY

Agriculture continued to dominate England's economy in the 1600s, although the share of total wealth it produced was doubtless shrinking. The development of industry and commerce by 1688 had been such as to contribute £13 million of a national income of £48 million.[1] Although neither Thomas Wilson nor William Petty gave comparable figures in his survey of wealth (in 1600 and 1665, respectively), it cannot be doubted that the eventual leveling off of agricultural profits diverted capital to industry and trade. Industrial change was also spurred by population growth, by the great expansion of markets produced by the Elizabethan and early Stuart trading companies and colonizing activities, and by the fate of wool and its textiles after 1551.

The Dutchman who observed English traders in the markets of Antwerp had clothiers in mind when he spoke of the English lust for profit: "If Englishmen's fathers were hanged in Antwerp's gates, their children would creep betwixt their legs to come into the said town." A petition of the Commons to Charles II a century later affirmed that wool and woolen textiles made up the principal foundation upon which the foreign commerce of England moved. Even in William III's day, 75 percent of England's exports were textiles. The preamble of a 1698 statute proclaimed them "the greatest and most profitable commodity of this kingdom, on which the value of lands and the trade of the

---

[1] Men in England in this period did not use words like "industrial" or "industrialization," and only rarely used "industry" to describe the making of products out of raw materials. They spoke of "trade" and "manufacture," and if we say "industry," we must not think of the modern usage. With the exceptions noted below, "industry," as used then, meant something more domestic than factories, machinery, and other fixed capital. The figures are from Gregory King, who gave statistical material, or what was then called "political arithmetic," in his *Natural and Political Observations and Calculations Upon the State and Condition of England* (London, 1696).

nation so chiefly depend." Whenever the economy faltered, wool was discussed as the cause. In the early Tudor period, high prices and the tremendous market for white broadcloth promoted a wave of criticism of graziers, clothiers, and textile merchants. Through much of the Stuart period, broadcloth exports were depressed. The loss of industrial employment brought another wave of criticism of the industry. All of these facts remind us of the fundamental role of textiles in English industry and commerce.[2]

Woolens and Worsteds

The industry had two main branches: broadcloth and worsteds. The basic difference between them was in the yarns used and the ways in which they were treated before the textile was actually made. Broadcloth was made from fine, short-staple wool, the cohesiveness of which was increased by carding.[3] It was then woven and "fulled," or soaped and beaten in a damp state. Fulling produced great matting of the warp and weft. The cloth was thus made warmer, more opaque, and more durable. Broadcloth contained much more wool per yard than either worsteds or the so-called new draperies. Worsteds were made wholly from long-staple wool that had been combed to straighten it. They were not felted; they depended on the strength of the warp and weft for their quality. Furthermore, worsteds were not fulled. Thus the fabric was lighter, less warm, and also cheaper. Fulling required a heavy investment of fixed capital in fulling mills and other machinery. The advantages of worsteds were partly aesthetic, since in them the woven pattern of the cloth was evident, whereas in broadcloth it was invisible.

In the period from 1520 to 1650, the two fabrics had sharply varied fortunes. Before 1550–1, broadcloth enjoyed its golden age: exports trebled between 1500 and 1550. After reaching the peak of an upward spiral that was aided by currency debasements and by the great supply of good short-stapled wool

---

[2] The quotation is in Peter Ramsey, *Tudor Economic Problems*; the statute is 10 Wm. III, c. 16. On wool and its textiles see P. J. Bowden, "Movements in Wool Prices, 1490–1610," *Yorkshire Bulletin of Social and Economic Research* (1952), IV, pp. 109–24; and his *The Wool Trade in Tudor and Stuart England* (London: Macmillan, 1962); G. D. Ramsey, *The Wiltshire Woollen Industry in the 16th and 17th Centuries* (Oxford: Clarendon Press, 1943); H. Heaton, *The Yorkshire Woollen and Worsted Industries*, 2nd ed. (Oxford: Clarendon Press, 1965); E. Lipson, *English Woollen and Worsted Industries* (London: Heinemann, 1953); T. C. Mendenhall, *The Shrewsbury Drapers* (Oxford: Clarendon Press, 1953); K. J. Allison, "The Norfolk Worsted Industry in the 16th and 17th Centuries," *YBSEcR* (1960), XII, pp. 73–8; and J. E. Pilgrim, "The Rise of the New Draperies in Essex," *University of Birmingham Historical Journal* (1961), VII, pp. 36–59.

[3] The process of passing the fleece between opposed sets of short metal teeth to gather the wool into rovings. The rovings are then spun into yarn.

resulting from the conversion to pasture, the level of sales declined throughout the rest of the century. With the exception of a short boom in broadcloth in the wake of the peace with Spain in 1604, shrinkage continued, and the industry decayed.

Worsteds enjoyed a reverse history. Their export languished before 1550. Early in Elizabeth's reign, however, worsted sales revived, in combination with sales of the new draperies, a variation of worsteds; and by 1650 worsteds had come to dominate the trade. Full worsted contained only long, straightened or combed fibers in warp and weft. In the combing of wool, short curly staples were caught by the pins of the comb. About one-sixth of the fleece was thereby lost, and since the use of short staples in broadcloth was forbidden by statute, these "pinions," or combings, could be put only into the cheapest, coarsest woolens. But they could also be carded and used in the weft of textiles, unlike either broadcloth or full worsteds. The new draperies were thus really lighter worsteds—bayes, sayes, serges, bombasines, shalloons, tammies, and many other "stuffs." These may have been produced in England early in the sixteenth century in insignificant quantities. But it was only after the collapse of the old cloth trade and the settling of foreign craftsmen in East Anglia that "stuffs" played a vital role in saving the industry.

Several factors help to account for the crisis in the textile industry and the transformation of that industry. One was the change in pasture practice we have already described. This increased the average size of sheep and the average weight of fleece.[4] The gain in weight brought with it a lengthening and coarsening of the staple. Broadcloth makers found it increasingly hard to obtain supplies of fine short-staple wool, especially in the traditional places in the Midlands. Highland supplies were both inadequate and costly. During the sixteenth century, Spanish short-staple wool usurped the place once enjoyed by its English equivalent. This development eventually doomed the broadcloth industry in the west of England and by the 1620s drove Somerset and Wiltshire clothiers to make "Spanish cloth," or medleys. This marked the decline of domestic broadcloths. By the 1630s, medleys were popular in European markets. The cloth industry of the southeast suffered a similar fate, with kersies and broadcloths from Kent, Hampshire, Berkshire, Sussex, and Surrey increasingly unable to meet Italian and domestic competition. In this area, too, the new draperies made up for lost business, since the local wool supplies were well suited to their production.

Even more fundamental than foreign competition and the change in English fleeces as a cause of decline in the sale of woolens was the structure of the industry itself. Capital was employed in a circulating stock of raw and processed

---

[4] 1.4 lbs. in 1350; 1.9 lbs. in 1550; 3.5 lbs. in 1700.

materials. Most cloth workers were supplied by entrepreneurs with materials and even tools. They were thus alienated from the final product and unlikely to rise either economically or socially through their labor. The Springs of Lavenham could employ whole village populations in cottage industry by putting out wool to be worked. But they therefore had little or no directly worked equipment of their own. Jack of Newberry[5] and William Stumpe of Malmesbury had pioneered the consolidation of fixed capital, by setting up factories earlier in the century. Stumpe had set his up on the site of an old monastery. The factory allowed close supervision and quality control while also reducing the amount of time and money lost in the transport of materials during different stages of production. Unlike most manufacturers, men with their own equipment had an incentive to maintain production, even in the face of shrinking demand. The others merely laid off their workers and reduced their circulating stock, which, by clipping wages and domestic buying, had the effect of deepening short-term fluctuations.

The poor position of rural cloth workers under most manufacturers was an adverse consequence of the slow shift of the industry to the countryside, where it was beyond city guild control. The guilds had regulated the scale of production and protected workers through the apprenticeship system. Rural industry did neither, since it took advantage of overabundant farm labor and a growing population of unemployed or underemployed people. The legislative efforts of boroughs to curtail rural clothiers failed. As a result, the overall vulnerability of the trade was ensured, and the increasingly regulation-fettered, older centers of production, where labor costs were high, were doomed unless they went over to the cheaper worsteds.

Manufacture of the cheaper worsteds had taken hold in England in the 1560s, especially around Norwich, in Norfolk, where the sale of full worsteds was in decline because they could not compete with Low Country varieties and were too high-priced for much of the domestic market. Dutch and Walloon immigrants brought with them the techniques for making the new draperies; labor was available, and so were plentiful supplies of moderately coarse long-staple East Anglia and Midland wool. Adaptation was easy in Norfolk, but it was less so in the Essex and Suffolk broadcloth areas, where worker resistance to "foreigners" and "inferior stuff" probably nourished the fears of men who as

---

[5] John Winchcombe's workshop was the subject of some doggerel verse in Thomas Deloney's novel *Jack O'Newberry*:

Within one room being large and long
There stood two hundred looms full strong
Two hundred men the truth is so
Wrought in these looms all in a row.

yet did not have the new techniques. By 1600, the lighter worsteds were dominant in Norfolk. Norwich cloth makers prospered while makers of older clothing and wool growers argued about the causes of their lack of prosperity. Then, slowly at first, in all of the old broadcloth areas—Wiltshire, Suffolk, Worcester, Yorkshire, and the Southeast or "Hampshire" industrial areas— the shift to the new draperies went forward.

The early 1600s thus constituted a period of adjustment and consolidation in the textile industry. There were few great innovations, but a rise in the scale of enterprise and an expansion in the range of goods compensated for the decline in the vent of fine broadcloths. Only dyed broadcloth held its own, except for the decade from 1604 to 1614. "Whites" faltered badly after 1614, and in the 1620s clothiers had to explore new possibilities. And those who did found a ready sale in the 1630s and 1640s. Jeremy Pottecary kept his laborers at work on high-quality colored cloth and stuffs, while his Wiltshire neighbors who stayed with whites failed. Medleys contributed to prosperity in the southwest, and the "immigrant style"—Norwich stuffs—spread from Norfolk throughout East Anglia. In the North, production of cheap goods was crippled temporarily in the 1640s by war damage in Bradford and Halifax, by epidemics, and by the interruption of wool supplies from the south. Nevertheless, the West Riding and Lancashire industries had been established, and their inexpensive fustians, linens, and cottons played a large part in the foundation of the "industrial north." Far to the southwest, around Tiverton and Exeter, in Devon, Irish and Spanish wools were used to make serges.

Thus, in every region of the country, the adaptation consisted chiefly of a limited change in technique rather than a change in technology or in the capital structures of industry. However, finer products more often than not reflected the role of big capitalists and the development of finishing plants with fulling mills and dyeing vats. Coarser goods were the product of many small masters, and their manufacture still embodied essentially the same processes that peasants used to make their own clothing. That home consumption of goods helped maintain overall levels of production may well be true. The inventories of goods that were attached to wills among all classes of men above the line of subsistence suggest that most Englishmen possessed a greater variety of goods in 1640 than they had in 1560, especially in utensils, plate, and good clothing. While we cannot be certain, it seems likely that the slippage in the percentage of all English exports represented by textiles, from about 90 percent in 1598 to just over 75 percent toward the end of the seventeenth century, gives too much emphasis to textile exports as a measure of the industry's health.[6]

---

[6] See the discussion of the export crisis on pages 265–73. The influence of this factor—foreign markets—on industrial production is fully treated there.

Coal, Iron, and the Pattern of Industrial Growth

That this may be so is especially evident from our knowledge of the rapidly rising coal industry. Like other new industries, coal was small in scale compared with textiles. But its methods and organization illustrate the revolution in industry that took place between Elizabeth's accession and the death of Charles I. And the pattern of its markets demonstrates how soundly domestic demand could anchor an industry. In fact, in light of developments after 1560 in the coal industry and in other industries whose need for cheap fuel it fed, it is no longer possible to see in the "revolution" of iron working and cotton in the 1760s the boundary separating industrial from agrarian England. The transformation was well under way in Elizabethan England, and it continued under the early Stuarts.

This fact a doggerel poet grasped in 1651 in his "Upon the Coal Pits about Newcastle upon Tine":

England's a perfect world! Has Indies too!
Correct your maps: Newcastle is Peru.

Allowing for the enthusiasm that made coal into black gold, the poet had a point. Between 1560 and the end of the seventeenth century, coal mining experienced a quantum jump in growth, the greatest period of which was concentrated between 1600 and 1650. The growth in overall production in all regions of Great Britain was fourteenfold during this time, while in the major fields of the northeast the growth was twentyfold. These leaps reflect the most spectacular economic happenings of the age.[7]

Contemporaries understood the vast increase in the scale of this extractive industry to be a response to fuel-supply problems and the rising cost of wagon-loads of wood. An Elizabethan observer said so pointedly in 1571: "The commodity of Newcastle and such like coals is known to be of more value than in times past, for wood being grown to dearth and the severity of it felt more every day, caused many of the said coals to be used for full in London and other places. . . ."[8]

The substitution of coal for wood, both in industrial and domestic use, was made imperative by the pressure of population growth and consumer-oriented industrial expansion. England's timber resources were not adequate to meet the need.

The increase in population was common to Western Europe. But in Eliza-

[7] See the Appendix, Figure 10.
[8] *SPD*, Eliz. 105, p. 30.

bethan England its effect on housing and industry was severe, and in the early 1600s population and industry were expanding faster in England than else-where—especially in London and a few provincial cities. This expansion brought into play a reciprocal economic action between the coal-supplying areas and the metropolis. London's people and industries required cheap and plentiful fuels. The expansion of coal supplies enabled Londoners to build houses and heat them economically. As the city gathered its teeming popula-tion, the brewers, salt makers, soap producers, and metalworking and food-processing craftsmen who served it drew fuel more and more heavily from the Northeastern and Midland collieries. Deeper shafts were needed, which intensified the need for capital. Coal transport necessitated wooden railways to get coal from the pitheads to the ever-bigger barges and the coastal trading ships. Hence each need spurred others, including the manufacture of tackle, sailcloth, cordage, and the manufacture of supplies of victuals for the sailors of the sea-coal runs. Without coal, industries meeting consumer needs and those serving coal extraction could not keep pace with the demand for cheaper services and goods. And without this tremendous demand, the concentration of capital required for a heavy mining industry would not have been justified by prices. While coal production alone cannot explain England's industrial leap forward, it is the most salient single element in the rise of a varied industrial sector in society during this period.

The challenge of meeting the increasing demand for coal was serious; it summoned the full capacities of the sixteenth-century revolution in tech-nology. This was as true in the processes of extraction as it was in those of using coal in other industries. As surface deposits played out and shallow pits failed, the London suppliers around Newcastle pressed to the limit the techniques of drainage, ventilation, and haulage, all of which placed limits on deep-working pits. To maintain such pits, with their tremendous capital expenditures, New-castle colliers (the Hostmen) organized a monopoly trade. This practice was increasingly resented in the late Elizabethan period. But only a good profit margin induced men to engage in the high-risk enterprise of expanding supplies. The Willoughbys of Nottingham left records that show how capital-intensive the industry was. In fact, operations in the sea-coal branch of the industry were revolutionary compared with the more local, land-coal enterprises of men whose workings did not supply mass markets. In the latter mining operations less than a dozen men, working without expensive machinery of any sort, mined small, shallow seams. Their product went over-land to strictly local markets. Costs and prices were kept down, and the small-scale industry served to dramatize the revolution in the London and the export pits.

Some landowners sought large profits in mineral exploitation. But for every success like the earl of Derby's at Preston, Lancashire, there were many failures.[9] Despite the failures, however, the record points to a significant augmentation of output and national wealth. More basic to this growth than the demand for domestic fuel was the use of coal industrially. In some industries, problems had to be solved before the future of coal was secure. For example, air pollution resulted from the domestic use of coal. This problem was partially alleviated by the production of special briquettes, by the use of anthracite, and by "charking" (reducing them to charcoal) gaseous coals before using them in hearths where inadequate drafts of air prevented whole coal from burning effectively. The attendant difficulty of transportation was offset by the sea route to London and by the improvement in the seventeenth century of both rivers and canals as inland waterways. The importance of superseding the costs of long-distance land haulage impressed even the Royal Society, which in 1675 sponsored a paper pointing out that it cost as much to haul a ton fifteen miles by land as it did to move 300 tons by water.

Once coal was on hand, some industries could use it without ado; this was largely true in smithing, salt boiling, soap making, brick making, and some metal trades. But potters, brewers, glassmakers, maltsters, and bakers complained about coal "tastes" and "smells" or discolorations in their products caused upon combustion by the gases emitted by coal. The mass demand for beer in London—brewers often had capital of £10,000 to £20,000—made it imperative to solve such problems and reduce the side effects of the fuel. Some masters used anthracite; this produced beer that Londoners liked because it was so sulfurous or "soft." Sir Robert Mansell used his patent in glassmaking after 1615 more constructively than most monopolists: his experiments produced crucibles that got rid of discolorations in molten glass. In dyeing processes and malting, the high price of wood fuels also stimulated inventions that advanced craft technology. The metal crafts in Wolverhampton and Birmingham prospered, and industries such as glassmaking and pottery grew in scale to an extent that would have been unimaginable in 1550. Hence cheap beer, window glass, containers of every description, household utensils, bread, and pretty clothes became more plentiful and were within the reach of more people.

By 1650, Londoners were using 40 to 50 percent of Newcastle's output of coal. They knew the names of great pits and spoke fondly of "Stella" and "Blaydon." They worried about England's relations with the Dutch, since they could be neither warm nor well supplied with luxuries and necessities if the sea coal that lay exposed to Dutch marine power were even temporarily made the prize of war. Outside London, men celebrated the "commodity of

---

[9] For example, the Beaumonts in Leicestershire and the Willoughbys at Wollaton, Gloucestershire.

Newcastle" in song and slogan. And in scattered places on the map, from Tynemouth to Pembrokeshire, where coal led all exports by 1660, the fortunes of merchants and middlemen were being made by the muscle of men alienated from the cycles of nature, by gnomes who worked in season and out at the seams of "black gold."

In most other branches of industry the period was characterized more by consolidation than by innovation. This was especially true in the mining of minerals other than coal and in the metallurgical industries, although we have seen how many consumer-goods industries produced important innovations in process because of the fuel crisis. We can conclude our description of industrial growth with a brief discussion of these developments, concentrating on iron making, where progress was typically in the scale of works rather than in their technology.

Iron making contributed to the new prosperity. Its development reduced English reliance on foreign goods while increasing the demand for ore, particularly ore from Sweden. Total investment was perhaps less than in coal mining, but the scale of enterprise was often spectacular, especially when blast furnaces became widespread and forced out the domestic bloomeries in the early 1600s.

The introduction of the blast furnace late in the fifteenth century radically increased production. This use of continental techniques in place of the English bloomery[1] transformed entirely the capital required in iron making. The typical furnace was vast compared with earlier forges. It rose to a height of 30 feet and had a square base 20 feet to a side. Walls of stone and brick, often as thick as 6 feet, contained and withstood the heat needed to melt the ore. This heat was obtained from bellows nearly as high as the furnace, driven by water from a dammed stream poured onto an overshot wheel.[2] Added to the cost of the business was the cost of the outlying buildings, structures to protect the mill wheel, and storage for fuel, ore, and pig iron. Such a furnace could produce up to 500 tons a year, in contrast with the small bloomeries, from which 20 tons was a good annual production. It required few tools, buildings, or appliances, and it employed a handful of manorial tenants. Even smaller blast furnaces produced four or five times the quantity of pig turned out in bloomeries. The new product was of higher quality and was also greater in volume per ton of ore than that obtained by earlier methods.

The changeover took place first in the old Sussex Weald center of the industry, chiefly in response to the rapidly expanding local market of London. The

[1] A large puddling furnace in which a mass of ore was deprived of its dross and shaped into oblong blocks or "blooms."

[2] The whole purpose was to force combustion of larger amounts of ore under the pressure of the blast. The resultant molten iron, or "pig," was separated from the slag at the bottom of the furnace.

motive was *quantity*, since cost per ton of bar-iron was not dramatically cheapened. The need for cast-iron goods and for drawn wire and nails to supply builders of homes in the metropolis expanded rapidly after 1550. The number of furnaces in the Weald increased from twenty in 1550 to fifty in 1580. Elsewhere, in the West Midlands, the forest of Dean, and South Yorkshire, development was at a slower pace before 1600; starts of bloomeries were recorded in Warwickshire as late as 1623. In fact, developments in iron making again illustrate developments in textiles and coal mining: new and old techniques and scales of operation coexisted, and often the choice between them was the choice between serving local needs and responding to the pull of larger, often distant, markets.

The decision to change methods of production was thus primarily a response to the extensiveness of demand and the availability of raw materials. The limit of freedom was chiefly the limit of timber supplies. This fact highlights what was basically conservative in an expanding trade. Although coal had long been used in calcining ore prior to smelting, in lead processing, in silver extraction, in wire drawing, in steel production, and, on a very small scale during the 1600s, even in iron smelting, timber was still the fuel used in almost all pig-iron production. In the Elizabethan decades, a crisis in costs and availability of fuel acted as a slight brake on expansion, but by 1640 the failures to convert to coal in operating the blast furnace contributed to the onset of stagnation in the English iron industry. As pressure from the metal trades in Sheffield and Birmingham was added to that from London, ironmongers found themselves unable to continue the upward spurt of production, even though profits were good.

As early as the 1540s, landowners with small furnaces had nearly exhausted their own estate timber. Sir William Sidney had invested between £200 and £300 during that decade and subsequently got a return on his money in three years. He reckoned his costs as running 75 percent below his selling price. When timber failed, however, such small-scale makers either leased their facilities to tenants with timber or joined "combines" or partnerships. Hence the fuel crisis itself produced innovation in the structure of the trade. Men linked together to command forests, furnaces, and forges. The production of iron became still more capital-intensive, partly because of the technological limitations of a process that was not surpassed until Darby used coke as a fuel in 1709.

Nonetheless, the transformation of the industry was impressive. Total production is not calculable, since many small bloomeries endured and left no records. The figures below represent a modern estimate of tons of bar-iron equivalents produced by blast in England up to 1600[3]:

[3] Pollard and Crossley, *The Wealth of Britain*, p. 109.

	1500	1540	1570	1600
Tons	140	1,400	7,000	10,000

It is unlikely that production rose much beyond 1660 levels by 1700; and total production in 1640 may not have risen 2,000 tons above 1600 levels.[4]

With the rise in production levels tapering off by 1600, the changes after that date and before the civil war were primarily in location and scale. The Sussex industry rapidly declined in the seventeenth century, while the northern and western centers swept ahead, with use of the blast furnace spreading rapidly after 1600. In part this chronology reflects the lag of other markets behind London's. But it also reflects the failure of Sussex streams to supply the water needed for the blasting of huge burdens of ore in the biggest furnaces. Just as the operators of fulling mills migrated to the great millstreams in the 1400s, so the furnaces and forges required the water power of the upland regions of England in the 1600s. Another factor in relocation was the exhausting of timber supplies in the Weald. The Midland masters had the ore, the timber, and the water. They formed vast combines to control these resources over wide areas. The Foley Partnership had fourteen works in the Stour Valley and a capital of £68,830 by 1660. Thus, although many small masters still maintained bloomery forges, iron making became a heavily capitalized industry on a scale quite beyond anything that might have been imagined in Sidney in 1540. The Foley works were as heavily financed as the largest coal mines, and only a technological lag prevented the steady expansion of what was already an "industrial enterprise" (in the later sense of the term).

In the other extractive industries and the secondary metal trades there were also important developments. Sometimes these resulted from a widespread demand for commodities based on raw materials whose distribution was limited to a particular region. The extractive industries grew up in that way: tin in Cornwall, lead in Derbyshire, iron in a few locations already named, and coal in the northeast, northwest, South Wales, and Scotland.[5] In the non-

[4] Wilson, *England's Apprenticeship*, p. 86. Wilson's figure for 1600 is 18,000 tons; for 1640, 20,000 tons. The difference lies in his use of bloomery and blast totals.

[5] For the extractive industries, metalworking, and secondary industries, see: John Gaugh, *The Mines of Mendip* (Oxford: Clarendon Press, 1930); H. Hamilton, *English Brass and Copper to 1800* (London: Routledge & Kegan Paul, 1926); G. R. Lewis, *The Stannaries* (Cambridge: Cambridge University Press, 1908); *The British Paper Industry, 1495–1860* (Oxford: Oxford University Press, 1958); D. L. Linton, *Sheffield and Its Region* (London: British Association for the Advancement of Science, 1956); A. P. Wadsworth and J. D. Mann, *The Cotton Trade and Industrial Lancashire* (Manchester: Manchester University Press, 1931); P. Mathias, *The Brewing Industry in England* (Cambridge: Cambridge University Press, 1959); R. Jenkins, *Links in the History of Engineering and Technology from Tudor Times* (Cambridge: Cambridge University Press, 1936); C. Singer, *The Earliest Chemical Industry* (London: Oxford University Press, 1948); E. S. Godfrey, "The Development of English Glass-making, 1560–1640" (Chicago: University of Chicago, 1957, unpublished thesis); D. C. Coleman, "Technology and Economic History," *EcHR* (1958), XI, pp. 506–14.

extractive industries, growth depended on the spurting demand for fine goods wanted by the rich and the great thrust of demand for ordinary consumer goods wanted by the increasingly affluent middle ranks of society. By the 1640s, colonial goods—sugar, tobacco, cotton, and dyes—had added to a list already containing fine textiles, pewter, glass, soap, and beer. Industries that depended on imported raw materials had to be centered upon the entry ports; this fact made for great growth around Bristol, Liverpool, Glasgow, and London.

But there were setbacks as well as advances. Tin production stagnated when it reached about 500 tons a year, kept down by a slowing demand for pewter. Bronze was being replaced by brass (copper and zinc), which also lessened the demand for Cornish silver. Copper, on the other hand, was subject to great demand, as brass church bells, cannons, and cannonballs hallowed the arts of war and peace. Lead for roofing, bullets, and shot stimulated demand in a populous and war-torn age. The output of the metal in Derbyshire rose to 12,000 tons by 1640; it was not much higher in 1800.

Looked at from the perspective of the whole period from 1540 to 1640, the growth of large-scale industry seems to have been heavily tied to technology in three main patterns of change. These we may summarize. First, there was the introduction and growth of heavily capitalistic industries unknown in England before the Reformation (paper mills, gun founding, sugar refineries, alum making). From the outset, these used more labor and materials than other trades. And they opened new avenues for industrial capital. Second, and more basic to industrial growth, was the use of advanced technical methods in old industries, often with the result of a leap in scale and capital requirements (in coal mining, iron making, copper refining, mailing, wire drawing, steel forging). Such trades produced innovations in organization, such as the Society of Mines Royal, the Foley Partnership, and the great wire works at Tintern. They also drew unprecedented numbers of workingmen into coal mining, and craftsmen from small villages into towns. Third, there was the discovery in certain trades of new methods that transformed old forms and habits of production (in brick making, glass making, pottery). The chief importance of these new methods was perhaps the immediate gains they provided in the visible standard of living of townsmen, whose houses were built better, were airier and brighter, and were supplied with a greater range of utensils than ever before. Changes in the making of textiles may also be included under the third classification, especially since the new draperies were essentially based on methods imported with foreign craftsmen.

The conclusion from all this may well be forcefully stated. No matter what the problems of making quantitative estimates may be, the nature of production and distribution was being altered. The acceptance of technical innovation facilitated the rise of large-scale industry, especially after 1570. This change in scale was also aided by the growth of markets and by transportation improvements vital to the cheap movement of heavy goods. Perhaps the coal, iron, and salt industries best illustrate the changes in scale and capital investments that characterize the general history of manufacture between 1540 and 1640; the salt works at South Shields employed about 1,000 men and thousands of pounds sterling by 1640. Brewing also illustrates the change; one London brewery in James I's reign had capital of £20,000. In shipbuilding, which had always been on a large scale, heavier cranes and sawmills began to be used in the 1600s, as the royal navy and the merchant fleets expanded rapidly under the combined pressures of colonization and an expanding economy. The example of textiles best illustrates the continued supremacy of the domestic workshop, but we have seen how factory conditions prevailed in the finishing operations of dyeing and fulling. The advantages of large-scale operation were evident even in textiles, under the pressure of population and the increasing consumption of clothing, bedding, and hangings.

Thus, while we do not know how many laborers were employed in capitalistic enterprises, we do know that the use of new tools, techniques, and machinery concentrated both labor and capital to a degree unknown in the 1520s. Nothing was more momentous for the future than these developments and the revolution in commerce to which they were both a response and a further stimulant. The lead in commercial and industrial affairs that England had in Europe by 1750 owed a great deal to the rapidity of change before 1640.

The Character of Elizabethan Commerce

In an earlier chapter, we showed how England's treasure by foreign trade grew in the late 1400s. In this chapter we have stressed the rapid growth of population and domestic markets in the 1500s and the changing patterns of production in several industries after 1540. Now it remains for us to treat more systematically the trade of England, its growth during much of the period from 1560 to 1640, and the significance of a profound crisis and depression in the cloth trade spanning the period from 1614 to 1640.

In so doing, we may conveniently separate domestic and foreign commerce only as long as we grasp their relatedness. For what England traded abroad was mainly what her land produced: sheep, cattle, grain, hops, minerals, and things made from them. The markets tended to merge in London, where the government increasingly thought of trade as national business. Therefore, in order to understand both commercial expansion and the recurrent crises that crippled trade, we must grasp the relationship of the home market, with London at its heart, to the role of foreign trade of England in an age of colonization; and, finally, the impact on English life of what we may call the "commercial revolution."[6] After 1600, English trade reflected the fact that economic development in Europe was shifting from the land empires of the south and center of the Continent to the overseas empires of the maritime powers—Spain, Portugal, Holland, England, and France. The eviction of the Hansa from London in 1598 and the chartering of the English East India Company signaled the shift.[7]

Any discussion of Elizabethan commerce must necessarily emphasize the degree to which its patterns and character bore the stigmata of the mid–Tudor ordeal. The great boom (1500–50) had ended in collapse in 1551–2. Currency manipulation in the 1540s and war had played their parts. The credit collapses at Antwerp in 1551–2 and 1557–8 were damaging. But war and the contraction of consumer demand in the Germanies helped turn credit and currency instability into a general commercial crisis. The third quarter of the century thus brought a protracted decline of overseas outlets for cloth. Figures for London cloth export show that the pre-1540 levels tended to become the rallying points for textiles, marred by two severe depressions—one in the early 1560s, the other in the early 1570s.[8]

Trade stagnated over most of the period at levels well below the earlier highs. Privateering, market closures, recurrent harvest crises, the Spanish war, and government caution about the role of industry in the economy combined to deepen the depression by 1586. Even the surge of exports in the 1590s and selective inflationary influences in other trades—especially metal goods and the products of extractive industries—were doubtful compensations for the broadcloth dislocations that helped produce the Poor Laws of 1597 and 1601. These facts help us to avoid being dazzled by the inflationary gains of landlords, the rise of conspicuous consumption, or the splendors of Elizabeth's court and the Armada. Plague, famine, and unemployment in the old textile industries produced a literature of anxiety. Fear of overpopulation became rampant again.

Yet it seems that commerce expanded between 1560 and Elizabeth's death in 1603. Concentrating on London shortcloth figures distorts our conception of trade, since no consideration is given to new textiles, to other products, or to the commerce of the outports.[9] Furthermore, progress was made in solving the instability of the Antwerp-German market, which had been sacked by

---

[6] The politics of commerce and colonization will be dealt with in Chapter Ten.

[7] The Venetians had left London in 1533 and Southampton in 1587. The Hansa lost privileges in 1552, forty-six years before the closing of the Steelyard.

[8] See the Appendix, Figure 11.

[9] See the demonstrations of this made in two critiques of F. J. Fisher's use of these data: Lawrence Stone, "State Control in 16th Century England," *EcHR* (1947), pp. 104ff., and J. D. Gould, *The Great Debasement* (Oxford: Clarendon Press, 1970), pp. 114–26.

Spanish troops in 1576 and blockaded by the Dutch in 1585. And there is clear evidence that the infrastructure of commerce developed some institutional strengths and skills vital to any sustained prosperity. Voyaging was on the rise. Colonial adventures had begun. New trading companies had started the development of new markets. Restrictive trading practices were called into question, and a slow conversion to policies favorable to industrial and commercial expansion influenced government actions. Taken together, these developments had the potential to help English commerce achieve better balance and reduce its dependence on the Dutch.[1]

The narrowness of markets and the domination of cloth in exports had prompted inquiries into the whole question of commerce in the wake of the collapse of the 1550s. In 1560, Thomas Colehill led an investigation into England's trade balance. The immediate result was a wave of patents to encourage new industries. The Newcastle Hostmen (colliers), the Mineral and Battery Company (lead), and the Society of the Mines Royal (copper) were all chartered in the 1560s. In 1582, Martyn's patent on brass making consolidated that trade in London. This early, beneficial use of monopoly patents has often been obscured by the later abuses of monopolies. But since government was trying to harness capital to new, high-risk enterprises, protecting innovations was essential to diversifying production and thus reducing the dangerous role of clothing exports in an unbalanced economy. The patents given to makers of window glass (Becker-Carré) and drinking vessels (Verselini) did not stifle initiative; nor did they direct privileges into the hands of men who merely sought to hurt established trades in exchange for profits made in supplying an impecunious queen with money.[2]

More important than giving aid to new products was securing markets for them. Before 1550, discussion of foreign trade really meant talk about the wool and cloth going to northern Europe. At home, road transport was very poor.

---

[1] G. D. Ramsey, *English Overseas Trade During the Centuries of Emergence* (London: Oxford University Press, 1957); W. H. Price, *The English Patents of Monopoly* (Cambridge, Mass.: Harvard University Press, 1913); R. Davis, *The Rise of the English Shipping Industry* (London: Macmillan, 1962); A. A. Ruddock, *Italian Merchants and Shipping in Southampton* (London: Oxford University Press, 1951); H. van der Wee, *The Growth of the Antwerp Market*, 3 vols. (Hague: Niijhoff, 1963); T. S. Willan, *The English Coasting Trade* (Manchester: Manchester University Press, 1938) and *River Navigation in England* (Oxford: Oxford University Press, 1936); P. Dollinger, *The Hansa* (Stanford, Calif.: Stanford University Press, 1970); R. K. W. Hinton, *The Eastland Trade* (Cambridge: Cambridge University Press, 1953); T. S. Willan, *Early History of the Russia Company* (Manchester: Manchester University Press, 1956); K. N. Chaudhuri, *The English East India Company* (London: Frank Cass, 1965); A. L. Rowland, *England and Turkey* (Philadelphia: University of Pennsylvania Press, 1924); K. G. Davies, *The Royal African Company* (London: Longmans, 1959).
[2] See Chapter Ten, where the debates on monopolies in 1601 and 1621 are discussed, as are exploration and colonization.

A rate of fifteen miles a day in the South and Midlands was the limit on over-land exchange. Given the sad state of inland river navigation, domestic com-merce was thus primarily a coastal trade. This fact determined the pattern and scale of many enterprises. A good example is the trade in home-grown grain. High London prices and easy water transport created severe problems for merchants and consumers in outlying districts. Advance buying by brokers in barley, peas, and beans created severe local shortages, as the privy council noted in 1565. Such shortages occurred again in the 1590s, when ruined har-vests threatened local subsistence. Yet the middlemen gathered skills and capital in such trades, and when new overseas markets became attractive, many brought capital and expertise to them.

Between 1560 and 1600, a remarkable harnessing of such resources changed the direction of overseas trade. The loss of facilities in Antwerp (after the 1565 closure) meant a loss of warehouses, privileges, financing, and European connections. In the 1550s, the Russia Company had been one response to such a closure. In the wake of the voyages of Chancellor to Archangel, this first joint-stock company set the pattern for ventures more closely knit than those of the old regulated groups like the Merchant Adventurers, although only trade with Persia proved profitable at first. In the 1560s and 1570s, the Levant and Barbary (North Africa) merchants sharply increased their activities, still without formal organization. Then, in 1581, the Levant Company formed under a crown charter. Three years later, the Barbary Company used the earl of Leicester's patronage to good advantage by securing privileges in North African markets. There too, in 1577, the joint-stock Spanish Company began systematic trade. Eleven years later, the Senegal Company began operations on a joint-stock charter. The company whose fame grew most in commercial history, the East India Company, gained a charter on December 31, 1600, under the sponsorship of George Clifford, earl of Cumberland, and some 215 knights, aldermen, and merchants. Early in 1600, the Arctic explorer John Davis took five ships to Sumatra and Java and so started England's great empire in the East. Some twenty years earlier, Englishmen had already made contact with the Moghul at Agra in the Punjabi.

The fact that only 8 percent of all English exports went to these new markets in the 1590s is no measure of their importance. These companies aggregated very large capitals and involved a wider circle of merchants and investors than did the regulated Staplers and Merchant Adventurers. Costs were very high. This was partly because voyages took longer and required heavier vessels. Hence the return on investment was slower and less sure than that from the short, well-developed Netherlands and Baltic trades. The demand for enlarged and prolonged investments also stemmed from the habit developed by joint-stock companies of redistributing capital after several voyages rather than after each one. Even regulated companies such as the Eastland Company (established in 1586), as well as the independent-minded members of the Merchant Adventurers who traded in French and Spanish wines, contributed to these developments.

Widening patterns therefore laid the foundations for the great seventeenth-century expansion, which was further shaped by colonization. In 1590, however, 75 percent of all export trade was carried on by Merchant Adventurers, privileged foreigners, or English interlopers lacking any privilege or organization. Textiles were still the commercial mainstay. Coal accounted for only .5 percent of the value of all exports, and tin and lead shipments had declined.

These and similar facts of trade were disquieting, despite the developments so promising for the future.[3] Imports in exchange for wool, leather, minerals, and textiles were numerous and costly. Luxury goods drained the supply of English bullion, which went especially to the East, where little in the way of English goods found a market. This was a dilemma for all concerned. If the government gave scope to practices restricting the carrying out of precious metals or the import of luxury goods that were traded for exports of cloth, retaliations abroad might cripple the sales of textiles, drive down employment, and increase the problems of poverty and dislocation that were already acute. Such a move would also certainly reduce domestic consumption, which was always a vital but inscrutable factor in prosperity. In the absence of multilateral credit arrangements, the outflow of bullion could itself depress internal trade. Some things imported were necessities. In 1565, linen and canvas made up 17 percent of all imports by value. Another 13 percent consisted of cloth-dyeing and -finishing materials. In bad harvest years, grain had to come in unrestricted. It was also impossible to maintain the merchant marine without Baltic naval stores. Wine was a heavy luxury liability, however, taking up 38 percent of the value of imports in 1570. Fine cloth constituted 6 percent of the imports,[4] while exotic foods made up 10 percent. The demand for these "deceitful wares" by politically powerful consumer groups frustrated efforts to right the unfavorable balance of trade.

Furthermore, England in the late sixteenth century did not realize the full benefits of its carrying trade. As late as 1570, about 25 percent of all exports went in foreign ships and 38 percent of imports came in that way. Hence the protests against the Hansa and Italian merchants. Moreover, a good part of "English" shipping was in reality foreign owned. Between 1550 and 1570 there had been serious decay in the merchant fleet. Vigorous government action in the form of subsidies began to reverse this situation after 1570. Fifty-

[3] There are no adequate statistics about imports available in index form. This derives in large measure from their heterogenous nature and the burdens of completion from diverse sources.
[4] Silk, for example, and cloth of gold and silver.

one ships of 100 tons or more were built *c.* 1570–6; between 1571 and 1582, the number of merchantmen increased by 50 percent. In the period from 1592 to 1595, another forty-eight large ships were built. Part of this stimulus came from the sea war against Spain, since there was not yet a fixed distinction between fighting "ships of the line" and the armed merchantmen. But long-distance trade was crucial in putting England in a position from which she might some day challenge Dutch dominion of the carrying trade.

The discussion of trading institutions, markets, domestic demand, and the merchant fleet shows the situation of some aspects of the commercial equation. We must also see how ill-equipped the infrastructure of commerce was.

Elizabethan trade was even more heavily London's trade than it had been in 1547. In that year, 90 percent of all cloth went out through the capital. Twelve years later, the figure was 93 percent. The trade of the provincial ports was in steady decline. As a result, capital, banking, and credit—which lagged behind continental practices in any event—were concentrated in London. Although places such as Ipswich and King's Lynn lacked credit facilities, their commerce was saved by local specialization in grain. Great Yarmouth's commerce was saved by sales of fish, and that of Exeter and Bristol only by desperate efforts to improve their harbors and capture trading privileges and capital for Atlantic voyages, for which they had advantages of location.

Finance depended on foreigners as much as shipping did. Flemish and Italian experts concentrated their brokerage work in London. Many outports had poor foreign-exchange capacities or none at all. Between London and provincial towns cash was transmitted too often, given the hazard of highwaymen. The coinage problems of the mid-century had upset confidence in sterling at home and abroad. Even the Elizabethan reforms did not fully restore trust.[5] Hoarding of good coins became a common practice among landowners. Crown loans were hard to place. These mutually reinforcing weaknesses combined to generate and maintain a crisis of liquidity that was only partially offset by the willingness of gentry and aristocrats to invest in commerce and by the successes of speculative privateering ventures. Limitations on the flow of capital augmented the ill effects of an often unfavorable trade balance, dependence on foreign expertise, the slow growth of domestic banking among goldsmiths, the weakness of the merchant fleet, poor inland transportation, London's unhealthy dominance of foreign and domestic markets, and the remnants of an anti-industrial policy.[6] This combination of ills was sufficient to offset the gains in markets and the encouragement given by patents to certain innovations.

English merchants under Elizabeth were still overly provincial; they relied

[5] See the discussion in Chapter Five.
[6] See Chapter Five.

too much on privileges in their commerce and remained crippled by a lack of expertise. Before the full benefits of expanded markets could be realized, Englishmen would have to master fully the European language of instruments of trade, double-entry bookkeeping, bills of exchange, bonds, policies of assurance, and bills of lading. No more than a start in this direction had been made by 1603; it is significant that the first commercial manual for instructing apprentice factors and agents appeared only in 1589, a full century after similar Italian models. The British merchant John Browne's *The Merchant avizo* was in part a cautionary tale. While proud of Bristol's imports of oranges, lemons, wine, paper, thread, "apes and japes and marmusets tayled," and her exports of cloth, swords, wool, knives, pins, and playing cards, he warned merchants' sons not to gape round-eyed at the astonishing world of wealth. Wealth came only to those who were godly and upright: "First seek the kingdom of God. . . . Be not greedy nor in lust after that, which is both displeasant unto God . . . and a shortener to thy life: which is wine, wealth, and women. . . ."

A Narrow Trade's Perils

With such advice on their minds and the death of Elizabeth heavy in their hearts, England's commercial classes welcomed their new monarch. But the reign of James I began under bad auspices. A fierce plague killed 30,000 Londoners in 1603. The gentry fled the city to country homes. The law courts adjourned. Postponements ruined major trade fairs, and the exodus of domestic experts and foreign specialists from the capital wholly crippled exports, dramatizing the bottleneck effect of London's domination of the economy's resources. Despite the regional nature of the agrarian economy and certain sectors of industry, London's development had promoted specialization. This of course promoted pride in local products on one level, while on another making for product exchange and dependency on London. Sir Thomas Roe expressed this situation pungently in a debate in Commons in 1640: "It is no good State, for a body to have a fat head, thin guts and lean limbs." Hence London's plague became a pox on the country's commerce and industry and set the mood of the new reign. The plague provides us with a start for a chronological account of commerce between 1603 and 1640, which we will follow by an analysis of the implications of that commerce.[7]

[7] On the commercial crisis, see especially B. E. Supple, *Commercial Crisis and Change, 1600–1642* (Cambridge: Cambridge University Press, 1959); A. Friis, *Alderman Cockayne's Project* (London: Oxford University Press, 1927); Ralph Davis, *A Commercial Revolution* (London: Macmillan, 1962); Robert Ashton, *The Crown and the Money Market, 1603–1640* (Oxford: Clarendon Press, 1960); C. Wilson, "Cloth Production and International Competition," *EcHR* (1960), XIII, pp. 209–21; and T. K. Rabb, *Enterprise and Empire: Merchant and Gentry Investment in the Expansion of England, 1575–1630* (Cambridge, Mass.: Harvard University Press, 1967).

One of the first acts of James I's initial Parliament was an effort to keep up wages and work in accordance with the terms of the 1563 legislation. But the alarm of 1603 yielded in 1604 to the boom ushered in by peace with Spain. An era of general optimism followed, buoyed by the Spanish-Dutch treaty of 1609, until 1614. London exports of shortcloths ran from 100,400 in 1604 to 127,200 in 1614. Peace had advanced commerce and freed capital from wartime uses; trade appeared more secure. The Jamestown settlement in Virginia in 1607 stirred colonial enthusiasm and appealed to investors. Restrictive monopolies were in part successfully attacked. Agitation for free trade was directed against the regulated companies and protected markets. London's spectacular continued growth spurred the home markets. Textile exports in 1614 were at 1550 levels. Prosperity stilled protest.

When the prosperity of the first decade of the seventeenth century yielded to lean times, London became the focal point of popular misgivings. As early as 1610, Londoners saw in the revival of broadcloth sales a potential repetition of the 1550s. Trade was still narrowly focused on the Netherlands and Germany, although worsteds had a market in France, Spain, and Italy. Gloucester had 15 percent of its work force engaged in making white cloth in 1608. If we can judge from a privy council inquiry into the depression of 1621–2, at least twenty-five other counties relied on cloth for some of their industrial employment. Hence any change that damaged the markets for cloth also threatened to create a major social disaster among landless, propertyless cloth workers devoid of other employment.

Sometime before 1614, this fact stimulated the imaginations of men who wished to see England completely finish cloth before exporting it. The argument was simple and attractive. The world needed English wool, cloth, and technique. If Englishmen dressed cloth completely, the added jobs required to do so would reduce social unrest and enrich the merchants, who then could sell "value-added" goods. Leyden dyers estimated that their process represented 47 per cent of the whole value of the English cloth they finished. Some English experts felt that finishing at home would increase by 50 to 100 percent the value of the traditional exports, thereby dealing a blow to Dutch dyers and weakening England's trade rival.

This in brief was the argument made successfully by Alderman Sir William Cockayne of London in 1614. He and a group of partners—the "projectors"—petitioned the king in July 1614, asking him to prohibit further exports of undressed cloth. James did so by proclamation, against his Council's advice. He also suspended the trading charter of the Merchant Adventurers. With Cockayne, the projectors obtained control of the trade to northern Europe. They were taking the gigantic gamble that the Dutch would buy finished cloth. Convinced by the arguments made at the crest of the boom, the crown overthrew England's greatest company and risked the prosperity of the six broad-cloth counties—Wiltshire, Somerset, Gloucester, Worcestershire, Oxford, and Hereford. The scheme promised to add new employment and to enrich the crown by £40,000 in customs. Cockayne had promised to export 50,000 bolts of dyed cloths in 1615.

The scheme rested on illusions. The capacity to dye 50,000 cloths did not exist. Neither did the capital to do so—at least not among the projectors. By 1616, with a three-year plan to export 6,000, 12,000, and then 18,000 dressed cloths, a retreat in strategy and a lowering of goals set in. Meanwhile, the projectors would take over the old stint of 30,000 broadcloths. This plan raised questions about the whole scheme. Was it really a bold move to save England from a narrow trade? Or was it in fact merely a ruse, by merchants already trading to the Levant, Russia, Italy, and the Baltic,[8] to edge out the old men of an established trade? By 1616, the projectors had offered membership to the old Merchant Adventurers, desperately in need of their capital, expertise, and reputation with clothiers. The Merchant Adventurers refused the offer, alleging Cockayne's scheme to be nothing but a fraud, and diverted their capital to the East India Company, to other trades, and to London's expansion and colonization schemes.

The result was disaster. England's old customers exploded Cockayne's myth of their need for English products. They refused to buy. By 1616, the projectors lacked every resource. They could not buy cloth, lacking capital. The six broadcloth counties wanted a vent. A full 25 percent of the looms were idle; sales of shortcloths were down to 88,200, a decrease of 37,000 in two years. In 1617, the old Merchant Adventurers won a complete victory and had their charter restored.

This led to some recovery by 1620. But between 1620 and 1624 the economy suffered a breakdown unprecedented in its extent and the reaction it drew. The Cockayne years had built up England's competitors. New fabrics had taken over old markets. Capital had been diverted into other trades and was not reinvested in broadcloth. The 1621 Parliament reported clothiers with a full year's inventory unsold. In 1622, a depression was in effect that lasted well into the 1640s. Poor harvests in the early 1620s raised the price of grain and ate into the domestic demand for all consumer goods. Unemployment in the cloth counties was widespread, and poverty led to riots, which threatened the stability of society in the six counties and also in Devon, Northampton, Dorset, Berkshire, and Hampshire. In 1625, the first year of Charles I's reign, there was an outbreak of plague such as had marked his father's accession. The outbreaks of 1625 were the worst of the period from 1600 to 1650. Thirty-

[8] The King's Merchant Adventurers, as Cockayne's group was known, had among the original members a heavy sampling of such men.

five thousand died in London. The courts recessed; Parliament adjourned to Oxford; fairs closed; and commercial communication all but ceased, disrupting what remained of production.

Contemporaries blamed the disaster on a variety of causes, foreign and domestic, natural and divine. Parliament passed measures that broke into restrictive monopolies and London's hegemony, hoping by freer trade to revive the outports. Royal proclamations aimed at maintaining production forced the buying of cloth. The East India Company had been dealt a severe blow by the Amboyna Massacre of 1623.[9] But the recovery, which began in 1624–5, owed little to these agitations, laws, and injunctions. Nor did it endure. Plague combined with the renewal of war with Spain to halt recovery. By 1626, recession was dominant, giving way to a depression that gathered strength from a new war with France. The cloth markets in both northern and southern Europe were disrupted, as were most other trades with the Mediterranean. During this period, artisan riots and merchant resistance to custom duties grew in strength. Not even the French peace of 1628 restored prosperity. Bad harvests damped domestic buying in 1630–1. Unemployment and the insecurity of trade marched hand in hand. Colonial commerce with new plantations[1] was not yet sufficient to relieve failures in Europe.

Consequently, "the eleven years' tyranny" of Charles I were years of almost unrelieved commercial depression. Every long-term commercial agreement lay exposed. The government resisted efforts to reduce costs and lower quality as competitive techniques. The Merchant Adventurers regained their full, restrictive monopoly privileges in 1634, and then had their monopoly extended to colored cloths and the new draperies. Political anxieties deepened the despair inherent in a troubled economy, especially when the crown's financial exigencies produced a stop of the Mint in 1640 and rumors of a debasement that would make coins 75 percent copper. The City cut off credit to Charles I in 1640–1, and when Parliament assembled in 1641, the crises in commerce reinforced the general mood of hostility and suspicion occasioned by the constitutional and religious struggles of the decade.

It is easy enough to recapitulate the forces that depressed the cloth trade and commerce in general. The competition from new products counted heavily, as did changes in taste, which hurt broadcloth consumption. Cockayne's scheme accelerated the dislocation and invited Dutch retaliation. Currency manipulation in Europe and the threat of debasement at home weakened foreign

[9] The Dutch governor of Amboyna put to death ten English traders, perhaps on false charges of conspiracy with some Japanese. The East India Company abandoned efforts to overtake the Spice Islands. Amboyna was one of the Molucca Islands.

[1] Plymouth, 1620–1; Massachusetts Bay, 1629; Maryland, Providence, and New Haven in the 1630s; and the West Indies in the 1640s.

markets, especially in Germany and Poland. The Thirty Years' War disrupted commerce and absorbed much-needed purchasing power. Paradoxically, the opening of new trade areas widened the demands for capital and drew off financing from established trades. These new markets were unable to provide the base for a changed commerce by 1640, whatever their richness was to be in the future. Agrarian crises also played a role, as we have repeatedly stressed.

It is difficult, however, to assess the nature of the instability of English commerce or to relate the forces to one another in a coherent explanation. And it is even more difficult to say whether such data as we have signify growth in the mercantile sector of the economy c. 1600–40. Finally, given the conclusions we *do* reach about this upheaval, we must ask, What were its consequences for the life of the English? How did economic activity reshape society between the Elizabethan Settlement and the onset of civil war in 1641?

The Elements of Instability

The questions we have raised have generated among historians some fierce disagreements. Some have believed that overseas trade was the key to instability and growth.[2] Others, including Eric Hobsbawm, have explained England's celebrated political stability and prosperity c. 1675–1800 in terms of the antecedent slow growth of the various domestic economies in combination with the expansion of international markets. Charles Wilson of Cambridge has viewed the change of face of the old agrarian economy in terms of "the dynamic of the time," which was commerce—albeit not exclusively foreign commerce.[3] More recently, W. E. Minchinton has reshaped Wilson's point of view, insisting that market growth may derive only from population expansion or rising real income in a stable population. Where markets do expand, the increase must be due either to natural population growth or the impact of empire building. Empire increases market size and may well augment real income among the people of the mother country. Minchinton has thus chosen to stress the importance of the revolution in agriculture at home, at least for the early seventeenth century.[4] About 1600, the domestic market probably consumed 90 percent of all production. Even in 1715, when 85 percent of English exports were industrial in character, only 33 percent of total industrial production went abroad.[5] It is therefore easy to exaggerate the significance of the depression in cloth and to make its effects a substitute for a more balanced view of the economy.

[2] Sir John Clapham and Paul Mantoux are good examples.
[3] Hobsbawm, *Industry and Empire*, p. 38; Wilson, *England's Apprenticeship*, p. x.
[4] See his *The Growth of English Overseas Trade*.
[5] Dean and Cole, *British Economic Growth*, pp. 41–2.

Crises in the English economy of the Tudor-Stuart era were not the result of modern cycles of overproduction and credit squeezes. English industry had little fixed capital. Its home market was relatively stable and was slowly expanding with population, although it was liable to setbacks induced by bad harvests. Thus it appears that industrial fluctuations depended to a large extent on the behavior of foreign markets. The breakdowns there, however, were *accidental*, turning on unpredictable events—plague, famine, and war—and were easily magnified by currency manipulations.

This combination of capital mobility and accident gave a latitude to capitalists that was lacking in rigid, industrialized societies. When a disaster struck, the merchant investor could easily redirect his investments. Producers of cloth could emulate the merchants in this respect and seek other employment for their capital. Laborers, however, had no such luck. Their sole asset was their marketable skill, which often was highly developed but of limited scope. Thus, in severe crises, the interests of capital and labor were utterly divergent. "Disinvestment" by clothiers was common, as we learn from Mr. Harbottle Grimstone's 1642 Commons oration on the situation in Essex. There were once-great clothiers, he said,

who now deal little or nothing in the same, but betake themselves to other ways of livelihood, some turning innkeepers . . . [while] those poor men, artificers, as weavers, combers and the like are brought many of them to beg their bread, and the rest to live upon the parish charge. . . .[6]

The mobility of capital and the fixity of labor were thus two crucial features of the commercial-industrial economy. At a time when credit mechanisms were inadequate, the free response of circulating capital to new demands often meant cash shortages in sectors of the economy that were already depressed. This problem of liquidity gave great importance to the question of bullion exports and trade balances, as we already know from the example of the luxury trades and the short-range impact of harvest fluctuations. Consumer purchases were tied to the relative inelasticity of grain demand; people bought cereals even in the face of steadily rising prices and the necessity to import some food. But increases in expenditures for food reduced the demand for every other commodity, apart from shelter. Food imports thus reflected liquidity, and inflation in wheat and barley prices set in motion a train of events that began with a decrease in cloth sales at home and often ended with a flight of capital abroad. The conjunction between these two events was especially clear in the 1550s, 1571–3, 1621–2, and 1629–31. Work levels and corn prices were thus inversely related, which was often the hard fact behind the wisdom

[6] Quoted in Supple, p. 12.

what made of the farmers' prosperity the laborers' poverty. The problem of the harvest was the problem of poverty in the society. Too many men depended on shifting work and on intentionally stinted production and sales. Too many men lived at the level of mere subsistence and had no great margin of income with which to meet rising food costs and also consume other goods. Inelasticity in cereal demand necessitated gross elasticity in the demand for textiles.

In the home market for industrial goods, there were built-in factors of instability. These tended to distort small crises and enlarge major ones. Yet it was not in England alone that cantankerous forces played.

The economy was also susceptible to external dislocations and stimulants. This was in part the lesson of the 1550s and the boom of 1604–14. And in a more drastic sense, this was also the lesson of the Cockayne fiasco. Englishmen learned that short-term slumps could permanently alienate some markets. Such alienation could spur the development of new products and the opening of new markets, under the pressure of competition. We have already seen how this happened in cloth production and marketing. The long-term lesson was certainly that commerce must develop away from reliance on the often fickle traditional textile marts of northern Europe. The Asian, African, and American trades, along with growth in the carrying trade and the rise in the re-exporting of colonial raw materials, would one day accomplish this. Certainly the agitation for free trade—in the 1570s and again in the crises of the 1620s—was led by groups of interloping Londoners and outport merchants hostile to the court, the brokers, and the middlemen and courtiers who supported London's hegemony.

Yet even these targets were proximate windmills for the new Quixotes rather than the real enemies responsible for the depressed state of trade after 1618. For the narrowness of trade in the old draperies had sometimes been beneficial. More to the point was the objection that cloth gave little work to shipping. The cloth was valuable but not of great bulk. Fishing on a large scale would have done more to increase the merchant marine and the industries serving it. This was evident from the experience of the Dutch, who had witnessed the reciprocity between American fisheries and Dutch enterprises in salt, shipbuilding, barrel making, and the coastal carriage of Europe's northern commerce. Ocean commerce was the "school of sailors." In England, this truth dawned first in the coastal sea–coal trade circles. The size of colliery ships plying the Newcastle–London run averaged sixty-five tons in 1600; by 1660, the average had risen to 250 tons. With the development of the Newfoundland Cod routes, total ocean-going tonnage grew from 25,000 in 1615 to 71,000 in 1660.

Astride all the lets and hindrances to the security and stability of commerce sat currency manipulations in Europe.[7] Changing at a dizzying pace after 1617, German, Polish, and other European currencies entered an era of instability that brought down the old European economy. Coins clinked together with less resilience to the tunes of glory that ushered in the Thirty Years' War. They were debased by recoinage or enhanced in value by fiat.

In the case of debasement, silver was actually taken out of coins, which were then circulated at their old face value. In the case of enhancement, a government achieved an upward revolution in untouched coins by saying that the circulating coins were worth *more* than their face value. In either case, when the manipulated currency was put in terms of a money of account, less silver was represented than previously. The real currency was priced higher than its silver content warranted. It was therefore overvalued on exchange, and traders naturally forced the "par" of exchange to move proportionally in a direction *unfavorable* to the manipulated currency. Englishmen wanted more debased or enhanced coins to balance the good silver in their currency.

For English trade, the consequences of this manipulation were disastrous, since the internal and external effects were opposite. Debasement reduces the amount of metal or silver price paid for goods in the host country, unless there is an exactly proportional rise of prices for goods and services. But David Ricardo[8] showed long ago that historically the inflations sponsored by currency manipulations did not rise proportionally. This was especially true of debasements, since governments rarely reissued the whole of the previously circulated medium, taking its *profit* in that way. There was thus a "laggard inflation." Currency was not depreciated to the full extent of its debasement so long as its quantity was not exactly proportional to its lessened intrinsic value.

After debasement, people in the host countries found domestic wares cheaper than they had been. Importers to these countries found themselves in a dilemma. If they sold their goods at the nominally prevailing prices, they realized less silver than before. This was apparent when they exchanged the depreciated

---

[7] The basic literature is still not synthesized, except in such texts as Pollard and Crossley, Wilson, and Ramsey. The following articles are fundamental to the interpretation given here: F. J. Fisher, "Influence and Inflation in Tudor England," *EcHR* (1965), XVIII, pp. 120–9; Y. S. Brenner, "The Inflation of Prices in England, 1551–1660," *ibid.* (1963), XV, pp. 256–84; W. G. Hoskins, "Harvest Fluctuations in English Economic History," *AgHR* (1964), XII, pp. 28–46; L. Stone, "Elizabethan Overseas Trade," *ibid.* (1949), II, pp. 30–58; E. Kerridge, "The Movement of Rent, 1540–1640," *ibid.* (1953), VI, pp. 16–34; D. C. Coleman, "The 'Gentry' Controversy and the Aristocracy in Crisis, 1558–1641," *History* (1966), LI, pp. 165–78; H. J. Habakkuk, "The Long-Term Rate of Interest and the Price of Land," *EcHR* (1952), V, pp. 26–45; L. Stone, "Social Mobility in England, 1500–1700," *Past & Present* (1966), No. 33, pp. 16–55; D. C. Coleman, "Labour in the English Economy in the Seventeenth Century," *EcHR* (1955), VIII, pp. 280–95; and the books of Hexter, Stone, and Simpson cited elsewhere.

[8] A British classical economist of the early nineteenth century.

currency for sterling, or when they sought to return the proceeds home by conversions through monies of account. To get sufficient silver, they had to raise their asking prices in the host currencies in order to make a profit at the new exchange rates. Hence Englishmen found that they either traded at a loss or priced themselves out of the market. One other way to survive, of course, was to *buy* goods in the host country, since English money then commanded more goods per shilling than it had before. But the consequence of this way was clear: a fall in English exports and a rise in imports. Whatever course the merchant pursued abroad induced acute dislocations in industry and employment at home.

The influx of cheap continental linens, cottons, fustians, and other products, encouraged by terms of trade favorable to importers, completed the destruction begun by Cockayne's project. Enhancement abroad bred depression at home. Capitalists diverted their money to importing. Politically and socially, the nadir was reached in 1622, when hostility to textile imports and to men who dealt in luxury goods culminated in riots in many places. And when *Die Kipperzeit* ended, in 1624–5, its consequences remained. The English textile industry never recovered from the decade of disasters. European currency manipulations ultimately revealed the consequences of the concentration and contradictions of English trade in northern Europe.

Toward a Diversified Trade

The crucial questions raised by this account of commercial crises and their causes remain. Was the decline in cloth export offset by growth in other sectors of the domestic trade, new foreign markets, shipping and invisible exports, or colonial profits? Were the years between the 1601 assault on monopolies and the City's suspension of credit to Charles I in 1640–1 years of overall growth or decline? Was there an overbalance in other data that represented advances pregnant for the future?[9]

Despite our pessimistic account of England's great industry and trade in cloth, the answer to these questions may well be yes! Some data will show why. We have pointed out that cloth contributed 90 percent of the value of England's

[9] R. G. Albion, *Forests and Sea Power* (Cambridge, Mass.: Harvard University Press, 1926); L. A. Harper, *The English Navigation Laws* (New York: Columbia University Press, 1939); W. R. Scott, *The Constitution and Finance of English Joint Stock Companies*, 3 vols. (Cambridge: Cambridge University Press, 1910–12); P. G. Dickson, *The Financial Revolution* (London: Oxford University Press, 1967); C. Wilson, *Profit and Power* (London: Longmans, 1957); B. S. Yamey, *Accounting in England and Scotland, 1543–1800* (Edinburgh: Sweet and Maxwell, 1963); W. MacCaffrey, *Exeter, 1540–1650* (Cambridge, Mass.: Harvard University Press, 1958); P. McGrath, *Merchants and Merchandise in 17th Century Bristol* (Bristol: Bristol Record Society, 1955); and R. Davis, *The Trade and Shipping of Hull, 1500–1700* (York: University of Hull Press, 1964).

exports as late as the 1620s. Total shortcloths sent from London reached 100,000 in 1601. This total had shrunk to 87,000 by 1640, having reached a peak of 127,000 in 1614. London's share of the whole cloth trade was put at 65 to 75 percent by F. J. Fisher. Thus the contraction between 1614 and 1640 represented a trade disaster for the country as well as for the City of London. Yet Professor Fisher has also argued that London's total trade grew from £720,000 in 1601 to £1,100,000 in 1640, while that of the country as a whole grew from a range of £.96 to £1.08 million in 1601 to a range of £1.6 to £1.8 million in 1640.[1] In part this was because of a great increase in exports of the new draperies, which by 1640 were worth as much as the diminished broadcloths. But other commodities helped, as can be seen in the official values of commodities other than old draperies exported from London by English merchants in 1640:

Woolen fabrics and hosiery	£454,914
Other English manufactures	26,973
Minerals	34,555
Agricultural produce	16,878
Re-exports	76,402

Between 1600 and 1640, shortcloth export values fell from £600,000 to £500,000; however, the value of other commodities rose from about £120,000 to £600,000 in the same period.[2]

In other words, the importance of the old draperies in the economy declined. Their share of London's exports declined from 72 percent in 1604 to 35 percent in 1640. The clear implication is that the narrowness of trade was being reversed. The quantity of shortcloths shipped to Spanish, African, and Mediterranean ports rose from 16 to 25 percent between 1614 and 1640. The distribution of goods other than shortcloths by English merchants based in London also showed this geographical transformation. The quantity sent to northern ports c. 1609–40 declined from 29 to 22 percent, while the figures for the Spanish, African, and Mediterranean trades rose from 45 to 65 percent.

The bilateral London–Netherlands (and outward to northern Europe) trade was yielding to patterns more balanced and hence less prone to short-term dislocations. Colonial commerce contributed to this trend. In 1620, imports of staple crops were small. Tobacco was only eighth in value, at £55,143 for a

[1] Depending on the adoption of either the 65 percent or 75 percent conversion base assumed by Fisher. See "London's Export Trade in the Early 17th Century," EcHR (1950), 2nd Ser. III, pp. 151–61.

[2] Professor Ralph Davis argued that Fisher's figures were far too low in every category. But he supported the idea of expansion; see A Commercial Revolution, p. 9. The table is from Fisher, EcHR, III, p. 154.

total poundage of 173,372. These figures had grown to £230,840 and 1,250,000 by 1640; tobacco had become England's leading import. The same thing happened with sugar. In 1615, 50,000 pounds had come in; the total in 1663 was 14,800,000. Home consumption was only 33 percent of the whole. Thus, in sugar as in tobacco, re-export trades developed on the basis of colonial products and imports. By 1650, 80 percent of all pepper sold in Europe and 67 percent of all calico went in English ships. The Iceland-Newfoundland fisheries employed 25 percent of all English seamen in 1640, despite the fact that development of the fisheries had not started in earnest until 1615. The total capital of the East India Company rose from £68,000 in 1601 to £400,000 in 1660, and reached over £4 million by 1700.

In place of the old bilateral trade, there grew up a series of routes, all of which ended in England: England–West Africa–West Indies–England; England–West Africa–New England–England; England–Newfoundland and Iceland–Mediterranean–England; England–the Carolinas–Hamburg or Stockholm–England.

There were many consequences from these developments. Perhaps the most significant were the growth of English shipping, the rise of re-export business, and the growth of the commerce of the outports. It was significant that capital was being invested in new raw materials and their carriage in English ships. It was significant, too, that capital was being accumulated, and that the management of capital showed increasing strength and sophistication. By 1640, re-exports of overseas goods equaled in value all nontextile English exports. This fact contributed little to industrial employment at first, since for the most part processing was still left to foreigners. But the challenge to Dutch domination of European carrying trade and finishing industries that was mounted in the second half of the century would have been unthinkable without these earlier developments. English tonnage grew from 115,000 to 340,000 between 1620 and 1635. The trade wars and navigation acts were real before men found the concepts to express them.

Customs (in pounds sterling)

Port	1614	1617	1672
London	105,131	121,887	503,312
Hull	7,664	5,904	22,527
Exeter	4,096	4,427	15,727
Bristol	3,599	3,568	56,922
Newcastle	3,781	2,957	8,889
Plymouth	2,316	3,462	14,102
Southampton	2,350	3,220	9,803
Lyme Regis	3,010	2,938	6,518

The diversification of trade mitigated the subordination of the outports, reversing the prevailing patterns of the period from 1570 to 1620 and helping to abate resentments focused on London. This development shows dramatically in Hull, Exeter, and Bristol, although it is less marked elsewhere, as we see by a glance at customs paid at English ports.

Thus, even in its infancy, the colonial expansion and opening of world markets cushioned the impact of the decline of the traditional aspects of the textile economy. More than that, the revival of the outports stimulated the development of internal transportation networks—especially the canal systems—as the major navigable river arteries and the great "river around England"—the oceans that were its defenses and its lifeline. Over 700 miles of navigable rivers and the best coastline in Europe made up in part for the still basically useless roads. Places like Bristol—which had only 15,000 people and perhaps 150 wholesale merchants in 1600—still did not rival London. But they became nodal points of specialized trades both foreign and domestic, despite repeated setbacks resulting from domestic political strife, war in Europe, and currency instability.

Even the damage done to the trust on which commerce thrived by the ruinous relations between the crown and London could not alter certain stubborn facts. Contemporary Englishmen lamented their depressions and industrial and commercial crises, their vision blurred by political crises. Yet commercial life and technique were advancing; capital accumulation was increasingly possible; routes, markets, and goods multiplied. Agricultural production was revolutionized. And, above all else, population had grown steadily since about 1480. No concentration on questions of money or finance can demote in rank the greater importance of the real economic changes that came as supplies and needs moved with population's upward spiral.

The consequences were many. New textiles expanded in production despite the so-called depression. Huge markets for metal goods loomed in the still feeble colonies, which were to have wage structures and a population ideally suited to English goods. The standard of living in America was high, even in the mid-seventeenth century, and it spurred domestic and foreign demand by providing employment in England and purchasing power abroad. Secondary industrial enterprises drew stimulation from the colonies also—a good example was the rise of Bristol sugar refining. The shipbuilding crafts prospered. Expansion stirred, and depended on coal and iron.

The nonindustrial effects were as significant. The re-export trades provided new capital outlets, helped development of entrepôt centers, and stimulated the merchant marine. Credit institutions and banking facilities were responsive to trade expansion, since merchants and bankers mingled in ventures and shared the responsibility of financing commerce. This mingling led, late in the century, to the Stock Exchange, the Bank of England, and the Funded Debt.

There was also impetus to educational reform once schools and colleges had to meet the demand for modern subjects, business skills, and allied expertise in geography, history, and modern languages. The establishment of Gresham's College in London symbolizes this impetus.

Since the benefits of size were not without limit, market profits were employed in new enterprises and philanthropic uses, such as agricultural improvement, banking, and the financing of new industries with merchant capital (soap, glass, sugar, brass, copper, and pottery) in Bristol, Liverpool, and Newcastle. This represented a break in the old pattern whereby merchant capital had found its way back to the land. Thus, a truly urban life developed in London and provincial towns, along with families permanently committed to the towns in which they prospered. Urban centers in the provinces became focal points of commerce, industry, and consumption. But the situation in London was without parallel.[3]

London's food markets groaned under the weight of wares from the rich market-gardening and dairy and meat farming of the home counties and more distant sources. Bermondsey, Battersea, Stepney, and Lambeth were in the rule of the Gardeners Company. Their apples, cherries, berries, pears, "herbes for food and Phisick," and varieties of vegetables were sold at good profits despite high rents for stalls. Townsmen relied on middlemen for their meals: butchers in Smithfield; mealmen and maltsters south of the river in Southwark; fishmongers at Cheapside and Billingsgate; bakers, chandlers, petty higglers, and great traders wherever they could set up carts or establish markets. Relieving the pressure of development in London by pushing into the suburbs became a necessary and profitable enterprise.

The metropolis was itself a congeries—of old parishes (the City), Westminster, and the suburbs. By 1620, its population was near the quarter-million mark. Fully 75,000 crowded into the City, bounded on the South by a mile of Thames-side docks, and reaching to the various medieval walls north of the river, forming in all a one-mile square. Already the "great Ditch" to the east was filling up with the rank industrial wastes of brewers, soap makers and salt boilers. The extramural parishes reached beyond the Bars, or gatehouses, northward and eastward, grasping Holborn, the Temple Shoreditch, Smithfield, and Whitechapel, the "liberties" that contained 113,000 people by 1605.

[3] On London's emergence as a great city, see F. J. Fisher, "The Development of London as a Center of Conspicuous Consumption," *TRHS* (1948), XXX, pp. 37–50; "The Development of the London Food Market," *EcHR* (1935), V, pp. 46–64; P. E. Jones and A. V. Judges, "London Population," *EcHR* (1936), VI, pp. 45–63; N. Brett-James, *The Growth of Stuart London* (London: Allen & Unwin, 1935); V. Pearl, *London and the Outbreak of the Puritan Revolution* (Oxford: Clarendon Press, 1961).

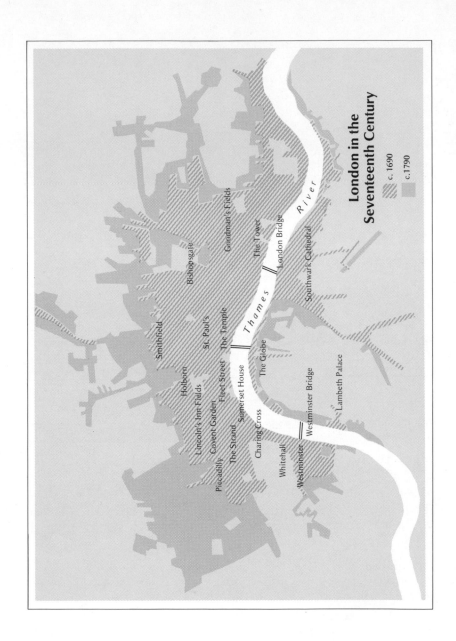

London in the
Seventeenth Century

c. 1690

c.1790

River
Thames
Goodman's Fields
The Tower
London Bridge
Southwark Cathedral
Bishopsgate
Smithfield
St. Paul's
The Temple
The Globe
Holborn
Fleet Street
Lincoln's Inn Fields
Covent Garden
Somerset House
Piccadilly
The Strand
Charing Cross
Westminster Bridge
Lambeth Palace
Whitehall
Westminster

Beyond these places, the so-called out-parishes held 36,000—many Dutch, Spanish, French, German, and Irish immigrants among them. London was thus two cities: a commercial metropolis tied to the rule of the City, and Westminster, the home of Parliament, the Court, and the great agencies of government. Beyond this political axis lay a rich profusion of poverty and prosperity: the townhouses and parks of the wealthy and the stinking workshops and slums of the London poor.

The great stretch of palaces along the river—Essex Place, Somerset House, Norfolk Place, York Palace—pointed the way from the City to Westminster and beyond, toward Kensington and Chelsea, where already in the Tudor age wealthy London citizens, courtiers, and crown officials had moved in search of quiet and the fresh air borne on the westerly winds that drove from those precincts furnace fumes, the stench of sea coal, night soil, and garbage. The gaggle of Stuart courtiers especially favored these areas, which became a symbol of the drift apart of the City and the Court on the eve of the civil war.

Among nobles and courtiers, we find some chief beneficiaries of the boom. Together with merchant capital, aristocratic assets financed the building of London. The Bedfords, Salisburys, and Hollands grew richer on slum profits. By 1650, the earl of Clare collected £2,800 in rents a year from the area around Drury Lane. Cecil, the earl of Salisbury, built the New Exchange in 1611 for £10,000; it was a department store for fancy goods. His colleague Bedford developed Covent Garden, from which a little northern walk still leads to Russell Square, where the British Museum and London University stand on Bedford lands. Rich "undertakers" like Hugh Middleton contracted to bring water from Hertfordshire to the City in 1609.

From Leadenhalls' great leather merchants to the poorest howler who found his wares on the streets, the metropolis was already a mercantile society. Merchant aristocrats made circulating capital master of the City. The great wholesalers held even the crown in thrall, to some extent, since they were its creditors.

All of this growth and excitement is perhaps a strange gloss on the fear, pessimism, and sense of decay that in 1640 marked much public oration and many printed treatises about the state of the realm. Those who lived through the decay of the old economy and the birth of a new one did not know the future. Moreover, as Hume so poignantly said: "Man fly not from present dangers to ones unknown." England in 1640 was torn by internal strife. Her disarray at home had made even the Scots formidable conquerors in 1639. The Dutch Republic still stood between England and both its suppliers and its customers in the markets of the free world. It had a near monopoly of bulk shipping, finishing industries, and capital facilities. Its own East India Company and Stock Exchange had no peers.

The English mercantile economists clearly saw such problems, as we know from the writings of Mun, Malynes, and Maddeson. But even in the 1620s these writers and others—Misselden and Robinson, for example—had realized the potential of commerce and written about it in lyrical terms. Perhaps Thomas Mun's *England's Treasure by Foreign Trade* best stated how the old disabilities could yield to new prospects. Although it was published posthumously in 1664, it was almost certainly composed in the 1630s and reflected Mun's work on the earliest trade commission—that of 1622–3. Buttressed by a good analysis of currency problems in relation to trade balances, Mun saw clearly the forces that were producing change in his own day. By the 1640s, the "economics of diversification"[4] had new champions in Sir Thomas Roe, Lewes Roberts, Henry Robinson, and William Goffe. They stressed that England must earn her way in the competitive world of trade, that in fact the country was in a war for trade, like it or not.

On the eve of the civil war, their writing mirrored England's place in an international economy. Price maintenance through restrictive practices by regulated companies was a dead doctrine. "The rather it concurs us all to sell good cheap," wrote Robinson in *England's Safety*. To beat the Europeans out of overseas markets became the goal. This objective would even compensate for "riotous consumption" at home. Industrial development as Goffe's rallying cry in 1641 shows how far England had come from Lord Burghley's day, when Elizabeth's treasurer practiced holding at bay any industrial expansion out of fear of unemployment and social disorders. Here we see in fact the forerunners of Petty, King, and Davenent, the "political arithmeticians" of the 1680s who looked on commerce as the most buoyant sector of the economy.

A new commercial and industrial network was growing up. The lines of communication stretched westward to America, southward to Africa and the eastern Mediterranean, under the Cape to India and the Far East. There had been a revolutionary diversification in production, not suddenly, but slowly, having gathered momentum in the 1400s. Chaucer, Langland, and Gower knew the wealth of the nation in wool walking rich pastures on the backs of sheep. Defoe knew another world:

Upon the whole, to sum it up in a few words. Trade is the wealth of the world; trade makes the difference between rich and poor, one nation and another; trade nourishes industry, industry begate trade; trade dispenses the natural wealth of the world, and trade raises new species of wealth, which nature knew nothing of; trade has two daughters, whose fruitful progeny in arts may be said to employ mankind, namely manufacture and navigation.

[4] Supple's phrase, in *Commercial Crisis and Change, 1600–1642*, p. 221.

The English were not yet a people of plenty in 1640. But their farms were producing more and better food than ever before. Despite the presence of hundreds of thousands of poor, the people on the whole were better housed, better clothed, and better fed in 1640 than they had been during the so-called golden age of the fifteenth century. There was as yet no immunity to the ravages of famine or plague or the subsistence crises (which still plague agrarian societies in our time). However, technology, commerce, and industry had begun the process by which that immunity was to be conferred. The century that separated Thomas Cromwell from his namesake Oliver was fertile in this regard, despite Smithfield's fires and the terrible wars the English made upon themselves. The factory that William Stumpe laid down on a monastic site faced the future.

Chapter Nine
BABYLON AND JERUSALEM

Behold, I will punish the kings and I will bring Israel back to his pasture, and he shall feed on Carmel . . . and his soul shall be satisfied . . . in Gilead.

JEREMIAH, 50: 17–19

Woe unto them! for their day is come, the time of their visitation. Hark, they flee . . . out of the land of Babylon, to declare in Jerusalem the vengeance of the Lord our God. . . . Behold a people cometh from the North, and a great nation. . . .

JEREMIAH, 50: 28, 41

The days come, that I will do judgment upon the graven images of Babylon. . . . Ye that have escaped. The sword, go ye . . . and let Jerusalem come into your mind.

JEREMIAH, 51: 47, 50

The prophetic voice rang clear in late Tudor and early Stuart pulpits. For in the realm of religion many Englishmen found themselves unwilling citizens of two cities—Babylon and Jerusalem. If it is not easy at this distance in time for us to know the Chosen People from the patriots of Bel, neither was it easy then. The Elizabethan Settlement had not really been the business of those devotees of Mammon to whom we lately paid attention. But it was even less a halfway house between Rome and Geneva, as it is so often said to have been. It was an accommodation of various brands of Protestantism. It quickly put Catholics out of hope that they could hold influence in the Church. The wave of deprivations in 1559 affected them rather than Protestant dissenters. This seems to have been less the queen's wish than a condition imposed by Parliament in return for supporting her.

It is indeed a striking fact of the politics of religion under Elizabeth that only two of her thirteen Parliaments originally met for reasons other than supply: those of 1559 and 1586. Both concerned themselves chiefly with religion, in accord with the government's intentions. And both were harshly anti-Catholic. Whatever was Roman was proscribed by law with increasing severity as the decades passed. If no very distinctive English theology existed before the rise of an Anglican one late in the reign, it was nonetheless true that the influences there were derived from Wittenberg, Zurich, Geneva, and Strasbourg, not from Rome. The "people of the North" no longer marched to free themselves from Rome. The enemy was within the House of Israel, a Catholic remnant and warring Protestants.

Indeed, the developments of the early Elizabethan years provided the outline of the contest for the soul of England. The Catholic recusant struggled to find a place in a Protestant society. The Protestants took upon themselves in different spirits the robes of the prophets. The Puritan elements faced a problem similar to that faced by the popish elements—that of finding living room in a society admitting no belief different from the established one. How these two minorities fared under the law will be our main concern in this chapter.[1]

Catholics at Bay

The old religion was unlike any Protestant one. Its appeal to the masses had been neither a drama of conscience nor doctrinal dispute, but a liturgical cycle marked by its rhythmic quality. John Bossy's description of it as a "social sentiment" is apt.[2] However, social sentiments need institutions for their maintenance. The impact of the Elizabethan Settlement completed the institutional wreckage begun with the monasteries, advanced by the chantries acts, and furthered by the conversion of the priesthood into a Protestant ministry. The existence of franchises had placed public authority in private hands. Their final disappearance in the aftermath of the rebellions in the North (1569–72), however, had ended the history of places immune to official scrutiny. The practical consequences of this determined the most important facet of Catholic life. It became dependent for its survival not on public institutions but on the seigneurial institutions of the countryside.

Aristocratic households were the institutions supporting the "sentiment." Sometimes whole villages, sometimes merely a mansion and its lands held out. Wherever good lordship provided a recusant master, the liturgical rhythms could survive. Lord Vaux made the point in 1581 when he claimed that his house had become his parish. What this amounted to was a geography of recusancy. For recusancy survived best in the still quasifeudal border areas. Where there was ease of access for the government, or a flourishing town life, or rural industry, or commerce of a maritime type, the faith was harder to keep. The cycle of feasts, fasts, and the Mass could be observed indoors, but public processions were too risky. The precedent of medieval proprietary churches was revived in the aristocratic enclaves. The lord recruited and controlled his chaplain and provided a shield against intrusive authorities. Obviously, the religious economy at issue was dependent on the loyalty of a closed household to its head. Conflict in the household exposed it to the discontented

---

[1] Although "recusant" in law means any sort of proscribed nonconformity, we shall reserve the term for Catholics.

[2] John Bossy, "The Character of Elizabethan Catholicism," *Past and Present* (1962), No. 21, pp. 39–59, contains the most thoughtful statement about the "old religion."

informer and government discovery. So, too, was it the case that women played a larger role in maintaining the faith than they had in the public church.

This character of Catholic life helps account for some notable facets of the Catholic community. Recusants who engaged in sharp economic practices injured their hope of going undetected. If some Catholic landowners were un-enterprising, this was perhaps an adaptive reaction meant to preserve the seigneurial bond. Most of the Catholic gentry remained aloof from the risings in the North and were later solidly against the Babington, Rye, and Gun-powder plots (1585, 1604, 1605). They were preoccupied with the household, intellectually conservative, dependent on those they patronized. Perhaps their loyalty to the sovereign derived from the similarities they saw in their respec-tive situations. The recusant and the monarch were equally suspicious of dis-turbers of the hierarchy. The Catholics reprobated papal politics because they were so vulnerable to betrayal from within and attack from without.

They had good reason to feel impotent and insecure. Between November 26, 1559, when Bishop Jewel preached his famous "Challenge Sermon," and the Gunpowder Plot of November 5, 1605, an increasingly harsh penal code made their life hazardous. This fact can be grasped from the summary table on pages 288–9.[3]

The government had consistently moved in the direction of impoverishing Catholics. It had also struck directly at the central institution of the Mass, by attacking the domestic source of priests—boys sent overseas—and by extending the treason law to returning missionary priests. There were also severe penal-ties for importing or keeping Catholic books. By the 1580s, even those who gave occasional conformity were liable to be stripped of lands and liberty. It is therefore somewhat wide of the mark to look at the 1559 acts and claim that the laws against Catholics were humane or tolerant, or that, if savage, they went unenforced.

No serious examination of the fate of the recusant will allow the view that Elizabeth's government was beneficent because it did not, like the Inquisition, cut windows into men's souls. In 1570, Cecil had tried to show that Catholics were not punished for their faith but for their breaches of the civil law; that they suffered no molestation "by way of examination . . . in their consciences,

[3] On the penal legislation and the problem of placing the size and geography of the Catholics see the following: Patrick McGrath, *Papists and Puritans under Elizabeth I* (London: Blandford, 1967); W. R. Trimble, *The Catholic Laity in Elizabethan England* (Cambridge, Mass.: Harvard University Press, 1964); J. S. Leatherbarrow, *The Lancashire Recusants* (Manchester: Manchester University Press, 1947); Martin Havran, *The Catholics in Caroline England* (Cambridge, Mass.: Harvard University Press, 1960); David Mathew, *Catholicism in England, 1535–1935* (London: Eyre and Spottiswood, 1948); and the two works I found most useful for hard data: Roger Manning, *Religion and Society in Elizabethan Sussex* (Leicester: Leicester University Press, 1969); and J. Cliffe, *The Yorkshire Gentry from the Reformation to the Civil War* (London: Athlone Press, 1969).

Table of Laws Touching Catholics

Statutory Penalties: Minimum and Maximum: Laymen and Priests[1]

Offense	1559	1563	1571	1581	1585	1593	1606
Using or causing the use of form of worship other than Prayer Book, or derogating from its reputation	6 months to life }P Deprivation 100 marks—all goods plus life for third offense }L						
Refusing oath of Supremacy	Barred from office, universities, etc. }L	Extended to teachers, barristers, attorneys					All goods, lands, life imprisonment }L
Refusal to attend church and conviction of those aged 16 and above	12 pence per absence }L		£20 per month or £260 per year }L	$\frac{2}{3}$ of all lands plus all chattels }L		Confined to home and 5-mile radius	$\frac{2}{3}$ of land }L
Sheltering a recusant				£10 per month			
Refusing to baptize children in parish							£100 }L

Offense	Penalty[1]	
Sending son to a foreign seminary	£20}L	£100}L
Seeking to reconcile a person to Rome (equal to treason)	Death⎫L Forfeiture⎭	
Going overseas to become a priest	Confiscation of all property	
Being ordained a "missionary" priest, if provable they sought to convert	Death	
Merely being ordained a Jesuit or "seminary" priest	Death	
Eligibility for office		Totally barred

[1] P signifies a penalty for clergy; L signifies a penalty for laymen.

for matters of faith."[4] The 1585 statute making it unnecessary, in order to convict a priest of treason, to show that he had tried to win subjects from their allegiance, seems more concordant with another view. Englishmen could be Catholics so long as they lived like Protestants, used Protestant rites, and did not believe what they professed to believe!

But that the laws were as important in practice as they were in theory we can know only by looking at some social facts. Three questions will bear scrutiny: How large was the lay Catholic remnant? how were they distributed geographically? what in fact were the consequences of the statutes among the various social classes? The data are imperfect, and any quantitative estimate in our period runs into numerous difficulties: inefficiency in detection, the conformity of some Catholics, the incompleteness of records, the problems of delineating the group studied, and the danger inherent in "official" figures from an age of persecution.

Yet some censuses of recusants do survive. In 1561–2, the Council prepared a list of 96 important Catholics, chiefly ecclesiastics, widely scattered through the kingdom. Two years later it gathered reports on the religion of the J.P.s. This more interesting census showed that, in the 21 returning dioceses, 293 justices out of the 941 surveyed were "unfavorable" in religion. We cannot, however, determine what part of the 293 were Catholics. Some data seem to indicate a large general Catholic population—for example, concentrations in traditional centers of conservatism. Among J.P.s counted in 1564, the proportion of men "unfavorable" was 12 out of 20 in Carlisle; 50 out of 78 in Chester; 43 out of 90 in Hereford; 46 out of 112 in Worcester; and 36 out of 85 in York. That most were Catholic is an inference that draws strength from the low incidence of "unfavorables" in known hotbeds of advanced Protestantism: 0 out of 42 in Canterbury; 7 out of 39 in Ely; 11 out of 81 in London.

It is from the 1570s that the most complete recusant records survive. In 1577, the privy council examined some 10 percent of 1,454 recusants, doubtless alarmed by the high proportion of landed gentlemen in the catch: 1 peer, 10 knights, 30 ladies, 102 esquires, 399 mere gentlemen, 36 priests, and 984 of lesser rank. The gentry constituted roughly 33 percent of the count. Compared with the whole number of the landed classes, about 15,000, recusants made up only over 3 percent of the landed elite. But their influence among inferiors could conceivably make them dangerous out of proportion to the number. A census of *convicted* recusants of 1582 numbered 1,839. The government again concentrated on men who "had rule in the countries."

When these data and those from two other surveys are seen in tabular form, arranged by counties and dioceses, what emerges most clearly is the geography

[4] The then Lord Treasurer Burghley returned to this theme in his *The Execution of Justice in England* (1583).

of recusancy.[5] The patterns support our description of Elizabethan and early Stuart Catholicism. Its rural character shows up well. And the report given to Cardinal Morone by Father Nicholas Sander in 1561 seems confirmed: the urban classes were chiefly Protestant, and what Catholic strongholds there were stood in the pastoral areas of the North and West marches.

This accords well with the evidence of literary sources, but does not tell us how large the total Catholic population was. Estimates from contemporaries are too diverse to be helpful, as are those of historians not working closely in the sources. Gondomar, the Spanish ambassador to England in 1617, thought there were 300,000 recusants in England and at least 600,000 " Church papists " —that is, conformists to the established religion. His estimate of the recusant population was close to 8 percent of the whole population, while his statement about all Catholics makes a total of 16 percent. Yet R. G. Usher placed the whole body of Romanists at only 5 percent, and the Catholic scholar A. O. Meyer placed the figure between 2 and 3 percent. Professor Arthur G. Dickens and Hugh Aveling have carefully collated the 1604 Yorkshire figures, which set the Catholic population at slightly more than 1 percent, about 3,500 in a total of over 300,000, in an alleged center of strength.[6]

Until we have closer studies on the county level, or diocese by diocese, it seems that no convincing estimate for the country can be made. What raises doubt about all previous estimates and the surveys made by the government is the lack of definition in the fact that in the wake of the Gunpowder Plot over 5,500 " papists " were convicted of various offenses; or the case of the bishop of Llandaff, who reported only thirteen recusants in 1577, while casually saying he could supply the names of over 200 more in his diocese.

Again, a recent study of the Yorkshire gentry has established that in 1604 there were 254 Catholic gentry in a class total of 641. In 1577, thirty-five gentry out of about eighty families in that rank were accused of Romish ways by the bishop of Chichester. If such numbers of a closely scrutinized class kept their faith, what should we think of the more anonymous masses? The obvious answer is that the total Catholic population may well have been very small. What gentry figures represent is the survival of Catholicism in part as a class phenomenon, which is entirely compatible with our view of its social character. The gentry household was a nourishing institution, supporting an extended

---

[5] See the Appendix, Figure 12.

[6] See especially A. O. Meyer, *England and the Catholic Church* (London: Kegan, Paul, Trench, Tribnen, 1916); R. G. Usher, *The Reconstruction of the English Church*, 2 vols. (New York: D. Appleton and Company, 1910); Hugh Aveling, "The Marriage of Catholic Recusants, 1559–1642," *J.Ecc.H.* (1963), XIV, pp. 68–83; and R. A. Marchant, *The Church Under the Law* (Cambridge: Cambridge University Press, 1969), for these questions and data given later on the work of the ecclesiastical courts.

"family" of blood relatives and servants. But it was under severe pressure and declining. That conclusion sits well with the picture of the best-studied diocese, York, where the number of recusants recorded in 1563 was 1,211, and where a 1627 visitation netted only 271. The largest of all censuses recorded only 8,630 recusants—the Bishops' Survey of 1603. If we allow a multiplier of four to compensate for family size, or even one of twenty, to extend the household beyond the blood, the 1603 recusants represented 1 percent of the population, or at best 5 percent.

The government had in fact chosen a good weapon with which to whip the recusant and fight the influence of the missionaries. The socioeconomic center of the faith was the gentry household. And it was against the gentry class that the government moved by statute. Their wisdom was somewhat akin to the modern theory of defending against guerilla war, which seeks to drain the sea in which the guerilla swims. The peasants were not the problem; the Elizabethan campaign sought chiefly to destroy the closed recusant economy by poisoning the sea in which the gentry lived.[7]

The first steps came soon after the opening of the reign. Despite assertions to the contrary, there was a systematic purge of the bench of J.P.s. The enforcement of Reformation lay in the local magistracy. J.P.s appointed by Mary were excluded from the 1558–9 commissions. By the mid-1560s, the following percentage of eligible Marian justices had been removed: Norfolk, 57 percent; Sussex, 61 percent; Northamptonshire, 59 percent. Vulnerable lesser nobility like Henry Strafford were hemmed in within their native shires. And by 1592, a Council order excluded recusants from the bench entirely. In some areas, notably Yorkshire, the government could not function without "popish gentlemen" in various commissions; but these were chosen from "Church papists," at least until the Gunpowder Plot brought legislation totally excluding from office Catholics of any variety. Only the vacillating but pronounced relaxation of law enforcement late in James I's reign readmitted them to local office. Increasingly, in most areas of the country, the Catholics became a leaderless, impotent minority. In Sussex, the proportion of Catholic officeholders fell from 50 percent in 1560 to 16 percent in the 1590s; notable among survivals were those in the burdensome, expensive office of sheriff. Striking at the J.P.s removed both a rallying point in country society and a potential for winking at orders from London. The often zealous Protestant replacements offered little hope of giving such quarter.

The impact of this campaign on the gentry and clergy was serious, especially

[7] Cliffe and Manning, already cited, are basic. So, too, are J. Gleason, *The Justices of the Peace in England, 1558–1640* (Oxford: Clarendon Press, 1969); A. Hassell-Smith, "The Personnel of the Commissions of the Peace: 1554–1564, A Reconsideration," *Huntington Library Q.* (1959), XXII, pp. 301–3.

in economic terms. In an age when estates in gentry hands generally grew, those of recusants often contracted. Among seventy-eight Sussex gentry families, the commonest cause of economic decline was religious nonconformity. Eleven of the twenty-three most declining families had heads who were clearly Catholic. Tax rolls show the persistence of doubled subsidy assessments for recusants, an Elizabethan device partly designed to further the transfer of social power from the Catholic nobility and gentry to the newer Protestant elites of that county. From the 1570s on, officials in Sussex zealously exercised their powers to clip Catholic wings. Unlike the dioceses of Bristol and Gloucester, where Church courts suffered from a systematic loss of jurisdiction, those in Chichester exercised an effective power in the 272 parishes of the diocese, at least among people below the rank of the greater gentry. Any local failures in dealing with the elite recusants were redeemed by the penal laws, which were used by conciliar power and the Court of High Commission in Ecclesiastical Causes. From one to a dozen people were always under sentence for recusancy in nearly every parish in Sussex. The struggle for the parish was being vigorously waged, and by the 1590s grudging clerical acceptance of the new liturgies was general. Widespread clerical resistance had diminished, especially in the 1580s, when the supply of Protestant ministers coming down from the universities met the accumulated demand that had once allowed 102 parishes to be devoid of incumbents. However, these results were not achieved quietly in this diocese, and the London government more than once had to decide between allowing a zealous bishop's persecution of crypto-Catholics and preserving peace in places along the Channel coast, where cooperation was vital to social order and national defense.

The hard core of Chichester's fifteen greater gentry recusant families and thirty lesser ones survived into the seventeenth century. But they were devoid of clerical allies and in a weakened position. Frequent prison confinements had ruined a few. Monthly fines of £20 had converted others. But it was the sequestration of property that had convinced most that the Mass was not worth the promised ruin of families. Family life had already been endangered by the selection of Protestant guardians for Catholic wards, by the penal laws, and by the treasonous context of papal sympathies. Thus, a slow process of forced conversion was visible even in the northern dioceses of York. Of 181 gentry families failing in the male line between 1558 and 1642, the danger was greatest among Catholics. A Catholic education meant a risky period abroad for the sons—at St. Omer or Douai. Only a small handful were tutored in native Catholic schools or by household teachers. The combined dangers and costs forced some staunch Catholics to send their sons to public grammar schools, especially after 1585, when heavy fines were imposed on parents who provided a Catholic education abroad. Striking at the pupil helped ensure that, in 1642, of the 247 college-educated heads of Yorkshire gentry families whose members numbered 679, only six had been to a Catholic college, university, or inn of court.

Economically, while taxes were generally a negligible charge on gentry incomes, and certainly not a major cause of financial difficulties before the civil war, Catholics liable for special levies suffered considerably from discrimination. Only 397 of 963 Yorkshire gentry families that were counted *c.* 1560–1640 suffered financial decline. In 1604, over one hundred of them were open recusants in a community of 254 identified Catholic families. There was in fact a strikingly forced reduction in Catholicism among the Yorkshire gentry between the Northern Rebellion and the civil war, as this table shows:

	Catholic families	Total number of families
1570	368	567
1604	254	641
1642	163	679

This reduction took place during an age of striking growth in gentry numbers and of popular recusancy in Yorkshire. The brief suspension of the penal laws in the 1620s did not restore the lost Catholic gentry. Indeed, even if the fugitive sons and daughters of the continental seminaries and nunneries had not been lost, the pressure of fines would in some cases have cast them into society's lower ranks. It was only in the 1630s, when Charles I's new system of moderated penal laws allowed recusants to compound for their estates on favorable terms, that recusant squires could avoid forced leasing of their own lands from courtiers and jobbers who had enjoyed easy pickings. Few Catholic gentry lost as much as 20 percent of their estates before 1640, but in 1638 a courtier observed that "no revenue of the King . . . comes in so speedily or certainly" as that resulting from discriminatory taxation. Of 271 families with Catholic sympathies in 1642, 102 paid such taxes. Not one had an income over £2,000 a year, and only 22 enjoyed over £1,000. There were 51 Protestant gentry worth upwards of £1,000 in 1642.

The idea of integrating lay religious dissenters into the framework of civil society on a basis of equality did not yet exist. After 1592, convicted recusants were confined in their houses or within a five-mile radius of movement. They were barred from office. Conformist husbands were made liable for the behavior of recusant wives and were fined accordingly. Public opinion demanded that Catholic mothers be forbidden to influence their children in matters of religion and that formal education be Protestant in character. What freedom of conscience was allowed was thus absolutely separated from freedom of religion. The demand for conformity forced Catholics into secret worship and implied the extinction of all but the heartiest of the upper-class faithful.

Neither the Jesuits nor the secular seminary clergy who came in the 1570s were able to gain ground in the "enterprise of England"—the task of maintaining Catholic faith. There was not an overt Catholic aristocracy in England comparable to the Protestant nobility of Valois France. There were no nobles able to marshal the forces of dissent, maintain a civil war, or successfully negotiate toleration of dissident religion. There were instead feeble plots, abortive risings, a generation of priests hidden in "priest-holes" ingeniously placed in country houses, and a mass of outwardly conforming laymen. In such a situation, the priests, clandestine presses, missions, and conspiracies made only the raw materials of a new Catholic martyrology. The temporary successes of conversion collapsed in the 1580s, before the onslaught of executions. Before 1587, only six priests had been put to death; in 1588, there were thirty-one executions. The continued war with Spain in the 1590s caused great pressures to be maintained against laymen as well, and efforts to dissolve lay Catholic allegiance to the queen led to eighty-eight further executions in the 1590s.[8]

Hence the survival of prominent Jesuits—John Gerard and Henry Garnet lived in hiding for twenty years—should not cloud the issue. Continued efforts to bring about a Catholic succession[9] drove apart the secular priests and the more militant men of the Society of Jesus. Some 400 seculars, of whom 154 were martyred by 1598, saw their efforts threatened by fourteen Jesuits, of whom only six had been executed. More important by far was the fact that militancy revealed a wide split between clerical and gentry politics. Father Parsons steadily condemned gentry allegiance to their sovereign and the "gentry priests" who disfigured the faith by living in disguise.[1] The laymen themselves knew that the merest hint of treason tightened the screw on their families and fortunes. Although only thirteen secular priests accepted an amnesty offer in 1602, on the condition of denying papal temporal authority, in the 1640s the patterns of Elizabeth's age bore fruit. Eighty-six of Yorkshire's recusant gentry hoisted the royalist standard; only ten maintained the parliamentary cause. James I had executed only twenty-five Catholics.

[8] On the Jesuits, other missionaries, and the impact of papal politics, see P. Hughes, *Rome and the Counter-Reformation in England* (London: Sheed and Ward, 1942); as well as J. H. Pollen, *The Institution of the Archpriest Blackwell* (London: Longmans, 1916); T. Clancy, *Papist Pamphleteers* (Chicago: Loyola University Press, 1964).

[9] For example, the book called *A Conference about the Next Succession* (1595), typical of the circle of William Allen and Robert Parsons.

[1] That is, the seculars.

Protestant Prospects

The problems presented to the government by the varieties of radical Protestants–styled–Puritans were complex. The papists had begun by supposing Elizabeth to be favorably disposed toward them. So had the more forward Protestants. Catholics had been quickly stripped of their illusions. But Puritans often held to the belief that Elizabeth would prove sympathetic, finally to learn the harsh truth Bishop Jewel had jokingly stated in 1559: "It is idly and scurriously said . . . that as heretofore Christ was cast out by his enemies, so he is now kept out by his friends." Nothing better shows the fallacy of teaching that the Reformation was the creature of the state than the history of Puritanism.[2]

In the conflicts between Puritan demands for true Christian liberty and government requirements of order, the imperfections of an imperfect society were writ large. This is so because the Puritans pursued reformation in polity, theology, and liturgy in a Church of England that in their eyes was but half-reformed.[3] Their reasons for doing so were deeply laid in the ground of the Elizabethan Church—in its parochial clergy and in its leaders. Hence our concern here will be less to trace the history of doctrinal broils or Puritan polemics than to show the social character of Puritanism in relation to the social character of the establishment against which Puritans railed. Our main focus will be on questions raised already in our study of the Henrician religious scene. The limit we impose on this discussion gladly cedes to another that boggy, treacherous territory of Puritanism and revolution.[4] Our concern will be to know why government conceded that policy in religion was bounded by its will but was given substance by what laymen and ministers practiced and preached in the dark corners of the land.

In order to give flesh to the skeleton of the argument, it will help to begin with angular facts. Most Englishmen never heard a Puritan sermon or went to "lectures" preached by radical, unbeneficed clergy. They did, however,

[2] The literature of Puritanism is too vast even to allow a brief "selection." The best book to date is Patrick Collinson's, *The Elizabethan Puritan Movement* (London: Jonathan Cape, 1967). Among the other indispensable books I would place William Haller, *The Rise of Puritanism* (New York: Columbia, 1938); Michael Walzer, *The Revolution of the Saints* (Cambridge, Mass.: Harvard University Press, 1965); C. H. Hill, *Society and Puritanism in Pre-revolutionary England* (London: Shocken, 1964); M. M. Knappen's *Tudor Puritanism* (Chicago: University of Chicago Press, 1939); John New, *Anglican and Puritan* (Stanford, Calif.: Stanford University Press, 1964); and C. H. and K. George, *The Protestant Mind of the English Reformation* (Princeton: Princeton University Press, 1961).

[3] *The Zurich Letters*, I, p. 17.

[4] Gerald Straka will deal at length with prerevolutionary Puritanism in the context of causal arguments about the Revolution: see his book *A Certainty in the Succession*, Volume IV of this History.

attend parish churches that were sick with diseases against which mere injunc-
tive purges had not prevailed. To purge the malignant humors in the ecclesiastical body of the realm was the self-appointed task of Puritan physicians.
Like the Reformation itself, the further demand for it was a response to
personal perceptions and experiences of disorder and the anxieties produced by
such experiences.

One of the major forces of discontent among the purifying opposition to
the Elizabethan Settlement of 1559–70 was the sectarian knot of returned
Calvinist emigrés. These Calvinists had failed to find many promotions, despite the fact that some of their number had obtained episcopal office.[5] The
Settlement itself had kept in vogue the "thirteen blemishes" condemned by
Thomas Sampson and Lawrence Humphrey[6] which included women baptiz-
ing in private houses, popish clerical habits, the disallowance of marriage for
the clergy, "exquisite singing in parts," organ music, a "mutilated and imperfect" communion, no liberty or preaching. These were the dregs of
popery! Men who had made sacrifices and gone abroad to escape such practices were outraged to find them surviving in England. They viewed with
distrust those of their company who accommodated themselves in office. They
were rueful that the second generation of bishops came from men more eager
to pursue careers than to establish Christ's kingdom—men with more academic ability and administrative talent than godliness. To the staunch Calvinists, quiet in the land seemed the wrong objective, the more so since the
Catholic revival of the 1570s walked hand in hand with Elizabeth's protection
of the queen of Scots. Had not the Lord taught his prophets to utter their
judgments against such wickedness?[7]

The lack of a reformed clergy was far more significant than jeremiads, however. Reformation was slow to take deep root in most parts of the country.
The official theological and devotional changes depended on local clergy to
give substance to the Word. Even where popular reformation had formed in
people a Protestant and antipapal attitude, the Church was not necessarily
transformed. Nor was the popular view of prelates necessarily changed.

The Elizabethan archbishop of Canterbury, Matthew Parker, spent only
£448 on servants' wages. But John Whitgift, his less austere successor, went
attended by 1,000 men, forty of them gentlemen wearing chains of gold. In
the diocese of Chichester, four successive bishops found themselves handi-
capped by jurisdictional disputes with powerful deans and vested lay interests.
One of them, Richard Curteys, favored clerical Puritans and forwarded

---

[5] Jewel at Salisbury, Sandys of Worcester, Grindal (London and Canterbury), Cox in Ely, Scory at
Hereford, and Pilkington in Durham.

[6] Two vocal Oxford academics, chiefly important in the 1560s.

[7] Jer. 1:16; Ezek. 2:6. "For they are a rebellious house. And thou shalt speak my words unto them."

prophesyings and other exercises in his diocese. Many laymen resented Curteys' extreme assertions of temporal power. Antiprelatic tracts and attacks on the Prayer Book helped to crystallize episcopal suspicions of radical reformers. Thereafter, Parker and other archbishops and bishops constantly sought aid from the Court and Council to forge an alliance against Puritan subversion. But waves of episcopal repression helped fashion a new radical critique of episcopacy. The perfect fruits of this were the brilliant tracts by Martin Marprelate. The more power passed from the progressive bishops into the hands of men unsympathetic to change, the wider the gap became between the bishops and a segment of the clergy supported by certain "precise" Protestant nobility and gentry.

Certainly, from the time of John Whitgift's election to Canterbury on September 23, 1583, the reforming elements in the Church of England looked not to the hierarchy for help. The fury of Marprelate's attack in the *Epistle* (1588), the *Epitome* (1588), and the reply to Bishop Cooper's answering *Admonition* (1589) in *Hay any Worke for the Cooper* (1589) helped discredit the Puritan cause and allied Presbyterianism. But the very savagery of the satirical attack also showed the deep sense of disorder felt by pamphleteers and ordinary people.

On the parochial level, old problems plagued the faithful.[8] Lincoln diocese was truly but half-reformed. One minister in eight was nonresident in 1576. Seventy-seven of a group of 466 studied were pluralists. Nearly 85 percent were not licensed to preach. Litigation in the Church courts was rising, despite attempts to curb their influence. In Norwich the peak was reached in the 1590s.[9] A similar pattern prevailed at York. Institution fees and first-fruits (first year's profits) played havoc with the fortunes of honest ministers seeking cures. Tithe cases and matrimonial and related causes steadily exposed lay life to clerical control. This we can readily see in data about cases in the consistory court at York between 1561 and 1639.[1] There was much heedless annoyance. Richard Neile, a Jacobean archbishop of York, irked parishioners by abolishing pews, the size of which had shown the social celebrity of their holders. Meanwhile, probates and administrations in his diocese had increased from 290 and 50 in 1540 to 970 and 675 in 1612–19. The correction courts were as

[8] See Marchant's *The Church Under the Law* and also his brilliant *The Puritans and the Church Courts in the Diocese of York, 1560–1642* (Cambridge: Cambridge University Press, 1960). For Chichester, see Manning, and for London and the other dioceses, see the items numbered 1905, 1915, 1920, 1978, 2017–19, 2033–36, and 2064, in M. Levine, *Bibliographical Handbooks: Tudor England* (Cambridge: Cambridge University Press, 1968). On the economic aspects see C. Hill, *The Economic Problems of the Church* (Oxford: Clarendon Press, 1956).

[9] The high of 436 cases in 1598 declined by quick stages: 1602=322; 1605=302; 1636=275. A new but slight rise to 298 in 1636 signaled Laud's campaigns.

[1] See the Appendix, Figure 13.

busy as ever, or busier. In Sheffield parish, Yorkshire, the number of offenders rose from 17 in 1590 to 46 in 1635. A year later, the Laudian regime raised the total to 147 new cases, with further charges against 32 excommunicates.

The courts continued to impose humiliating penances, in which sinners appeared before the community bareheaded, barelegged, and barefooted, in white sheets, to make a declaration of errors. Thus, even in minor matters, the nascent Anglican Church put laymen under the law with severity. The visitation system constantly expanded, and in 1590 it assumed the form of a circuit system not unlike the common-law itineraries. Fees rose steadily, partly in response to general inflationary pressure, partly because many court officials, from the chancellor downward, were laymen rather than pluralist clergy.

What made the Church law especially offensive was the degree to which there was discrimination against the poor and weak in cases of alleged sexual immorality, bad language, drunkenness, or breaking of the Sabbath. The law was not socially blind. The use of the benches of socially prominent men to punish poor men encouraged contempt of court. Nearly 77 percent of all persons presented at court in Ely in 1619 were amenable to court order. But figures for Gloucester and Bristol do not mirror the degree of obedience seen in York and Ely. In Norwich diocese, cases in which the last resort of excommunication was applied reached 1,600 in 1627, and rose to 2,100 in 1633. York seemed to average about 1,500 excommunications a year, Chester about 2,000. The three dioceses together covered 23.8 percent of the territory of England and Wales and perhaps 25 percent of its population. A conservative estimate thus places the number of excommunicates at 5 percent of the total population, with losses due to family ties raising the number to perhaps 150,000, or 15 percent. The Puritans suffered most under the law and used it as evidence that the Church harbored a vast bark of irreligion.

The Puritans' claim was especially true in London diocese. From the time of Elizabeth's accession until her death there had been a steady rise in court presentations and in the proportion of those cited who submitted to discipline. Bishops Grindal, Aylmer, Sandys, and Bancroft were vigorous upholders of the law, especially where curates, their assistants, and nonconformists were concerned.[2] The serious contempt that had marked obedience in the early Tudor courts was gone; but Puritans were not satisfied. Attacks on their ministers worked a hardship on them. And as early as 1577–83, citizens deprived of the pastors they favored transferred from church to church in pursuit of godly worship, as we shall see. Requirements that lecturers assist in administration were a good device to unmask Puritans who rejected parts of the liturgy. But this device set some parishioners against others, since discipline depended on a

---

[2] Grindal excepted, London bishops showed scant sympathy toward Puritans.

network of informers, especially where the chief offenses were not reading prescribed homilies or royal injunctions. What must men eager to purify the church have thought of the *Second Book of Homilies* (1562), wherein there were three sermons "of repentance and true reconciliation" and six prescribed "against disobedience and wilful Rebellion"? Preaching seemed bent more to the support of authority in a divided society than to the gospel of salvation.

Pricks to Conscience

This neglect of preaching showed that the church was storing up trouble for itself. The many shifts in religious policy before 1558 and the rapid turnover of bishops during the same period could themselves have produced chaos. The repeated deprivation of clergy who would not swear oaths created a spiritual vacuum in many parishes. The struggle for the parish in Chichester made 16 percent of the cures subject to deprivation. Bishops Barlow and Curteys reported many churches devoid of sermons for periods of seven to twelve years. Others complained of the general lack of learned and godly clergy who were able to preach effectively. Since the universities did not provide a stream of staunch Protestant preachers overnight, the policy of deprivation for nonsubscribers exacerbated the existing ills of pluralism. Archbishop Parker experienced great difficulties in filling benefices in Canterbury between 1559 and 1575. Even the strong Grindalian, Curteys, could not make good the deficiency by his support of "lectures" and a policy of calling down Cambridge Puritans to preach in Sussex.

The general problems of pluralism and nonresidence were still great. Competition for benefices was as keen among careerists as it had ever been. The standard of conduct of impoverished curates marched with their low incomes. Because of impropriations,[3] only four benefices in Chichester diocese were worth above £30 in 1580. A church living was as much a piece of freehold property as it had been in 1530. Town parishes were generally more inadequately served than rural ones, and the stipends for them were lower. The situation was similar in East Anglia and in the Marches parishes of Cheshire, Shropshire, and Herefordshire. In Lancashire in 1599, there were only four licensed preachers of repute. And in Wales, the bishops of Llandaff, Bangor, St. Asaph's, and St. David's cited 90 percent of the Elizabethan clergy as being unable to preach. By 1640, an irritated M.P. could claim that there were only thirteen qualified preachers in 1,000 Welsh parishes. Even London, so much praised for the plenty of its preachers in a sermon at Paul's Cross in 1571,[4] had

[3] The annexation of an ecclesiastical benefice to a corporation or person, usually not the resident minister. The result was to drain off part of the income.

[4] "When I came out of the country hither to the City . . . I came into another world, out of Darkness into Light. For here is the Word of God plentifully preached." The preacher was Edward Bush.

grave problems. Puritan radicals were systematically jailed in the parish of the Minories without Aldgate. Where Coverdale and Crowley had enjoyed Edward VI's liberty to preach further reformation, under the patronage of the dowager duchess of Suffolk, later authorities moved to break up the "plumbers' hall conventicle" that had thrived in the period before 1568. John Field[5] and four other preachers in succession were imprisoned.

Persecutions bewildered and angered the dedicated Protestant laymen, who thought them a strange way to plant God's Word. The government seemed to be turning away deliberately from the missionary enthusiasm of earlier years. Edward VI appointed six hot-gospelers to convert Wales, Lancashire, Yorkshire, the Borders, Devon, and Hampshire, bringing the Word to the people. Archbishop Parker urged the queen and the Council to use their like to forward reform. Sir William Paulet, the Lord Treasurer, recommended sending three missionaries to Yorkshire and two to Durham. The Council acknowledged in 1569 that in many places "the people are hopelessly backward in religion," not because of willful disobedience but because of the insufficiency of preaching. Durham in 1560 had few able lecturers. Grindal thought his York clergy wicked and impious. Bernard Gilpin, the "apostle of the North," who preached extensively in the area beyond the Trent, found there "a thousand pulpits covered with dust." As late as 1587, John Penry sought the queen's help to evangelize Wales, "the most barren corner of the land."

These facts did more than anything else to bring about the Puritan condemnation of Elizabeth's settlement. They gave the color of truth to a 1586 description of Chichester:

In the same Citie are manie which are greatly aggrieved . . . by reason of the want of good and able ministers there to do the Lords message faithfullie. For it is much to be lamented to see the state and condition of the same Citie, which hath in it viij parish churches, and never a minister in any of them that is able to teach and exhort the people . . . and the common people are overgroune as it were a wilderness for lack of instruction. . . .

Perhaps the root of the problem was more economic than attitudinal, more the effect of the structural deficiencies noticed before the Reformation began than of perverse official will. The diocese of Chichester in 1585 provides some good evidence of this. Of 118 clerics in the archdeaconry of Chichester, 34 had university degrees, 21 had left university without one, and 5 had only grammar school educations; for the rest, the record is silent. The 1603 visitation of 67 incumbents shows only 29 priests in Lewes archdeaconry with degrees.

[5] The great organizer and driving spirit of the "classical" presbyterian-oriented movement of the 1570s and 1580s.

The 1585 financial records of the diocese show that few livings were worth more than £16—at most, 17 out of 118. Only 35 of the clergy visited in 1585 preached; 22 of them were graduates. Fully a third of the preachers were graduates in livings worth more than £16. By contrast, 32 of 33 unschooled curates and incumbents who did not preach held livings worth less than £11 a year. Of the 20 *tradesmen* filling cures, only one preached, and only one received more than £11 a year. Forty-three of the 118 livings were encumbered by impropriations.

No effort to discourage rude artisans and servingmen from the ministry would succeed where benefices paid less than £15. Nor would holders of benefices leave off plying other trades. The 1566 *Book of Advertisements*, issued by the government, enjoined quarterly sermons in every parish church. Incumbents described in Chichester records in the 1570s and 1580s frequently were styled "tailor," "draper," "grazingman," "surgeon," "weaver," or "sheareman." That they preached regularly defies belief. And as time wore on the likelihood of their doing so was reduced by events. The 1585 total of 43 impropriations in Chichester archdeaconry and 32 in eastern Sussex grew to 153 in the mid-seventeenth century. The direct relationship between impropriations and inadequately educated incumbents was well known to Puritans in Sussex. So was the fact that many Church of England gentry were the predators.

The subjugation of the vicar to the squire had long been a familiar pattern in social politics. Of 79 known patrons of livings in Sussex in 1603, 63 were laymen. That the Chichester data are representative of a broader trend we need not doubt. Christopher Hill's study of the economic problems of the Church showed that the original secularization of land had stripped the Church of 40 percent of its patronage of benefices. Although the Church was even in 1646 far from bankrupt—there were still episcopal lands worth £676,387 and chapter lands worth £1,170,000[6]—an economic abyss opened between the intention and the achievement of reform.

Many said openly this was because the disciplinary power of the Church had been undermined by poverty in the parish and the concomitant loss of initiative at the pulpit level. The ceaseless government raids on benefices had not been reversed by Edward VI. Under Elizabeth, a golden stream flowed through the Court, with the fortunate grabbing what they could, and became a torrent under the impact of rising prices and raging appetites. The earl of Leicester was steward to four bishops, all the while milking their revenues and making shift to promote radical reformers. Tithes were sold to laymen with the courtiers' aid. Twenty-five percent (2,216 of 8,200) were sold up by

[6] The sale price paid for them after their confiscation and distribution by parliamentary commissions.

Elizabeth's orders. James I bargained an additional 1,453, thus bringing the
level of alienations to nearly 50 percent of the total. Taken with the Henrician
and Edwardian grants, nearly 75 percent of all English parishes had been at
least partially stripped of income needed for the cure of souls. Richard Hooker,
mindful that covetous officers looted God's storehouse, in book three of his
Laws of Ecclesiastical Polity raised unto an avenging Heaven this cry: "Let there
be some stay, some stint in spoiling. . . ." Were that wish not granted, in the
fullness of time the Church would, like some great tower, fall, brought down
by the "thirst of unsuitable minds."

Englishmen weary of sordid transactions and hopeful of salvation could not
tarry to hear Oliver Cromwell style his revolution "the thing of God and his
working. . . ."[7] From the beginning of Elizabeth's reign, they reacted to their
views of the Church's shortcomings. And the character of their objections
reflected what was basic to their religious experience at the parish level.

The religious center of Puritanism grew out of criticism of the Church of
England. Despite evidence of corruption, this criticism was not that the
Church was corrupt. Rather, it was that the Church presented to the world
the face of a vast hierarchy of propertied men—men too much concerned with
tithes, offices, support of the monarchy, mundane law, legal fees, and extorting
from the faithful the last egg, and too little concerned with preaching, pastoral
care, and bringing to simple congregations the balm of God's healing Word.

This is not to say that Puritanism and emergent Anglicanism were without
sharp theological differences. But awareness of such divergences was not sharp
before Hooker wrote his *Laws of Ecclesiastical Polity*. Hooker showed that the
Church of England maintained traditions not clearly taught in the Bible but
not in conflict with scriptures. He understood that, apart from a small body
of separatists, most Elizabethan and early Stuart Puritans regarded themselves
as members of the Church of England. Although the early lack of a clear
notion of Anglican orthodoxy clouded the issue, most Puritans felt they shared
a common set of beliefs with men whose ceremonies they found superstitious.
Thomas Cranmer, John Whitgift, John Field, Thomas Cartwright, and Walter Travers had all acknowledged themselves to be members of the Church of
England. Even the Welsh gospeler John Penry wished nothing more than to
be the Church's apostle in his native country. The rich legacy of the English
Reformation also counted its treasure in the works of John Wycliffe, William
Tyndale, Heinrich Bullringer, John Calvin, Thomas Cranmer, Peter Martyr,
and John Knox. Thus, it would have taken an arrogant man to argue for the
exclusion of the Puritans. They were men who seemed to allege no articles or
creed apart from the terms of the Elizabethan Settlement.

[7] From a speech for Parliament, January 22, 1655.

Two generations of controversy and the great works of the radical apologists had not produced a Puritan theology wholly at odds with Elizabethan establishment thought. This may explain why recent students disagree as to the characteristic note of Puritan doctrine and the degree of difference between it and "Anglican thought." Some profess to see no special "Puritan Calvinism" regarding predestination or sacramental doctrine, and choose instead to stress its "spirit" or "temper." Charles H. and Katherine George and Ronald A. Marchant certainly emphasize this view, showing that "party strife" was less about doctrine than about ceremonial and liturgical detail—the surplice, the sign of the cross in baptism, genuflection at the name "Jesus." In their view, even the arguments about ecclesiastical polity can be comprehended in such terms—whether the government of the faithful ought to be by bishop or presbyters. Whitgift himself had argued, in opposition to the presbyterians, that bishops were convenient but not prescribed.

Yet the Puritan manifesto of 1572, *An Admonition to the Parliament*, referred to conflict over "great matters" rather than things trivial or indifferent, and this was some twenty years before Hooker's great book. Recently, John New has argued that there were early basic doctrinal splits between Anglican and Puritan conceptions of God, nature, the corruption of man's nature, and the economy of salvation. The Anglicans rested secure in the merit of human efforts toward salvation, while the Puritans spoke with contempt of the Pelagian or Arminian "free-willers." Thomas Cartwright certainly held dissident views on baptism; and many Puritan thinkers excluded "sinners" from the grace of communion. Above all, as Archbishop Laud once remarked, the Anglicans gave a priority to the altar that the Puritans granted only to the pulpit.

Thus, as Elizabeth's reign yielded to that of James, or James I's to that of his son, some say that Anglicanism and Puritanism were different religions. But it seems closer to the truth to say that Puritanism stood for a body of dissident opinion *within* the established Church, held by men who wanted to jettison the freight of tradition, men more rigidly scripturalists and in terror of Catholic elements. For Puritans were mainly the left wing of a revolutionary Church that was still not firmly set in its later, historic mold; and in their number were conservatives who were only marginally at odds with the Settlement and radicals who would be content only with the Book and the discipline.

To pursue the issue of division further would be to prefer a new scholasticism to the solid social reality of how Puritans, lay and clerical alike, lived in the new order. It is more useful to locate Puritans in their local communities. There we may look at the behavior of the "godly," as they liked to call themselves. This view will help us grasp why their neighbors derisively called them puritans, precisians, saints, and scripture men. To the godly, such epithets confirmed that their Protestantism was less form than substance. To their comfortable critics, the terms expressed distaste, fear, and anxiety over the possibility that radical reforms would upset the order of society, or at least change its shape in ways inimical to the critics' preferences for quiet, deference, and hierarchy.

The Rise of Puritan Dissent

The Puritan movement in English society stood solidly anchored on a tripod, the three legs of which were mass sentiment, support among the landed classes, and widespread clerical endorsement. The clerical leg is the best documented, whereas the support of the masses is the least thoroughly explored. Yet it is clear that Puritanism was much less a movement dominated by clergy than was once thought. The radical Protestant element in lay society was not subordinate to ministers. Indeed, Elizabethan and early Stuart Puritanism in its ministerial aspects was often a response to the felt needs of lay nonconformists possessed of their own religious values and experiences. It was from this lay set of experiences and values that much clerical nonconformity drew sustenance. And it was clearly at the parish level that the conditions prevailed that were to dissolve the bonds of the Church's basic unit and drive popular Protestantism toward the idea of congregational independence. Thus, Puritan experience rather than Puritan doctrine best accounts for the threat Puritanism posed to the ideal of a unity of Church, polity, and society.

It is not easy, however, to base this account in precise statistical formulations. Local studies are too thin to allow a good demographic or geographic analysis, much less an occupational one, that fits the godly precisely into a schematic social structure. Yet we do have much evidence from court records, visitations, Puritan records of their own organizing activities, inquiries by central government, and literary sources. And these allow some comment beyond the 1572 remark that "not every fortieth person . . . is a good and devout gospeller."

Strong Puritan pockets existed in areas traditionally associated with heterodoxy in other days—London, Essex, East Anglia, the Weald of Sussex and Kent, parts of the Midlands, the West Country, and Lincolnshire, as well as towns and ports of every region. The counties of Suffolk, Northamptonshire, Middlesex, and Norfolk rank high in the records, as do the towns of Coventry, Leicester, Cambridge, and Bury St. Edmunds. In the newer industrial centers —Newcastle, Halifax, and Manchester—and in March towns like Worcester, Hereford, and Chester, large knots of commercial and industrial peoples adhered to "godly practices." Thus, the often-alleged conservatism of the Celtic fringes and of Yorkshire must be set side by side with favor shown the Protestant religion in areas that could not easily be reached by government agents and places where mass urban sentiment allowed dissidents to entrench themselves and made their detection onerous to the community. It is worth noting that Protestant nonconformity found a secure urban base even in cities in the North, where the Catholic cult could not be openly used. This fact seems to reinforce our notion of the slenderness of the Catholic population in Yorkshire. Had the recusants really been as numerous as they were alleged to be, it is difficult to believe they would have been forced underground. The distant London government could not have crushed a faith solidly based in the masses.

There is also evidence to render suspect the old idea that Puritanism was a "middle-class" phenomenon, or was peculiar to any trade, calling, or class. If Puritanism was not merely a clerical Protestantism, it was even less confined to the industrious sort. It thrived in rural communities and in great cities. It was not regional in character. Given the fact that only the Puritan groups in London, Oxford, Cambridge, Essex, Suffolk, Northamptonshire, and Warwick were regularly active in the 1580s in the national movement of conferences aimed at establishing a presbyterian system, the proper inference is that the presbyterian classical movement was narrowly based, not that Puritanism as a whole was strong only in those areas. This inference would seem to be supported by the widespread gentry support of Puritan ministers in Kent, Sussex, Lancashire, Yorkshire, and Leicestershire, which we hear of repeatedly in accounts of Elizabeth's reign. Moreover, a census of Puritan ministers *c.* 1600–1610 shows significant concentrations of support in other areas.[8]

Lay prophesying and clerical exercises were widespread in the dioceses of Exeter, Gloucester, Chichester, Lincoln, Winchester, Bath, Lichfield, and St. David's, especially during Grindal's primacy. Only the queen's order to suppress prophesying, given on May 7, 1577, forced the appearance of names of suspect nonconformists in place of the good gospel-Christians Grindal had praised for their missionary zeal. Twenty-five Kentish gentlemen complained of this suppression. Throughout the reign there was parliamentary agitation against the crown's policy of gagging gospel preachers. In the 1584 session, members heard the pleas of Sir Thomas Lucy (Warwickshire), Sir Edward Dymock (Lincolnshire), and Geoffrey Gates (Essex). The organizers of the *classes*—presbyterian-oriented cells—kept records giving evidence of local support in Cornwall, Surrey, Berkshire, Buckinghamshire, Ely, Devon, and Oxfordshire, in addition to the places already mentioned. Even after rigorous action against the Puritans in the 1590s had destroyed elements of leadership and invoked the recusancy laws against dissidents on the left, early Jacobean evidence suggests no large-scale change in the ubiquity of Puritanism.

[8] See the Appendix, Figure 14.

The Yorkshire documents are especially impressive in this regard. Prosecutions for radical Protestant nonconformity rose steadily in Yorkshire between 1558 and 1640. This increase was perhaps a reflection of the decline of sympathy among lay and ecclesiastical governors there, especially in the 1620s and during the Laudian regime of the 1630s. The Pilgrim Fathers had their roots in the county or its border areas, having been driven toward separatism and emigration by vigorous persecution. A solid core of parsons came under repeated court citations, and the family of Henry Ireton, Cromwell's great general, was represented in numerous presentations in the parish of Attenborough. Clergy presented in York deaconries between about 1560 and 1640 ran close to 265, with another seventy-eight in the deaconry of Nottingham. Seventy-three laymen in the single parish of Great Budworth were presented in 1633 for Protestant nonconformity!

In Sussex, there was not much separatist enthusiasm. But a large group of Puritan ministers attended to the needs of laymen there, often under great pressure from the government's campaign against them. Despite harassment, the orthodox rector of Ashurst gloomily recorded that laymen "cared not if he did present them," since "it is but a matter of twelve pence." The 1581 escalation of fines to £20 a month discouraged some. But Puritanism thrived in the towns, judging from the distribution of cited ministers in urban parishes in the decades after 1580. Royal and episcopal action had failed to break the movement there, at least until 1605, when Archbishop Bancroft successfully deprived ten ministers. Yet Chichester had at least thirty-three known Puritan ministers between 1583 and the 1605 purge out of a total of some 200 beneficed clergy and curates. And that 16 percent does not include sympathizers who had not been cited. These Sussex data correct the impression of a failing Puritan movement that is often derived from the fact that fewer than ninety beneficed clergy in the nation preferred deprivation to subscription and conformity when James I and Archbishop Bancroft turned on the Puritans in 1604–5, after the Hampton Court Conference.

We must now look more closely at Puritanism in the parish to discover the relations between the laity and their ministers.[9] This will make clearer the characteristic politics of Puritan dissent. For even when ministers and laymen rejected presbyterianism and separatism, Puritanism remained and grew in strength in English society.

[9] P. Collinson, "John Field and Elizabethan Puritanism," in *Government and Society in Elizabethan England*, edited by S. T. Bindoff, C. Morris, and J. Hurstfield (London: Athlone Press, University of London, 1960), pp. 127–62; H. G. Owen, "A Nursery of Elizabethan Nonconformity," *JEccH*, (1966), XVII, pp. 65–76; A. T. Hart, *The Country Clergy, 1558–1660* (London: Phoenix House, 1958); Albert Peel, *The First Congregational Churches: New Light on Separatists in London* (Cambridge: Cambridge University Press, 1920).

John Field himself had recognized that "the people . . . must bring the discipline to pass which we desire" if parliamentary politics failed to convert the government to presbyterian polity. His "people" were men who had the economic independence to pursue the costly course of dissent. The minutes of the Dedham classis of Essex show little concern for the poor, except when the headboroughs and the clergy relieved want among "forward poor men" or chastised others "every way disordered" and of "naughty disposition." The truly poor disappear from our sources because poverty set a line that all but excluded men from active work in the life of a congregation. However, above what Patrick Collinson called that "median line," householders, their families and friends, servants, and the extended entourages of landed men catechized, prophesied, exercised, and in general shared in the experience of moving the local minister to lead in the direction the faithful wished to go.

We get a good view of the situation of a Puritan parish in the Minories without Aldgate. This was a nursery of nonconformists under the government's nose in London. The parish was a natural link between radical advocacy within the Church and discussion of change outside its doors. It was the center of activity for clergy in the vestments controversy of 1565–6 as well as for nonsubscribing clergy afterward. The embryonic London classis met twice weekly there, drawing support from men like Seth Jackson, Robert Gates, Christopher Coleman, and the separatists Broune and Robert Patterson. John Field was jailed during his ministry there. Incipient conventicles harbored nascent separatists and Puritans anxious to remain in the Church to work for its reform. The popular base for their activities was strong; there was a large emigrant French and Dutch Calvinist core, worshiping in "strangers' churches." The grey duchess of Suffolk enjoyed the advowson nominally in crown control, and she had made Coverdale, Broune, and Patterson her religious voice. Constitutionally, the parish lay outside the London bishop's reach, in the liberty of St. Clare. It claimed donative privileges to nominate its own minister. A situation in which the parishioners themselves were the "patron" bypassed the ordinary machinery of presentation, institution, and induction.

If made good, this claim converted the benefice into a congregational property and the minister into a hired stipendiary. Here were all of the problems presented to Church and State by Puritanism: the resistance of laymen to clerical domination, the basic contradiction that separated lay concerns from the clerical elitists (and presbyterians) who suffered little lay supervision of their work, and the threat to social order inherent in any populist or quasi-democratic reversal of initiative at the parish level. No wonder the government destroyed this "plumbers' hall conventicle." It is even less strange that Field and other presbyterians organized a ministerially led radical movement beyond the parish framework.

The drive for congregational control of the character of the minister and his teaching could not always be won by aristocratic patronage or exercise of the privileges of St. Clare. Splits often existed among lay factions with diverse beliefs and tastes. Sometimes grandees like the earls of Leicester and Huntingdon used their power to settle matters. Victory did not always come easily, however. If the opposing forces were balanced, conflict resulted.

Hath not Minge brought Ashford[1] from being the quietest town . . .? What hath Casslocke done at Chart? What broil and contention hath Fenner made in Cranbrook, and all the rest likewise in their several cures?

These were complaints about Puritan clerics who disrupted the calm of their parishes. Other cases show laymen who, finding the incumbent minister in their parish unacceptable, visited other parishes in pursuit of spiritual nourishment. Bishops' act books indicate that "gadding about" arose from the belief that a service without a sermon was no service. Thomas Woodhan of Purleigh, Essex, admitted in 1585 that he had sought an acceptable service at Langdon, Maldon, and Danbury. Three Colchester parishioners of St. Nicholas protested the "simplicity" of their minister and went elsewhere to worship. Early on, Puritans earned a reputation for setting communities at variance.

Where clerical ignorance was no hindrance to good sermons, one course open to objectors was that of persuading the minister to adjust his opinion and conform less to what distant authority wished than to what his close flock accepted. Ministers of every opinion short of separatist sectarianism were open to persuasion in this manner. Their notion of the Church was the old one of a visible church of preaching and sacraments. To drive away laymen concerned more about the Word than the sacraments was a grievous fault. Lay efforts to move the minister to provide a preaching cure of godly character thus coincided with ministerial beliefs that the gospel had to be brought to every parishioner. If disordered or lewd parishioners withstood the influence of a Puritan minister, he could deny them the sacraments. But this alternative strained the hope of extending the gospel to the whole of society. If, on the other hand, a minister scandalized a sincere, godly bunch of parishioners, their subsequent flight to another minister threatened to dissolve the wider notion of the commonwealth based on the parish.

Hence the whole character of early Puritanism was colored by the ideal of comprehensiveness, even where that ideal was not achieved. Only the persistent refusal of government to support radical Protestant preaching drove English Puritans to emphasize inner piety, assurance, ethics, and personal discipleship. These goals combined to change the concept of covenant from a

---

[1] All of the instances cited here are from Kent.

social idea to something embracing smaller, "voluntary" societies. When that happened, the household became the essential unit of religion, replacing the parish. The way was open to the emergence of knots of dissenting households independent of the life of the established Church. Neither congregationalism nor independency was the *starting* point for radical Protestant thought derived from Calvinist tenets. It was the parochial experience that forced Puritans into a choice between the safe harbor of working within the Church for modest changes and the dangerous far shore of despairing separatism.

Separatism made difficult every social transaction in a society organized as English society then was. Whether the godly forsook alehouses, bowling greens, dances, and plays, considering them little hells, or so avoided the society of less godly men as to forsake all intercourse with them, their way was hard. Exclusiveness meant a loss of fellowship, neighborliness, and comfort in village society. And in towns or their suburbs, the demands of covert exercises could prove hard to reconcile with success in business or obedience to government. "If you can trot to sermons, we will make you trot to courts," was the threat of an Essex archdeacon's official.

The social difficulty of dissent thus helps to put in context two factors most representative of the organized attempts of Puritans to remain in the established church: the classical movement and its politics, and the Puritan lectureships that thrived between 1560 and 1640. We cannot narrate in detail the first nor study in depth the second. But some effort to show the nature of Puritan politics will further illuminate the social context of religious experience. And the lectureships give emphasis to the fact that Puritans sought the means to convert the whole of English society, even when it was clear that the citadel of public power stood against the effort.

A Struggle for Control: Law and Gospel

The first decade of Elizabeth's reign had made it clear that no general welcome would be given exiled radicals, except such of them as the responsibilities of office would make more conservative. The government gave some scope to detached intellectuals. But it also stressed that the minister's task was to accept the Settlement and avoid potentially schismatic radicalism. This was largely the position taken by politicians sympathetic to Puritanism—the earls of Warwick and Leicester, Lord Rich, and the earl of Bedford. Few were as uncompromising as the duchess of Suffolk or those conciliar enthusiasts, Sir Walter Mildway, Sir Francis Walsingham, and Henry Hasting, third earl of Huntingdon. What this meant was that no man in the established Church, Parliament, or the universities was free to advocate structural changes. Such advocacy was deemed a threat both to episcopacy and monarchy. Puritan impulses to test institutions by scriptural authority and lodge appeals against lay power and its satellite ecclesiastical authority were unacceptable.[2]

This became clear between 1565 and 1593. Puritan campaigns in the 1560s against clerical dress and the "Jewish priesthood" enjoyed widespread support in sermons at Paul's Cross and Westminster. Men warned against a government that prescribed "one piece of popery" and so might prescribe others. The official response was to close Paul's Cross to radicals and condemn extravagant Biblicism. The once-sympathetic bishops closed ranks with the queen, and Puritans found it vital to seek help outside the hierarchy. The bishops were in fact commissioners for the Supremacy rather than agents of revolution. *The Brief Discourse against the Outwarde Apparell* and other early manifestoes had revealed a coherent Puritan party enjoying a base in London, the counties, the Council, and Cambridge and Oxford. But lawyers were not yet so evident in the movement as they were in the decades after 1580. The first purges sent into the wilderness of the unbeneficed some Puritan lights. Liberty of preaching was dead.

Whatever fears government nurtured in the late 1560s were multiplied in the 1570s. English presbyterians became the ministerial leaders of Puritanism. Men like John Field and Walter Travers, dissociated by force from parochial security, made the "church in London" the conventicles of stipendiary curates who "lectured" to hearers. This gave a base of support independent of the establishment. Such stipendiary curates, successors of the friars as popular preachers, had created a novel nuclear movement. They voiced their demands in the manifesto *An Admonition to Parliament* (1572), which tied their London group to Thomas Cartwright, the Lady Margaret Professor of Divinity in Cambridge, and Oxford radicals like Thomas Wilcox. While protected at first in the donative curacy of the Minories, these men had developed proposals to revolutionize the Church of England. They gave only spiritual functions to bishops and consigned the welfare of the poor to deacons. Real authority lay in the local ministers, as Cartwright had said in his 1570 lectures. There was to

[2] For the account of developing attitudes and conflicts, see Horton Davies, *The Worship of the English Puritans* (Westminster, London: Dacre Press, 1948); D. J. McGinn, *The Admonition Controversy* (New Brunswick, N.J.: Rutgers University Press, 1949); M. Maclure, *The Paul's Cross Sermons, 1534–1642* (Toronto: University of Toronto Press, 1958); I. Morgan, *The Godly Preachers of the Elizabethan Church* (London: Epworth Press, 1965); E. S. Morgan, *Visible Saints* (New York: New York University Press, 1963); V. J. K. Brook, *Whitgift and the English Church* (London: English University Presses, 1957); S. J. Knox, *Walter Travers* (London: Presbyterian Historical Society, 1962); D. J. McGinn, *John Penry and the Marprelate Controversy* (New Brunswick, N.J.: Rutgers University Press, 1966). See also Mark Curtis, "The Hampton Court Conference," *History* (1961), XLVI, 1–16; E. S. Morgan, *The Puritan Family* (London: Harper & Row, 1966); and H. Trevor-Roper, *Archbishop Laud* (Oxford: Clarendon Press, 1950); Sir J. E. Neale, "The Elizabethan Acts of Supremacy and Uniformity," *EHR* (1950), LXV, pp. 304–32.

be a presbytery in each church, the congregation being free to choose the minister.

The 1571 Parliament launched the career of the many bills brought in by Puritan M.P.s to purify ceremonies and to reform the Prayer Book. Many members supported the two aims, but few would openly challenge episcopal authority. In 1571, John Whitgift led the anti-Puritan forces in Convocation. The 1572 failure of several bills that would have tolerated congregational freedom by protecting Puritan ministers and their lay patrons apparently led Field and his lieutenants beyond moderate reform to the open advocacy of an "equality of ministers." If bills on rites could not be passed or even debated without the queen's assent, then they would utter God's word in other places. "Is a reformation good for France? And can it be evyl for England? Is discipline meet for Scotland? And is it unprofitable for this Realm?"

This appeal to Parliament and to wider public involvement set the tone for the future efforts of Field and his sympathizers. It also revealed the deep disagreement that was to split apart the mass of Protestants and the presbyterians. Most Englishmen accepted Christian magistracy as essential in a monarchy. A polity of equal ministers might suit a free city like Geneva, where the rule of magistrates was excluded by the notion of church and commonwealth as distinct spheres of authority. But in England, the crown needed the bishops. The crown would tolerate no doctrine that rent the social fabric down which its authority and that of bishops reached to the local level in carefully graded intervals. The issue joined between Field, Cartwright, and Whitgift in their polemics gained depth in the *Second Admonition* (1572), the *Answer to the Admonition* (1572 or 1573), the *Reply to an Answer* (1573), *Defense of the Answer* (1574), and Walter Travers' *Full and Plain Declaration of Ecclesiastical Discipline* (1574).

Interestingly, no ballads survive to testify to much popular interest in the debate. This may mean that there was little popular support for radical ecclesiology. Lawyers were less concerned about the classis and its power over local churches than they were about being deprived of a good minister. As a direct result of the radical campaign for reform, the leadership went underground in and about London, where it was established as a "conference of brethren" by late 1572. The tendency among these brethren was to elevate the pastor above the people and the classis above the congregation. This ran contrary to the Tudor history of lay anticlerical sentiment. Field himself emphasized obedience to the ministry. Hence, despite the remarkable organizing ability Field showed in the 1570s and 1580s, the clerical aristocracy of the classis and synod failed to move laymen as effectively as popular exercises did. Popular exercises at least promised to "purify" the Church within the legal limits of the system, whereas presbyterianism bore the stigma of revolution in an already divided society.[3]

Authorities might have cooperated with an effort to provide godly men with pulpits and thus raise the standards of the parochial clergy, had it not been for Elizabeth's suppression of prophesying and Whitgift's campaign forcing subscription to all of the Thirty-Nine Articles (1576–83), which made most Puritans aloof from the presbyterian movement. Puritanism became a national movement less by virtue of its spectacular parliamentary failures and the machinations of the classis than because the political elite accepted its major motifs and the colleges soon established Protestant "seminaries."

From 1565 to 1575, 230 new Cambridge ministers and forty from Oxford exhibited Puritan learnings. Even Whitgift's persecutions, as well as Bancroft's and Laud's after 1605, could not alter the facts. If the newer generation of prelates was hostile toward the slow revolution in religious life, the revolution nonetheless enjoyed massive support at every level of society. The queen's closest advisers (Burghley, Leicester, and Pembroke) gave aid to circumspect parliamentary actions, stopping short of abetting the new presbyterian drives of 1581–7. They warned Elizabeth of the danger of the great campaign of suspensions that was begun in 1583[4] and renewed in the 1590s, in 1605, and again in the 1630s.

When the takeover bid had clearly failed, resort to compromise moved the politically alert Puritans. But as the Hampton Court Conference in 1604 was to show decisively, even the tolerant and agreeable James VI was limited in his freedom to negotiate concessions that were objected to by a hostile hierarchy. This limitation reinforced Puritan efforts to control the parish and thus immunize ministers against the virus of the recusancy statutes. The nobility, gentry, and urban elites followed eagerly. They saw parochial Puritanism as an extension of their own drive to make the shire and its ruling elites more weighty than the bishops in church governance. If the parish could be reformed through the power of lay patrons, church government would be brought into harmony with the will of the magistrates in town and county. This central purpose was in fact a step on the long road leading toward the curtailing of ecclesiastical dominion. And those taking that step could allege Wycliffe's words and Thomas Cromwell's regime as landmarks. No campaign had broader lay support than the campaign for freedom from the temporal dominion of churchmen.

The vision that counted was the peripheral vision of the world of local

---

[3] The subsequent legislative history of the Book and the discipline lies outside the scope of this book, as does the internal history of the "classical" movement.

[4] Nearly 400 ministers refused subscription between 1583 and 1584, with large groups in Suffolk, Essex, Kent, Lincolnshire, and Chichester.

government. In the shires, the microcosms of the English Commonwealth were making their own sense out of the Reformation. The landed classes tied their allegiance to an informed piety; they were serious, moderate, lawful for the most part, well educated, and content to remain conformist while steadily helping to make room in the parish ministry for ministers of their own persuasion. Only Laud tried to undo this system of "puritan government" at the local level. And his efforts helped to deepen the general discontent of a nation cursed by disease, famine, and war. The change would not sit well in a world of squires and aldermen whose fathers had taught them to "gadd aboute," walk to sermons, distrust the bishops and the crown's commissioners, and buy up tithes and advowsons as a means of controlling their ministers.

The Protestant governing classes preferred an indivisible union of church and state because they possessed the basis of power in both. The presbyterian doctrine of separating the magistracy from religious concerns was thus not only unhistorical but also contrary to their interests. Godly preaching anchored the commonwealth—which they ruled. Hence what was vital was to control the pulpit and divest prelates of real power. Confining the clergy to preaching the gospel sat well with lay desires and their reading of scripture. The justices were in fact and self-concept the crown's chief agents. Bishops who set themselves against the gentry were thus viewed as subverters of the crown's authority.[5] Good bishops were "conformable" and thus respected in their dioceses. This ideal left little scope for the old style of bishops, and it gave the government of the Church into the hands of various groups in search of the least common denominator of their interests: ministers, congregations, and the powerful lay leaders of society.

A society already prone to faction thus found in Reformation politics a new source of fracture. And its ruling groups desperately sought agreements, even if only of a negative kind. There would be little tolerance given men such as Dr. Peter Turner, who in 1585 brought in a bill to replace the Prayer Book with the Genevan *Form of Prayer*, into which Field had pasted a scheme of presbyterian rule. The Commons refused permission to read Dr. Turner's "bill and a book," no matter how sympathetic they were to complaints against the clergy. Still less would they smile on revisions of the *Book of Discipline* or such further supplications as Anthony Cope's 1587 "book and a bill." The queen and her successors blocked every presbyterian thrust. M.P.s eager to hear evidence of clerical corruption submitted by the classis turned a deaf ear toward the call for any revolution in ecclesiastical polity.

By the time of the Armada, then, the real struggle for religion lay wholly in the parish and the pulpit. Some men turned toward the lure of separatism.

[5] As resisters to Wolsey's amicable loan made clear in 1525, and the plotters against Cranmer did in 1543, in the Prebendaries' Plot.

Others spent themselves in the hopeless but brilliant campaign of the Marprelate tracts, the groaning labor of the Millenary Petition (1603), the Hampton Court Conference (1604), and lucid pamphlets of counsel such as Stephen Edgerton's *Advice Tending Toward Reformation*. But Commons' bills in 1604 to provide for a learned and godly ministry drew the taunt that "religion was no business" of that house. They also provoked Bancroft to issue canons designed to determine whether the Puritans were "either joined with them or severed from them." Some Puritans would not remain in England under such terms. They found the road to Amsterdam, Leyden, and America. Others stayed, in disillusion and discomfort, never again to face the crown as a coherent, radical party.[6]

Preaching Under the Law

As it happened, Archbishop Grindal's ill-fated defense of certain spiritual exercises against Elizabethan repression had been a step on the right road. Grindal had himself painfully gathered patristic and scriptural sources on the role of prophets and prophesying.[7] He knew that serious laymen demanded liberty of preaching. Where the discipline of the Word was not heard, sacraments were not rightly administered. Dean Hutton of York had abhorred the exercises, but had shrewdly said the matter extended beyond "a cap and a surplice" to "bishops, archbishops, and cathedral churches." Not that he thought all Puritans were presbyterians. But he did think that liberty of preaching would come to that.

And it was true that in the idea of liberty of preaching, other facets of Puritan thought stood clarified. For the sermon was the vehicle of Biblicism and hostility to the old liturgies and rites. As the 1571 Settlement hardened, what had before been advocacy turned into reproach. Puritan sermons were a barrier to enforcement and a cry for change. The struggle for liberty of preaching and control of the pulpit had after all the potential to do what political approaches had not done: change the Prayer Book or revolutionize the structure of the Church, de facto if not de jure.[8]

---

[6] Subscription to the 1604 Canons was required. Estimates of deprivation vary from about 300 (Usher) to about ninety (Collinson).

[7] His notes bore the heading *quod prophetia sit retinenda*—"that prophesying might be allowed."

[8] Paul Seaver, *The Puritan Lectureships: The Politics of Religious Dissent, 1560–1662* (Stanford, Calif.: Stanford University Press, 1970), is fundamental. On aristocratic patronage, see C. M. Cross, "Noble Patronage in the Elizabethan Church," *Historical Journal* (1960), III, pp. 1–16, and the biographical studies already cited. The most valuable studies of patronage in this context, however, are in W. K. Jordan, *Philanthropy in England, 1480–1660* (New York: Russell Sage Foundation, 1959); *The Charities of London* (New York: Russell Sage Foundation, 1960); *The Charities of Rural England* (New York: Russell Sage Foundation, 1961).

Many Puritans became involved in complex campaigns based on their understanding of the relationships between the functions of patronage and the economics of the Church. Their knowledge was nothing occult; these things were as well known to their Elizabethan and Stuart enemies. But the advantage the Puritans took of certain structural weaknesses in the Church offered a lesson that only Laud and his allies in the policy of "thorough"[9] learned by heart. The leakage of ecclesiastical resources into lay hands had weakened unity and discipline. Pluralism, nonresidence, clerical poverty, and the associated problems of learning and the sufficiency of ministers constituted the Trojan Horse in the war the Puritans waged against Troy's redoubts.

The lack of patronage and inadequate incomes had bedeviled generations of eager priests and parsons. Where patronage had been used for such ends as were inimical to good ministry by incumbents who resided and exercised their cure of souls, advowsons could become, in the hands of Puritans, instruments for reformation. Where direct control over nominations was lacking, however, the institutional arrangement known as the lectureship was more basic. The laity could hire a Puritan to preach in churches not in use for regular services. They would give laymen control over the sort of sermons they heard. They could choose the lecturer and pay his stipend. They could dismiss him. The bishops' only effective answer would lie in their power to refuse licenses to the unbeneficed preachers. The lectureship was an ad hoc institution more fateful for the future than the presbyterian classis, more respectable than the Marprelate press, and more sinuous than even the greatest legislation. Lawyers, ministers, cobblers, and merchants did pool their funds to purchase outright impropriated livings in the 1620s. But the lectureship became the enduring success of popular Puritanism.

Paul Seaver's study of the London lectureship rightly contrasts the situation in the capital and the countryside. London's livings were 70 percent in the hands of crown and Church, while elsewhere perhaps 80 percent of parish benefices were in the gift of laymen. Hence the opportunity for direct Puritan patronage was small in London and great beyond the metropolis. The struggle for the souls of men in the city was won by the lectureship, which also thrived elsewhere. But in rural England and most provincial towns, direct Puritan control of advowsons was the prize sought. Impropriations and lecturers thus helped Puritans to realize article nineteen of the famous Thirty-Nine: "The visible Church of Christ is a congregation of faithful men, in which the pure word of God is preached. . . ." Most bishops bent their efforts to realize the royal dictum that "it is good for the Church to have few preachers."[1] William

---

[9] This policy, associated with Laud and Strafford, originally described the rigor of Irish administration; it later came to mean strong, efficient order and rule in state and church.

[1] The words were Elizabeth's.

Laud's later complaint that Puritans elevated the pulpit above the altar drew its strength from a widespread fear that too much preaching was a danger to calm and unity. This was so because the majority of Puritans were willing to take half a loaf. They supported preaching, even without the discipline. To most believers the lecturers (and their own nominees in benefices) promised help in living in the social setting in which they found themselves. Life in the visible church mattered to ordinary men more than some future sectarian paradise.

Lecturers rarely refused a benefice when one was offered. For them, as for the hierarchy, the parish was the center of religious life. Where authority prevented a Puritan parochial life in the ordinary sense, however, recruiting and financing an alternative ministry based in the parish seemed more promising than personal "gadding."

In all of this, formal theology played only a small part. Experience had made central the relationship of preacher and congregation, and shown also the necessity of invading traditional rights of property. Thus Puritanism in practice meant economic action. The revival of parliamentary Puritanism in the 1640 Parliament is itself the best evidence for thinking that effective sanctions against the hierarchy owed more to their material bases than to brilliant but premature revolutionary struggles. Even Bishop Bonner in Mary's reign had continued old lectures at St. Stephen's Westminster, insisting only that they be "scholastic."

Indeed, Edward VI's regime had made a closer knit of the fibers of religious reform and the lectureships at St. Paul's. The skein ran back through Thomas Cromwell's preaching appointees toward Colet. Apart from the special cathedral lecturers, the institution was, however, basically parochial in London and in the provinces. Where large urban populations existed, this common variety of sermon profoundly affected the religious life of town corporations. Christopher Hill has shown this with regard to one group of notably "parliamentarian" boroughs for the 1640s. Beyond his fifteen, it is noteworthy that 36.8 percent of England's 201 parliamentary boroughs had hosted at least one Puritan lectureship. The evidence indicates the radical origins of most such lectureships. It also supports the case that the towns of England were rapidly falling away from the Church of England in the two generations before 1625. The town preacher emerged as the dominant clerical figure, and he was answerable less to churchmen than to the urban elites.

Archbishop Laud's reaction to this danger was astute. The 1629 *Instructions* he gave to bishops had provided no preacher be allowed to preach unless he was willing to take on the full cure of souls. Laud also campaigned to assure that "no layman . . . have power to put in or put out any lecturer. . . ." His dissolution of the Feoffees for Impropriations[2] met directly the danger of lay efforts to control advowsons. But Laud found it harder to upset the lecturers. Their Puritanism was backed by medieval custom and the collective power of the town corporations. Indeed, the ability of government to strike at direct patronage of cures was an incentive to endow lectureships rather than subsidize impoverished benefices. The privy council could urge Bristol's mayor and aldermen to direct common purse funds from three preachers to the poor ministers in 1593. But about 1600, the assessment of £44 for parochial support —about £3 for each incumbent—compared badly with the £30 paid each lecturer. Sometimes the sources tell us of the Puritan origin of lectureships— for example, in Northampton in Henry Hasting's day.[3] We are more usually left with mere surmise from official opposition or the disposition of the lecturers themselves.

Leeds, Halifax, Bradford, Newcastle-upon-Tyne, Plymouth, Beverley, Hull, Dedham, Colchester, Yarmouth, Lynn, Ipswich, Norwich, and Sudbury began supporting radical lecturers early in Elizabeth's reign. How important this was politically we may perhaps infer from another set of facts: 70 percent of M.P.s from the seventy-four boroughs supporting preachers were for Parliament in the civil war; 80 percent of the borough members who resided in their elective place sided with the rebels. Whether radical preachers corrupted the corporations or merely expressed their disaffection is a pretty question. Laud and Charles believed Puritan preachers to be the root of their trouble in the cities. Perhaps! But had they thought urban alienation to be more widely based than its clerical elements, they might have used a weapon other than suppression of the preachers. Their repeat of Elizabethan tactics— and the continuity of hostility to lectureships needs stressing to dispel the myth of Elizabethan tolerance and Stuart despotism—only increased discontents in already disaffected areas.

This can best be seen in London. Surely in that great wen on the face of England neither patrons of lecturers nor the ruling corporation produced the City revolt of the 1640s. Yet lectureships, like London politics, expressed the sentiments of parishioners and local vestries. As early as 1581, when Bishop Aylmer ordered a sermon to be delivered in every parish twice a week, ostensibly to counterattack the seminary priest revival, the Corporation of the City told Aylmer that local enterprise had long since seen to it. Thirty-one lectureships existed before then;[4] and in the next decade 29 new ones were established. Seven more parishes followed suit in the 1590s. By 1600, over 100 sermons were

[2] A group of Puritans that used pooled capital to buy up impropriated livings when these came on the "commodity" market in London and elsewhere.

[3] The third Earl of Huntingdon.

[4] In thirty parishes plus the Temple.

given by lecturers in over 50 parishes. The peak came in 1630, when 54 more parishes had already founded preachers,[5] bringing the total to 116 parishes, nearly 90 percent of the urban total.

There is in this a tremendous irony. The primary motive of laymen providing sermons was to remedy deficiencies in preaching. This self-help was making the London ministry a preaching ministry. But the century-long rise in clerical standards was doing the same among incumbents, as this table shows:

Time	Percentage of graduate incumbents	Percentage licensed to preach
1560	47	44
1586	61	79
1601	75	88

In the 1630s, the nongraduate was all but gone. Of seventy-five clerks admitted to cures between 1627 and 1632, only thirteen were without degrees. Yet disaffection grew.

This should call to mind our argument that merely increasing the level of educational attainment would not in itself have solved the church's structural problems. Over 60 percent of London's incumbents were graduates in 1586; but 46 percent were also pluralists! Neither greater competence nor rigorous administration by Arminian prelates accomplished a reduction below 38 percent in 1640. Absenteeism among men of the Arminian persuasion merely combined the ideological problem of voluntarism and the structural problems of the Church's economic situation.

Vestries continued to study candidates and to hear trial sermons by prospective lecturers. Then, as sovereigns made sheriffs by pinpricks in the lord chancellors' lists, the common sovereigns of the parish made preachers. This made a mockery of the 1580 and 1604 requirements that tried to exclude radicals by requiring sacramental administration. Where the vestry also had the advowson, they could in effect make their favorite their minister as well. Famous Puritan preachers found cures in thirteen such parishes.

Most lecturers, however, did not have benefices. Not that it mattered economically. Popular lecturers were often "pluralists," especially where salaries were slender. Their stipends rose more rapidly than did the value of benefices over the whole period from 1500 to 1650. Lecture wages tripled from 1583 to 1660. Food prices rose only 70 percent. Increases in the value of benefices lagged well behind the rising cost of living throughout the Tudor and early Stuart periods. The average value of all London benefices was only £84 in the 1650s, up from about £19 in 1535.

[5] Nine by 1610; another twenty between 1611 and 1620; a further twenty-four by 1629.

Even the disparity in these figures is misleading, however. Thomas Crook enjoyed over £60 a year from two Elizabethan lectureships. Nathaniel Walker had £100 from his three in the 1620s. Donors were readily adding to the stipends, keeping them ahead of the inflation of living costs. Professor W. K. Jordan has shown how eagerly Londoners gave to establish lectureships even in far-off Cheshire, Lancashire, and Yorkshire, sometimes in their native county but often without that spur.[6] The efforts were especially intense in the 1580s and 1630s. The timing probably reflects the pressures resulting from the Puritan political failures of Elizabeth's reign and Laud's great challenge to dissidence.

Since at least 60 percent of the 700 known lecturers in London between 1560 and 1662 were Puritans, Laud's repression was not misdirected. Over 400 lecturers came to London from beyond the Home Counties. Some 23 percent were from London itself or the Middlesex suburbs. Fully a third of the total migrant element came in from Yorkshire, Essex, Norfolk, Kent, Leicestershire, Gloucestershire, and Northamptonshire—well known as Puritan seed-plots. That 23 percent originated in the metropolitan area, however, is most significant. In 1640 only 5 percent of the whole population of England and Wales lived there. Only 8 percent of London's lord mayors were native, 11 percent of liveried merchants, 4 percent of retailers, and 7 percent of the professional classes. London gave lecturers more plentifully than men in other callings. Moreover, only 42 of its 95 native lecturers ended their days in London livings.

It gave generously to the countryside. It was also parasitic. We know that 283 lecturers among the 538 whose last preferment is known (54 percent) held London livings at their death. As in political and economic life, the City had an influence on religious dissent out of proportion to even its great size. Sixty-five percent of known Puritan lecturers had their last preferment there. Their number included 82 percent graduates. This was a challenge to the literate Anglican clergy. Furthermore, such facts seem to support the hypothesis that university colleges helped make Puritanism more than a sectional eccentricity. Graduate Puritan lecturers were highly mobile. They went hither and yon in response to the felt needs of their congregations, and London was clearly the hub of their wheel's motion.

Success in the regular ministry was not easily had by Puritans. Only 24 percent of Puritan lecturers had obtained a benefice between 1560 and 1579, while 92 percent of known Church of England lecturers got benefices. During Whitgift's time, ironically, things got better; 75 percent of Puritan lecturers (67

---

[6] Yorkshire and Lancashire led the nation—London aside—in the percentage of charitable endowments for lectureships: Lancashire with 42 percent of all funds, Yorkshire with 31 percent. London merchants were the leading benefactors, on aggregate terms.

percent of Anglicans) had held other preferments before first taking a London lectureship. Less than 20 percent of the Anglicans lectured again, however, while over 50 percent of the Puritans had no benefice and remained in lectureships. After the accession of James I, nearly 75 percent of the Puritan lecturers eventually obtained benefices. Hence it is possible to argue that the scores of lecturers active in London at any one time were merely the tip of the iceberg.

During the long history of Elizabethan and Stuart efforts to root out the lecturers, Puritan prudence and imperfections in ecclesiastical machinery of discipline allowed them to survive. This was partly the result of connivance by royal officials who disliked the ticklish questions put to moderate Puritans. Lord Burghley had once denounced Whitgift's 1583 questions as "curiously penned, so full of branches . . . as I think the Inquisitors of Spain use not so many . . . to trap their prey." It proved impossible to dry up the demand for an evangelical ministry and even harder to destroy the supply. Qualified subscription to episcopal articles and occasional conformity helped intended victims escape even the furor in the wake of the Hampton Court Conference and the Gunpowder Plot of 1605.

The reasons for the failure of ecclesiastical discipline are many and complex. Suspensions of unbeneficed preachers licensed during their good behavior were equivalent to deprivation.[7] But preachers and beneficed Puritans profited from the situation of the Church in society. The archdeacons of a diocese had the most intimate contact with the Puritan clergy. Every archdeacon was judge and administrator, supervising inductions, taxes, inspections of clerical orders, preaching licenses, and the parochial work of sinners requiring punishment *pro salute animae*. It was also through the Puritan cleric that the Church supervised the laity. The local clergyman was expected to give information against suspected laymen; to supervise confessions; to administer penances; and to exhort parishioners to take part in public purgations and, above all, avoid excommunication. The clerk was both informer and court assistant, at least in theory. In practice, he was the shield obscuring the vision of archdeacons.

The Dedham classis in 1584 had admonished one Essex archdeacon to free ministers from his courts. It was better to have discipline of them in the congregation; still better to sever the bondage of laymen to such courts. Failing that, it was common in Essex parishes for the godly to appoint poor, illiterate men as juries to gather evidence for visitations. Their incompetence as church wardens gave eyes and ears that were blind and deaf. Inferior judges, already weighed down by the burdens of the Settlement, were thereby deprived of effective agents.

It was also the case that Puritanism grew vigorously just at the moment that

---

[7] "*Quamdiu se bène gesserint*" (during good behavior) was the controlling phrase in such licenses.

the hierarchy found itself preoccupied with Catholic recusancy. Further, juris-dictional competition was rife, and this enlarged the loopholes through which Puritans found their way to safety. Competition lowered the efficiency of the correction machinery, which was not in any case helped by the excessive publicity of procedures that were dependent on parochial good will in the first place. Neglect of duty was as helpful here as positive collusion, as the ruse of appointing illiterates as church wardens demonstrated. Finally, in the three-year intervals between episcopal visitations, the overburdened inferior officials were happy enough to practice salutary neglect. Nonconformists thus easily evaded discipline.

After 1610, few lecturers were cited until James' *Book of Sports* (1618) and the opening of the Thirty Years' War in Bohemia sharpened the temper of Puritan criticism. Then, a new campaign was fed by the vehement Puritan resistance to royal pacifism and the pursuit of a Spanish match for Prince Charles. This new repression climaxed in the *Directions* of 1622; these sup-pressed discussion in sermons of the doctrine of election and the royal preroga-tive! Only ten of seventy-five Puritans lecturing in London were cited, how-ever. And by 1628 there were at least 121 lecturers at work, of whom more than half were "godly."

These preachers, like the growing country party among the laity, railed against the foreign policy that put Rome and Hapsburg before the fate of European Protestantism. They preached mightily against fashionable Armin-ianism and its open resort to popish liturgy and ceremony. The reply of Charles I had been to promote Laud to Canterbury, in effect to spread the challenge from the City—that "receptacle of the Grandees of the Puritan Faction"—to the kingdom as a whole.

The issue was joined between unequal forces, however. Laud held a steward-ship that was sadly diminished materially and unpopular spiritually. The Puritans had widespread popular support; only one of the eighteen Puritan lecturers Laud cited among the City's seventy was effectively silenced. Most "acknowledged" their errors and so went free, usually unreformed, and eager to preach against the hated ceremonialism of the archbishop. When in 1640 Laud issued the first new canons since 1604, his campaign had manifestly failed to achieve the unity and conformity sought by crown ministers since Elizabeth's earliest days.

Indeed, as he launched his last campaign, Calybute Downing, vicar of Hackney, took a reading of London temperatures. He preached to the people outdoors, in the Artillery Garden, and there allowed how "for the defense of religion . . . it was lawful to take up arms against the king." The crown had failed to separate the preachers from their popular base. It had never been strong enough to attack wholesale the system of lay patronage of dissent.

Piecemeal efforts to do so had brought little more than the alienation of vestries, merchants, gentry, and nobility—men who saw in royal policy another manifestation of the fundamental challenge to property rights already evident in other ways.

Such actions were condemned even by the royalist peer Viscount Falkland, when in 1641 he accused the Laudian bishops of defiling the Church, advancing superstition, and sacrificing Protestantism overseas to vain ambitions. These, he warned, were actions "as unpolitic as ungodly." There were more preachers at work in 1640 than at any time since 1625, inciting to arms against a government that would neither preach rightly nor suffer to live in peace those who would. Had Laud lived to know this sentence of Lord Macauley he would have appreciated it, although the historian spoke it not of him but of the Puritans:

A government which, not content with repressing scandalous excesses, demands from its subjects fervent and austere piety, will soon discover that, while attempting to render an impossible service to virtue, it has in fact only promoted vice.

Chapter Ten
GOVERNMENT AND SOCIETY REVISITED

Your Lordship must remember that in the policy of this Common Wealth, we are not over-ready to add increase of power and countenance to such great personages as you are. And when in the country you dwell in you will need enter into a war with the inferiors therein, we think it both justice, equity and wisdom to take care that the weaker part be not put down by the mightier.

LORD BUCKHURST to Gilbert, earl of Shrewsbury, 1592

This letter from an Elizabethan councillor to one of the Catholic earls reveals that the peace of the realm was still being broken by magnates in 1592. In Nottinghamshire, the Talbots and Stanhopes had feuded for years before the privy council was alarmed enough to intervene; the intervention apparently came because the Talbot earls' religious loyalty was doubted. Yet even in 1592 the government was cautious. It preferred nourishing the gentry's power to making any frontal assault on greater aristocrats. And it hoped that a lengthening period of peace would generate habits conducive to order in the country. Operating through the courts was a surer method of dealing with the factious elements of society than was quickly spending the royal capital of coercion. So said Buckhurst openly, giving in his letter a valuable clue to the still unsettled state of the social order.

In 1640, it was evident that royal efforts to preserve order in the commonwealth had not succeeded. Social disturbance was inherent in the Puritan challenges to episcopal power and parochial discipline. The resistance of Lord Buckhurst's favored gentry to secular motifs of government made it impossible for Charles I to balance the power of the noble aristocrats with that of the squirearchy. The assumption that religion was a force making for order in society had been overthrown by the Reformation, which had created a new geography and politics of faith. The government gave no scope to sectarian fellowship. And the diversification of the economy that had taken place since 1520 had ruined some of the customary deference to landed men without yet perfecting new amalgams able to bind together civil elements and those somewhat wild and unruly. The realignment of government and society was unfinished.

Our chief object up to this point has been the isolation of aspects of the social body. Our purpose, however, has been dynamic rather than static. We have sought to show the complex material bases of the dominant political and social structures of the English countryside. And we have included institutions of religion because we do not suppose them to be exempt from the pressures of the corporal interests that link even matters of conscience and taste to the soil and the marketplace. It remains for us to look again at England's ruling classes, concentrating on that period in which her aristocracy achieved a new degree of articulation in politics, found its voice in Parliament and the executive, and refounded its power in the control and manipulation of regional and local office.

How elements of this reconstructed aristocracy used their aggregate power and position in the City and county to turn out the Stuart king Charles I belongs to another volume. But the story of how England's grandees came to repossess the power to challenge the crown brings this history full circle. It also requires that we set aside some generally misleading typological devices that segregate the various elements of the governing elites. Excessive searches for the origins of the civil war that began in 1641 have led to unbalanced assessments of the role of the gentry, the crisis of the aristocracy, the supposed collapse of the civil service under the Stuarts, and the triumph of bourgeois parliamentarians and Puritan lawyers. It has even been claimed that Oliver Cromwell's final victory over Charles I was akin to that of Copernicus over Ptolemy. If we turn aside from such grand themes, we stand a good chance of seeing the transition of power as it happened; not as the outcome of a simple historical dialectic but as the unforeseen and utterly unintended result of social changes the shape and nature of which are yet only partly known—and perhaps only partly knowable.

Crown and Aristocracy in the Reformation Era

The condition of government and society in Henry VI's day was one of uncertain balance. The lack of legitimate partisanship, of a lawful "party" of opposition, and the weakness of bureaucracy gave more scope to monarchs than Charles II was ever to enjoy in the Stuart Restoration. Yet our own analysis of the achievement of York and Tudor casts doubt on the image of "new monarchy" achieving peace among factious lords to whom the ways of the administrator and courtier were foreign. Kings and queens did radically alter the political atmosphere by their will and character; this was as true under Charles I as under Henry VIII. But between the time of Wolsey's ministry under the second Tudor and Laud's under the second Stuart, more had changed than the dynasty and the diversion of a churchman's gaze from Rome to Lambeth. The English political system had matured in the course of the revolt against Rome. Institutions had multiplied, as the government sought the means to do social work that was once done by the Church or had not previously been considered a proper concern of government. The means available to government had also increased, although not enough to fund both the works of war and those of peace in a dizzy time of inflation. And the long-term consolidation of power by the landed classes finally shaped a system of power relationships that was to survive for at least three more centuries.

The politicians who came to power under Edward VI were no soldier-gangsters contesting for the crown—such an image applies to a Shakespearean class of predators that is more literary than historical. Somerset and Northumberland were in fact career servants of the crown in the full tide of their maturity. Like Paget, Sadler, Peter, and Wriothesley,[1] they were neither young nor inexperienced men, but governors who in 1547 had served the crown an average of 16.7 years. The largest part of their fellow ministers, like those who had served Mary, Elizabeth, James I, and Charles, were of gentry origins. They had married women of gentry families and settled into the landed elite among the greater gentry or the nobility newly minted in reward for habitual loyalty.[2]

It was in the chaotic conditions of the mid-Tudor crisis that the service aristocracy, laboriously built on the ruins of the feuding magnates, proved itself in government. Indeed, the pattern of power being gained in exchange for service was more a mutation of familiar stock than a new creation. Just as Henry I and Edward III had built their monarchies in part on the shifting sand of noble loyalty, Tudor and Stuart rulers made it their practice to "butter the rooks' nest"—to tie to the interest of the dynasty and to the royal Supremacy those masters of practices who constituted the widened aristocracy of land and office. That there was little major change in the structure of royal politics between 1520 and 1640 we can best see by looking more closely at some salient facts about the English aristocracy of that period.

England was governed at the center by the sovereign and a council of grandees composed of crown servants drawn from the ranks of the titled nobility, the gentry, and the professional classes—chiefly lawyers and experts in finance. The displacement of the "old peerage," which was so marked a feature of government in the fifteenth century, quickened pace in the sixteenth. In 1547, there were only twenty-two families whose titles antedated 1509, only nine of

---

[1] Each was a secretary of state under Henry VIII.

[2] See the studies by Jordan, *Edward VI*; Emmison, *Tudor Secretary*; and Slavin, *Politics and Profit*. But the best work on the emergent Reformation political aristocracy is Wallace MacCaffrey, "England: The Crown and the New Aristocracy, 1540–1600," *Past and Present* (1965), No. 30, pp. 52–64; and L. Stone's great book, *The Crisis of the Aristocracy, 1558–1641* (Oxford: Clarendon Press, 1965). See also Helen Miller, "Subsidy Assessments of the Peerage in the Sixteenth Century," *BIHR* (1955), pp. 15–34.

which were truly ancient. The only one of that nine who enjoyed a measure of power under Edward VI was Henry Fitzalan, the earl of Arundel.[3] The politically important nobility of the crisis period had all been raised to their titles for service in one of Henry VIII's great crises—the divorce, the pilgrimage, or the years of the great wars. They were a majority of the lords, representing some thirty-five titles in all. Even if we add the fifteenth-century creations to the old peerage, this group of twenty-two families with twenty-six peers was wholly banned from power, chiefly because of a lack of ability and because of distrust of their religious conservatism. Only Arundel was in the circle of executors or assistants designated in Henry VIII's will. Where were Bohan and Mowbray, to say nothing of Talbot, Clifford, Neville, Scrope, Zouche, Latimer, Ogle, de la Warr, and Abergavenny? Not in the Council. Only four old peers were admitted in Edward's reign.

The old peerage was neither employed at the center of government nor trusted with power. Nor did its members marry with the politically active new peers; only four such matches were concluded, along with five alliances with gentry and one tie to London merchant capital. For the most part, the old peers became inbred to an increasing degree, their insularity increased by a lack of education at the universities. Only Arundel, Clinton, and Grey attended Cambridge or Oxford, in sharp contrast with the new peers who made their way upward by combining, in varying proportions, humanistic education, legal training, and administrative service.[4] Only seven of the old peers were intransigently Catholic in religion, but only five others were eager Protestants. The contempt in which the old peers were held by their newly powerful compeers shows best in the way they were neglected when it came to the disposition of rewards. The total value of their estates in 1553 was about £56,000, up by only 2.3 percent from 1547, according to Professor W. K. Jordan's calculations.

The "Henrician" peers who were raised in the political struggles and were crafty enough to survive them attained the bounty of the crown. Of the thirty-one peerage families that we may properly call Henrician, the ten raised before the divorce crisis gained least in wealth or power. The heirs of what was historically another age, they were not impressive in ability, were excluded from authority in Henry's will, were kept out of the Council, and were not enriched greatly,[5] receiving altogether less than £5,000 in crown lands, with one family —the Wentworths—accounting for £3,884. Contrasted with that ten, the dozen families that rose with the Reformation movement supplied the execu-

---

[3] The twelfth of the line (1511–81).

[4] For example, of the Tudor secretaries of state, only Cromwell and Sadler were not university men; Pace, Paget, Petre, Wriothesley, the Cecils, Smith, and the Elizabethans all were.

[5] Conyers, Somerset, Manners, Mounteagle, Morley, Sandys, Vaux, Bray, Wentworth, and Windsor.

tive board that had been charged in Henry's will. They came to the peerage directly from gentry ranks. Their careers were built on Rome's ruin, and they were fittingly enriched with monastic lands as well as with the profits of office. These Henricians and the even fresher Edwardian peers supplied the center of gravity for Edwardian and Elizabethan politics and became, in the persons of their heirs, the main contestants for power in early Stuart England. The great political dynasties of early modern English history were not Elizabethan creations for the most part.[6]

Russell, Parr, Dudley, Seymour, Paulet, Wriothesley, along with the revived Howards and the Cecils, Herberts, Pagets, Riches, and Thynnes—these were the families, made in the Reformation upheavals, whose future was to give to modern London streets and squares names associated with great country palaces: Bedford, Northampton, Leicester, Hertford, Southampton, Salisbury, Pembroke, Holland, Bath, and Norfolk. Both the staunchly Protestant Herberts and the conservative Wriothesleys tasted power, shared it, and fought to preserve their grasp of it. They also shared gentry roots and did not stint in their efforts to maintain ties with the large class of wealthy, able gentry. They sought education eagerly, often for themselves and always for their sons. The majority became politically Protestant in the mid-Tudor era and remained ardently so thereafter.

They had not been greatly enriched by the Henrician distributions of Church wealth, at least not before the last phase of grants and gifts—in the war years 1542–7. But under Edward VI, they carved vast fortunes to support their new dignities. They did this nominally at the king's will, but in fact because they controlled the levers of power. In fewer than seven years, the newer nobility absorbed about £166,000 in crown lands by gift, with £159,000 going to the leading dozen of the junta. Almost 40 percent of the crown gifts were given to them. The crown also sold them parcels of abbey and chantry lands at terms of purchase of less than 5 percent, with the median value of transactions being over £700. In return for the nearly £425,000 consequently paid in, the members of this small group had by 1558 augmented their estates by an amount equal to 6 percent of the value of all lands held by nobles. Almost 67 percent of all grants were made to alleviate the political crises of 1549 and 1553; over £290,000 changed hands in the latter year alone.

Yet there is a grave danger in giving undue emphasis to the new nobility in any analysis of the burgeoning aristocracy of land and office. During the late Henrician and Edwardian years, crown lands were also purchased by 688 men below noble rank. Seventy-seven of these men were courtiers or crown servants in intermediate offices; they bought nearly 20 percent of all alienated

---

[6] The Cecil elevation to the peerage was the greatest exception.

crown lands. Within their ranks, nineteen councillors, executors, and administrators below the grandee level got 7 percent of the total. Another forty-eight men, including judges, ambassadors, department heads, and other chief agents at the center, gained nearly 11 percent of the total. The peers got 40 percent of all outright gifts of land. They were not, however, so dominant in *purchases* of landed property in England and Wales. Land purchase by new and old nobility was less substantial than that by gentry servants of the crown. When we include the other elements in the total of 688 known purchasers, gentry who were not directly court-connected obtained over 50 percent of all crown lands alienated in the Henrician and Edwardian periods. Brokers, merchants, and yeomen bought about 20 percent of this total.

The conclusion seemingly warranted by such data is that the tendency to concentrate wealth in gentry hands, already so marked in the 1520s, was accelerated by the Reformation. Moreover, not quite 3 percent of all manorial wealth changed hands during this time. Any effort to see in this spate of alienation the emergence of a wholly new landed elite or a narrowing rather than a broadening of the apex of the pyramid of wealth and power would be seriously misleading. In London, Kent, Yorkshire, Wiltshire, Northamptonshire, Gloucestershire, and Somerset, which were the regions most affected, there was little social or economic dislocation, much less a displacement of one ruling class by another. Long-term movements, already two centuries old, were confirmed. Over 67 percent of all new alienations went to men who were already lords of at least one manor. And about 50 percent of the purchasers resided in the county or shire in which they added lands to their estates. London capital was involved in many large transactions, but this fact was less evidence of undue bourgeois movement out to the land than of London's dominance of liquid and speculative finance.

In retrospect, the Edwardian lands that changed hands were worth nearly £900,000 in capital value—an amount evenly divided between gifts and sales. Gifts (and some sales) to favored recipients topped off the accumulation of power by the newer nobility. But sales consolidated the even greater local aggregate influence of the gentry and the established urban elites. Over 58 percent of all outright grants by gift went to the grandees and important crown servants. There was a modest amount given to sustain old peerages, but this was chiefly a tactic used by the duke of Northumberland to bolster his power. The inner ring of politicians, powerful gentry supporters in the counties, and senior bureaucrats formed the hard core of the major beneficiaries of largesse. But the lesser gentry bought over 40 percent of the total amount alienated by the crown; the success of this still land-hungry class was simply a reciprocal function of the great responsibility and authority given to it by government in the whole period of this study. The lesser gentry were able to buy their continued place in the sun, whereas others had merely to petition for gifts. The merchant classes had strikingly less success; they accounted for only 2.6 percent of all gifts and 20 percent of purchases.

A few men rose strikingly beyond their contemporaries, often gaining groups of manors in huge combinations, as this list clearly shows:

Northumberland	88
Somerset	63
Pembroke	51
Admiral Seymour	48
Paulet	28
Russell	15
Clinton	13

But the chief consequence of these gains was not, perhaps, the spectacular shift in power within the nobility, or even the constant consolidation of gentry wealth, but the dispersal of crown lands.

This dispersal reflected the weakness of a regime beset by recurrent political crises. By buying loyalties in such an expensive way, Edward's agents were paying the current costs of government out of capital, a policy that had been practiced by Lancaster, reversed by York, and temporarily suspended by the Tudors. This policy meant a diminution in the reality of crown power absolutely; particularly in light of the advances made by the classes with which English rulers shared power, the decline was more striking. The meaning of the facts is hard to escape. Despite the great strides taken by reforming kings and ministers between 1460 and 1540, Tudor governments had not effectively solved the problem of meeting the costs of expanding government on a regular basis. A poverty no less stark than that facing Henry VI confronted Elizabeth I and her Stuart successors. The increasing power of government was not the achievement of an absolute monarchy but the result of effective cooperation between the sovereign and the elites of land, office, and trade. The personal rule of Charles I testified to this truth when the great officers of state and their subordinates could not supply the means to effect a policy that was unsupported by large elements of the governing classes.

The brutal facts of the quest for power that had thrust into aristocratic hands 64.86 percent of all disposed crown lands had debased the coin of royal strength. The £832,000 alienated between about 1547 and 1553 constituted nearly 75 percent of the expropriated wealth of the monasteries and equaled the value of all chantry lands. In the secular polity, as in the ecclesiastical, authority and power kept pace with material resources. In a society still rooted in the soil, perhaps 10 percent of all landed wealth had changed hands rapidly. The crown's fiscal and political weakness could not help but have a profoundly disturbing impact on the bonds that linked to it folks in the dozen shires and counties most deeply involved in the process.[7]

The Elizabethan Political Scene

To look at the Elizabethan political scene is to see the proof of our proposition about the transition of power. The new ideology of Protestantism tied the aristocratic classes to the policy of the Supremacy and its material fruits. But the Reformation itself did not derive from definitions in theology. And it took more than religious politics to validate the tradition of deference to the sovereign. Ephemeral forms of association jostled with more lasting forms (bonds of association and Parliaments) to focus action and belief on the area where the crown's sole power and prerogative met the collective strength of the politically articulate. The Tudor notion of obedience was strong but not enough so that it hid the growing independence of an aristocracy finding its voice with the help of the crown. The Edwardian and Marian crises, coupled with Elizabeth's first dozen years, made credible the idea of a conscious sharing of power between crown and aristocracy. "Party" leaders arose: William Cecil and the earl of Leicester in the 1560s, Sir Robert Cecil and the earl of Essex in the 1590s. They held influence in the Council, attracted followers at court, and joined men together in parliamentary interests.[8]

A wider, although uncertain, area of free discussion had been shaped by events between 1529 and 1570. The queen, in doctrine never an autocrat, was in practice the focal point of a changing political system. Public pressures, channeled from local elites to their conciliar and parliamentary brethren, often transgressed the unspoken boundaries of the past era. This frequently drove Elizabeth and the Stuarts to declare what they would not share: marriage, foreign policy, and religious change. But the increasingly articulate elites steadily pushed back such frontiers, turning this way and that and stopping short of transforming the art of intrigue into a naked contest for power. Ironically, factions that had threatened to disrupt the Council in the 1560s

[7] Devon, Dorset, Essex, Gloucester, Hampshire, Kent, Lincoln, Norfolk, Somerset, Warwick, Wiltshire, and York.

[8] On the power of the Council, factions, and the "political scene" *c.* 1560–1640, see Sir J. E. Neale, "The Elizabethan Political Scene," *Proceedings of the British Academy* (1948), XXXIV, pp. 97–117; W. MacCaffrey, "Elizabethan Politics, the First Decade," *Past and Present* (1963), No. 24, pp. 24–42, "Talbot and Stanhope: An Episode in Elizabethan Politics," *BIHR* (1960), XXXIII, pp. 73–85; W. MacCaffrey, "Place and Patronage in Elizabethan Politics," in *Government and Society*, pp. 95–126; A. J. Slavin, "A Sixteenth Century Struggle for Property and Profit," *BIHR* (1965), XXXVIII pp. 31–47; and A. G. B. Smith, "Portrait of an Elizabethan: Sir Michael Hicks," *History Today* (1964), XIV, pp. 716–25.

were stilled until the 1590s, but other factions arose that were of more permanent significance. We have seen one fruit of this development in the parliamentary politics of the Puritans. More important perhaps were the "succession" politics that flowed from Elizabeth's evident lack of dynastic ambition.

The political scene for a very long time after 1570 had been framed by three things: the dimensions of the mid-Tudor crises; the regiment of childless women; and the revolution in the nature of politics that both helped to bring about. The Yorkist and early Tudor achievements of security abroad and stability at home had vanished in the 1530s. Public order and the security of private property were often more ambitions than achievements. The crown seemed again unable to force a balance between private power and public need. Henry VIII had perhaps not intended to weaken the crown in his drive to free England of Roman authority. However, with Cromwell's help he had made government a revolutionary machine. The crown no longer sought to conserve the society of its ancestors; it now tried to reshape the society in which it ruled. This broke the cake of political custom, and nowhere more certainly than in religious reformation. The center of political gravity thus altered visibly: the crown in Parliament became more important than the crown acting alone. The community of the realm had always judged great matters. It now seemed to claim the right to do so, if not all at once before 1603, certainly by degrees *before* 1640.

The Council proved less and less able to bridge the gap between crown and community. This is the meaning we ought to give to the winning of initiative in policy by the Commons. Between opinion-mongering aristocrats in the provinces and their ideological cousins in the Council, there ran increasingly the notion that the representative function was better left to the "country" assembled at Westminster than to the Court and Council. Every dispute dividing the Protestant elites and the crown's intimate agents tore at the fabric of the old system. Great matters of state and the petty interests of men were too closely linked to allow convenient separation. A national politics dominated by the aristocracy was emerging alongside the politics of personal monarchy.

The chief manifestation of the old system lay in the inner workings of the politics of favorites and interests. Sir John Neale has shown that a mere understanding of the administrative framework misleads to a degree. Government had trouble compensating its agents for their work, especially since salaries were drowned in the rising tide of inflation. Payments in the form of fees and gratuities had become as fixed as salaries. And this situation ensured that open bribery would compete with subtler inducements, in every contest for land, office, or privilege. It was common knowledge that the cost of government to a suitor varied according to his conscience—depending on whether an officeholder aspired to Heaven, Hell, or Purgatory! The facts promoted the value of even the most local stewardship. And this indisputably aided monarchs who were trying to preserve personal power.

The force of material gain moved the social wheels. In fact, government came to groan under the weight of unofficial imposts and the profits they created at the expense of the governed. Where a word from king or queen made a career and a fortune, the stuff of politics, petty as it was, gave to the sovereign a measure of control that was not to be sniffed at. Wherever there were lands to lease or sell, offices to fill, elections to be contested, patents to be had, licenses and monopolies to seek—there the crown in its majesty could ally the elites to its own interests and balance rival factions. "A suit is well-ended where a man is well-friended" was the maxim of the age. Within the inner ring of councillors and among the most obscure placemen in admiralty ports, this maxim held force. Spenser said as much, in *Mother Hubbard's Tale*:

Full little knowest thou that hast not tried
What Hell it is in suing long to abide;
To lose good days that might be better spent;
To waste long nights in pensive discontent.

Government and society felt patronage's refreshing rain. No politician was too great to be another's suitor. Offices were bought and sold. That is why Wyatt could enlist men in rebellion to forestall their loss of offices to Spaniards. And that is also why ordinary country men, recalling the age of James I's darlings, asked whether justice could prevail in a regime of favorites. Here was a dilemma for sovereignty. To stop the flow of favors would be to stop government itself. How to control it was therefore the problem. The well-advised policy of the crown was to spread patronage widely, to use it to avoid overmighty men at Court or in Council. In the absence of both a fully professional civil service and the means to pay for one, controlled factions of suitors played a vital political role. Faction necessarily focused on the queen or king, and it seemed inescapable that patronage in its disposition affected policy in its formation. Leicester's men were the proponents of intervention in the Netherlands. Essex's followers feared his Irish expedition would put him out of sight and hinder their suits. The earl himself said he was not so poor a grammarian as to think he could, like a substantive, stand alone. His more than 20,000 followers suffered from his failure to heed his own wisdom and joined his rebellion in 1601 out of desperation. From the point of view of an aristocratic faction leader, Holland and Ireland could be keys to a little kingdom.

Since controlling access to the ruler was a chief stratagem, the court battles to win places in the privy chamber were not the vain exercises that they might appear to have been. Packing the chamber in James I's time was as great a coup as packing a Parliament in Newcastle's day, or the sheriff's list in the days of Henry VI's duke of Suffolk. The role of politics in a system partly under a personal monarchy and partly under a parliamentary aristocracy was to focus ambition at the source of power. The task facing the sovereign was to keep factions in balance and to minimize corruption. Elizabeth failed to do either in the last decade of her reign. She preferred the heirs (which were often the sons) of old councillors, often regardless of their ability. Perhaps familiar faces lessened the shock of aging by minimizing the appearance of change at Court and Council. Neither birth nor merit dominated, and the able Sir Robert Cecil was seconded in rank by less gifted careerists of Charles Howard's stripe: a competent soldier, a shrewd pluralist officeholder, a newly minted Elizabethan earl, and an increasingly corrupt administrator of the navy. What Elizabeth failed to check in Cecil, James utterly failed to do with regard to Carr and Villiers.[9]

The danger of vicious factional rule that had so plagued Henry VI's reign had not been relegated to the back room of history. Nor had the competed-for spoils decreased in attractiveness. The effort to tie the elite to the crown as a pacific governing class grew along with the prizes to be distributed. In 1587, Lord Burghley drew up for Elizabeth a list of more than 800 rich landowners and another list consisting of about 1,500 magistrates in England and Wales. This combined aristocracy of fewer than 2,500 men represented political society, according to Burghley. He knew most of those on both lists. He also knew how small a part of the whole the five dozen or more peers were. National and local politics had to be cemented from such lists, or from a larger one that included younger sons of little patrimony blessed with education and ambition. Few on either list would otherwise have caught a sovereign's eye. Fewer still were ideologues. Most of them wanted neither great dangers nor truly great rewards. Almost without exception they wanted land, office, and honors.

We have already seen how the demand for land was met. Office had expanded with economic change and the crown's invasion of functions that were once private. There had arisen a horde of minor fiscal, judicial, administrative, and executive posts in the central government, perhaps in obedience to Parkinson's law.[1] Many were sinecures or entailed little work. At local levels and in

---

[9] See David Willson's account of the machinations of Jacobean favorites, in *James VI and I* (Oxford: Oxford University Press, 1967); and Joel Hurstfield, "Political Corruption in Modern England," *History* (1967), XLII, pp. 16–34; and "Corruption and Reform under Edward VI and Mary," *EHR*, LXXVIII, pp. 25–51.

[1] C. N. Parkinson, *Parkinson's Law, The Pursuit of Progress* (London: J. Murray, 1958). The "law" states the hypothesis that bureaucracies have inherent capacities for self-expansion.

regional government centers, men who had been placed in office competed for the profits of politics. The Court itself had 1,000 persons employed early in James I's regime. There could not have been fewer than 2,000 gentlemen-placemen at any time in Elizabeth's reign, including those in the nearly 200 top posts in the central government. Pushing competition among the men on Burghley's lists was the natural condition.

Great ministers of Cecil's loyalty used their vast powers to advance good men—or at least such as had gratitude—to bishoprics, clerkships, or a share in some monopoly privilege. Hundreds of offices were worth at least £50 a year, a sum that easily matched the income of a lesser county gentleman of the squirearchy. Some annuities were worth far more than their face value. This was true of Sir George Howard's. He sold *half* of an office worth £200 officially for £500 cash and £600 in canceled debts. Minor posts in royal parks, chases, castles, and forests often brought in small fortunes, when they were carefully exploited. We know of at least one Elizabethan stewardship valued at £4 in salary but worth nearly 500 marks in fees, bribes, and "sweeteners." There lay the danger. Inadequately supervised, the system encouraged reckless competition and ruthless exploitation.

Money, Favorites, Patriots: The Politics of Poverty

The problems given scope by this system of fee and favor were especially evident under the first two Stuarts. This was not because their regimes were necessarily more corrupt, but because James especially lacked Elizabeth's political talent for compromise as well as the insulating shield of her virginal pose. James was alternately bookish and wildly sensual and addicted to hunting. His son Charles had a definite talent for the details of administration but none for politics. Neither could check the system of fee and favor by which their government worked.[2]

Indeed, James aggravated the difficulties. Wanting to be good to the Church, he forgot its poverty in his own necessity and constantly called on clergymen for loans and benevolence, while using its remaining endowment for patronage. Wanting to reform government on the civil side, he constantly entrusted

---

[2] Stone and Willson are relevant here. But by far the most important work is G. Aylmer's *The King's Servants* (London: Routledge & Kegan Paul, 1961); seconded by M. Prestwich, *Cranfield: Politics and Profit under James I* (Oxford: Clarendon Press, 1966) and R. H. Tawney, *Business and Politics under James I* (Cambridge: Cambridge University Press, 1958). On the revenue questions, see the works of F. C. Dietz already cited, as well as R. Ashton, *The Crown and the Money Market* (Oxford: Clarendon Press, 1960); on the sale of titles, see L. Stone, "The Inflation of Honors, 1558–1641," *Past and Present* (1958), No. 14, pp. 45–70; Joel Hurstfield, *The Queen's Wards* (London: Jonathan Cape, 1958).

high office and the control of patronage to unworthy favorites. His lofty motives gave way before his infatuation with Robert Carr and George Villiers. The country was shocked by repeated tales of debauchery. It was even more troubled by the luxuriant growth of corruption among officeholders and the dispensers of the prerogative. Discussion in and out of Parliament often focused on the causes of scandal: the king's role in shielding the killers of a favorite's mistress in the famed Overbury case; the campaign to force the great Coke from the judiciary; the failure to give support to the Protestants in the Rhineland; and the bribery case against Lord Bacon. But in one way or another these incidents were closely connected with the financial plight of the crown or the degree to which a regime of favorites deepened the burden.[3]

The powerful landed classes gaped at the financial crisis. Lord Dorset, James' first treasurer, had increased the nonparliamentary revenue from £247,000 in 1603 to £366,000 in 1608. But expenditures in 1603 soared to £544,000, leaving a deficit of £178,000. Meanwhile, borrowing at 10 percent, James continued heedlessly to give away resources not really his. In 1608, the debt stood at £597,337. Salisbury (Sir Robert Cecil) paid off some notes during his stint at the treasury by raising revenues. James did not materially reduce expenditure, however. Instead, he sold lands for a total of £426,151. He also made resort to impositions on trade, which proved upsetting to commerce and merchants. Salisbury in 1610 reported ordinary revenue at £460,000 per annum. The debt was down to £160,000, but outlays had risen to £600,000! He advised the king to seek a remedy in Parliament by proposing to the Commons "the Great Contract." In return for a permanent annual revenue of £200,000, James would abandon certain feudal rights, especially the much-hated wardship and purveyance for the household, and would also guarantee land titles to purchasers. Agreement, however, proved impossible to obtain, for both king and Commons raised their demands.

Salisbury's death in 1612 and the previous failure of the contract gave control to Carr and a knot of nobles. There were sharp contests between the followers of Carr and the Howards on one side, and the so-called patriots on the other, headed by the earl of Pembroke, the archbishop of Canterbury, and Ellesmere, the Lord Chancellor. But the crown grew poorer as Carr waxed rich. By 1614, the debt stood at £680,000. The spending departments were nearly £500,000 in arrears in payments. Trade was in decline. Carr was rumored to have made £90,000 by patronage manipulations in 1612, out of which he allegedly offered James a loan of £22,000 to help buy necessaries! The fall of Carr brought no relief. In 1617, ordinary revenue nearly balanced expenditure for government. But a deficit of £137,000 was built out of Christmas revels—a

---

[3] Fontenay, a contemporary, observed James' three great failings: an inability to estimate his poverty; an indiscreet love for favorites; laziness and indifference in affairs.

trip to Scotland; gifts to the rising star, George Villiers; and spending to garnish the hunting lodge at Theobalds.

Not even the calling of the great London financier Lionel Cranfield to the treasury helped. Before his rise to the earldom of Middlesex in royal service, Cranfield had made a fortune in trade, banking, exchange manipulations, offices, and monopolies. Having catered to the needs of aristocrats through the luxury trade, he knew the values of the jewels "which scarce Caligula wore on his birthday" but James showered on Buckingham. James judged Cranfield as he did merchants—as men who did not scruple to make fortunes out of public losses. Yet no government since Edward I's time had been able to disregard the tycoons of the City. This was true not because of any overdrawn opposition of commercial men to royal policy. Indeed, financial distrust did not imply political hostility. What mattered was that the crown and the money markets needed each other. And this had never been truer than in those early seventeenth-century decades, when the opportunities for colonialization, speculation, and manipulation of trade grew with the embarrassment of the government's treasury.

Cranfield knew this from his personal experiences. He had enjoyed profiteering from cloth-export patents, crown land sales, and a monopoly on the retailing of certain wines. He had held shares in the 1604 lease on the Great Farm of the Customs, an arrangement by which a distressed government sold to business syndicates the right to collect royal customs. In exchange for these shares, James had received advance capital payments and certain fixed annual rents. Yet no element of bureaucratic corruption was more detrimental than this arrangement. It linked favorites (as patrons) to officeholders and capitalists in a mutual exploitation of fees and favors. Between the first lease (1604) and the expiration of the third (1624), profits rose steadily, as City men borrowed at lower rates than they gave in turn to the crown. The Dorset and Salisbury reforms were in part aimed at this system as well as at the land sales that liquidated future capital for present needs. When Cranfield became Surveyor-General of the Customs in 1613, he was also a partner in the various farms. He was not above maintaining conflicting interests in his rapid rise to higher office.[4]

The problem was as much political as fiscal, centering as it did in the monarch's integration of court politics with the civil service. Cranfield's description of this system as "the manor of England" properly stressed the royal view that the ordinary revenue of the crown was in principle an enlarged version of private-estate management. If that segment of the aristocracy

[4] By 1616, he was Master of Requests; by 1618, Master of the Great Wardrobes; by 1619, Master of the Court of Wards and Chief Navy Commissioner; by 1620, privy councillor; by 1627, Baron Cranfield and Lord Treasurer.

identified by Lawrence Stone as suffering a crisis between 1558 and 1640 could live by mortgages, why not the king?

Taxation was not the real test of a Stuart finance minister any more than it had been for Wolsey or Cromwell. The real test was the ability to manage standing taxes and land revenues so as to avoid entirely the recourse to parliamentary grants. The crown's failure to realize that goal helps in large measure to explain the grave conflicts over finances in the early Stuart era. Not just the imperfection of the machinery of government was to blame. There was an area of procedural uncertainty, of course; but this was magnified, at least in official eyes, by the occasional nature of the financial need, and by resentment on both sides. Ministers found the necessity of revising their theory frustrating, especially when demands for economical measures were ignored by their master. And the Commons too often acted with its heart in its pocket. The Great Contract had been a vain attempt to remove from the system this stress.

Elizabeth had grasped that the crown's financial system was in effect not an estate but a trust fund beset by public claims. However, James I was a learned fool in finance. He was the victim of the system he inherited from Gloriana, as well as of economic and social movements beyond his control. Inflation had raised prices by about 50 percent between 1603 and 1614. Yet even as late as 1620, the swollen expenses of state business were less at fault than heedless extravagance and display. Cranfield reminded James that Elizabeth had avoided giving treasure in profusion. She had preferred instead expensive sentiments: to wit, that she would rather have thrown £10,000 into the sea than have heard of the death of her schoolmaster, Roger Ascham. James gorged himself in every excess of the fashionable world. He loved orgies of patronage and consumption.

These meant that after Robert Cecil's death in 1612 the annual deficit was about £500,000. Cranfield's remedies included economy proposals, cuts in pensions, sales of forest lands, monopoly patents put up for grabs, household rationing, and allocation of funds to departments of state made in accord with specific priorities. But even adding to the list of expedients the sale of titles of nobility was inadequate. Moreover, like new taxations, the sales occasioned conflict. It may well have been true, as was often claimed, that not one-hundred men were £100 poorer by virtue of royal taxation. Nonetheless, the politically potent classes protested new levies. And the established nobles and gentry bitterly protested the "inflation of honors" that the crown used as a commodity for fiscal reasons.

In monarchical societies, titles of honor are a distinctive feature. As wealth multiplies and becomes more widely distributed, such titles cease to be the sole means of achieving status. Yet titles then become more eagerly sought after. The competition for them seems to reflect a new balance between the aristocratic ideal of stable hierarchy in a mobile society and the reality of mobility in that society. The College of Heralds had emerged in response to the pressures of the burgeoning gentry. But it was in the years from 1560 to 1640 that the competition for grants of arms and titles of nobility peaked, encouraged through James I's expedient of selling them. Grants were made for as little as twenty-two shillings (in the case of London's hangmen in 1616) and for as much as £10,000 (in the case of the baronies conferred on Sir John Holles and Sir John Roger in 1616).

The pressure that debased the coin of privilege had always come from within the elite. But Elizabeth had been sparing in her creation of knights, despite rapidly growing pressures of population. There was, however, no such reluctance under James or Charles, even when we allow for the lulls in the activity of creating knights from 1610 to 1614 and during the mid-1630s. The number of knights during the queen's reign had fallen to 550. Over 25 percent of these were created by Essex in Ireland. James dubbed 1,161 in the first year of his rule. Cranfield had bought the right to nominate six for £373! Financial needs after 1614 drove James to sell about 120 knighthoods a year until his death. Under Charles, this yearly average fell to 45 c. 1626–30 and to 22 c. 1631–40. In 1641, however, more than 100 knighthoods were sold in a clear response to renewed political stresses.

In 1611, the rank of baronet was invented and sold. This new and marketable hereditary dignity ranked just below the baronage in titular precedence, filling the gap between knights and peers. James' intention was to sell only 200 such titles, and only to families that had been armigerous for three generations and that owned lands worth £1,000. A pledge was exacted from recipients saying that they had not sought the honor by giving gratuities to courtiers. Recipients were also bound to pay for three years the support of thirty soldiers in the Irish colony at Ulster. Actually, payment of £1,095 was openly made at the Exchequer. The first seventy-one appointments passed without scandal. But Sir Paul Bayning paid £1,500 cash for his, and he was a mere London merchant. By 1618, the making of baronetcies was granted to courtiers for resale to the best bidders. Subsequent sales showed a sharp correlation to the monetary and political crises of the Stuarts.

The creation for sale of baronetcies debased nobility and caused rising men to undervalue mere gentility. It also occasioned bitter disputes over patronage, precedence, and the profits of office open to favorites. It was becoming apparent that the financial debacle implied a deepening political crisis and a collapse of a sense of dignity that was vital to the loyalty and spirit of the landed classes.

The damage done through the knighthood and the baronetage was greater in scale but less significant in the eyes of the true nobility than the attack launched on their own ranks. The forty-four peers of 1500 had been only slightly expanded in number by 1603, owing to the proportion of extinctions and creations. The revolutionary political necessity of the 1530s and 1540s first broke the pattern of Tudor caution. Before the Reformation, the Tudor kings had carefully raised men who augmented the luster of nobility while domesticating the peers as a whole. We have observed how grants were made to servants of demonstrated merit and loyalty—to administrators, lawyers, and soldiers. Elizabeth retained this policy, and after rewarding great servants of her early, troubled years (Cecil, Dudley, Paulet), she made only one new peer after 1573.[5]

The Stuarts transformed the nobility in two stages. The first came before 1615 and was a necessary response to political pressures, although it was not without some fault. Arabella Stuart had obtained a blank patent in 1605, and filled it in for £3,000 in favor of Sir William Cavendish. But it was only in 1615 that the wholesale disposal of honors at the top began. This apparently reflected the need of the favorite George Villiers, who used every device to build his faction en route to his dukedom of Buckingham. During his lifetime the number of peers expanded from 81 to 126. The number of earls rose from 27 to 65. There were political rewards, of course, some of them even merited: Lords Bacon, Dudley, and Conway. One may even allow this merited status to Buckingham's party in the 1628 Parliament. But many had only the merit of their money. The 1616 instances of Roger and Holles are examples, as are the several titles that in 1624 were sold for about £30,000. The cash went chiefly to the duke's friends and relatives.

Clearly, more was at issue than James Stuart's weakness or the later dependence of Charles on "Steenie," his beloved Buckingham. We witness in the sale of titles of honor the mechanics of the sale of offices, monopolies, and other patents of profit. The whole of government was infested with the plague of gratuities, bribes, favoritism, sinecurism, and corruption. The monarchy found the pressure of its needs greater than the strength of its resources. Yet kings who reckoned the threat of presbyterianism in slogans like "No bishops, no King" failed to see how the debasement of honors stripped virtue of its reward.

Plato had taught that in a good state it was more important to preserve the rewards fit for lovers of virtue than to find ways to placate merely acquisitive men happy with goods. What the earl of Clare correctly called "the temporal simony" of the royal regime was in fact merely the counterpart of weaknesses in structure that made simony and pluralism the besetting sin of churchmen and the chief weakness in God's House. The immediate effect of sales fostered by need was a market ruined by driven-down prices. The long-

---

[5] There were some elevations within the peerage. But only the Armada hero Howard of Effingham leaped the barrier separating nobility from the knightly class.

range effect was reduced respect for the monarchy. Persons "of great extraction" felt bitter and cheapened. The edge of ambition among service-minded men was often dulled by pollution in the prize. Their lack of incentive rather than their finances constituted one of the critical bases of the crisis of the aristocracy. And the crisis was more political and social in character than it was economic. The temporary abolition of the House of Lords in 1649 attests in part to the erosion of earlier decades. Moreover, the creation of so enlarged a peerage further reduced the political power of the crown, adding to the earlier impact of the Reformation. Hereditary baronets and nobles were less at the crown's mercy than mere knights whose dignity was not heritable. There was a consequent diminution of pressure on a segment of the service class of the crown.

Lord Bacon alleged another effect. Titled men were of necessity conspicuous consumers. Hence the inflation of honors consigned a greater share of the income from office and landed capital to unproductive uses. This effect in turn increased pressure on the system of rewards and services, added to the burden of royal extravagances, sharpened competition for profits, and embittered the ordinary taxpayers who did not benefit from the system. Lawrence Stone has rightly seen in this effect a cause of enmity between court and country as well as of incitement to faction. The taunts flung at the de la Poles in the fourteenth century echoed around Cranfield in the seventeenth. The crown was soiled by the service of insolent merchants. The crown perhaps derived some comfort from the inflation of honors; its minimum profit between 1603 and 1629 was about £620,000. It is questionable, however, whether such gains were worth the enlarged hostility of some aristocrats.

Lord Bacon's observation on this point, which was that the sale of honors implied a sort of indirect tax on nonbeneficiaries, is also worthy of scrutiny. Was it not the case that the whole of society had wealth systematically transferred from it to the administrative cadres and favorites? Was not the structure of government a huge network of hidden taxes on those who often received little security in return? £77,000 a year for the household in 1621; £57,000 for the navy; £28,000 for the wardrobe—in those expenses Cranfield found waste to the tune of £22,000, £20,000, and £13,000, respectively. Vested interests resisted reductions, as they did reform in the Chancery, in the administration of justice, and in the Court of Wards. This entrenched opposition among its own servants then drove the crown between the Scylla of taxes approved by the Commons and the Charybdis of forced loans, "benevolences," and the "ship money" of the 1630s.[6]

The frequent early Stuart drafts of budgets and crown accounts were not

---

[6] The 1622 loans netted £117,000, not quite 75 percent of the parliamentary subsidy of 1621.

made to inform a public of royal extravagances. Nor were commissions investigating fees, annuities, pensions, and salaries convened for reasons external to the administration itself. But the constant talk of "necessity" on the king's behalf made it certain that Parliament would debate such matters and even demand the resignation of ministers, sometimes wisely (Bacon) and sometimes foolishly (Cranfield), before passing on to harsher judgments of impeachment (Buckingham) and death (Laud and Wentworth). The El Dorado of reform and solvency was as far off for James in 1624 and Charles in 1640 as it had been for Henry VI in 1453. The debt reached £1,000,000 in James' last year. The Thirty Years' War would have pressed hard on even a fiscally sound monarchy headed by prudent men. But James never did heed Cranfield's plaintive counsel to cut expenses: "Every footman can raise money . . . by the king's power, with the alienation of his subjects' hearts, but that is . . . far from service. . . ."

Early in Charles I's reign, investigations of the household, wardrobes, armory, ordnance, revenue offices, and law courts revealed widespread corruption. In the Exchequer, where 90 percent of royal revenue was audited, over 40 percent of all expenditure was accounted for in the spending of the royal household! Parliament expressed its grief and outrage over this situation in its sessions in 1626 and 1628. Yet the financial ruin of the crown had been only occasionally parliamentary business. Parliament had met for a total of four and one-fourth years between 1603 and 1629; it would meet not at all for the years 1629–40. The Commons, malcontent and hostile, had granted taxes only in 1621, 1624, and 1628, chiefly because of war pressures. Popular views on religion, foreign affairs, and war could not readily be traded against taxes to fashion accommodations and to reduce tensions. Therefore, the parliamentary classes themselves came to seek other means to control the crown's policies and the extent of its demands.

The Personal Rule of Charles I

That is reason enough why our emphasis has been on the ordinary means of government and its makers rather than on the spectacular colloquies at Westminster. As we shall soon see, the House of Commons was growing powerful enough to contest initiative in policy with the crown. But Parliament was not yet part of the daily machinery of government. That is also why the main thrust of reform and criticism fell on the most evident, continuing institutions—on the Court and the administration. These were the government, especially during the "personal rule" (1629–40). Indeed, it is during Charles I's so-called tyranny, when there were no Parliaments, that we can best look closely at the struggle for government between the crown and the parliamentary classes. Our vision is not dazzled by proceedings at Westminster.

While Thomas Wentworth (Lord Stafford) breathed new life into the governance of Ireland and Laud attempted to reform the religion and economics of the Church, Charles showed a determination to reform the domestic administration. His reasons were a mixture of pieties about a king's responsibility and a shrewd determination to settle political conflict by avoiding the most palpable occasion for it. Parliament was indispensable if taxation by the consent of the elites was the sole remedy for financial ills. But if other avenues to solvency could be built, the crown might escape the clutches of that risky partnership. The alternate roads lay through two difficult terrains, the one marked extraordinary and nonrecurrent receipts, and the other marked ordinary receipts of the crown. The politically articulate classes, however, were suspicious of such road building, and in the end complicated royal easements with their own claims of rights of way.

Constitutional historians have cut from the whole cloth of the conflicts of the 1620s and the 1630s the cloak of a crisis of the constitution issuing inevitably in civil war: the Petition of Right, the Ship-Money, the Five Knights case, the doctrines of Sir Edward Coke, John Hampden, "King" Pym, and a host of lesser lights. It is perhaps more to the point to pass over in silence the outcome of the struggles—civil war—and focus instead on its unfolding nature.

This we can in some measure do by looking at a table showing increases in selected ordinary revenues from 1631 to 1641 during the five-year periods 1631–5 and 1636–41.

Increases Expressed as Annual Averages

Source of revenue	1631–35	1636–41
Great and petty customs farms	£210,000	£245,000
New impositions (customs)	53,091	119,583
Other new impositions	9,500	60,092
Coal duties and farms	8,400	18,400
Payments from soap-makers	—	29,128
Forest dues	—	17,951
The Mint	5,984	24,428
Wards and liveries	53,866	75,068
Totals	£340,841	£589,650

At first glance, the table seems to indicate some spectacular success in building the new roads to solvency. An increase of almost 60 percent occurred from the first period to the second. There were in addition extraordinary receipts of about £240,000, chiefly from heavy direct taxes and forced loans devoid of popular sanctions. Ship money assessed between 1636 and 1641 yielded about

£107,000 a year. This was an amount larger than any previous direct tax in peacetime, even when allowances are made for failures to collect 20 percent of the levy in 1639 and 79 percent in 1640.

It is the evidence of resistance, however, that casts a pall over the achievement of increasing total revenue from £700,000 in 1631 to £1,150,000 in 1640. For resistance called into question the settled temper of obedience. It exacerbated the relations between sovereign and subject. Moreover, the feat tended to obscure the fact that heavy sales of land had decreased standing revenues from estate management. That was precisely the area of private enterprise that had promoted Yorkist and early Tudor solvency.

Nor was there real compensation in the sales of offices and other crown boons. The sum paid annually in the 1630s for sales and unofficial fees varied between £373,000 and £277,000. This was a burden on society. It transferred the cost of government from the governors to the consumers. The benefits went directly to certain upper-class people—peers, gentry, lawyers, merchant-monopolists, and bureaucrats. The cost was perhaps equal to 33 percent of all crown income, and its distribution stemmed from a system weighted against the provincial people and the poor.[7] A cost of government equal to 33 percent of its regular, visible cost, greater than any single source of revenue, was thus a major part of the whole fiscal and political system. Fee taxation and official salaries together amounted to £660,000 in 1636, or about 70 percent of the sovereign's income. The gentry were especially prominent among the payees, although not many were its beneficiaries. This realization caused some consternation in their ranks, since the transfer of wealth from society at large to its official and courtier classes was not traditionally reckoned as the chief function of government.

Indeed, the real effect may have been a transfer not across class lines but within the political elites. Sixty-eight percent of the king's servants were gentry, while only 30 percent were landless merchants or professional men serving chiefly in the less important offices. Officeholding—and with it a share in the profits of the social system— visibly affected 20 percent of the whole peerage, perhaps 12 percent of the knights, 6 percent of all esquires, and less than 2 percent of the lesser gentry. Only about 4 percent of the population was armigerous (1625–42). Hence the vast bulk of Englishmen paid for a system from which they did not profit. The roughly £590,000 to £760,000 a year changing hands because of office raised a small part of the whole elite to a position of power, wealth, and status superior to their not-so-favored equals.

This may easily be seen by looking at a table of incomes attributed to the elites in 1633.

[7] Calculations from this point forward are based on the maximum estimated cost, crown income, etc.

Suggested Landed Incomes, c. 1633

Rank		Total	Average per person
122	peers (English)	£732,000	£6,000
26	bishops	25,000	950
305	cadets, Irish peers, baronets, etc.	460,000	1,500
1,800	knights	1,440,000	800
9,000	esquires	4,500,000	500
14,000	gents	2,100,000	150

The roughly £9,300,000 in landed income enjoyed by the ruling classes was part of a "national income" of perhaps £30,000,000. This means that the top estimate of £760,000 in the cost of officeholding constituted about 8 percent of the whole income of the landed classes from land, or about 3 percent of the national income.

The conclusion warranted by these data is not that officeholding in the old regime in England created a ruling elite. It certainly did help to distinguish a group of ruling families within the elites because of nonlanded incomes and the prestige conveyed by office. In the case of the gentry, office contributed about 7.7 percent of their total income; but only one man in seventeen enjoyed the increment. English society was not "controlled" by a single economic class, either under Elizabeth or the early Stuarts. But the aristocracy of office was vital to its control. It was also of substantial significance in elaborating the social hierarchy. Politics in its local and national forms had been the natural outgrowth of a long process of upward social mobility and land distribution. But the form national politics assumed in the generations after the Reformation bore a special relationship to the new elements of growth and change deriving from Henry VIII's revolution. This was less a revolution in the mode of government than it was a revolution in what government aspired to do and in the means available to it. The struggle to control both means and motifs lies behind much of the so-called constitutional crisis, as the crown sought to manipulate its servants in circumstances increasingly favorable to the attempt.

The shape of society in its lower and middle ranks was earlier the subject of our discussions of social and economic change in town and countryside. Here we have necessarily focused steadily on the top rungs of the social ladder. This focus is entirely appropriate if we hope to attain an understanding of government and politics that is dynamic rather than static. For descriptions of institutions and narratives of constitutional crises have the disadvantage of not revealing to us the bases of the oppositions that flower in rhetoric and armed conflict.

Yet to say that wealth and power are the stuff of governance and the motor of politics merely repeats a truism. What remains is a discussion of the role of yet another force making for mobility and for the determination and loss of political balance. It will be necessary to look more closely at education— another facet of the social character of the aristocracy. For the English governing classes were as much an elite of education as of land, office, and status. Power went to school in the age of Elizabeth.

Government and Society: The Impact of Education

If it is true that government by Charles Stuart failed because the confidence of the ruling elites had been lost and initiative had passed to the Commons before 1629, the increasing political articulateness of some Englishmen was learned behavior, not a birthright or something achieved in the furnace of rebellion. The men who undid Charles I's personal rule were not in that regard superior to his servants. The whole of the upper classes, court, and country, both Puritan and Anglican, had flocked to the colleges, grammar schools, law schools, and universities in the Tudor age. The society of the 1630s was not divided between progressive opponents of the monarchy and its duller partisans.[8]

The proportion of university-educated men in Charles I's central government was high, which was merely a reflection of the domination of the educated, landed, magisterial classes in society. Fifty-five percent of crown servants with university education derived from families of the squirearchy or upper gentry. The corresponding figure for legal education is 47 percent. Only 31 percent of the serving sons of fathers lower than esquire rank had university training. Only 37 percent had been to the Inns of Court. But almost all administrative clerks in London had some "higher" education, just as 92 percent of the Anglican clergy were graduates by the 1640s.

Between 1558 and 1640, the universities and Inns of Court became the haunts of noblemen, cadets of peerage families, gentry of all ranks, and prosperous bourgeoisie. The universities had once been chartered ecclesiastical corpora-

[8] The following works not previously cited have been most valuable in estimating the impact of higher education in government and society: L. Stone, "The Educational Revolution in England, 1560–1640," *Past and Present* (1964), No. 28, pp. 41–80; also, in the same journal: M. Curtis, "The Alienated Intellectuals of Early Stuart England," No. 23 (1962); Joan Simon, "The Social Origins of Cambridge Students, 1603–1640," No. 26 (1963); W. Prest, "Legal Education of the Gentry, 1560–1640," No. 38 (1967). Also, J. H. Hexter, "The Education of the Aristocracy in the Renaissance," in *Reappraisals in History* (Evanston, Ill.: Northwestern University Press, 1961); K. Charlton, *Education in Renaissance England* (London: Routledge & Kegan Paul, 1965); Joan Simon, *Education and Society in Tudor England* (Cambridge: Cambridge University Press, 1966); Mark Curtis, *Oxford and Cambridge in Transition* (Oxford: Clarendon Press, 1959); and Hugh Kearney, *Scholars and Gentlemen* (Ithaca, N.Y.: Cornell University Press, 1970).

tions training priestly servants of crown and church. The Reformation wrought great changes. It began the transformation of the collegiate system that was ultimately to make the colleges dominant in the universities and the elites dominant in the colleges. The gradual replacement of clerics by laymen in central and local government had begun in the thirteenth century. The Reformation accelerated the pace of change, and the landed elites especially responded to the lure of service by equipping themselves with the necessary learning. Professor Gleason has shown this decisively in his study of the educational backgrounds of the justices of the peace.

Many factors operated in the appointment of justices: the word of assize judges, personal friendships, family prestige, ambition, the government's needs in a region, and country politics. By the 1530s, however, education—whether "liberal" (humanistic) or legal—was increasingly necessary. Just as the need for a suitably educated clergy took time to provide, so did it take time to remodel the commissions and make over local authorities. The problems of ecclesiastical power and civil power were parallel and related. Open Catholics, presbyterians, and the wholly ignorant were excluded from commissions—or at least almost so, remembering Justice Shallow! In 1562, only a few commissioners in Kent, Worcester, Norfolk, Somerset, Yorkshire's North Riding, or Northamptonshire had been enrolled in either a university or an Inn of Court. By 1636, all but eleven of Kent's eighty-five justices had such training. The corresponding proportions for Worcestershire are 10 out of 35; for Northamptonshire, 9 out of 57; for Somerset, 8 out of 63. This meant that in seventy-five years there had been a transformation of the local governing classes with regard to training. From a group primarily feudal and chivalric in education, with a minimum of literary discipline, had come a class of lawyers and humanistically trained men. A reversal in upper-class attitudes toward education had taken place, doubtless in response to the demands after 1529 for a broader secular civil service. A cultural revolution was in progress within the aristocracy, and its consequences can be seen in the personnel of government at every tier, including the House of Commons.

The "third university" (the Inns of Court) was as important as Cambridge and Oxford in this revolution. It provided an education calculated to serve the considerations of property and the preservation of social order. Hence it is no surprise that men went there often without thinking of legal careers. A first-rate technical training in the law could put a man on the train to court. It certainly helped in estate management, business, and politics. Between 1558 and 1640, the Inns of Court—Gray's, Lincoln's, Inner Temple, and Middle Temple—grew in size to an average of about 200 members each. By 1640, nearly every local governor had spent time in an Inn, if only to be able to cope with the extra work required of justices as the result of the various experiments of the period 1629–40. Of these experiments, the Poor Law and the Book of Orders (1626) added out-of-session burdens to regular Quarter Sessions, according to books such as Michael Dalton's *The Country Justice* (1618).

The primacy of the Inns of Court meant that the country benches, the one hundred or so lords, and the 450 members of the Commons had similar educational backgrounds, ties of kinship, related property interests, and a firm hold on local office and country politics. At least 306 of the original members of the revolutionary Long Parliament had been to one of the four Inns. Although their total number of admissions never rose above two-thirds of the total for either Oxford or Cambridge, most members of the Inns were decidedly upper class. Whereas about 40 percent of all Oxford and Cambridge students were of aristocratic (gentry and nobility) origins, well over 80 percent of all matriculants at the Inns came from the upper social strata.[9]

Their ambitions clearly reached socially and politically beyond the narrow confines of the common law. When the community of the realm gathered at Westminster in 1584, 24 members of the Commons were sons of peers and 13 were closely related to peers; 240 of the 460 M.P.s were gentry, while 75 were in legal and administrative office, with 53 actual lawyers in the House. The "quality" of the 1584 Commons, so ferocious in debating the queen's security and Puritan religion, stood in the fact that 145 of its men were university educated, compared to 67 in 1563. In the same two decades, the number of members educated at the Inns of Court jumped from 108 to 164. By 1593, Parliament had a lower chamber with 161 university men, 197 who had been to read law (or at least to live where it was read), and 106 who had prefaced the Inns with a spell at Cambridge or Oxford.

The stark upward trend was not planned, despite schemes to that effect introduced as early as 1558. Nor did it mean that students always took degrees or passed the bar before launching a political career or cutting a figure in the countryside. In the 1584 Commons, only fifty-four men took a first degree and only sixty-four were called to the bar. But the educational surge was vital to the standing of the House of Commons. In 1593, 43 percent of its members knew the liberal arts in some measure, and 54 percent knew either the law or what was taught in the new-fangled civil seminaries on the Thames and the River Cam. Moreover, half the gentry in the 1584 Parliament also held local office. The same evidence of birth, marriage, estates, and practical experience that had always characterized the corporate solidarity of the ruling aris-

[9] On the "quality of the House," see Sir J. E. Neale, *The Elizabethan House of Commons* (London: Jonathan Cape, 1949); Mary Ransome, "Some Recent Studies of the Composition of the House of Commons," *Birmingham Historical Journal* (1957), VI, pp. 37–63; D. Brunton and D. H. Pennington, *Members of the Long Parliament* (London: Allen & Unwin, 1954).

tocracies of England now extended to their education. By 1640, 57 percent of the Commons was composed of university men. The technical requirements of public service in all its branches were shifting, and the ever-adaptable English aristocracy was doing what was required to maintain a dominant social position.

Armed with causes, such men took advantage of their education and the solidity of their power base in the counties to challenge the crown in its control of Parliament. Sir John Neale, Wallace Notestein, and many others have shown how, in the evolution of the Commons, the period from the 1590s through the 1640s was critical—for the committee system, for the rise in the number of members speaking in any debate, and for the advances in the technique of legislation that increasingly made it difficult for the councillors and agents of the king in the House to control its course. From the mid-Elizabethan Parliaments on, the grip of the councillors and other royal officials gave way before the pressure of nonofficial members. This development was most stimulated by the growth of political consciousness arising out of the Reformation. But it was greatly helped by the use of procedural mechanisms favorable to the participation of many men—committees especially. There were in every Elizabethan and early Stuart House "committee men," those who were seldom heard in debate but were specially adept at preparing bills for the scrutiny of the House.[1]

All of these changes doubtless were aided by the poor political sense of James I; and it was during the scattered sessions of his reign that one may speak of the crown as having lost legislative initiative. But neither royal indolence nor the turbulence of the Jacobean era and its issues account wholly for the changes. If the Commons was coming of age, if its members learned how to divide labor between the debaters and the committee men, this was the result chiefly of the long-term shift in political focus and political power. The House was no mere knot of great men surrounded by apathetic country gentlemen. Such gentlemen there doubtless were. But the recent students of the Commons have been at pains to show how the extant committee lists illustrate the eagerness of many members to sit on the crucial second-reading committees, where laws were finally shaped in most instances, and where the weight of the whole House told against that of the crown's officers. The "noughts" against which

---

[1] See especially W. Notestein, *The Winning of the Initiative* (Oxford: Oxford University Press, 1925), and *The House of Commons, 1604–1610* (New Haven, Conn.: Yale University Press, 1971); and also Robert Zaller, *The Parliament of 1621* (Berkeley: University of California Press, 1971); T. G. Barnes, *Somerset, 1625–1640* (Oxford: Clarendon Press, 1961), despite its focus on one county in the "personal rule." The older studies of Mitchell and Willson on the rise of opposition and the role of privy councillors are still worth reading, as well as D. Eusden, *Puritans, Lawyers, and Politics* (New Haven, Conn.: Yale University Press, 1958).

QUEEN ELIZABETH I IN PARLIAMENT.
From the 1682 edition of Sir Simon d'Ewes' Journals of the Parliaments of Queen Eliza-beth. *Courtesy the British Museum.*

the truthteller raged in the 1405 treatise by Mum and Soothsegger, quoted earlier in this book, had given place to a well-educated class of members united by their sharing of local power, unease about royal spending habits, fundamental Protestantism, and astute manipulation of procedure. Two hundred years of profound social change had forced the most able elements of England's political classes to undergo profound behavioral adjustments.

A certain part of the nobility and the gentry failed to make the adjustments, on account of obstinate preferences for the age of blood and iron, indolence, or the legal prescriptions that derived Catholics' education and office at home. But even the nobility gathered its offspring in fashionable schools—Eton, Winchester, and St. Paul's. Professor Jordan sampled ten counties in which there were only thirty-four schools open to the laity in 1480. In the year 1660, there were 305 new endowments and 105 foundations not endowed but "open" in the same counties. From 1560 on, the gentry and other upper-class clientele flocked to them. Peers even attended local schools. As concentration on a few choice places took hold, yet another powerful factor making for dominance of the landed classes appeared—social exclusiveness based on the best schooling. The titled nobility, however, lost out in the struggle; the peak of peers in the Inns and universities came in the 1570s, when nearly thirty were at Oxford, Cambridge, or the London Inns. The pattern of their education moved decisively in the direction of the European grand tour after 1570.

The upshot of this differentiation in educational experience was a confirmation of experiences that distinguished the titled nobility from the rest of the aristocracy. The old intellectual and managerial elite of the clergy had given way to the lay aristocracy. Within its ranks, the gentry and a scattering of peers pursued the course required to man the diplomatic corps and the civil service. The secular rulers were in the process of becoming a power elite in which neither birth alone nor great wealth was a sufficient basis on which to claim political privilege. The new magnates and their gentry affiliates had little in common with stereotyped images of literary cavaliers. Although they did advance literature, painting, and other arts—above all architecture—through their lavish building programs, the English aristocracy was notable in this period chiefly for the functional adaptations it made to the new demands of society. The educational system gave to some peers, and to the leading gentry especially, a tremendous advantage over the poorer gentry, who could afford neither the formal education nor the European tour in the contest for power and profit. English landed society, already so divided between the rich and the poor, was now divided also between the educated, rich, officeholding, and politically powerful members of the elite and their coarser, duller, and less puissant neighbors.

Had the educational revolution wider social implications? Was the aristocratic demand for a suitable political education the counterpart of a demand for vocational training by the sons of clergy, bourgeoisie, and the professional classes? How did education affect the general nobility of society after 1500? What impact, if any, did a shift in the type and availability of education have on the balance and stability of society? These questions are easier to put than to answer.

Thomas More supposed in 1533 that over half of his countrymen were literate. The open Bible was a powerful stimulus toward reaching that level of literacy. But less noble motives to learning played a part. Of 204 men given death sentences by the Middlesex justices (1612–14), 47 percent pleaded benefit of clergy by reason of literacy, a skill gained in petty school. More than 60 percent of the householders in the village of Limpsfield were literate in 1642, as opposed to 20 percent of the servant class. Whether these or similar data justify any conclusion about general literacy seems doubtful. But some conclusion may be drawn from the fact that by 1650 charitable impulses had ensured the existence of one school for every 4,400 persons. Nobody in England then was more than twelve miles from a school of some sort. But the unevenness of data drawn from primary and secondary school evidence prohibits any firm conclusions.

The evidence for higher education is clearer. Professor Stone and others have by prodigious efforts extracted from limited data about student matriculation the total range of admission and population at Cambridge and Oxford. We know that a wave of expansion set in by the 1540s, reached a peak in the 1580s, declined steadily thereafter until 1604, and then picked up and rose until 1640. The civil war triggered a lasting decline that characterized the Restoration and eighteenth-century university life. The Inns of Court reveal a similar pattern. The result is summarized in the table below.

Entrants to Higher Education

Decade	Universities	Inns of Court	Private and abroad	Total
1560–69	650	80	50	780
70–79	780	79	50	910
80–89	770	103	40	910
90–99	652	106	40	800
1600–9	706	119	40	860
10–19	884	140	50	1,070
20–29	906	120	50	1,080
30–39	1,055	137	50	1,240
40–49	557	109	100	770

Even in the peak decade of the 1630s, not more than 1,200 men were able to pursue a higher education. Some 430 of these prepared to swell the clerical ranks, while 160 studied for a career in law and thirty for nonprofessional purposes. In a population of roughly five million (*c.* 1640), the male cohort reaching the mean entry age of seventeen would have been about 55,600 in any one year. Fewer than 2.25 percent of all Englishmen could reasonably expect to be taken into the higher education complex. The educational revolution was narrowly based in aggregate terms and by social composition. The Inns admitted only 2 percent of all applicants from bourgeois backgrounds, and only 10 percent from legal or clerical families. Over 70 percent of the Middle Temple admissions went to elder sons of landed men.[2]

Judging from Oxford matriculation books, the university was a more open society. Between 1575 and 1639, 50 percent of the Oxford matriculants were gentry, 41 percent were plebeian, and 9 percent were from clerical homes. This breakdown is somewhat deceptive, however, since about 25 percent of the gentry were from towns, while many proper gentry were younger sons being groomed for the professions, the Church, and trade. There is thus some evidence, even within the pyramid itself, that opportunity for entry into the elites was expanding. But too much should not be made of this evidence; entries to Caius College, Cambridge, between 1560 and 1640 showed a strong tide for the gentry. And astute foreign observers stressed the dominance of the colleges by wellborn men.

Artisans, shopkeepers, and boys with fathers in the professions did, however, constitute 40 percent of the intake of St. Johns, Cambridge. This was possible chiefly because of the provision of some 500 new scholarships and numerous charitable bequests in both universities. Within the limited numbers we are discussing, the change in opportunity was great. But wholesale upward social mobility through education was far in the future. If we compare the situation in 1640 to the far more meager intakes of the pre-Reformation era, however, we may speak of a revolutionary situation. Even by comparison with the modern English industrial society situation, the same holds true. The Robbins Committee Report on Higher Education in 1963 showed that only 1.2 percent (1900) and 2 percent (1938) of eighteen-year-olds of both sexes entered university.

Between 1540 and 1640, there had been a dramatic increase in opportunity. This was seemingly the consequence of the social, religious, economic, and political developments that we label the Reformation. Yet the situation achieved by the overthrow of the dominant clerical culture of the waning Middle Ages was not democratizing. To say it was would involve us in a wild

---

[2] The figure stood closer to 85 percent in 1570; the sons of lawyers accounted for the shift.

misuse of language. Opportunity within families enlarged, as it had in the nation. The incentives of wealth and power now lay in the path of clever men, whatever their birth, despite the strong hold of the landed classes on the levers of politics. Land was changing hands at an unprecedented pace.[3] Indeed, the rise and fall of the land market showed a curve very like that of educational intake. The growth of popular Protestantism intensified the demand for lay literacy and clerical learning.

The universities in 1450 had been a subculture of the Church. The sixty Oxford halls included thirty devoted to the training of legists in canon law. A survey of Cambridge B.A.s awarded in 1489 reveals that twenty-two out of thirty were baccalaureates in canon law. Between 1300 and 1550, the proportion of graduates in the clergy of Exeter Cathedral rose from 20 percent to 67 percent. But throughout the period, nearly 67 percent of all graduates took degrees in canon law. Such data merely reflect the origins of the schools under the control of monastic and mendicant orders. The largest foundation and the richest were both monastic: Canterbury, Durham, and Gloucester at Oxford. Colleges for the secular clergy had been smaller and impoverished, and had reflected chiefly the gradual extension of the parochial system to frontier regions in England—Exeter, Brasenose, and Merton, among others.

By 1540, the base on which such a structure of education had been raised had been swept away. Cromwell's revolution had abolished a profession (canon law) and thus the *raison d'être* of many colleges. The training of parish clergy had been on the rise in the universities before the 1530s, under humanist and other pressures. But the changes of the first decade of total Reformation forced a shift in the social base of the system. The halls suddenly vanished, as the colleges rose overnight to dominate the universities. The demise of the canon law schools and the rise of the common law Inns was closely connected with the downfall of the monasteries. But the secular clergy were only the most immediate, and not the most important, beneficiaries of the revolution.

The crown moved to fill the void left by the collapse of the orders. By 1540, it had founded regius professorships in medicine, law, classical languages, and theology. Henry VIII and Edward VI also spent lavishly on royal colleges; Trinity and Christ Church were rightly called "academic palaces" by one admirer, and Peterhouse and Corpus Christi at Oxford likewise flourished. The immediate result of all this attention from the crown was a crisis of organization from which the collegiate system emerged supreme. The colleges were modeled on Reformation assumptions and reflected the crown's supremacy, the problems of the secular clergy, and the rapidly expanding secular educational needs of laymen. The colleges facilitated closer supervision than had

---

[3] That is, since the period 1340–1440.

the halls; this supervision was especially vital to the parents of gentlemen for whom the college would now be a training ground more important than the old apprenticeship in chivalry that once had been served in the great hall of some aristocrat.

There was also a marked shift in the curriculum as the humanist core of the liberal arts was remade to reflect the growing secularism of society. The tutorial system emerged, with its stress on rhetoric and religion of the sort proper to Protestant laymen. Control and discipline replaced the uproar of the medieval lecture hall. And in this respect as in so many others, the transformation of higher education provided institutions well suited to play the role in educational reform that the Council had played in other areas. Between 1530 and 1570, the first great waves of gentry hit the colleges. They represented the force of modernization, reflecting the shift from the demand for a narrowly technical education suitable for clerical careerists to the goal of moral and intellectual preparation of the lay leaders of society. A humanist and radically Protestant bias marked this shift, as did the class bias so pronounced in the intake of students.

It is hard to see these shifts as less than mirror images in the universities of the changes suffered in the larger society. England had been a nation dominated by churchmen and military aristocrats, in which canon law, buckler, and sword had been the finest expressions of power. But by the time of Henry VIII's death, the transformation of knights of blood and iron into aristocrats who lived by service of a more pacific kind was complete, or very nearly so. The Elizabethan earl of Essex was the exception that proved the rule, an atavist in his ways. The profession of gentlemen mixed service with the accumulation of capital as its chief reward. And the colleges, inasmuch as they retained a clerical aspect, became after 1560 Protestant seminaries for the education of the parochial clergy. The senior officials of the colleges were clerks: heads, tutors, and bursars. The chancellors, however, were laymen. The dominant senior faculty was still made up of theologians; but their theology was new, Protestant, and often radical.

The colleges had in fact begun to compete successfully with ministerial and episcopal households as training places for government servants of lay status. They were thus involved in the status revolution we have been studying. Attendance in a college marked the gentleman off from other men and in this way completed the demarcation begun in the late 1300s and early 1400s with the less mannered insistence on titles of distinction. Gentility stood by education as much as by the lack of a visible means of support! And it had important consequences in law, where it affected punishments; in politics, where it prepared one's place in county society; and in religion, where it oriented the gentry toward radical Protestantism. The gentlemanly way of life late in

Elizabeth's reign required a suitable education for the fullest alloying of power with responsibility and status. This requirement made higher education a channel of mobility for yeomen, artisans, and those of merchant origins; the army, the Inns, and service in the developing colonies were other such channels. The shift had been in progress since about 1400; it was certainly no Tudor phenomenon. But its maturation was a result of the revolution of the 1530s.

Epilogue

It is necessary that noble men and gentlemen . . . be able to put
their own case in law, and to have some Iudgement in the office
of a Justice of peace and Sheriffe; for through the want thereof the
best are often tymes subject to the direction of farre the Inferiors.

SIR H. GILBERT Queen Elizabeth's Academy

This book had its beginning in my curiosity to know more about the relations between economic and political changes and how these combined to make the fortunes of government and society in England. Economic and demographic causes of shifts in the value of land and labor proved more amenable to exact expression than did shifts in the mental attitudes that often marked shifts in government. Yet, in retrospect, it seems clear that it is not merely convenient to focus as we have done. Man's material culture determines his self-awareness. And often his struggles to relieve the profound anxieties that human consciousness and self-awareness promote is centered in the ceaseless struggle to command the environment by using the total adaptation we call culture.

Our study has thus been of the adaptations by which a single traditional agrarian society moved slowly toward the margin of modernity. The overall acceleration of change in England between 1340 and 1640 profoundly altered the balance of forces in that traditional society without establishing new stable relationships. The precariousness of the emerging balance was signaled in the fourteenth century by peasant rebellion and dynastic struggle; in the fifteenth century by civil wars and more widely based revolts; in the sixteenth century by the social revolution we call the Reformation and the series of major rebellions between 1536 and 1570; and in the first half of the seventeenth century by the subsistence, despite the reputation of Elizabeth's reign for "settlement," of the deep malaise that was to sweep Oliver Cromwell to power and Charles I to his coffin. Happily, those seventeenth-century events belong to the historian who will explain how stability did emerge from the crises of that period.

Historians have proclaimed many revolutions and have been prone to the notion that each "era" delineated by them was responsible for setting society back on a stable base. It is to be hoped that no reader of this book will come away thinking that Edward of York or Henry VII did things so conclusively. Nor, hopefully, will he credit the notion that Henry VIII and Thomas Cromwell achieved the "revolution" that created a *modern* sovereign state in place of the tottering, decadent, reprieved *medieval* halflife of the waning Middle Ages. No vast trench dug across the space of time between 1485 and 1534 marks the boundary of two recognizably different societies, in a political, constitutional, economic, social, or religious sense. The mid-Tudor crises seem conclusive evidence for the ephemeral nature of Cromwell's bold schemes. The Reformation was not a set of solutions to problems. It was not yet the accomplishment of a decade, or even of several decades. Not even the seeming stability achieved in the guise of the Elizabethan age—especially in the 1570s and the early 1580s—effectively hid the gaping gulf growing between men of different minds in religion along with the implications that religious doctrine had for both foreign and domestic policy. Above all, it is manifest that successive governments never did solve the problems of the general economy and of finding the means to fund administration in a way that was both convenient and politically wise.

The century after 1529 was one of even greater mobility and change than the troubled hundred years ended by the fall of Cardinal Wolsey. Hierarchies of status were jostled by those of income, as wealth alone became a claim to power in towns and even in certain provincial settings. The peerage as a class suffered a transformation punctuated by several great crises—in income, utility, and power. But it survived, adapted to new conditions, and in its most agile members held its place at the head of the governing aristocracies. The apparent hold on power attained by the gentry and certain professionals before 1520 grew more solid, despite regional dislocation (in 1536 and 1569 in the North; in 1549 in the West), the uncertainty of the Tudor dynasty after 1547, and the demonstrable contest within gentry ranks. The urban oligarchies certainly tightened their grasp of power in the 1500s. Even the clerical estate had ups as well as downs: witness the reactions in the 1580s, after 1604, and again in the 1630s, under Whitgift, Bancroft, and Laud.

What is less clear is how the power of the crown fared throughout the period. From strength to strength it did not go. But it certainly waxed in strength, in relationship to the politically valid classes *c.* 1500–40, before suffering some eclipse between 1547 and 1570. The loss of supporting influence in the clerical estate, especially in Parliament, was permanent; and this made the Elizabethan achievement of apparent stability before the Armada a greater illusion than it otherwise might have been.

It is hard to resist saying that the government after 1540 was primarily a strong monarchy in a weak phase. This, however, is vastly different from saying that it was a weak, feeble monarchy, that Englishmen were badly led, that justice was poorly served, or that administration was utterly incompetent in the generations reaching from Thomas Cromwell to his lineal descendant Oliver. The distribution of ability and intelligence in the monarchy was more than modest. But the same can be said about the political elites who found the regime of one ruler and then another less perfect than they had been made to hope. Coupled with changes that are known to have been detrimental to social stability—demographic change, continued epidemics, violent inflation, war, corruption of the system of fee and favor—it is perhaps less to the point to ask why the monarchy failed in 1641 than to admire the ability of that imperfect society to aspire to the revolutionary tasks it had made its goals in the 1530s. England in her time of troubles expanded into new continents, evicted Rome, withstood Spain, reduced injustice in its most palpable forms, domesticated a violent, factious aristocracy, aspired to educate common men, controlled pests, defeated the cycle of agrarian insufficiency and consequent starvation, relieved the poor, regulated trade, and found the time to achieve greatness in literature, painting, music, and occasionally the art of government by consent. These are not the successes of fearful men in a decadent society.

The fact is that some of them were achieved because a narrowly based elite was strengthened at all levels of government. From the parish vestry to the county commissions, governance fell into the hands of the "better sort." They were an elite partly monied, partly landed, partly official in character, and at least partly educated. The county community, like the country community, had embraced both Mammon and Jehovah. In some counties, a caucus of titled magnates ruled. But in most, domination was by rigidly stratified landed families of lesser pretense, with magnates waiting in the wings, after the Restoration, to help build a genuine political stability. The gentry, who suffered most from the utter breakdown of order in every civil war between 1450 and 1650, made the most impassioned reaction against whatever lawlessness there had been. They were the chief force of law and order in 1640, as they had been in 1460, 1549, and 1570. Neither peer nor peasant lost as much in war as did those who stood in favor, wished for temperate politics, and worked to realize order in local government.

The gentry presumed that Parliament spoke with the voice of reason and the mind of justice. When it was adjourned—and it usually was—the guarantee of fundamental rights and fundamental law, of property itself, inhered in their class. The causes that Coke, Selden, Eliot, and other heroes of resistance to the claims of administration reveled in were cases in which law and politics seemed to join ethics, religion, and equity. They argued that government was not yet the realm of mere gain, however much power might be a function of government. They also spoke for the educated governing classes who accepted the tradition wherein obedience was tempered by respect for order, by a longing to trust authority, and by a certain knowledge that some things were bad not because they were forbidden but because they were evil in essence. This distinction between things *mala quia prohibita* and others *mala in se* was translated into practice slowly. But parliamentary history shows clearly that from Henry IV's time on, the liberties of subjects and rights of persons stood by God's will rather than the king's. The assumptions that law was in accord with national principle and that God's reason governed true laws grew dear to the gentry and their lawyers in proportion to the number of trespasses against them. So society ought to be governed; when it was not, the judgment of God fell on kings as well as ministers.

How that judgment fell in England and for what causes we leave to the historian of the civil war. Our concern has been merely to discern the shape of the society in which that war came, and to establish that English society was indeed in precarious balance in 1640, as it had been in 1450. Lucky is the society that, under severe stress from forces largely beyond its control, strikes a perfect balance between useless imitations of its own past and innovations helpful in the present or productive for the future. Englishmen in this era suffered much from their mimicry of old ways, but what is more, they also often experimented brilliantly.

Appendix

FIGURE ONE

Prices and Population Before 1350[1]

Wheat Prices in Terms of Silver, 1160–1339[2]	
1160–79	100.0
1180–99	139.3
1200–19	203.0
1220–39	196.1
1240–59	214.2
1260–79	262.9
1280–99	279.2
1300–19	324.7
1320–39	289.7

Various Commodity Prices, 1200–1350, with Population[3]			
	1200–1249	*1250–1299*	*1300–1349*
Wheat	63	87	100
Barley	59	87	100
Oats	61	89	100
Rye	70	88	100
Oxen	60	79	100
Sheep	87	101	100
Salt	52	72	100
Population[4]	2.04–2.57	2.57–3.30	3.3–3.7

[1] After Postan and *The Cambridge Economic History of Europe*, II, 166.

[2] 1160–79 is the index base of 100.0.

[3] 1300–50 is the index base, by 50-year periods.

[4] In millions, expressed as a decimal.

Some Population Data[1]

England (without Wales, Scotland, Ireland, 1086–1690)

Year	Population
1086	1.100
1348	3.757
1350	3.127
1360/1	2.745
1369	2.452
1374	2.250
1377	2.223
1400	2.100
1430	2.100
1603	3.780
1690	4.080

Population in England, 1100–1600, as Percentage of Maximum

Year	Population	Percentage of Maximum (1337)
1050	.92	25
1100	1.10	30
1150	1.85	50
1200	2.04	55
1250	2.57	70
1300	3.30	90
1350	3.70	100
1400	2.20	60
1450	2.20	60
1500	2.67	72
1550	3.26	88
1600	3.70	100

---

[1] After Russell, expressed in decimals of 1,000,000. Hollingsworth, *Historical Demography*, app. III, figures 8–10, assumes larger death rates and lower replacement rates.

FIGURE THREE

Real Wages, Prices, and Rents

	Wheat-price/Wage Ratio, 1320–1479[1]		
Decades	Indices, Wheat	Indices, Wages	Ratio of Wages/Wheat[2]
1320–39	100	100	100
1340–59	88	94	107
1360–79	99	105	106
1380–99	72	122	169
1400–19	76	116	153
1420–39	71	105	148
1440–59	59	101	171
1460–79	52	82	158

Rents at Bigod Manor, Norfolk[3]	
Years	Pence per Acre
1376–8	10.69
1401–10	9.11
1422–30	7.78
1431–40	8.02
1441–50	7.72
1451–60	6.26

[1] Winchester Estates, adopted from Postan by B. H. Schlicher von Bath, *Agrarian History of Western Europe*, pp. 140–51. All rates expressed in grams of silver, to compensate for currency debasements.

[2] The real wage here is taken to be the gain in purchasing power expressed in a proportion of money wages to grain prices.

[3] Adopted from Lord Beveridge and Davenport.

FIGURE FOUR

Grain and Animal Prices

Bidecennial Averages: Sheep Products Compared to Wheat[1]			
Decades	Wheat	Wool	By-products
1320–39	100	100	100
1340–59	88	98	97
1360–79	99	96	89
1380–99	72	97	99
1400–19	76	103	89
1420–39	71	101	86
1440–59	59	109	101
1460–79	52	113	105

[1] 1320 taken as base year, adopted from Beveridge, expressed in index numbers based on grams of silver.

Decades	*Decennial Averages: Sheep and By-products*[2] Wheat	Wool	Skins	*All By-products*
1450s	100	100	100	100
1460s	99	109	126	105
1470s	100	107	99	101
1480s	102	113	130	107
1490s	91	96	93	101
1500s	109	93	100	102
1510s	114	119	126	118

[2] 1450 taken as base year.

FIGURE FIVE

Triennial Averages of Cloths Exported from London[1]

Years	Cloths	Years	Cloths
1500–2	49,214	1530–32	66,049
1503–5	43,884	1533–5	83,043
1506–8	50,373	1536–8	87,231
1509–11	58,447	1539–41	102,660
1512–14	60,644	1542–4	99,362
1515–17	60,524	1545–7	118,642
1518–20	66,159	1550	132,767
1521–3	53,660	1551	112,710
1524–6	72,910	1552	84,968
1527–9	75,431		

[1] See F. J. Fisher, "Commercial Trends and Policy in Sixteenth Century England," p. 153, in *Essays in Economic History*, vol. I. Note the annual figures, given to emphasize the broken boom. Fisher's figures give shortcloth.

Comparisons of Exports of Wool Sacks and Cloths[1]

Decade	*Averages Per Annum by Decades* Wool	Cloths
1350–59	32,000	5,000
1390–99	19,000	37,000
1500–9	5,000	82,000
1540–50	5,000	118,000

[1] The woolsack of standard size weighed 364 pounds. The discrepancy in averages between these figures (Peter Ramsey, *Tudor Economic Problems*, p. 48) and Fisher's derive from Ramsey's use of broadcloth statistics for the country as a whole; Fisher measured London exports only. The broadcloth was by statute 24 yards long. But real cloths were often 30 or 45 yards in length. Customs officials converted actual cloths into standard measures for levy purposes.

FIGURE SIX

Titles, Benefices, and Clerical Incomes

Titles and Benefices Given by Religious Houses 1514–1521, Lincoln Diocese[1]

House	Order	Number of Titles Given 1514–20/1	Number of Presentations Made of Those to Whom Titles Given 1514–20/1	Number of Presentations Made of Those with Other Titles 1514–20/1
Bardney	Benedictine	9	1	2
Crowland	Benedictine	2	0	6
Godstow	Benedictine	1	0	7
Ramsey	Benedictine	1	0	6
Garendon	Cistercian	44	0	0
Heynings	Cistercian	11	0	0
Louth Park	Cistercian	2	0	1
Chicksands	Gilbertine	1	0	4
Nocton	Augustinian	16	0	1
Osney	Augustinian	16	0	4
Ulverscroft	Augustinian	18	0	2
Northampton St. James	Augustinian	17	0	0
Croxton	Premonstratensian	1	0	0
Axholme	Carthusian	1	0	0
Totals		140	1	33

Distribution of Clerical Incomes

Gross Income			Net Income	
Rectors	Vicars		Rectors	Vicars
41	44	Up to £4 19s 11d	20	14
279	336	£5–£9 19s 11d	63	26
297	119	£10–£14 19s 11d	46	17
87	25	£15–£19 19s 11d	24	5
129	21	Over £20	21	4

[1] Source: M. Bowker, *The Secular Clergy in Lincoln Diocese,* for these tables and those in Figures Seven and Eight.

FIGURE SEVEN

Ordinations and Absenteeism

| Diocese | Ordinations in Five Dioceses Compared | | |
	Average Number of Ordained Priests including Religious at one Ordination	Number of Parishes as a Fraction of the Number of Parishes in the Lincoln Diocese	Estimated Average of the Total Number Ordained at one Ordination if size of Diocese same as Lincoln
Lincoln	30	—	30
Exeter	13	1/3	39
Hereford	7	1/7	49
Bath & Wells	10	1/4	40
Ely	8	1/16	128

Causes of Absenteeism, Lincoln Visitations	
To take benefices in plurality	97
University study or office	30
Chaplain, private service	21
Church administration	24
Pilgrimage	2
Parish depopulation	8
Reason not known	119

| Archdeaconry | Duration of Absenteeism, Lincoln Visitations | | | |
| | Number of Parishes and Date of First Report of Absenteeism | State of those Parishes and Date at Second Visitation | | |
		Nonresident	Resident	Unknown
Lincoln	51 cases in 1500	14(1519)	20(1519)	17(1519)
Huntington	19 cases in 1507	8(1518)	5(1518)	6(1518)
Leicester	4 cases in 1489	2(1518–26)	2(1518–26)	
	12 cases in 1498	5(1518–26)	7(1518–26)	
	14 cases in 1509/10	7(1518–26)	7(1518–26)	
	52 cases in 1518	20(1526)[1]	19(1526)[1]	13(1526)
Totals	152	56	60	36

FIGURE EIGHT

Offenses of Clergy in Lincoln Diocese

	1500–10,[1] *1,359 Parishes Visited in Six Archdeaconries*	*1514–21,*[1] *1,006 Parishes Visited in General Episcopal Visitation*	*Corrected occurrences*[2] *if all 1,700 Parishes Reported in Proportion to Survival*	
			1500–10	*1514–21*
Offense: Moral				
Having a woman	8	126	10	213
Irregular clothes and hair	2	0	3	0
Unacceptable behavior	0	7	0	12
Farming-sheeprunning	0	3	0	5
Offense: Pastoral				
Irregular services	2	17	3	29
Sacraments wrongly administered	5	12	6	20
Failure to preach or visit sick	1	7	1	12
Too old to perform duties	0	5	0	8
Offense: Fabric Maintenance		*175 Churches*		
Church or Chapel decayed	—	88	—	850
Vicarage or rectory	—	23	—	223
Cemetery	—	44	—	425
Vestments, books, vessels	—	29	—	283
Composite Table, Unbeneficed Clergy, 1500–21				
Incontinence	10	12	12	20
Irregular services and sacraments	1	8	1	14
Sleeping outside parish	2	5	3	9
Failure to preach and visit	0	1	0	2
Ignorant	0	1	0	2
Irregular clothes and hair	0	2	0	3
Irregular behavior	0	17	0	29
Inadequate: No reason	0	2	0	3

[1] The figures represent parishes visited in several visitations, within the decades sampled, for which reports survive.

[2] These figures represent the proportional total of abuses, on the assumption of a visitation of all parishes, with the same reported incidence.

FIGURE NINE

An Index of Prices and Wages, 1260–1650[1]

Decades	Prices[2]	Wages[3]	Decades	Prices[2]	Wages[3]
1260	80.0	62.8	1450	101.8	101.0
1270	101.0	50.0	1460	104.1	97.0
1280	92.7	55.3	1470	95.3	106.5
1290	101.2	50.0	1480	116.0	88.9
1300	98.7	55.5	1490	98.7	100.9
1310	141.6	50.5	1500	104.3	96.4
1320	122.8	*55.9*[4]	1510	111.2	90.3
1330	93.3	60.0	1520	148.0	68.5
1340	95.6	53.1	1530	155.1	*60.0*
1350	128.5	*49.0*	1540	192.1	*61.0*
1360	141.5	57.0	1550	289.2	*48.0*
1370	130.8	66.0	1560	278.7	59.5
1380	107.8	77.3	1570	314.6	*60.5*
1390	108.6	77.2	1580	357.0	57.7
1400	110.4	*69.6*	1590	472.0	46.1
1410	113.2	90.2	1600	473.9	42.6
1420	103.7	97.2	1610	518.4	37.9
1430	115.1	88.1	1620	515.8	38.8
1440	100.7	99.0	1630	615.8	—
			1640	617.4	*48.0*

[1] Adopted from E. P. Phelps Brown and Sheila V. Hopkins, "Seven Centuries of the Prices of Consumables, Compared with Builders' Wage-rates," *Economica* (1956).

[2] The price of a composite unit of consumables, including cereals, meat, fish, butter, cheese, drink, fuel, light, and textiles.

[3] Wage-rate of building craftsmen in southern England, expressed in the composite consumable units.

[4] Each figure in italics denotes a decade mean based on four or less years.

FIGURE TEN

Coal Production[1]

Region	Estimated Annual Production of Coal in Tons	
	1551–60	1681–90
Durham and Northumberland	65,000	1,225,000
Scotland	40,000	475,000
Wales	20,000	200,000
North and West Midland and the North	65,000	850,000
Cumberland	6,000	100,000
The West	10,000	100,000
Forest of Dean	3,000	25,000
Devon and Ireland	1,000	7,000
Totals	210,000	2,982,000

[1] Source: Nef, *The Rise of the British Coal Industry*, I, p. 19.

FIGURE ELEVEN

Triennial Averages of London Shortcloth Exports[1]

Years	Exports	Years	Exports
1536–8	87,231	1568–70	93,681
1539–41	102,660	1571–3	73,204
1542–4	99,362	1574–6	100,024
1545–7	118,642	1577–9	97,728
1550	132,767	1580–82	98,002
1551	112,710	1583–5	101,214
1552	84,968	1586–8	95,087
1559–61	93,812	1589–91	98,806
1562–4	61,188	1592–4	101,678
1565–7	95,128	1598–1600	103,032

[1] Single year averages for the 1550–1 highs. The figures are adopted from Fisher.

FIGURE TWELVE

The Geography of Catholicism in Post-Reformation England

Region	Census of Non-conformists, 1577[1]		Privy Council Census of Convicted Recusants, 1582[2]	Bishops' Survey of Recusants, 1603[3]
	Total	Suspected Recusants		
South and Southeast	132	76	154[4]	734
Southwest, West, and Welsh Marches	201	101	303	1,286
Wales	15	8[5]	—	712
London	390	99[6]	129	318
North	246	132	973[7]	3,111
East Anglia	63	40	199	801
Midlands	407	174	81[8]	1,668
Totals	1,454	630	1,839	8,630

[1] By dioceses, with the universities and Inns of Court and Chancery separately listed.

[2] By counties and shires.

[3] By dioceses.

[4] Only Kent and Southampton returns.

[5] The Bishop of St. David's alleged that he could supply another 200 names!

[6] Fifty-nine accounted for in the Inns.

[7] No data for Cumberland and Carlisle.

[8] Returns for Warwickshire and Oxfordshire only.

FIGURE THIRTEEN

Causes Entering the Consistory Court of York[1]

Year	Tithe	Defamation	Matrimonial	Totals
1561–2	13	1	7	213
1571–2	54	60	31	211
1581–2	72	114	46	306
1591–2	96	170	36	357
1601–2	133	159	20	350
1611–12	143	164	12	379
1621–2	130	107	12	290
1626–7	132	134	5	305
1634–5	101	159	7	308
1638–9	126	127	4	305

[1] Years begin on the first day of the Michaelmas term. The acts for 1631 are in too bad a condition to be examined. "Rates" include church, curate's, and parish clerk's rates.

FIGURE FOURTEEN

Census of Puritan Ministers

	Number of Names Noted, 1603	Number Threatened with Deprivation, 1605	Number of Names available from Other Lists, 1605
London–Middlesex	35	22	30
Essex	43	43	57
Suffolk	33	50	71
Norfolk	20	—	28
Northamptonshire	29	—	51
Hertfordshire	9	40	17
Rutland	3	—	—
Lincolnshire	12	—	33
Leicestershire	9	—	57
Huntingdonshire	1	—	—
Bedfordshire	3	32	16
Buckinghamshire	9	—	33
Nottinghamshire	5	—	20
Oxfordshire	6	9	9
Sussex	18	30–40	47
Lancashire	17	—	21
Warwickshire	3	27	44
Kent	1	—	23
Wiltshire	3	—	31
Surrey	2	—	21
Devon/Cornwall	6	41	51
Hampshire	2	—	—
Worcestershire and Monmouthshire	2	—	—
Dorset	—	—	17
Staffordshire and Derbyshire	—	—	34
Somerset	—	—	17
Cheshire	—	—	12
Totals	271	294–304	740

Bibliography [1]

Chapter One   THE PRECARIOUS BALANCE

BERESFORD, MAURICE. *The Lost Villages of England*. London: Lutterworth Press, 1954.

———. *New Towns of the Middle Ages*. London: Lutterworth Press, 1967.

CARUS-WILSON, E. *Medieval Merchant Venturers*. London: Methuen, 1954.

HALLAM, H. E. *Settlement and Society*. Cambridge: Cambridge University Press, 1965.

HILTON, R. H. *A Medieval Society*. Oxford: Clarendon Press, 1966.

HOSKINS, W. G. *The Midland Peasant*. London: Macmillan, 1957.

POWER, EILEEN. *The Wool Trade in English Medieval History*. Oxford: Clarendon Press, 1941.

POWER, E., and M. M. POSTAN. *Studies in English Trade in the Fifteenth Century*. London: Routledge & Kegan Paul, 1933.

RAFTIS, J. A. *Tenure and Mobility*. Toronto: The Pontifical Institute, 1964.

RUSSELL, J. C. *British Medieval Population*. Albuquerque, N.M.: University of New Mexico Press, 1940.

SEARLE, ELEANOR. *Lordship and Community*. Toronto: The Pontifical Institute, 1972.

TAWNEY, R. H. *The Agrarian Problem in the Sixteenth Century*. London: Longmans, 1912.

THIRSK, JOAN. *English Peasant Farming*. Cambridge: Cambridge University Press, 1967.

[1] The works cited here represent only a small part of the main literature given in chapter footnotes. In some instances I have taken this opportunity to recommend very recent books.

THRUPP, S. *The Merchant Class of Medieval London*. Chicago: University of Chicago Press, 1940.

Chapter Two   THE LOSS OF ORDER

BALDWIN, J. F. *The King's Council in the Middle Ages*. Oxford: Oxford University Press, 1913.

CAM, HELEN. *Liberties and Communities in Medieval England*. Cambridge: Cambridge University Press, 1944.

GRAY, H. L. *The Influence of the Commons on Early Legislation*. Cambridge, Mass.: Harvard University Press, 1932.

JACOB, E. F. *The Fifteenth Century*. New York: Oxford University Press, 1961.

KINGSFORD, C. L. *Prejudice and Promise in Fifteenth-Century England*. Oxford: Clarendon Press, 1962.

MCFARLANE, K. B. *The Wars of the Roses*. London: British Academy, 1965.

MCKISACK, MAY. *Representation of English Boroughs in the Middle Ages*. Oxford: Clarendon Press, 1932.

SCOFIELD, CORA L. *The Life and Reign of Edward IV*. 2 vols. London: Frank Cass, 1967.

STOREY, R. L. *The End of the House of Lancaster*. London: Barrie, Rockliff, 1966.

WILKINSON, BERTIE. *The Constitutional History of England in the Fifteenth Century*. London: Longmans, 1964.

Chapter Three   THE RESTORATION OF ORDER

BEAN, J. M. W. *The Decline of English Feudalism, 1215–1540*. Manchester: Manchester University Press, 1968.

CHRIMES, S. B. *Henry VII*. London: Eyre-Methuen, 1972.

ELTON, G. R. *Tudor Revolution in Government*. Cambridge: Cambridge University Press, 1953.

PICKTHORN, K. *Early Tudor Government*. 2 vols. Cambridge: Cambridge University Press, 1934.

PUTNAM, B. *Early Treatises on the Practice of the Justices of the Peace*. Oxford: Clarendon Press, 1924.

RICHARDSON, W. C. *Tudor Chamber Administration, 1485–1547*. Baton Rouge, La.: Louisiana State University Press, 1952.

STOREY, R. L. *The Reign of Henry VII.* London: Blandford Press, 1968.

WERNHAM, R. B. *Before the Armada: The Growth of English Foreign Policy, 1485–1558.* New York: Oxford University Press, 1966.

WOLFE, B. P. *Yorkist and Early Tudor Government.* London: Historical Association, 1966.

Chapter Four   THE REFORMATION

BOWKER, M. *The Secular Clergy in Lincoln Diocese, 1495–1520.* Cambridge: Cambridge University Press, 1968.

CLEBSCH, W. A. *England's Earliest Protestants.* New Haven, Conn.: Yale University Press, 1964.

DICKENS, A. G. *The English Reformation.* New York: Schocken Books, 1964.

————. *Lollards and Protestants in the Diocese of York, 1509–1558.* Oxford: Oxford University Press, 1959.

ELTON, G. R. *Policy and Police: The Enforcement of the English Reformation in the Age of Thomas Cromwell.* Cambridge: Cambridge University Press, 1972.

FERGUSON, A. B. *The Articulate Citizen of the English Renaissance.* Durham, N.C.: Duke University Press, 1965.

KNOWLES, DAVID. *The Religious Orders in England: Vol. III, The Tudor Age.* Cambridge: Cambridge University Press, 1959.

LEHMBERG, S. E. *The Reformation Parliament.* Cambridge: Cambridge University Press, 1969.

MCCONICA, J. K. *English Humanists and Reformation Politics.* New York: Oxford University Press, 1965.

MOZLEY, J. F. *Coverdale and His Bibles.* London: Longmans, 1953.

OGLE, A. *The Tragedy of the Lollard's Tower.* Oxford: Clarendon Press, 1948.

SAVINE, A. *English Monasteries on the Eve of the Dissolution.* Oxford: Clarendon Press, 1909.

SCARISBRICK, J. J. *Henry VIII.* Berkeley, Calif.: University of California Press, 1967.

SLAVIN, A. J. *Thomas Cromwell on Church and Commonwealth: Selected Letters, 1523–1540.* New York: Harper & Row, 1969.

SMITH, L. B. *Tudor Prelates and Politics.* Princeton, N.J.: Princeton University Press, 1953.

THOMPSON, A. F. *The Later Lollards.* Oxford: Clarendon Press, 1965.

Chapter Five THE WALL OF AUTHORITY BROKEN

BINDOFF, S. T. *Ket's Rebellion*. London: Historical Association, 1949.

DODDS, RUTH and MADELEINE. *The Pilgrimage of Grace . . . and the Exeter Conspiracy*. 2 vols. Cambridge: Cambridge University Press, 1915.

FLETCHER, A. *Tudor Rebellions*. London: Longmans, 1968.

JAMES, M. E. *Change and Continuity in the Tudor North*. York, Eng.: Borthwick Institute, 1965.

JORDAN, W. K. *Edward VI*. 2 vols. Cambridge, Mass.: Harvard University Press, 1968–70.

RIDLEY, JASPER. *Thomas Cranmer*. Oxford: Clarendon Press, 1962.

ROSE-TROUP, F. *The Western Rebellion of 1549*. London: Macmillan, 1913.

SLAVIN, A. J. *Politics and Profit*. Cambridge: Cambridge University Press, 1966.

WHITNEY-JONES, R. D. *The Tudor Commonwealth Men*. London: Athlone Press, 1969.

ZEEVELD, W. G. *Foundations of Tudor Policy*. London: Methuen, 1948.

Chapter Six THE MONSTROUS REGIMENT OF WOMEN

EMMISON, F. G. *Tudor Secretary: Sir William Petre*. Cambridge, Mass.: Harvard University Press, 1961.

GARRETT, C. H. *The Marian Exiles*. Cambridge: Cambridge University Press, 1938.

HALLER, WILLIAM. *Foxe's "Book of Martyrs" and the Elect Nation*. London: Jonathan Cape, 1963.

HARBISON, H. E. *Rival Ambassadors at the Court of Queen Mary*. Princeton, N.J.: Princeton University Press, 1940.

LOADES, D. M. *Two Tudor Conspiracies*. Cambridge: Cambridge University Press, 1965.

MacCAFFREY, WALLACE. *The Shaping of the Elizabethan Regime*. Princeton, N.J.: Princeton University Press, 1968.

MATTINGLY, GARRETT. *The Armada*. Boston: Houghton Mifflin, 1959.

NEALE, SIR J. E. *Elizabeth I*. London: Jonathan Cape, 1934.

———. *Elizabeth I and Her Parliaments*. 2 vols. London: Jonathan Cape, 1953–7.

PRESCOTT, H. M. F. *A Spanish Tudor*. New York: Constable, 1940.

Chapter Seven THE REVOLUTION IN AGRICULTURE

DARBY, H. C. *An Historical Geography of England Before A.D. 1800*. Cambridge: Cambridge University Press, 1948.

GRAY, C. M. *Copyhold, Equity, and the Common Law*. Cambridge, Mass.: Harvard University Press, 1963.

GRAY, H. L. *English Field Systems*. Cambridge: Cambridge University Press, 1915.

KERRIDGE, ERIC. *Agrarian Problems in the Sixteenth Century*. London: Allen & Unwin, 1969.

———. *The Agricultural Revolution*. London: Allen & Unwin, 1967.

ORWIN, C. S. *The Open Fields*. Oxford: Oxford University Press, 1954.

SIMPSON, ALAN W. B. *An Introduction to the History of the Land Law*. Oxford: Oxford University Press, 1961.

———. *The Wealth of the Gentry*. Chicago: Chicago University Press, 1961.

THIRSK, JOAN, ed. *The Agrarian History of England and Wales: Vol. IV: 1500–1640*. Cambridge: Cambridge University Press, 1967.

———. *Fenland Farming in the Sixteenth Century*. Leicester: Leicester University Press, 1953.

Chapter Eight THE GROWTH OF A MERCANTILE SOCIETY

ASHTON, R. *The Crown and the Money Market*. Oxford: Oxford University Press, 1960.

COURT, W. H. B. *The Rise of the Midland Industries*. Oxford: Clarendon Press, 1938.

DOLLINGER, P. *The Hansa*. Stanford, Calif.: Stanford University Press, 1970.

HINTON, R. K. W. *The Eastland Trade*. Cambridge: Cambridge University Press, 1953.

LEWIS, G. R. *The British Paper Industry, 1495–1860*. Oxford: Oxford University Press, 1958.

MATHIAS, P. *The Brewing Industry in England*. Cambridge: Cambridge University Press, 1959.

PEARL, VALERIE. *London and the Outbreak of the Puritan Revolution*. Oxford: Oxford University Press, 1961.

RABB, T. K. *Enterprise and Empire: Merchant and Gentry Investment in the Expansion of England, 1575–1630*. Cambridge, Mass.: Harvard University Press, 1967.

RAMSEY, G. D. *English Overseas Trade in the Centuries of Emergence.* London: Longmans, 1957.

———. *The Wiltshire Woollen Industry in the 16th and 17th Centuries.* Oxford: Oxford University Press, 1943.

SCHUBERT, H. R. *A History of the British Iron and Steel Industry to 1775.* London: Longmans, 1957.

SUPPLE, B. E. *Commercial Crisis and Change, 1600–1642.* Cambridge: Cambridge University Press, 1959.

SWEEZY, P. M. *Monopoly and Competition in the English Coal Trade, 1550–1750.* Cambridge: Cambridge University Press, 1938.

WILLAN, T. S. *The English Coasting Trade.* Manchester, Eng.: Manchester University Press, 1938.

Chapter Nine BABYLON AND JERUSALEM

CLIFFE, J. *The Yorkshire Gentry from the Reformation to the Civil War.* London: Athlone, 1969.

COLLINSON, P. *The Elizabethan Puritan Movement.* London: Jonathan Cape, 1967.

HAVRAN, MARTIN. *The Catholics in Caroline England.* Cambridge, Mass.: Harvard University Press, 1960.

HILL, CHRISTOPHER. *The Economic Problems of the Church.* Oxford: Clarendon Press, 1956.

———. *Society and Puritanism in Pre-revolutionary England.* London: Secker and Warburg, 1964.

MANNING, ROGER. *Religion and Society in Elizabethan Sussex.* Leicester: Leicester University Press, 1969.

MARCHANT, R. A. *The Church Under the Law.* Cambridge: Cambridge University Press, 1969.

———. *The Puritans and the Church Courts in the Diocese of York, 1560–1642.* Cambridge: Cambridge University Press, 1960.

MCGRATH, P. *Papists and Puritans under Elizabeth I.* London: Blandford, 1967.

NEW, JOHN. *Anglican and Puritan.* Stanford, Calif.: Stanford University Press, 1964.

PEEL, A. *The First Congregational Churches: New Light on Separatists in London.* Cambridge: Cambridge University Press, 1920.

SEAVER, PAUL. *The Puritan Lectureships: The Politics of Religious Dissent, 1560–1662.* Stanford, Calif.: Stanford University Press, 1970.

TREVOR-ROPER, H. *Archbishop Laud.* Oxford: Oxford University Press, 1950.

TRIMBLE, W. R. *The Catholic Laity in Elizabethan England.* Cambridge, Mass.: Harvard University Press, 1964.

WALZER, M. *The Revolution of the Saints.* Cambridge, Mass.: Harvard University Press, 1965.

Chapter Ten GOVERNMENT AND SOCIETY REVISITED

AYLMER, G. A. *The King's Servants.* London: Routledge & Kegan Paul, 1961.

BARNES, T. G. *Somerset, 1625–1640.* Oxford: Oxford University Press, 1961.

CURTIS, MARK. *Oxford and Cambridge in Transition.* Oxford: Clarendon Press, 1959.

HURSTFIELD, JOEL. *The Queen's Wards.* Cambridge, Mass.: Harvard University Press, 1958.

NEALE, SIR J. E. *The Elizabethan House of Commons.* London: Jonathan Cape, 1949.

———. *Essays in Elizabethan History.* London: Jonathan Cape, 1958.

NOTESTEIN, WALLACE. *The House of Commons, 1604–1610.* New Haven, Conn.: Yale University Press, 1971.

PULMAN, M. B. *The Elizabethan Privy Council in the 1570s.* Berkeley, Calif.: University of California Press, 1971.

RUIGH, R. *The Parliament of 1624.* Cambridge, Mass.: Harvard University Press, 1971.

SIMON, JOAN. *Education and Society in Tudor England.* Cambridge: Cambridge University Press, 1966.

STONE, LAWRENCE. *The Crisis of the Aristocracy, 1558–1641.* New York: Oxford University Press, 1965.

TAWNEY, R. H. *Business and Politics under James I.* Cambridge: Cambridge University Press, 1958.

WILLSON, D. H. *James VI and I.* Oxford: Oxford University Press, 1967.

WILSON, CHARLES. *Queen Elizabeth and the Revolt of the Netherlands.* Berkeley, Calif.: University of California Press, 1970.

ZALLER, ROBERT. *The Parliament of 1621.* Berkeley, Calif.: University of California Press, 1971.

Index

Abingdon Abbey, estates of, 13

Acts of Parliament: Annates, 143, 145; Appeals, 143; Articles of the Faith, 182, 206; attainders, 93–4; chantries, 167, 170; dispensations, 143; enclosures, 16–17; First Fruits and Tenths, 145; franchise reform, 57; Justices of the Peace (J.P.s), 29–30, 60–61, 111–13; monastic dissolution, 145–6, 163; recusancy, 287–90, 294; resumption, 63–4; *Six Articles,* 148; subsidy, 102–3, 159, 174; succession, 143, 189; *Supplication of the Commons,* 142–3; Supremacy, 143–4, 158, 205; treasons, 159, 165, 208–9, 287 (repeal of, 170); Uniformity, 171–2, 182, 204–5; uses, 98

Admonition to Parliament, An, 304, 311

Advowson, 130

Agrarianism, 3–4

Agricultural prices, 3–4, 15, 17–18, 215–16

Agricultural Revolution, 229–44

Agricultural techniques, 6, 13–14, 222–3, 230–31, 239–40

Agricultural wages, 8, 24, 239–44

Aldgate, London parish of, 308

Alva, duke of, 209

Amboyna Massacre, 268

Anticlericalism, 121–3, 127–37, 140, 141–3, 178

Appropriations, 129–30, 300

Arable crops: extent of, 8, 231–3; specialized practices for, 218–30; yields per acre of, 6. *See also* Farming

Aristocracy: composition of, 8, 31–2, 342; crisis in, 340–44; crown and, 91–3, 98, 157, 328–34; expenditures by, 12–13, 279; habits of as landlords, 160; households of, 159–61, 286–7; incomes of, 5, 8, 11, 12, 348; patronage relations of, 80; political power of, 30–31, 334–5, 337; recusant, 286–7

Armstrong, Clement, 19

Ascham, Roger, 201

Aske, Robert, 157, 162

Askewe, Anne, 168

Assarting, 6

Attainder, 93–4

Aveling, Hugh, 291

Aylmer, John, 187

Ayscough, Bishop William, 68

Bacon, Sir Francis, 104

Barbary Company, 262

Barnes, Friar Robert, 147

Beauchamp, Richard, Earl of Warwick, 30

Beaufort, Bishop Henry, 54

THE PRECARIOUS BALANCE: ENGLISH GOVERNMENT AND SOCIETY
BY ARTHUR JOSEPH SLAVIN

ARTHUR JOSEPH SLAVIN, Professor of History at the University of California at Los Angeles, has written and edited numerous books and contributed extensively to scholarly journals. On the Tudor period, his books include *Politics and Profit* (1966); *Henry VIII and the English Reformation* (1968); *Humanism, Reform and Reformation* (1969); *Thomas Cromwell on Church and Commonwealth: Selected Letters, 1523–1540* (1969); and *Tudor Men and Institutions* (1972). Professor Slavin received his B.A. from Louisiana State University and his Ph.D. from the University of North Carolina. He served as an Assistant Professor at Bucknell University from 1961 until 1965, when he joined the U.C.L.A. faculty. Among the honors he has received are designation as a Guggenheim Fellow and election as a Life Fellow to the Royal Historical Society of Great Britain. At present he is working on a book about Thomas Cromwell.

A NOTE ON THE TYPE

THIS old face design, BEMBO 270, has such an up-to-date appearance that it is difficult to realize this letter was cut (the first of its line) before A.D. 1500. At Venice in 1495, ALDUS MANUTIUS ROMANUS printed a small 36 pp. tract, *Petri Bembi de Aetna ad Angelum Chabrielem liber*, written by the young humanist poet PIETRO BEMBO (later Cardinal, and secretary to Pope Leo X), using a new design of type which differed considerably from that of Jenson's. The punches were cut by FRANCESCO GRIFFO of Bologna the designer responsible six years later for the first italic types. A second roman face followed in 1499 and this type design, based on the first, and used to print the famous illustrated *Hypnerotomachia Poliphili*, was the one which, after adaptation by Garamond, Voskens and others, resulted finally in Caslon Old Face.